Maud Devos and Jenneke van der Wal (Eds.)
COME and GO off the Beaten Grammaticalization Path

Trends in Linguistics Studies and Monographs

Volume 272

COME and GO
off the Beaten
Grammaticalization Path

——

Edited by
Maud Devos and Jenneke van der Wal

DE GRUYTER
MOUTON

ISBN 978-3-11-048473-1
e-ISBN 978-3-11-033598-9
ISSN 1861-4302

Library of Congress Cataloging-in-Publication Data
A CIP catalog record for this book has been applied for at the Library of Congress.

Bibliografische Information der Deutschen Nationalbibliothek
The Deutsche Nationalbibliothek lists this publication in the Deutschen Nationalbibliografie;
detailed bibliographic data are available in the internet http://dnb.dnb.de.

© 2014 Walter de Gruyter GmbH, Berlin/Boston
Typesetting: Frank Benno Junghanns, Berlin
Printing: CPI buch bücher.de GmbH, Birkach
♾ Printed on acid-free paper
Printed in Germany

www.degruyter.com

Foreword

From 2007–2011, the Belgian Science Policy funded an inter-university cooperation on Grammaticalization and (Inter)subjectification (GRAMIS), between the Universities of Ghent, Antwerp, Leuven, Louvain-la-Neuve, Hannover and the Royal Museum for Central Africa in Tervuren. We, the editors, were both involved in this project at the RMCA, where we studied the processes of grammaticalization and (inter)subjectification in the Bantu languages, spoken in sub-Saharan Africa.

Maud Devos drew on her earlier profound studies of the language Shangaci when she discovered a rather unexpected grammaticalized use of the verb 'go'. Inspired by this new and fascinating grammaticalization path (see the Introduction to this volume, as well as Devos and Van der Wal 2010), Maud developed a more general interest in the grammaticalization of motion verbs. It appeared to her that verbs of 'come' and 'go' are often taken as 'most basic', 'in deictic opposition' and known to develop into tense/aspect markers, whereas this is certainly not exceptionless – a conclusion also drawn by Wilkins and Hill (1995). We hence examined data on the semantics and grammaticalized uses of verbs of 'come' and 'go' in a number of Bantu languages, presenting the results at the International Conference of Historical Linguistics in Osaka (July 2011). More importantly, we organized a workshop to bring to light the less well known paths of grammaticalization of these verbs crosslinguistically, within the 44th meeting of the Societas Linguistica Europaea, held in Logroño (Spain) in September 2011. This workshop attracted much international interest and was a great success in bringing scholars together working on the lexical semantics and grammaticalization of 'come' and 'go'.

With the interest of these researchers and the quality of the papers presented, we felt that the results should be published together, the outcome of which is the current book. We would like to thank the authors for their efforts, their cooperation and their patience. Furthermore, we are grateful to the external reviewers of the papers: Daniel van Olmen, Johan van der Auwera, María José Rodríguez Espiñeira, Matthew Juge, Amina Mettouchi, Iren Hartmann, Jacques Bres, Mario Squartini, and Claus Pusch.

Maud Devos
Jenneke van der Wal

Brussels and Cambridge
February 2014

Contents

Conclusion

Contributors

Philippe Bourdin
York University, Toronto
pbourdin@yorku.ca

Ana Bravo
University of Murcia
ana.bravo@um.es

Robert Carlson
Africa International University
robert_carlson@sil.org

Kelsey Daniels
Graduate Institute of Applied Linguistics
klsydnls@gmail.com

Maud Devos
Royal Museum for Central Africa
maud.devos@africamuseum.be

Adina Dragomirescu
University of Bucharest and
"Iorgu Iordan – Al. Rosetti"
Institute of Linguistics
adina_drag@yahoo.com

Anna Giacalone Ramat
University of Pavia
annaram@unipv.it

Caterina Mauri
University of Pavia
caterina.mauri@unipv.it

Egle Mocciaro
University of Palermo
egle.mocciaro@gmail.com

Alexandru Nicolae
University of Bucharest and
"Iorgu Iordan – Al. Rosetti"
Institute of Linguistics
nicolae_bibi@yahoo.com

Andrea Sansò
University of Insubria
andrea.sanso@uninsubria.it

Jenneke van der Wal
University of Cambridge
jennekevanderwal@gmail.com

Maud Devos and Jenneke van der Wal
Introduction

1 Motivation

Verbs glossed as 'come' and 'go' are known to evolve into grammatical markers of tense and aspect (see e.g. Bybee, Perkins, and Pagliuca (1994), Bybee and Dahl (1989), Heine and Kuteva (2002)). Examples (1) to (4), taken from different Bantu languages, illustrate this. In (1) and (2), verbs expressing 'come' are used in constructions marking immediate past and remote future. The utterances in (3) and (4) illustrate the use of 'go' to express the habitual and a 'tomorrow' future.

(1)   Sesotho (Doke and Mofokeng 1957: 204, gloss added)

    u-tswa-rɛk-a
    SBJ$_{2SG}$-COME.FROM-buy-FV
    'I have just bought.'

(2)   Mwera (Harries 1950: 98 cited in Botne 2006: 161)

    many'any'i   ci-ga-jie-w-a
    NP$_6$.grass   FUT-PP$_6$-RFUT(<come)-die-FV
    'The grass will die.'

(3)   Zulu (van Eeden 1956: 567, gloss added)

    u-ye   *a-vuk-e*   *ekuseni*   *kakhulu*
    SBJ$_1$-GO.SBJV SBJ$_1$-wake-SBJV in.the.morning very
    'He usually gets up very early in the morning.'

(4)   Hunde (Mateene 1992: 25, cited in Botne 2006: 174)

    tw-eéndé-birangir-a   mu-kátsi
    SBJ$_{1PL}$-FUT(<go)-call-FV   NP$_1$-woman
    'We will call a woman tomorrow.'

However, 'come' and 'go' verbs are also known to travel down less common grammaticalization paths. The verb *entta* 'go' (cf. (5a)) in Shangaci, a Bantu language from Mozambique, is a case in point. It has evolved into a marker of verb focus, as in (5b): *entta* does not function as an autonomous lexical verb here but has the effect of focussing the immediately following verb *rezula* 'sweep', contrasting it with other activities like 'pulling out the weed'.

(5)   Shangaci (Niger-Congo, Bantu)

    a. lexical use of -*entta* (Devos and Van der Wal 2010: 46):

        mwaw-éntt-é   *vaaí*   *taána?*

        SBJ$_{1PL}$.PST-go-PFV where yesterday

        'Where did you (pl) go yesterday?'

    b. grammatical use of -*entta* (Devos and Van der Wal 2010: 53):

        miíyó   *koów-áampel-e*   *o-khuruúp-a*

        I   SBJ$_{1SG}$.PST.OBJ$_{2SG}$-tell-PFV NP$_{15}$-pull.weed-FV

        'I told you to pull out the weed

        weéyo *w-entt'*   *o-rézuúl-a*   *mi-yaní* *z-áawe*

        you   SBJ$_{2SG}$-GO-PFV NP$_{15}$-sweep-FV NP$_4$-weed PP$_4$-POSS$_1$

        but you just swept it.'

The uncommonness and the apparent loss of motion semantics in the above grammaticalization path prompted us, first, to reconsider the lexical semantics of motion verbs in Shangaci and other Bantu languages and, next, to look for other less common grammaticalization paths starting from Bantu 'come' and 'go' (Devos and Van der Wal 2011). In order to broaden our perspective and to add insights from people working on languages for which historical sources exist we decided to organize a workshop (held at the 44th meeting of the Societas Linguistica Europaea in Logroño) on lesser known grammaticalization paths travelled by 'come' and 'go' in familiar and less familiar languages. The papers presented at that workshop are gathered in the present volume. Grammatical targets different from tense and aspect have been mentioned in the literature (see e.g. Nicolle 2002, Ebert 2003, Bourdin 2008, Devos and Van der Wal 2010 and Heine, Claudi, and Hünnemeyer 1993 and Heine and Kuteva 2002 for an overview) but, as far as we know, no single book volume has been dedicated to the topic. Bringing the less usual targets together is, of course, typologically interesting and it will broaden our understanding of the possible grammaticalization paths of a particular set of source items (cf. also Maisak 2005). More importantly, however, we believe that a study of more unusual targets of 'come' and 'go' verbs will increase our insight in grammaticalization processes in general as they force us to rethink certain aspects of grammaticalization. The present volume focuses on four such aspects. It should be clear from the start that not all papers discuss all four aspects to the same extent. However, the authors certainly had the focal points enumerated below at the back of their mind when developing their papers and the conclusion at the end of this book will serve to bring them to the fore again.

2 The broader questions addressed in this volume

2.1 Lexical semantics and persistence

It is generally accepted that the lexical meaning of a source item "persists" to a greater or lesser degree in the newly developed grammatical function. Hopper and Traugott (2003: 95), for example, claim that "it is unlikely that any instance of grammaticalization will involve a sudden loss of meaning" and that it is therefore "incumbent on the researcher to seek a plausible set of inferences that enable changes to occur". They also make clear that bleaching or loss of lexical meaning is characteristic of the later stages of grammaticalization only. This "persistence" (Hopper 1991: 22) of the original lexical semantics is the reason why Lichtenberk (1991: 505) in his study of the development of movement verbs in Oceanic languages consistently asks himself "what there was in the meaning of the source element that enabled the new function to develop." It should be clear that to be able to appreciate the role of persistence in grammaticalization the lexical semantics of source items need to be well understood. However, we find, on the one hand, that source elements are typically described as general in meaning, which appears to downplay persistence effects, and, on the other hand, that their lexical semantics are often presupposed or taken for granted.

Lexical meanings that enter into grammaticalization processes are typically referred to as basic, universal, general and frequent. Semantically, source items tend to be described as *basic*. Bybee, Perkins, and Pagliuca (1994: 9), for example, claim that "lexical units that enter into grammaticization [...] usually represent [...] the basic semantic features of their domains. Thus 'come' and 'go' are the motion verbs chosen most often for grammaticization." Heine, Claudi, and Hünnemeyer (1991: 33), also stress the basicness or prototypical nature of source concepts. In addition, they indicate that source items are similar to what is known as "basic vocabulary" in that they are less prone to replacement than other lexemes and represent universal notions, which also makes them good candidates for a universal set of semantic primitives.[1]

---

1 Neither 'come' nor 'go' are included in Wierzbicka's (1996) semantic primes, whereas 'move' is.

On a more pragmatic level, source items are said to be *general* and *frequent* in use, the latter characteristic plausibly being a concomitant feature of their basic and general nature (cf. also Heine, Claudi, and Hünnemeyer 1991: 38). Both Bybee, Perkins, and Pagliuca 1994 (1994: 9–10) and Hopper and Traugott (2003: 100) take it that lexical items that enter into processes of grammaticalization must first be semantically general(ized). This implies that they are already fairly abstract in content and have gained a wider distribution. Maisak (2005) basically refers to the same thing when suggesting that source items have a 'meta-linguistic' potential, i.e. the possibility of metaphorically referring to notions different from their core meaning. As an example of generalization of meaning, Hopper and Traugott (2003: 102) refer to the Latin verb *ambulare* 'walk' which grammaticalized as a future marker only after it was generalized in its French cognate *aller* 'go'.

One of the questions that this study of lesser known grammaticalization paths starting from 'come' and 'go' wishes to address is whether these motion verbs reflect the basic, universal and general nature typically associated with source items. Part of the question is instigated by Wilkins and Hill (1995), who show that 'come' is not a lexical universal and in doing so pave the way for more research on the basicness of 'come' and 'go'. Next, just as Wilkins and Hill (1995) question the basicness of 'come' and 'go', the present volume aims to take a closer look at their supposed generalness and whether it leaves room for persistence. As an illustration, Swahili has a grammaticalized construction consisting of the habitual of the verb *enda* 'go (to)' followed by a consecutively marked semantic main verb and expressing epistemic possibility (cf. (3a)). Surprisingly, the same meaning can be expressed by substituting *enda* 'go (to)' by *ja* 'come' (cf. (3b)), even though the latter construction occurs less frequently.

(3)   Swahili (Niger-Congo, Bantu) (Zawawi 1988: 130)

a. *yeye hu-end-a   a-ka-fik-a   leo*
   he   HAB-go-FV SBJ$_1$-SUBS-arrive-FV today
   'He might arrive today.'

b. *yeye hu-j-a   a-ka-fik-a   leo*
   he   HAB-come-FV SBJ$_1$-SUBS-arrive-FV today
   'He might arrive today.'

This variability could be explained by referring to the generalization of the concerned motion verbs prior to grammaticalization. However, an important question still is whether the original lexical meanings of 'come' and 'go' restrict the usage range of the grammaticalized constructions.

Studies dedicated to grammaticalized uses of 'come' and 'go' often assume that it is the deictic nature of the verbs that is responsible for their grammaticalization. Sweetser (1988), for example, when discussing the grammaticalization of English *going to* into a marker of future tense claims that "lexicalization of motion away from the deictic centre makes 'go' the perfect choice for movement away from the present in time". However, Wilkins and Hill (1995) convincingly show that, contrary to what is commonly assumed, 1) 'go' is not universally deictic (see also Langacker 1990: 155) and 2) 'come' and 'go' are not in a universal deictic opposition. Botne's (2005) study of motion verbs in the Bantu language Chindali fully supports these findings. Whereas Chindali has a deictic motion verb encoding motion towards the location of the speaker (i.e. *iisa* 'come'), it has no motion verb dedicated to the expression of motion towards a location different from the deictic centre. Instead, there are up to four (i.e. *tiila* 'GO from source, *fuma* 'go from SOURCE', *buuka* 'GO to goal' and *ya* 'go to GOAL') non-deictic motion verbs that can, in appropriate contexts, fulfill the role of deictic 'go'.

Seeing that deixis cannot be presupposed for 'come' and 'go' verbs, an important question will be whether the motion verbs that take part in the grammaticalization paths discussed in the present edition, are really deictic. Next, if deixis can be established, we still need to find out whether deixis is crucial in the grammaticalization process in question or whether other semantic features come into play. Motion verbs, in general, and 'come' and 'go' in particular, typically involve a Source, a Path and a Goal (Fillmore 1997, Talmy 1985). Deixis, i.e., whether or not the Goal of the motion can be identified with the deictic centre, is an important variable in motion schemes pertaining to 'come' and 'go' verbs. However, other variables may be equally important. First, motion schemes typically involve a "spatial reference point" (Fillmore 1997: 81, based on his 1965 & 1966 papers). This becomes more clear when comparing the examples in (4) and (5), taken from Fillmore (1997: 80).

(4)   *He went home around midnight.*

(5)   *He came home around midnight.*

In (4) the use of *go* implies that the motion starts at midnight and the spatial reference point coincides with the Source. In (5), on the other hand, *come* indicates that the motion ends at midnight and the spatial reference point coincides with the Goal. In the same vein, Taylor (1988: 506–507) describes *go* as having Source focus and *come* as having Goal focus. This is different from a third feature, which Botne (2005: 45) refers to as Salience. According to him Chindali 'come' and 'go' verbs can differ solely in whether or not they mark the Goal, the Path or the Source as the most prominent and relevant part of the motion scheme. To illustrate, Chindali has two verbs expressing motion towards a specified Goal: *buuka* and *ya*, the crucial difference between the two being that in the case of *buuka* the motion is salient (cf. GO to Goal), whereas in the case of *ya* the Goal is salient (cf. go to GOAL). Interestingly, it is the verb with Salience of Goal (*ya*) which grammaticalizes as a future marker (Botne 2005: 74).

2.2 The role of the co-text

So far, we have only considered discrete lexical items as inputs to grammaticalization processes. However, it is well-known that whole constructions rather than individual lexemes grammaticalize. As Bybee, Perkins, and Pagliuca (1994: 11) put it, "in tracing the origin of grammatical meaning, we must attend to the syntax and morphology of the source construction and not simply to the referential meaning of its lexical items". In the present volume special attention is paid to the syntactic contexts in which 'come' and 'go' verbs grammaticalize.

As suggested by Bourdin (2008: 42), who notes that auxiliation and serialization are especially favored structures in the grammaticalization of 'come' and 'go' verbs to textual connectives, it will be interesting to see whether semantically similar targets involve similar source structures. Moreover, some papers address the question how influential the distributional context is to the grammatical meaning. Bybee, Perkins, and Pagliuca (1994: 11) suggest that the distributional context is crucial. Rather than stating that a single source concept can give rise to different grammatical targets (as do, for example Heine, Claudi, and Hünnemeyer (1991: 38)), they prefer to say that each target derives from a specific source construction involving the same lexeme. Alternatively, different targets can actually be seen as distinct steps on the same grammaticalization cline, a situation we turn to in Section 2.3. A quick glance at grammaticalization paths followed by cognates of the Proto-Bantu verb **gènd* 'walk, travel, go' supports this. The verb is known to develop into a future tense marker, as in (6), as well as into a progressive aspect marker, as in (7) and (8). However, the constructions leading to future and progressive are crucially different with **gènd* being followed by an infinite and a finite verb form, respectively.

(6)   Kikae (Niger-Congo, Bantu) (Racine-Issa 2002: 127)
       kw-end-a-tend-a   *u-shez-a*
       SBJ$_{2SG}$-go-PRS-do-FV   NP$_{11}$-play
       'Are you going to play?'

(7) Ruwund (Niger-Congo, Bantu) (Nash 1993: 859)
   tal   *âap,*   *m-êm*   *m-ènd*   *m-ììcik*
   look.IMP PP$_{16}$.DEM$_B$ NP$_6$-water PP$_6$-go.FV PP$_6$-spill.out.FV
   'Look here, the water is spilling out!'

(8) Kagulu (Niger-Congo, Bantu) (Petzell 2008: 144)
   ni-gend-ag-e   *ny-ambik-a*
   SBJ$_{1SG}$-go-IPFV-FV   SBJ$_{1SG}$-cook-FV
   'I was cooking.'

2.3 Direct and indirect paths

A distinction is made between unusual targets of 'come' and 'go' involving direct paths versus indirect paths. The latter are of two types. First, the unusual targets can be derived from more usual targets of grammaticalization processes and thus involve changes pertaining to the second part of the definition of grammaticalization as formulated by Hopper and Traugott (2003: 231) in which it is said that lexical items, once they have developed a certain grammatical function, can "continue to develop new grammatical functions" (cf. 'expansion' in Haspelmath 2004: 33). A difficult issue with respect to such indirect paths is when to identify a given grammatical meaning as a new one (i.e. how to define discrete events of grammaticalization).

Second, the path can be indirect because of a change in the lexical semantics of the motion verb in question. As was mentioned in (1) it is generally assumed that lexical items that are subject to grammaticalization have undergone generalization and can, thus, be used in many contexts. In the present edition we apply the term 'indirect path' to those cases where the lexical meaning that enters the grammaticalization path no longer pertains to Motion. It might not always be easy to distinguish between indirect paths of the first and of the second type since there is arguably no easy way to distinguish between lexical meaning change and grammatical meaning change (cf. also Hopper and Traugott 2003: 102). We turn to the latter in Section 2.4.

2.4 Meaning changes

What kind of meaning changes are involved in the grammaticalization of 'come' and 'go' verbs? Recent grammaticalization studies tend to agree that, rather than involving loss of semantic content or 'semantic bleaching', the early stages of grammaticalization involve a change in meaning often referred to as 'pragmatic strengthening' (e.g. Hopper and Traugott 2003: 76). Pragmatic strengthening occurs when a source construction used in a specific context invites an inference, most typically through metonymy or metaphor. If this inference occurs often enough it can become routinized and then conventionalized (i.e., semanticized). In sum, in the early stages of grammaticalization meaning change is instantiated by mechanisms of pragmatic strengthening and generalization. The overall change in meaning from (lexical) source to (grammatical) target has been said to typically involve 'subjectification', or in Traugott's terms an increasing tendency to express the speaker's subjective perspective on the situation (see the overview in Traugott 2010).

The papers in this volume address several issues relating to meaning changes in the early stages of grammaticalization. First, it considers the role of metaphor and/or metonymy. Metaphorical processes are often seen as crucial in grammaticalization processes starting from source items with spatial properties (via the SPACE = TIME metaphor). Emanatian (1992: 3), for example, argues that "Chagga verbs for coming and going may imply a future interpretation [...] by expressing present 'motion' of the actors on a path of action through time, directed toward the future." And she adds that "this, of course, is spatio-temporal metaphor." However, together with an increasing interest in the co-texts (cf. syntactic contiguity) of lexical source items, metonymy (cf. semantic contiguity) has gained importance in grammaticalization studies. Another question is whether the unusual targets of 'come' and 'go' involve subjectification and whether intersubjectification (Traugott and Dasher 2002, Traugott 2003), i.e. an evolution towards meanings that are increasingly concerned with the interaction between speaker and hearer, is ever attested in the early stages of grammaticalization starting from 'come' and 'go' verbs. And if such is the case, does it necessarily follow subjectification?

Until now, we have only considered meaning changes pertaining to the early stages of grammaticalization. Of course, the second part of the definition of grammaticalization relating to 'expansion' or the development of new grammatical functions out of older ones also involves changes in meaning and these have received much less attention in the grammaticalization literature (see Kranich 2010). In cases where unusual targets of 'come' and 'go' verbs develop out of more usual targets, do we see the same mechanisms of pragmatic inferencing and generalization at work and do we find cases of generalization leading to desemanticization? Or, do we find evidence for Kranich's (2010: 103) claim that secondary grammaticalization typically involves a loss of subjective meaning, an evolution she refers to as 'objectification'? Also, can we adhere to Hopper and Traugott's (2003: 102) claim that a difference between grammatical meaning changes and lexical meaning changes is that the former do not show narrowing in meaning? Complicated grammaticalization networks might bring about near-synonymous grams leading to specialization and narrowing of meaning (cf. also Haspelmath 2004: 33 on 'retraction' rather than 'expansion').

3 The contributions to this volume

The papers are organized following the grammatical targets of 'come' and 'go' source items: the first three papers involve grammaticalization paths leading to passives. The next two papers discuss targets pertaining to the domain of mood and modality, whereas the remaining four discuss 'come' and 'go' verbs evolving into discourse markers. In terms of methodology, the grammaticalization paths in question are addressed 'in depth', 'in width' or by a combination of both approaches. An in-depth approach leans on a historical corpus when such is available or on synchronic variation in the absence of historical data. In-width approaches are more typologically oriented and concern representative samples of the world's languages. Below we give summaries of all nine papers.

3.1 Passive

In Italian the verb *venire* 'come' has undergone a grammaticalization process to passive auxiliary in the periphrastic construction with a past participle. Giacalone Ramat and Sansò address two questions about this process and provide answers on the basis of a historical corpus study as well as crosslinguistic data.

The first question they address is which among the various constructions in Old Italian is the most plausible forerunner of the modern passive construction. Two candidate constructions are discussed: 1) the action in the verb happens to an encoded involuntary experiencer ('to him came left open his room' = 'he happened to leave his room open'), and 2) the entity encoded by the subject undergoes a change of state ('they came thin' = 'they had become thin'). The authors argue that the second candidate is the forerunner of the passive construction, because the dynamic interpretation of the passive, representing both the process and the final state, is more compatible with the dynamic character of the change-of-state function. This also explains the restriction of the passive to non-compound tenses, that is, tenses that favor a dynamic rather than stative interpretation.

The second question is to what extent this path is determined by the original lexical semantics of *venire* 'come'. Although there is persistence of the dynamic semantics of the construction that grammaticalized to the passive, this construction did not contain the original lexical verb *venire*. That is, *venire* first developed into a change-of-state predicate ('become'), and in the context of a passive-oriented past participle this verb was reanalyzed as a passive auxiliary.

The authors conclude that the original meaning of the motion verb *venire* 'come' did not have an influence on the development of the passive auxiliary, because it was a step-wise, indirect development. This conclusion is strengthened by their crosslinguistic survey: in all the languages with a passive construction consisting of 'come' + past participle, the verb for 'come' has also developed a change-of-state meaning, suggesting that this is a necessary and common grammaticalization stage for the passive construction to develop.

Mocciaro examines the development of Italian *andare* 'go', which – like *venire* 'come' – is a passive auxiliary in Modern Italian. Like Giacalone Ramat and Sansò, she argues that the grammaticalization process is an indirect one: *andare* + past participle first developed into a resultative construction, which consecutively developed a passive reading.

On the one hand, this development has much in common with the path described for Italian *venire* 'come', as both first develop the metaphorical extension of a change-of-state meaning and only then acquire the passive function because of the inherently passive interpretation of the participle. On the other hand, there are important differences in both the development and the current restrictions on the use of this passive construction, which Mocciaro analyses in terms of deixis and source-orientation of the motion verb *andare*.

First, *andare* + past participle specialized to a negative value of 'loss' or 'destruction', whose origin can be traced back to Early Italian according to Mocciaro. This may be related to the second property, which is the unintentional character of the construction: when the *andare*-passive focuses on the negative semantics, the agent is defocused (and in general people do not wish to be seen as agents in negative events). On a scale of agentive responsibility, then, the passive with *essere/venire* has an expressed or implied agent, the reflexive *si*-passive has a more defocused agent, and the passive with *andare* does not have an implied agent at all, Mocciaro argues. These two properties – the negative semantics and the non-intentional character – justify the existence of the *andare*-passive in the spectrum of passive constructions, albeit in a very restricted domain.

A third interesting property concerns the restrictions in the temporal-aspectual domain. The pure passive reading of the construction *andare* + past participle especially arises when the auxiliary is in a perfective tense. When used with an imperfective tense, the result is a (passive) deontic/necessive reading. This, Mocciaro argues, represents a secondary, metonymical extension of the passive meaning, based on the goal-orientedness of the participial context, where the state described in the participle is reached (perfective, passive) or is yet to be reached (imperfective), i.e. needs to be reached (passive-deontic).

Dragomirescu and Nicolae take the Romanian verb *veni* 'come' under close scrutiny, finding three different grammaticalized uses: 1) passive auxiliary, 2) copula and 3) inceptive verb.

One of the important issues Dragomirescu and Nicolae address is the possibility that the passive arose by contact with Italian or was inherited from Latin. Based on research of a historical corpus of Romanian, they find that *veni* was involved in two different passive constructions. The first one came about as the result of language contact with Italian, being attested in a translation from Italian from the end of the 17th/beginning of the 18th century, and sporadically in texts influenced by or translated from Italian up until the end of the 19th century. This construction never entered the mainstream usage, and is not present in the current language. However, the current colloquial and productive *veni*-passive has different uses from the older construction, and it arose independently of the Italian *venire* passive. Furthermore, the authors show that the current Romanian *veni*-passive cannot be a continuation/inheritance of an (alleged) Latin *venire*-passive.

The current use of the *veni*-passive differs from the older use and from the *be*-passive in that it has a deontic or iterative meaning in the present tense (e.g., 'comes placed in box' = 'it has to be placed in a box'). Interestingly, this aspect of meaning is absent when the auxiliary is in a perfective tense, when the past participle must be interpreted as a secondary predicate (e.g., 'it has come in the state of being placed in a box').

As with the Italian *andare* 'go' (Mocciaro) and *venire* 'come' (Giacalone Ramat and Sansò), Romanian *veni* is used as a change-of-state verb, but it has evolved beyond that and now functions as a bona fide copula, in parallel with *fi* 'be'. The difference between the two – and perhaps the reason why *veni* as a copula came into being – is that *veni* underwent a change from 'change of location' to 'marker of indirect kinship relation' (cousin, nephew, brother-in-law, etc.), which is a semantically more restricted use than the general *fi*. This shows the persistence of the original motion and deictic centre, where the relation expressed by the copula must have been arrived at via an indirect way. Hence, for terms expressing a direct kinship relation (mother, father, brother, etc.) only the copula *fi* can be used, not *veni*.

The motivation for the multiple grammaticalization of *veni* rather than one of the other motion verbs in Romanian, is the combined effect of the lexical semantics and syntax of the verb. Already in Old Romanian *veni* was highly polysemous, more so than the other candidates, and could hence be used in many contexts. Its syntactic restriction to unaccusative use favors its reanalysis as a passive auxiliary.

3.2 Mood and modality

Bourdin's paper is a cross-linguistic study of ventive and itive verbs developing into necessive markers.

The author makes a first distinction between grammaticalization paths that involve an intermediate stage as a future marker and those that do not. In Dehu (Austronesian) and in Kru languages (Niger-Congo) a generic motion verb and a 'come' verb, respectively, turn into markers of non-epistemic necessity via an intermediate stage as a future marker.

In languages where future marking does not play a role a further distinction is made between ventive and itive passives co-encoding necessive modality and ventives that go necessive directly. In Italian and Indo-Aryan languages itive passives can in certain contexts express necessity. In Romanian ventive passives show a similar evolution. The direct path is encountered in Scottish Gaelic, Irish and some non-Slavic Circum Baltic languages. In these languages the ventive source verb is robustly deictic. This is not the case in Russian, which attests a strikingly similar grammaticalization path, although the source verb is less strongly deictic.

Although the different pathways involve diverse semantic mechanisms (metaphor, metonymy and /or language iconicity), Bourdin claims that, ultimately, they all owe their existence to the goal-orientedness or deictic nature of the source verbs. He goes on to argue that when similar paths are traveled by weakly deictic or adeictic motion verbs, as is the case in Dehu and Russian, this can be accounted for by a "next-best-tool principle".

Based on a convenience sample of 200 languages, Mauri and Sansò show that 'come' and 'go' are frequent sources of directive markers. Although this grammaticalization pathway is a relatively well known one (see Aikhenvald 2010 and Heine and Kuteva 2002), the paper indicates that the development cannot simply be explained by referring to the (presupposed) telic and change-of-state nature of the source verbs, notions that are often brought up when explaining the grammaticalization of 'come' and 'go' into markers of TAM or case relations.

Instead, the authors argue that 'come' and 'go' enter the process of grammaticalization because they imply displacement, and displacement is often a necessary preliminary action to realize an order. It is this frequent co-occurrence that triggers their reanalysis as directive markers.

Mauri and Sansò then go on to show that the original lexical semantics do constrain the extensions of the reanalysis. More specifically, the deictic component of their meaning explains why 'go' shows a preference for second person imperatives, whereas 'come' is restricted to first person plural directive constructions.

3.3 Discourse markers

Daniels describes the various discourse-related uses of *venga* 'come' in present-day Peninsular Spanish as the outcome of two distinct grammaticalization paths 1) optative > discourse marker of acceptance and discourse marker of conversation ending, and 2) imperative > discourse marker of disagreement.

Although both paths appear to involve an (almost) complete loss of motion semantics (as is the case in example (5b) from Shangaci), Daniels' careful study of historical corpora as well as sources of current-day use shows that the semantic loss is accompanied by pragmatic strengthening as metaphorically or metonymically construed pragmatic inferences become conventionalized. Furthermore, Daniels also shows that pragmatic strengthening and semantic weakening go hand in hand with an increase in syntactic independence, which is typical of discourse markers.

Finally, a short cross-linguistic excursion shows that 'come' often develops discourse related uses but that we need more discourse data on more languages to evaluate the commonness of the evolution.

Bravo discusses one grammaticalization path of Spanish *ir* 'go', which happened in two stages: it developed first into a resultative marker (IRres) and only then into a focus marker (IRfoc). The resultative IRres crucially developed from *ir* as a motion verb (as in *ir a París* 'go to Paris') and not from purposive *ir* + infinitive (as in *ir a comprar pan* 'go to buy bread').

Bravo proposes that IRres has not grammaticalized into an auxiliary, but is a deficient lexical verb that takes a second verb as its complement. It still has the same semantics of motion, with or without displacement, where the subevent is now interpreted as the resultant state. The resultative construction is found as early as the 13th century.

The use of *ir* as a focus marker (IRfoc) is argued to be a separate and further grammaticalized construction that did not appear until the 18th century. Syntactically, IRfoc occupies a position in the left periphery of the sentence and heads a focus projection. In semantic-pragmatic terms, IRfoc developed out of ambiguous contexts where the contextually clear negative evaluation of the metaphoric goal of *ir* (e.g. 'she went to give her beauty to an extremely ugly man') allowed for a scalar ranking of the implied alternatives (e.g. less ugly people), which comes down to a focused interpretation ('of all the people she had to marry this one'). The underlying syntactic structure as a focus marker is at some point more economical than the motion verb + inferences, Bravo argues, which is why reanalysis happened, followed by the semantification of the focus interpretation, leading to the current use of *ir* as a focus marker.

Carlson discusses the grammaticalization of the 'go (to)' verb *shyε* in Supyire, which travels two independent grammaticalization pathways. The first one which ends in an allative auxiliary is well-attested cross-linguistically. The second and probably more recent one concerns an intriguing development into an intensifying serial verb.

The 'go'-derived intensifier either strengthens a gradable concept within the sentence (as in 'he is really big') or intensifies the speech act (statements, polar questions or directives) as a whole (as in 'he really is big'). The specific function of the speech act intensifier depends on the type of speech act involved. An epistemic function coincides with the strengthening of an assertion in the face of the addressee's disbelief and a deontic function is served when a directive or an interrogative is strengthened in the face of the addressee's reluctance to act/answer.

Carlson claims, with the help of insights from a native speaker, that the motivation for the use of 'go' as an intensifier can be found in a metaphorical mapping of 'farther away from the speaker' on 'more than usual'. The author goes on to argue that the speech act intensifying function probably developed out of the strengthening use. Given that no historical data are available, this hypothesis is backed up by several bridging examples.

Devos' paper starts out with a description of the lexical semantics of nine motion verbs in Shangaci. They form an unstable network of related meanings. The instability is reflected by the presence of two near-synonymous verbs of 'going (to)', one derived from a generic verb of motion ('to walk', 'to travel') and the other from a verb expressing 'leave from'. Devos suggests that the lexical changes typically involve an increase in goal-orientedness.

In the second part of the paper Devos looks at grammaticalization paths starting out from these motion verbs. It turns out that four of them grammaticalize, together leading to seven different grams. Some travel the more or less beaten path (towards future and co-hortative markers), whereas others have less common targets as they develop into pragmatic markers.

One of the 'go' verbs has textual uses (mostly marking sequences and episode boundaries) as well as interpersonal (disapproval) uses. Surprisingly, the verb expressing 'enter' developed very similar uses as it can also mark episode boundaries and indicate surprise. The verb expressing 'come' has mainly text-structuring uses as a purpose marker and a floor holder.

In the remainder of the paper, Devos attempts to reconstruct these developments based on synchronic variation, sketching the plausible semantic and syntactic changes involved. Although 'go' and 'enter' have similar targets, the suggested grammaticalization paths are very different. 'Go' develops textual and interpersonal uses through the metaphorical mapping of distance in space on distance in time and emotion, respectively. The grammaticalization of 'enter', on the other hand, appears to involve an intermediate stage as an ingressive marker. In the case of 'come' the context plays a crucial role and Devos suggests that its development into a purpose marker is motivated by metonymy.

4 Aim

Wilkins and Hill's (1995) article entitled 'When go means come, questioning the basicness of basic motion verbs' has been a key inspiration for the current volume. The article ends with an important appeal for further research, which, to the best of our knowledge has not been properly addressed so far. As their research indicates that common working assumptions about 'come' and 'go' regarding their universal and deictic nature do not work, there is an obvious need to "reconceptualize research into grammaticalization paths from COME and GO verb sources" (Wilkins and Hill 1995: 251). The present collection of papers aims to do so by looking at lesser known grammaticalization paths of 'come' and 'go' verbs in typologically divergent languages. We have chosen to concentrate on less beaten paths because unusual targets almost automatically invite questions about the nature of the source items, and in the case of 'come' and 'go' about the presupposed notions of basicness and deixis. In the conclusion at the end of this book we compare the broader questions with the findings of the papers and hope to come up with some answers and an agenda for further research.

Abbreviations

FV	final vowel
HAB	habitual
NP	nominal prefix
PP	pronominal prefix
RFUT	remote future
SUBS	subsecutive

References

Botne, Robert. 2005. Cognitive schemas and motion verbs: COMING and GOING in Chindali (Eastern Bantu). *Cognitive Linguistics* 16 (1): 43–80.
Botne, Robert. 2006. Motion, time and tense: On the grammaticalization of 'come' and 'go' to future markers in Bantu. *Studies in African Linguistics* 35 (2): 127–188.

Bourdin, Philippe. 2008. On the grammaticalization of 'come' and 'go' into markers of textual connectivity. In María José López-Couso & Elena Seoane (eds.), *Rethinking grammaticalization: new perspectives*, 37–59. Philadelphia: John Benjamins.

Bybee, Joan & Östen Dahl. 1989. The creation of tense and aspect systems in the languages of the world. *Studies in Language* 13 (1): 51–103.

Bybee, Joan, Revere Perkins & William Pagliuca. 1994. *The Evolution of Grammar*. Chicago: University of Chicago Press.

Devos, Maud & Jenneke van der Wal. 2010. 'Go' on a rare grammaticalisation path to focus. In Jacqueline van Kampen & Rick Nouwen (eds.), *Linguistics in the Netherlands* 27, 45–58. Amsterdam: John Benjamins.

Devos, Maud & Jenneke van der Wal. 2011. What lexical semantics tell us about the grammaticalisation of 'go'-verbs in Bantu. Presentation at the 20th International Conference on Historical Linguistics, Osaka, 25–29 July 2011.

Doke, Clement & Sophonia Machabe Mofokeng. 1957. *Textbook of Southern Sotho Grammar*. 3rd ed. Cape Town: Maskew Miller Longman.

Ebert, Karen H. 2003. 'Come' and 'go' as discourse connectors in Kera and other Chadic languages. In Erin Shay & Uwe Seibert (eds.), *Motion, Direction and Location in Languages: In honor of Zygmunt Frajzyngier*, 111–122. Amsterdam & Philadelphia: John Benjamins.

Emanatian, Michele. 1992. Chagga 'come' and 'go': Metaphor and the Development of Tense-Aspect. *Studies in Language* 16 (1): 1–33.

Fillmore, Charles J. 1997. *Lectures on Deixis*. Stanford, CA: CSLI Publications.

Haspelmath, Martin. 2004. On directionality in language change with particular reference to grammaticalization. In Olga Fischer, Muriel Norde & Harry Perridon (eds.), *Up and down the cline. The nature of grammaticalization*, 17–44. Amsterdam & Philadelphia: John Benjamins.

Heine, Bernd, Ulrike Claudi & Friederike Hünnemeyer. 1991. *Grammaticalization. A conceptual framework*. Chicago & London: University of Chicago Press.

Heine, Bernd & Tania Kuteva. 2002. *World Lexicon of Grammaticalization*. Cambridge: Cambridge University Press.

Hopper, Paul. 1991. On some priciples of grammaticalization. In Elizabeth C. Traugott & Bernd Heine (eds.), *Approaches to grammaticalization*, vol. 1, 17–35. Amsterdam: John Benjamins.

Hopper, Paul & Elizabeth Closs Traugott. 2003. *Grammaticalization* (2nd edition). Cambridge: Cambridge University Press.

Kranich, Svenja. 2010. Grammaticalization, subjectification and objectification. In Katerina Stathi, Elke Gehweiler & Ekkehard König (eds.), *Grammaticalization. Current views and issues*, 101–122. Amsterdam: John Benjamins.

Langacker, Robert W. 1990. Subjectification. *Cognitive Linguistics* 1 (1): 5–38.

Lichtenberk, Frantisek. 1991. Semantic change and heterosemy in grammaticalization. *Language* 67 (3): 475–509.

Majsak, Timur A. 2005. *Grammatikalizacija konstrukcij s glagolami dviženija i glagolami pozicii*. [Grammaticalization paths of motion and posture verbs: a typology]. Moskva: Jazyki slavjanskix kul'tur.

Nash, Jav Arthur. 1993. *Aspects of Ruwund grammar*. Urbana-Champaign: University of Illinois dissertation.

Nicolle, Steve. 2002. The grammaticalisation of movement verbs in Digo and English. *Revue de Sémantique et Pragmatique* 11: 47–67.

Petzell, Malin. 2008. *The Kagulu language of Tanzania. Grammar, texts and vocabulary*. Köln: Rüdiger Köppe Verlag.

Racine-Issa, Odille. 2002. *Description du Kikae, parler swahili du sud de Zanzibar, suivie de cinq contes*. Leuven: Editions Peeters.

Sweetser, Eve E. 1988. Grammaticalization and semantic bleaching. In Shelly Axmaker, Annie Jaisser & Helen Singmaster (eds.), *Berkeley Linguistics Society 14: general session and parasession on grammaticalisation*, 389–405. Berkeley: Berkeley Linguistics Society.

Talmy, Leonard. 1985. Lexicalization patterns: semantic structure in lexical forms. In Timothy Shopen (ed.), *Language Typology and Syntactic Description III: Grammatical categories and the Lexicon*, 57–149. Cambridge: Cambridge University Press.

Taylor, Kenneth A. 1988. We've got you coming and going. *Linguistics and Philosophy* 11 (4): 493–513.

Traugott, Elizabeth Closs. 2003. From subjectification to intersubjectification. In Raymond Hickey (ed.), *Motives for Language Change*, 124–139. Cambridge: Cambridge University Press.

Traugott, Elizabeth Closs. 2010. (Inter)subjectivity and (Inter)subjectification: A Reassessment. In Kristin Davidse, Lieven Vandelanotte & Hubert Cuyckens (eds.), *Subjectification, Intersubjectification and Grammaticalization*, 29–71. Berlin & New York: Mouton de Gruyter.

Traugott, Elizabeth Closs & Richard Byrd Dasher. 2002. *Regularity in Semantic Change*. Cambridge: Cambridge University Press.

Van Eeden, Bernardus Izak Christiaan. *Zoeloe grammatika*. 1956. Stellenbosch, Grahamstad: Die universiteituitgewers en -boekhandlaars.

Wilkins, David P. & Deborah Hill. 1995. When "go" means "come": Questioning the basicness of basic motion verbs. *Cognitive Linguistics* 6 (2/3): 209–259.

Wierzbicka, Anna. 1996. *Semantics: Primes and Universals*. Oxford: Oxford University Press

Zawawi, Sharifa M. 1988. *Kiswahili kwa kitendo, 1: learn our Kiswahili*. Trenton NJ: Africa World Press.

Passives

Anna Giacalone Ramat and Andrea Sansò
Venire ('come') as a passive auxiliary in Italian[1]

1 Introduction:
venire + past participle in present-day Italian

In present-day Italian there are two periphrastic passive constructions. One is formed with the auxiliary *essere*, 'be', + the past participle (ex. (1)). In the other construction, the auxiliary that combines with the past participle is *venire*, 'come' (ex. (2)).[2]

(1) *Il*   *barista* **fu**   **colpito**   *per errore.*
     ART.M.SG barman be:PST.3SG hit:PPT.M.SG for mistake
     'The barman was erroneously hit.'

(2) *I*   *due* **vennero**   **trascinati**   *via.*
     ART.M.PL two come:PST.3PL drag:PPT.M.PL away
     'The two were dragged off.'

---

1 This article is the result of joint research. Andrea Sansò has written Sections 1 and 2 and Anna Giacalone Ramat has written Sections 3 and 4. The financial support of the Italian Ministry of Education is gratefully acknowledged (MIUR grant no. 2008EHLWYE-004, "Language Contact and Change in the Evolution of Functional Categories from Latin to Romance languages: Theory and description"). We would like to thank Egle Mocciaro and an anonymous referee for their insightful remarks on a previous draft of this article.
2 *Venire* in Italian is a deictic motion verb whose basic meaning is "to move towards the speaker". It is opposed to *andare*, 'go', which means "to move away from the speaker's site". *Venire* has a number of other non-motion (mainly metaphorical) uses in which the idea of 'coming' to the speaker (from outside or from a different place) can be still perceived: e.g. *prende la vita come viene*, 'he takes life as it comes', *mi è venuto il mal di testa*, 'I've got a headache' (lit. 'headache has come to me'), *l'anno che verrà*, 'the coming year/next year'. It also means 'to come out'/'to turn out' when followed by adjectives and adverbs, as in *è venuto bene/male* 'it came out well/badly', *è venuto alto* 'it turned out tall'. Also *andare*, 'go', can be used in combination with the past participle in passive constructions. Its use as a passive auxiliary, however, has a number of semantic idiosyncrasies that cannot be mentioned here (the reader is referred to Giacalone Ramat 2000 and Mocciaro, this volume). As the glosses in examples (1) and (2) clarify, the past participle in the two passive constructions always agrees with the patient subject. However, for the sake of simplicity, we will only make use of the gloss PPT in the remainder of this article.

The two construction types are interchangeable in a number of contexts: in both (1) and (2) replacing *venire* with *essere*, and vice versa, yields perfectly grammatical sentences, which are also appropriate in the contexts from which (1) and (2) are drawn. There are, however, some significant syntactic and semantic differences between the two constructions. A prominent syntactic difference, for instance, concerns the compatibility with compound tenses (i.e., tenses that require an auxiliary – either *essere* 'be' or *avere*, 'have' – plus a past participle; Squartini 1999; Giacalone Ramat 2000): both *essere* and *venire* can be combined with simple tenses (present, future, imperfect, simple past), whereas only *essere* is allowed with compound tenses (perfect, pluperfect, future perfect; cf. (3a) vs. (3b)):

(3)　a.　*Il　portone　era　stato　chiuso.*
　　　　ART　main.door　be:IPFV.3SG　be:PPT　close:PPT
　　　　'The main door had been closed.'

　　　b.　**Il　portone　era　venuto　chiuso.*
　　　　ART　main.door　be:IPFV.3SG　come:PPT　close:PPT
　　　　'The main door had been closed.'

From a semantic point of view, the periphrastic passive with *venire* is highly favoured with telic predicates in imperfective contexts, "for the stative meaning of *essere* impinges on the possibility of being interpreted as denoting a dynamic event" (Squartini 1999: 346; cf. (4a) and (4b)); in progressive contexts too, *venire* is the most natural choice, for it triggers a dynamic interpretation while *essere* only admits the stative interpretation (cf. (4c) and (4d)):

(4)　a.　*??Il　giovedì　il　portone　era/è　chiuso*
　　　　ART　Thursday　ART　main.door　be:IPFV.3SG/be:PRS.3SG　close:PPT
　　　　al-le　21.
　　　　at-ART　21
　　　　'On Thursdays the main door was/is closed at 9 p.m.'

　　　b.　*Il　giovedì　il　portone　veniva/viene*
　　　　ART　Thursday　ART　main.door　come:IPFV.3SG/come:PRS.3SG
　　　　chiuso　al-le　21.
　　　　close:PPT　at-ART　21
　　　　'On Thursdays the main door was/is closed at 9 p.m.'

　　　c.　*In　quel　momento　veniva　chiuso　il　portone.*
　　　　in　that　moment　come:IPFV.3SG　close:PPT　ART　main.door
　　　　'At that moment the main door was being closed.' [passive interpretation]

d. *In quel momento era   chiuso   il   portone.*
   in that moment   be:IPFV.3SG   close:PPT ART main.door
   'At that moment the main door was closed.' [stative interpretation]

The grammaticalization of the periphrasis 'come + past participle' into a passive construction is quite unusual across languages; in the vast majority of cases, periphrastic passives (a construction type particularly widespread in Indo-European languages) are formed with a form of the verb 'be' (English, Spanish, Lithuanian etc.) or 'become' (German, Polish, etc.) plus the past participle. In this paper we sketch the historical scenario through which "come + past participle" has emerged and established as a passive construction in Italian. We aim to fill the gap in the comprehension of this historical process by providing an in-depth diachronic corpus analysis and by discussing which among the various constructions of Old Italian in which the verb *venire* is followed by a past participle is the most plausible candidate as the forerunner of the present-day Italian construction. Moreover, we aim to assess to what extent this path is determined by the original "ventive" meaning of *venire*, and whether there are any cross-linguistic similarities in the handful of languages in which a passive construction formed with the verb *come* + the passive participle is attested.

The paper is organized as follows: in Section 2 we deal with the situation of Old Italian and Italo-Romance varieties. In 13th and 14th century Tuscan, two constructions are attested in which the verb *venire* combines with the past participle. Although none of these constructions has a clear passive meaning, both share various properties with passive constructions: one construction type, for instance, can be labeled "uncontrolled eventive/resultative" and encodes situations in which a final state is reached without the control of the main volitional participant; in the other construction type *venire* in combination with participles and adjectives has developed a 'change-of-state' meaning roughly paraphrase-able as 'become'. The aim of Section 2 is to single out which of these constructions is the most plausible forerunner of the present-day Italian passive with *venire* and clarify the mechanisms through which this source construction has been reinterpreted as a passive construction. Providing an answer to this question also requires us to deal with two related questions, namely (i) whether the original lexical semantics of *venire* is involved or not in this development and (ii) which is the role of language contact, given the fact that in other Italo-Romance vernaculars (e.g. in Venetan and Venetian) we do find instances of the passive construction with *venire* as early as the 13th century. In Section 3 we extend our analysis to a handful of other languages in which passive constructions with the same building blocks (a verb meaning 'come' + a past participle) are attested. Data from these languages show that in many cases in which the verb meaning 'come' is used as a passive auxiliary it has also developed a change-of-state meaning. This fact leads us to posit a "change-of-state" meaning of the verb *come* as a necessary intermediate step on the grammaticalization path of the construction *come* + past participle as a passive construction. Section 4 concludes.

2 The origins of *come* as a passive auxiliary in Italian

In this section, we sketch the historical development of the Italian passive construction formed by *venire* + the past participle. As will be documented below, the earliest clear examples of this construction in the Tuscan vernacular (and in the Tuscan-based literary variety) can be dated back to the 15th century. In 13th and 14th century Tuscan documents there are, however, two non-passive constructions in which the verb *venire* is accompanied by the past participle, whereas in other vernacular varieties of the same centuries there is a construction *venire* + past participle that can be considered a passive construction in its full right. The geographic distribution of these constructions allows us to sketch a plausible diachronic scenario through which the present-day Italian passive construction has developed out of its source and has established itself in the standard, Tuscan-based literary language.

2.1 The situation in Old Italian vernaculars

In Old Italo-Romance vernaculars of the 13th/14th century there are various construction types in which the verb *venire* is followed by the past participle. In this section, we will analyze the semantic and syntactic properties and the geographical distribution of each construction type. In Section 2.2, we will put forward our hypothesis, based on a large diachronic corpus of Italian, on how one of these construction types might have evolved into a passive construction.

The first construction type (henceforth, Construction type #1) encodes an event in which a human entity is involved. This entity (encoded as an indirect object, the case typically reserved for experiencers in Italian) is agent-like in nature but non-volitional: he/she happens to perform a given action / obtain a given result in an involuntary fashion (Squartini 2003: 25; Ambrosini 2000: 560); the entity encoded as subject of this construction is the entity, if any, involved in the action as patient/undergoer, and therefore the construction has a passive flavor, though differing from other passive constructions of Old Italian because it does not allow to encode the agent as an oblique argument introduced by the prepositions *da* and *per*, 'by/through'. The abstract structure of the construction is given in (5):

(5) **CONSTRUCTION TYPE #1:**

HUMAN ENTITY X$_{\text{[indirect object]}}$ + *VENIRE* + PAST PARTICIPLE + [SUBJECT]

The subject slot in (5) may also be filled by a complement clause with verbs of saying/thinking and other similar predicates (cf. (9)) and the construction is possible with intransitive as well as intransitively used transitive predicates (cf. (8a)–(8b)); lack of volitionality is often reinforced by adverbs such as *per ventura* 'by chance', but they are by no means necessary for an involuntary interpretation to hold.

(6) **venne-gli**   **lasciata** *aperta la sua camera per*
come:PST.3SG-to.him leave:PPT open ART his room for
dimenticanza.
oversight
'He unadvertently happened to leave his room open.'
(*Tavola ritonda*, Florentine, 1st half of the 14th century, ch. 23, p. 83, r. 25)

(7) *mi* **vengono** **toccate** *le membra di Pirro.*
to.me come:PRS.3PL touch:PPT ART limbs of Pyrrhus
'I unadvertently touch Pyrrhus' limbs.'
(Ceffi, *Epistole eroiche*, Florentine, 1320/30 – ep. Ermione, p. 78, r. 27)

(8) a. *e avvegnadiochè mortalmente gli* **venisse** **peccato**
and although mortally to.him come:SBJV.IPFV.3SG sin:PPT
'and although he happened to commit mortal sin' (lit.: 'to mortally sin')
(*Teologia Mistica*, Sienese, 1356/67; 84, col. 1.18)

b. *a Sagramorre* **venne** **mirato** *in quella parte.*
to S. come:PST.3SG look:PPT in that part
'Sagramorre happened to look in that direction.'
(*Tavola ritonda*, Florentine, 1st half of the 14th century – 166.13)

(9) **venne**-*li* **pensato** *d' andare in Grecia*
come:PST.3SG-to.him think:PPT of go:INF to Greece
'he happened to think of going to Greece'
(Legg. G. di Procida, Tuscan, 1282–99, p. 43, r. 22)

Giacalone Ramat (2000: 139) calls this construction "dative construction". Squartini (2003: 25) adopts the label "anticausative". According to Ambrosini (2000: 560), the semantics of this construction involves "un incrocio tra le modalità eventiva e risultativa dell'azione" (*a blend between eventive and resultative modality*). A more transparent label accounting for both these semantic components could be UNCONTROLLED EVENTIVE/RESULTATIVE. Construction type #1 is only attested in Tuscan vernaculars.

A sub-type of Construction type #1, with the same building blocks but attested with only a restricted class of verbs (*fare*, 'make/do', *fallire*, 'fail', *fornire*, *compiere*, 'accomplish'), has a meaning roughly paraphraseable as "x (eventually) manages [or doesn't manage/fails] to do/perform a given action": the semantic component "lack of volitionality" is somewhat off the stage with respect to the resultative component, and this subtype has a high degree of idiomaticity/substantivity. This sub-type too is only attested in Tuscan vernaculars:

(10) e   questo certo gli   **venía**   **fatto,** s' io non
      and this   surely to.him come:IPFV.3SG do:PPT if I   NEG
      fossi   *fuggito de-lle   loro mani*
      be:SBJV.IPFV.1SG flee:PPT from-ART their hands
      'and he would have surely managed to reach his goal, if I hadn't fled away from them'
      (Guido da Pisa, *Fatti di Enea*, Pisan, 1st half of the 14th century, ch. 13, p. 25, r. 16)

The second construction type (henceforth Construction Type #2) in which *venire* is followed by a past participle has the abstract structure in (11):

(11) **CONSTRUCTION TYPE #2:**

     SUBJECT + *VENIRE* + PAST PARTICIPLE/ADJECTIVE

This construction type encodes an event in which an entity undergoes a change of state. The entity involved in the change of state (encoded as subject) is generally non-volitional and is characterized by low control. The past participle/adjective refers to the resulting state, and the verb *venire* has evolved into a change-of-state predicate. The agent cannot be overtly encoded in this construction, and there is no entity that can be construed as an experiencer as in Construction type #1.

Michaelis (1998: 76) adopts the label "fientive/anticausative" for this construction type. The construction can be better characterized as a change-of-state construction, which focuses on the attainment of the new state but maintains the possibility, when *venire* is in the appropriate tense (e.g. the present, the imperfect or the simple past), of referring to the process leading to it (it is therefore different from a pure resultative construction, intended, in Nedjalkov & Jaxontov's terms, as a construction referring to "a state implying a previous event" [Nedjalkov & Jaxontov 1988: 6]). Construction Type #2 occurs with both simple and compound tenses of *venire* and is robustly attested in both Tuscan and northern vernaculars. In the OVI corpus (see the Appendix) compound tenses are attested only when *venire* is followed by an adjective (as in (16)):

(12)   E   bene   sia   egli molto fiero,   non per tanto
       and   although be:SBJV.3SG he   very   ferocious   NEG for this
       viene   **privato**   molto tosto come egli è
       come:PRS.3SG domesticate:PPT very soon as   he   be:PRS.3SG
       preso.
       capture:PPT
       'And although it (=the elephant) is very ferocious, nonetheless it becomes
       domesticated soon after it is captured.'
       (*Tesoro di Brunetto Latini volgarizzato*, Florentine, end of 13th century –
       Book 5, ch. 54 – p. 171, r. 16)[3]

(13)   *Chatone fu*   *paghano e*   *uccise*   *se medesimo con sua*
       Cato   be:PST.3SG pagan   and kill:PST.3SG himself   with his
       propia mano per non **venire**   **sottoposto** *al-la   signioria di*
       own   hand for NEG come:INF   submit:PPT   to-ART   lordship of
       Julio Ciesare.
       Julius Caesar
       'Cato was pagan and killed himself in order not to become subject to Julius
       Caesar's lordship.'
       (*Chiose falso Boccaccio*, *Purgatorio*, Florentine, 1375 – Ch. 1, p. 288, r.19)

---

3 The construction *venire* + past participle in (12) could be misinterpreted as a passive construction (*viene privato* = is domesticated). However, the example in (12) is drawn from the Tuscan adaptation of the Old French version of the same text, and its non-passive nature emerges clearly once it is compared with the original version of the text, given in (i):

(i)   *Et   jà*   *soit*   *olifans si fiers,*   *neporquant il*
       and   although be:SBJV.3SG elephant so ferocious nonetheless he
       devient   *privez*   *tantost comme il est*   *pris.*
       become:PRS.3SG domesticate:PPT soon   as   he be:PRS.3SG capture:PPT
       'And although the elephant is very ferocious, nonetheless it becomes domesticated
       soon after it is captured.'
       (Brunetto Latini, Le livre dou tresor, Old French, 13th century – Book 1, part 5, ch. 189)

(14) *E   allora gli cavalieri tutti **vennoro**   **smarriti***
     and then ART knights all   come:PST.3PL loose:PPT
     'And then all the knights lost their ways.'
     (*Tavola ritonda*, Florentine, 1st half of the 14th – 352, 23)

(15) *per queste doe cose   elli **vengnirave**   **pigri et enviciadi***
     for these two things they come:COND.3PL lazy and spoil:PPT
     'because of these two things they (i.e. the servants) would become lazy and
     spoiled'
     (Paolino Minorita, Venetian, 1313/15, ch. 64, p. 92, r. 23)

(16) *Illi   erano   **vegnudi** tutti molto **magrissimi.***
     they be[AUX]:IPFV.3PL come:PPT all   much thin:SUPERL
     'They all had become very thin.'
     (Jacopo della Lana, *Purgatorio*, Bolognese, 1324–28, canto 23, 28–36, p. 474,
     col. 1, r. 3)

In Tuscan vernaculars of the 13th and 14th century, and especially in the
Florentine vernacular, out of which standard Italian has evolved, Construction
types #1 and #2 are the only attested construction types in which the verb *venire*
is followed by the past participle. However, once we broaden our horizons to
other vernaculars, we easily find instances of *bona fide* passive constructions
with *venire* + the past participle outside the Tuscan area.[4] This is the case, for

---

4 We have counted only a few examples of *bona fide* passive constructions with *venire* in
Tuscan documents of the 14th century. Two of them come from the same text (exx. (ii)–(iii)).
Example (iv) is drawn from a letter sent by a Sienese merchant, Andrea de' Tolomei, living
in Bar-sur-Aube, to his relatives in Siena: such documents are particularly interesting from a
linguistic point of view, because in many cases they contain the earliest attestations of words
and constructions that are attested in the "official" literary language decades later, and often
vividly testify the complex dynamics of language contact among different Italo-Romance varieties and between Italo-Romance varieties and other (Romance and non-Romance) varieties.
The passive construction with *venire* is also occasionally found in the speech of authors heavily influenced by Venetian and Venetan vernaculars (as in example (v), which exemplifies the
use of the Tuscan vernacular by a Paduan writer, Antonio da Tempo). All in all, however, the
scantiness of *bona fide* passive constructions with *venire* casts serious doubts on the actual
currency of this construction in 14th century Tuscan.

(i)   *e   la fraternita   de'   portatori di Firenze, la quale*
      and ART brotherhood of.ART porters   of Florence REL
      viene   ***chiamata*** *compagnía e   fraternita   de la   casa*
      come:PRS.3SG call:PPT company   and brotherhood of ART house
      di misericordia di messer sancto Giovanni Baptista
      of mercy   of sir   saint   John   Baptist

instance, of Venetian and Venetan vernaculars, where passive constructions with the auxiliary *venire* are attested as early as the late 13th century (see exx. (17)–(18)). In Old Emilian too the passive with *venire* is attested, though somewhat later (ex. (19)).

(17) *in lo   logo o'   che **ven**   **dito**   lo   Casal de Roberti*
      in ART place where REL come:PRS.3SG call:PPT   ART Casal de Roberti
      'in the place that is called *Casal de Roberti*'
      (*Designazione di terre nel ferrarese*, Venetian, 1253)

(18) *un çovene fazando mal no   **vegniva**   **corecto**   da-l   pare*
      a   young   do:GER   bad NEG come:IPFV.3SG   correct:PPT   by-ART father
      'a young man who behaved badly was not reproached by his father'
      (Paolino Minorita, Venetian, 1313/15, ch. 55, p. 79, r. 8)

(19) *La soa   lengua ge   **ven**   **roxegà.***
      ART POSS:3SG tongue to.him come:PRS.3SG crunch:PPT
      'His tongue gets crunched.'
      (*Atrovare del vivo e del morto*, Emilian, 1375, I, st. 35, v. 4, p. 154, r. 12)

The linguistic picture of 15th century Italy is slightly more complex: while local vernaculars continue to be used in both literary and non-literary documents,

---

'and the Confraternity of Porters of Florence, which is (hereby) called Company and Fraternity of the House of Mercy of Saint John the Baptist...'
(*Statuti fiorentini*, Florentine, 1317, 118.18)

(ii) *le buone cose   che a-l   decto   luogo di misericordia **vengono***
      ART good   things REL to-ART aforementioned place of mercy come:PRS.3PL
      ***date,**   salubrevolemente e   devotamente siano   date*
      give:PPT with.wholesomeness and devoutly   be:SBJV.3PL give:PPT
      'the good things that are donated to the aforementioned charitable institution should be donated with wholesome heart and devoutly.'
      (*Statuti fiorentini*, Florentine, 1317, 118.24)

(iii) *(e) **vene**   **venduta** la   soma intorno di quaranta (e) quatro l.   (e)*
      and come:PST.3SG sell:PPT   ART load around   44   liras and
      cinq(ue) s.
      5 scutes
      'and a load (of pepper) is sold at 44 liras and 5 scutes'
      (*Lettera di Andrea de' Tolomei*, Sienese, 1269)

(iv) ***vien**   **depinto**   in nominanza falsa*
      come:PRS.3SG depict:PPT   in reputation false
      '(the loser) gets false reputation (lit.: is depicted with false reputation).' (Antonio da Tempo, *Rime* (ed. Grion), Tuscan-Paduan, 1332, 57, v. 2, p. 168)

a new standard literary language based on the two most influential Tuscan writers of the 14th century (Petrarca and Boccaccio) begins to develop and is increasingly adopted by Northern Italian writers operating within northern Italian courts. These writers also maintain various non-Tuscan linguistic and orthographic peculiarities that can be mostly attributed to contact with the local vernaculars of their courts (Tavoni 1992: 91; Marazzini 1994: 224). If we look at the geographical distribution of the passive construction with *venire* in the 15th century, a fact emerges rather clearly: the construction in question is attested almost exclusively in the Tuscan-based literary language of Northern Italian writers (see examples (20)–(21)), while it is still only sporadically used by Tuscan writers (a rare example from an autochthonous Tuscan text of the second half of the 15th century is given in (22)). Based on this geographical distribution, the construction cannot be said to be an autochthonous Tuscan construction, and can be hypothesized to have penetrated into literary Tuscan only as a consequence of its massive use by writers operating within northern Italian courts. Indeed, Tuscan writers begin to adopt it massively as late as the first half of the 16th century (see exx. (23)–(24)).

(20) *E,   quel che è   peggio, ogni om **vien**   caleffato.*
     and that REL be:PRS.3SG worse   each man come:PRS.3SG mock:PPT
     'And, what is worse, each man is mocked.'
     (Boiardo, *Orlando Innamorato*, Ferrarese, 1495-1, 12, 35)

(21) *Quandò ... poter-mi   dir   tuo   mi   **vien**   concesso*
     when   can:INF-me say:INF yours to.me come:PRS.3SG accord:PPT
     'When I'm allowed to call myself yours...'
     (Niccolò da Correggio, *Rime*, Emilian, 2nd half of the 15th century)

(22) *il   suo   popolo ... **veniva**   conculcato da-gli uomini*
     ART POSS.3SG people   come:IPFV.3SG trample:PPT by-ART men
     'his people was trampled by other people'
     (*Bibbia Toscana*, Tuscan 1471-8.596.8)

(23) *che   non **venga**   oppresso / Da-gli armenti, da gregge,*
     COMP NEG come:SBJV.3SG tread:PPT   by-ART herds   by flock
     o   d' uman   piede.
     or by human foot
     '(make sure that the meadow) is not trodden by herds, flocks or by human foot.' (Luigi Alamanni, *Della coltivazione*, Florentine, 1546)

(24) *Il che   nientedimeno   pare   a   me   che   **venga***
  REL   nonetheless   seem:PRS.3SG to me COMP come:SBJV.3SG
  compreso *in   quella   spezie   che   pone   lo   inventore*
  comprise:PPT in that   species REL posit:PRS.3SG the inventor
  per   la   cosa   trovata
  for ART thing found
  '[talking about metonymy] which in my view should be classified similarly
  to those cases in which the inventor stands for the thing invented.'
  (Giambullari, *Regole della lingua fiorentina*, Florentine, 1551)

2.2 *Venire* + past participle: reconstructing a grammaticalization path

The presence of various constructions with a quasi-passive meaning (be it resultative or anticausative) in Italian vernaculars from the 13th to the 15th century raises the question as to which construction represents the most plausible source of the passive construction, and whether the original semantics of motion of the verb *venire* is involved in this diachronic pathway. As is well-known, both anticausative constructions and resultative constructions are attested as sources of passive constructions cross-linguistically (Givón 1981; Haspelmath 1990, among many others): as a result, in the literature on *venire* + past participle as a passive construction in Italian there have been various proposals on its source and on the mechanisms leading to its emergence. In what follows, we will reconstruct the diachronic scenario leading to the emergence and establishment of the passive construction on the basis of the analysis of a large corpus of Italian documents from the earliest written records to the 17th century, whose results have been summarized in Section 2.1.

In construction type #1 "the deictic orientation of *venire* expressing the idea of 'coming' in an unexpected and surprising way toward the recipient" (Giacalone Ramat 2000: 141) is still present, i.e. the original lexical semantics of *venire* is somewhat retained. This semantic component seems to be related to another use of *venire* in Old Tuscan, in which it functions as a happening verb followed by the complementizer *che* to encode sudden events, often seen from the perspective of the main character or the narrator, as in example (25).

(25) *Qua(n)do   **vene**   che   noe   avate   piue   bisogno   di   lui*
  when   come:PRS.3SG COMP NEG have:SBJV.2PL more need   of him
  'Should you happen not to need him anymore'
  (*Lettere lucchesi*, 112.16; Tuscan, 1301)

The unexpected character of the action/event does not seem to characterize the target construction (i.e. the passive with *venire*). The lack of any semantic component of unexpectedness in the Italian passive with *venire* makes Construction type #1 an implausible candidate as a source of the passive construction. Moreover, the most agent-like entity in Construction type #1, i.e. the human entity which inadvertently happens to perform an action, is construed as an experiencer rather than as an oblique agent, as in the passive construction: this fact makes the reconstruction of a hypothetical pathway from Construction type #1 to the passive construction of present-day Italian highly improbable, forcing the advocates of such a pathway (e.g. Rohlfs: §735; Ambrosini 2000: 560; see also Giacalone Ramat 2000: 140–141) to admit a sudden demise of the dative experiencer in concomitance with the passive reinterpretation of the source construction.

In construction type #2, on the other hand, the original semantics of motion is somewhat less prominent: the verb *venire* has developed into a change-of-state predicate (roughly paraphraseable as 'become'/'get') which focuses on the transition into the new state encoded by the participle/adjective, while also embracing the event or process immediately preceding the attainment of that state when the verb is in the simple present, the imperfect, or the simple past. This is a common development, well attested in various languages (see below, Section 3).

The data discussed in Section 2.1 seems to suggest that Construction type #2, in which *venire* is used as a change-of-state predicate with an adjective or an adjectivally-used participle with inherently "passive orientation" (in the sense of Haspelmath 1994: 153), is the most plausible forerunner of the passive construction: the passive construction is already fully developed in 13th century Venetian, where only construction type #2 is attested (construction type #1 being limited to Tuscan vernaculars). In its 13th and 14th century attestations, Construction type #2 is much more widespread with adjectives than with participles. When used with participles, the passive orientation of the participle is responsible for the reinterpretation of construction type #2 as implying an external agent, as the participle maintains the argument structure of the verb from which it is derived (e.g. if the elephant *becomes domesticated* there must be someone who domesticates it). If this hypothesis is correct, in the emergence of the Italian passive with *venire* the same process of reinterpretation that characterizes the emergence of passive constructions with "become"-auxiliaries would be at play (e.g. Polish, Wiemer 2004: 301; German, Riehl 2001: 482–483; Vogel 2006: 119–132); moreover, in the auxiliation process the meaning of the verb in the source construction persists in the target construction: *venire* as a change-of-state predicate maintains its dynamic character, resulting in a target construction which can be characterized as a (more) actional passive which differs from the (more) stative passive construction with *essere* 'be' in terms of dynamicity/stativity.

The characteristics of the source construction are also able to explain why in present-day Italian the passive construction with *venire* is only limited to non-compound tenses. Construction type #2 has a somewhat double nature: when the verb *venire* in the source construction is in a compound tense (as in example (16)), the construction only focuses on the resulting state (they had become very thin ≅ they were very thin), whereas when the verb is in the simple present, the simple past (*passato remoto*) or the imperfective past (*imperfetto*), it embraces both the final state and the process leading to it. It is only with tenses favouring a dynamic interpretation (process + final state) that the passive interpretation emerges, resulting in a dynamic passive contrasting with the (more) stative passive with *essere*, which in simple tenses is often ambiguous between a dynamic and a stative interpretation (cf. Section 1).[5]

Squartini (2003: 27–28) puts forward a different hypothesis on the emergence of the passive with *venire*: he proposes that the forerunner of the passive construction in Italian is the use of *venire* with a meaning roughly paraphraseable as "result"/"turn out to be", as in example (26). This use of *venire*, which is widely attested in the 17th century, and which Squartini exemplifies by means of passages taken from 17th century treatises, "convive con le prime attestazioni di passivo e [...] rappresenta un plausibile candidato come stadio intermedio nel processo di grammaticalizzazione" (Squartini 2003: 28; "coexists with the earliest attestations of the passive and represents a plausible candidate as an intermediate stage in the grammaticalization process").

(26) *D' un modulo e mezo* [...] *(gli intercolumni) vengono*
      of one unit and half   ART intercolumns come:PRS.3SG
      troppo   ristretti.
      too.much restrict:PPT
      'The intercolumns turn out to be too much restricted if they measure one unit and a half.'
      (17th century Italian, from Squartini 2003: 28)

The meaning of *venire* in (26), however, is subtly different from the meaning of the verb in construction type #2: while in (26) the event is seen from the vantage point of the final state encoded in the participle (*ristretti*) and there is no reference to

---

5 An anonymous referee points out to us that the present-day syntactic restrictions of the passive with *venire*, which do not characterize the supposed source construction, seem to contradict the expansive nature of grammaticalization: in our view, they are fully motivated in a grammaticalization process in which the emerging construction has specialized as a more dynamic passive in contrast with the other passive construction with *essere*.

the process leading to that state (i.e. the construction is a pure resultative), when *venire* is used as a change-of-state predicate (as in examples (12)–(16)) both the process and the change of state are in focus. Squartini (2003: 30) also coherently states that a re-categorization of the source construction in terms of Aktionsart is necessary for a source construction denoting a state such as the one exemplified in (26) to become a passive; in our proposal, however, this is not necessary, as the source construction is not simply a resultative construction but a dynamic construction which already implies both the process and the resulting state.

The geographic distribution and chronology presented above (and schematized in Table 1) seems to suggest that the passive construction has developed in Tuscan (and in standard Italian) as a result of contact with northern vernaculars (especially the Venetian vernacular), and the adoption of the passive construction from the model language (Venetian) has been fostered by the existence of the source construction (i.e. Construction Type #2) in the replica language (in the sense of Heine & Kuteva 2005), i.e. Tuscan, as testified by examples (12)–(14). At any rate, if this areal pattern is correct, it is not entirely appropriate to look for the plausible forerunners of the passive construction in Tuscan documents of the 17th century, as Squartini does. Instead, the source construction of the passive must be looked for in 13th/14th century Venetian and Venetan vernaculars, from where the passive with *venire* seems to have spread to other Italo-Romance vernaculars: the data discussed above show that the only plausible candidate in Venetian/Venetan varieties is construction type #2, the meaning "result/turn out to be" of the verb *venire* being not attested in 13th and 14th century Venetian.

Table 1. The chronology of the three construction types with *venire* ('come') + past participle (/adjective) in different Italian vernaculars. #3 indicates the passive construction with *venire*. The broken line indicates sporadic occurrences.

	13th century	14th century	15th century	16th century
Venetian/Venetan vernaculars	#1: not attested #2: ———————————— #3: ————————————			→ →
Emilian vernaculars	#1: not attested #2: #3:		———————— ——————	→ →
Tuscan variety (Tuscan writers)	#1: —————— #2: —————— #3:		— — — — — —	→ → →

3 *Come* as a passive auxiliary: a cross-linguistic survey

The grammaticalization of the periphrasis 'come + past participle' into a passive construction is quite unusual across languages. The vast majority of periphrastic passives (a construction type particularly widespread in Indo-European languages) are formed with a form of the verb 'be' (English, Spanish, Lithuanian etc.) or 'become' (German, Polish, etc.) plus the past participle. Siewierska (1984: 126) lists Italian, Kurdish, Maithili and Kashmiri as languages in which there is a passive construction with a form of the verb 'come'. However:

–   in Maithili the auxiliary of the passive *ja* means 'go' rather than 'come' (Yadav 1996: 210);
–   the Kurdish and Kashmiri constructions are structurally different from the Italian passive with *venire*: in Kashmiri the passive is formed with the ablative form of the infinitive plus the auxiliary verb *yun* 'to come' (Wali & Koul 1997: 208); in Kurmanji Kurdish too the verb *hatin* 'come' is followed by the infinitive of the main verb (Thackston 2006: 67):[6]

(27)   NORTHERN KURDISH, Awroman dialect (MacKenzie 1961: 195, quoted by Bourdin 2008)

    watuw   *dē*   ***hēt-a***   ***kušt-in***
    that.way FUT come-ALL kill-INF
    'That way he will be killed.' (lit.: 'that way he will come to the kill(ing).')

Passive constructions formed with the same building blocks as the Italian construction ('come' + past participle) are however known from a handful of languages. For instance, they are quite widespread in various circum-Alpine Romance and German varieties: Surselvan and other Rhaeto-Romance varieties (Haiman & Benincà 1992; Ebneter 1994); Cimbrian (Schweizer 2008: 844–845; Tyroller 2003: 122); Bavarian (Wiesinger 1989); Swiss German (Bucheli Berger 2005); Walser dialects in Switzerland and Italy (Gurinerdeutsch, cf. Russ 2002: 115; Pomattertitsch, cf. Dal Negro 2004: 96; Gressoney Walser, cf. Zürrer 1982: 93). In many of these varieties the verb *come* has also evolved into a change-of-state predicate

---

6 Passive constructions in which a form of a motion verb is combined with the infinitive/verbal noun are by the way attested in various languages (Neo-Aramaic dialects, cf. Khan 2008: 754; Fassberg 2010: 120; Scottish Gaelic, Gillies 2009: 268; Tajiki, cf. Perry 2005: 249; see Bourdin 2008 for a survey)

(= *become*, German *werden*; Zinsli 1970: 151; cf. Schweizer 2008: 844–845 for Cimbrian; Russ 2002: 115 for Gurinerdeutsch; Dal Negro 2004: 96, and cf. (30b)).

(28) SURSELVAN (Ebneter 1994: 418)

> *el ei   vegnius   cattaus*
> he be:PRS.3SG come:PPT find:PPT
> 'He has been found.'

(29) CIMBRIAN (Tyroller 2003: 122)

> *di   tokkn   khemmen   getoalt*
> ART pieces come:PRS.3PL divide:PPT
> 'The pieces are divided.'

(30) POMATTERTITSCH (Dal Negro 2004: 96)

> a. *der salam chun   röwä gässä*
>   ART salami come:PRS.3SG raw   eat:PPT
>   'Salami is eaten raw'

> b. *wir sin   älli grossi cho*
>   we   be:PRS.1PL all   old   come:PPT
>   'We have all become/grown old'

In the Alpine German speaking communities, the area using *kommen* instead of *werden* (Bucheli Berger 2005; Iwar Werlen p.c.) includes the western region in the Canton of Fribourg ("Senslerdeutsch"), the whole German speaking part of Valais, the Walser settlements in Italy and Ticino and parts of the Grisons (not only Walser dialects). The availability of the change-of-state meaning of the motion verb *kommen* might have fostered the grammaticalization of *come* + past participle into a passive construction, but these varieties have also been in contact with Italian and Italo-Romance varieties for centuries, and the chances that passive constructions with *come* + past participle have developed in these languages as replicas of Italian (or Italo-Romance) models are high (Zinsli 1970: 144; Mayerthaler & Mayerthaler 1990: 390–391 and Wiesinger 1989: 262–264 for southern German varieties). Since passive constructions in European languages are commonly formed with *be* or *become* as auxiliaries, Heine and Kuteva (2005: 86) identify this Alpine area as a grammaticalization area (see also Ramat 1998: 227–28), whichever language provided the model construction.

Passive constructions based on the verb 'come' + the past participle are also attested outside the Circum-Alpine area. In Romanian (and particularly in southern dialects), for instance, the construction *come* + past participle can be considered as a passive construction with special ingressive or imminent meaning (Alexandru Laurentiu Cohal, p.c.; see also GALR 2008: 137), as in example (31a). *Come* in Romanian is but one of a set of modal and aspectual semi-auxiliaries (*must, wait, go*, etc., cf. (31b)) that can be combined with the past participle (which is responsible for the passive orientation of the construction) to yield a full range of modal and aspectual meanings.

(31) ROMANIAN (Alexandru Laurentiu Cohal, p.c.)

　　a. *Masa*　　*vine*　　　　　*pusă*　　*de ei*　　*în colţ*
　　　　table:DEF　come:PRS.3SG　put:PPT　by　them　in　corner
　　　　'The table is going to be put by them in the corner.' (imminent/ingressive)

　　b. *Masa*　　*trebuie*　　　*pusă*　　*de ei*　　*acolo*
　　　　table:DEF　must:PRS.3SG　put:PPT　by　them　there
　　　　'The table must be put by them over there.'

　　c. *Apa*　　*vine*　　　　　*mare*
　　　　water:DEF　come:PRS.3SG　big
　　　　'The water grows big/deep'

Normative Romanian grammars analyze this set of constructions as resulting from the suppression of the verb *be* (*must be done > must done; comes to be done > comes done* etc.); however, according to Dragomirescu & Nicolae (this volume), the development of *veni* into a passive auxiliary in Romanian presupposes the evolution of this verb into a change-of-state predicate, which is well-attested in the history of Romanian (cf. (31c)).[7]

Venir is a passive auxiliary also in Spanish (cf. Green 1982), although the passive construction with *venir* appears to be less grammaticalized than the Italian construction, and appears to be used under the following two conditions

---

7 Dragomirescu & Nicolae (this volume) do not provide any information on when the construction exemplified in (31a) came into existence, and characterize it as typical of the popular language. They present and discuss a few examples from Romanian texts from the late 17th century onwards in which the passive periphrasis *veni* + past participle is frequent, and consider the presence of the construction in these texts as due to the Italian influence (the author being Italians working in royal courts). However, they are rather skeptical as to the possibility that the present-day Romanian construction be explained as an effect of language contact with Italian, mainly because of aspectual and modal differences (the 17th and 18th century construction is not characterized by any modal flavor and unlike the construction exemplified in (31a) admits the overt expression of the agent as oblique).

(Francisco Ruiz de Mendoza, p.c.): (i) the past participle must have a clear resultative meaning; (ii) from the speaker's point of view, there is a participant that is (either positively or negatively) affected by the action (for this reason it tends to collocate with *le* 'to him/her', *les* 'to them', *nos* 'to us', *me* 'to me'); in (32a) it is almost impossible to omit *le*, while the *ser* counterpart (*le fue dada*) loses the resultative focus and the subjective impact of the result of the action on the affected participant. The same applies to (32b). Although a diachronic survey of the grammaticalization of *venir* as a passive auxiliary in Spanish is still missing, it is worth noting that in Old Spanish the verb *venir* had already developed a change-of-state meaning, as example (33) testifies (cf. Pountain 1984; Söhrman & Nilsson 2008: 169)

(32) SPANISH (Francisco Ruiz de Mendoza, p.c.)

a. *su   popularidad le   vino   dada   en   gran parte*
   his   popularity   to.him   come:PST.3SG give:PPT in   great part
   por sus sonados   matrimonios
   for   his renowned   marriages
   'To a large extent his popularity was the result of his high-profile marriages.'

b. *la   carta le   vino   devuelta sin   más*
   ART letter to.him   come:PST.3SG return:PPT without more
   explicación
   explanation
   'The letter was returned to him without any explanation.'

(33) OLD SPANISH (Söhrman & Nilsson 2008: 169; Pountain 1984: 102)

Ricos   son   venidos   todos los sos vasallos
rich   be:PRS.3PL   come: PPT all   ART his vassals
'All his vassals have become rich'   (*El Cid*, 1853; 12th century)

Moving further away from the Romance area, passive constructions with the same building blocks as the Italian construction are attested in Maltese, in Latvian and in Marathi. In Maltese the presence of the construction is most likely due to Italian influence, as suggested by Borg & Azzopardi Alexander (1997: 214):

(34) MALTESE (Borg & Azzopardi Alexander 1997: 214)

It-tabib   ġie   afdat   bil-każ
ART-doctor come:3SG.M trust:PPT.M.SG with.ART-case
'The doctor was entrusted with the case.'

In the Tamian dialect of Latvian spoken in Svētciems (Gāters 1977: 133) the verb *nākt*, 'come', is used in combination with a past participle in the passive construction (see ex. (35)). *Nākt* has also developed the meaning 'become' in this variety (Gāters 1977: 133; Wälchli 1996: 90 and p.c.), and thus the construction in question is not much different from similar constructions in other varieties of Latvian in which two different verbs (*tikt* and *tapt*), respectively meaning 'get (somewhere)' and 'become' (Holvoet 2001: 368–369), are used:

(35)   LATVIAN (Tamian dialect spoken in Svētciems; Gāters 1977: 133)

    Pêc   tam   nāk   adic   papêc
    after   that   come:PRS.3SG   elevate:PPT   heel
    'then the heel is elevated'

Finally, in MARATHI, both *come* and *go* can combine with the past participle to form passive constructions with slight differences in meaning (Pardeshi 2000: 132). Interestingly, the verb meaning 'come' in Marathi (*yēṇēṃ*) also means "to become; to have attained or reached any condition or character" (Molesworth 1857: 677, *sub vocem*):

(36)   MARATHI (Pardeshi 2000: 133)

    uttarpradeshA-tIl   kalyANsing   yanche   sarkAr   baDtarfa
    Uttar_Pradesh-in   Kalyansing   his   government:N   dismissal
    kar-NyAt   A-l-e
    do-PPT   come-PFV-N
    'The Kalyansingh government in Uttar Pradesh was dismissed.'

4 Conclusion

The data presented in Section 3 unequivocally show that the verb 'come' has developed a change-of-state meaning in many (if not all) languages in which a passive construction with 'come' + the past participle is attested. The path leading from a verb meaning 'come' to a grammatical meaning involving "change of state" is indeed quite widespread across languages (Heine & Kuteva 2002: 74–75). In Toqabaqita, for instance, *mai*, 'come', signals "that a participant reaches, enters the state designated by the verb with which it occurs in a verb complex. The state is conceptualized metaphorically as a location and reaching the state as reaching a location" (Lichtenberk 2008: 224). Moreover, the path 'come' > change of state appears to be quite common in creoles (cf. ex. (38)).

(37) TOQABAQITA (Austronesian, Lichtenberk 2008: 224)

Fanua neqe sui   naqa, nia fungu na=mai   qana kuburu.
place this EXHST PFV   3SG be.full PFV=come GENP storm
'All of this place, it had become full of the storm.' (That is, 'the cyclone had spread all over the area.')

(38) FRENCH GUYANA CREOLE (Corne 1971: 90, quoted from Heine & Kuteva 2002: 74)

i vini   malad
he come sick
'He has become sick.'

An intermediate change-of-state stage is also postulated for the grammaticalization path *come > copula* attested in a few languages (e.g. Sri Lanka Malay; cf. Nordhoff 2011; Vlach Romani, cf. Boretzky 1997: 119–122). The grammaticalization path in (39) has been proposed by Nordhoff to account for the development of the copula in Sri Lanka Malay:

(39) 'come' > resultative [*he (be)came a teacher*] > stative
      [copula: *he is a teacher*]

According to Nordhoff, in the first stage of the grammaticalization path in (39) the original motion meaning is lost and what remains is the change of state from A to B; the second stage in (39) appears to have been fostered by a number of predicates in which there is a "reciprocal entailment between the stative reading and a prior ingressive/resultative one" (Nordhoff 2011: 121) (e.g. predicates of profession/membership in a professional class)

(40) SRI LANKA MALAY (Nordhoff 2011: 106)

a. *oorang mlaayu siithu=dering dhaathang=apa cinggala*
    man   malay   there=ABL   come=CP   Sinhala
    raaja=nang=le   ana-banthu
    king=DAT=ADDIT PST-help
    'The Malay men came from there and helped the Sinhalese king.'
    (lit.: 'The Malay men having come from there, (they) helped the Sinhalese king')

b. *Se=ppe   baapa   dhaathangapa Jinaan Samath*
    1SG=POSS father COPULA   Jinaan Samath.
    'My father was Jinaan Samath.'

The in-depth diachronic analysis of the path of grammaticalization of *venire* + past participle in Italian has shown that the original meaning of *venire* (motion towards the speaker) plays no role in the development of the passive construction: it is the change-of-state meaning of *venire*, well-attested in 13th and 14th centuries Italian and Italo-Romance vernaculars, that is ultimately responsible for the development of the construction into a passive construction. The grammaticalization process discussed in this paper, therefore, does not significantly differ from the process leading to the emergence of *become*-passives in German and other languages (Wiemer 2004: 301; Riehl 2001: 482–483; Vogel 2006: 119–132): the inherently passive orientation of the past participle is responsible for the reinterpretation of a change-of-state construction, possible with both adjectives and adjectivally-used participles, as a passive construction.

The irrelevance of the original motion meaning of 'come' to the grammaticalization process in question is corroborated by the fact that in all the languages examined in which a passive construction formed with *come* + past participle is attested, the verb meaning *come* has significantly developed a change-of-state meaning. Although in some cases (Circum-Alpine languages, Maltese), a contact-based explanation for the emergence of the passive construction is to be preferred to an explanation postulating independent developments, the cross-linguistic data discussed in Section 3 conspire towards the conclusion that the availability of a change-of-state meaning of *come* is a propelling (if not a necessary) factor in the development of passive constructions formed with *come* + the past participle.

Abbreviations

ABL = ablative; ADDIT = additive; ALL = allative; ART = definite article; COMP = complementizer; COND = conditional mood; CP = conjunctive participle; EXHST = exhaustive; GENP = general preposition; GER = gerund; N = neuter; NMLZ = nominalization; PPT = past participle; PRS = present tense; SBJV = subjunctive; SUPERL = superlative.

Sources

The OVI Corpus
    http://gattoweb.ovi.cnr.it/ (accessed March 2012)
Biblioteca Italiana
    http://www.bibliotecaitaliana.it/ (accessed March 2012)

References

Ambrosini, Riccardo. 2000. Sulla sintassi del verbo nella prosa toscana del Dugento, ovvero Tempo e aspetto nell'italiano antico. *Lingua e Stile* 35: 547–571.

Boretzky, Norbert. 1997. Suppletive forms of the Romani copula: *'ovel/avel'*. In Yaron Matras, Peter Bakker & Hristo Kyuchukov (eds.), *The typology and dialectology of Romani*, 107–132. Amsterdam: John Benjamins.

Borg, Alexander J. & Marie Azzopardi-Alexander. 1997. *Maltese*. London: Routledge.

Bourdin, Philippe. 2008. What, if anything, counts as a grammaticalization pathway? The case of so-called ventive and itive passives. Paper presented at the International Conference *New Reflections on Grammaticalization 4 (NRG 4)*. Leuven, July 2008.

Bucheli Berger, Claudia. 2005. Passiv im Schweizerdeutschen. *Linguistik Online* 24 (3). www.linguistik-online.de (accessed August 2011)

Dal Negro, Silvia. 2004. *The decay of a language. The case of a German dialect in the Italian Alps*. Bern: Peter Lang.

Ebneter, Theodor. 1994. *Syntax des gesprochenes Rätoromanischen*. Tübingen: Niemeyer.

Fassberg, Steven E. 2010. *The Jewish Neo-Aramaic dialect of Challa*. Leiden: Brill.

GALR 2008 = Guţu Romalo, Valeria (ed.), *Gramatica limbii române*, vol II. Bucharest: Editura Academiei Române.

Gāters, Alfred. 1977. *Die lettische Sprache und ihre Dialekte*. The Hague: Mouton.

Giacalone Ramat, Anna. 2000. On some grammaticalization patterns for auxiliaries. In John Charles Smith & Delia Bentley (eds.), *Historical Linguistics 1995*, Volume I: *General issues and non-Germanic languages*, 125–154. Amsterdam: John Benjamins.

Gillies, William. 2009. Scottish Gaelic. In Martin J. Ball & Nicole Müller (eds.), *The Celtic Languages*, 2nd edition, 230–304. London: Routledge.

Green, John N. 1982. The status of the Romance auxiliaries of voice. In Nigel Vincent & Martin Harris (eds.), *Studies in the Romance verb*, 97–138. London: Croom Helm.

Haiman, John & Benincà, Paola. 1992. *The Rhaeto-Romance languages*. London: Routledge.

Haspelmath, Martin. 1994. Passive participles across languages. In Barbara Fox & Paul J. Hopper (eds.), *Voice: Form and Function*, 151–177. Amsterdam: John Benjamins.

Heine, Bernd & Tania Kuteva. 2002. *World Lexicon of Grammaticalization*. Cambridge: Cambridge University Press.

Heine, Bernd & Tania Kuteva. 2005. *Language contact and grammatical change*. Cambridge: Cambridge University Press.

Holvoet, Axel. 2001. Impersonals and passives in Baltic and Finnic. In Östen Dahl & Maria Koptjevskaja-Tamm (eds.), *The Circum-Baltic languages. Typology and contact*, Vol. 2: *Grammar and typology*, 363–389. Amsterdam: John Benjamins.

Khan, Geoffrey. 2008. *The Neo-Aramaic Dialect of Barwar*. Volume 1: *Grammar*. Leiden: Brill.

Lichtenberk, Frantisek. 2008. *A Grammar of Toqabaqita*. Berlin: Mouton de Gruyter.

Marazzini, Claudio. 1994. *La lingua italiana. Profilo storico*. Bologna: Il Mulino.

Mayerthaler, Eva & Willi Mayerthaler. 1990. Aspects of Bavarian syntax or 'Every language has at least two parents'. In Jerold A. Edmondson, Crawford Feagin & Peter Mühlhäusler (eds.), *Development and Diversity. Language variation across time and space. A Festschrift for Charles-James N. Bailey*, 371–429. Arlington (Texas): Summer Institute of Linguistics.

Michaelis, Suzanne. 1998. Antikausativ als Brücke zum Passiv: *fieri*, *venire* und *se* im Vulgärlateinischen und Altitalienischen. In Wolfgang Dahmen, Günter Holtus, Johannes Kramer, Michael Metzeltin, Wolfgang Schweickard & Otto Winkelmann (eds.), *Neuere Beschreibungsmethode der Syntax romanischer Sprachen*, 69–98. Tübingen: Narr.

Molesworth, James Thomas. 1857. A dictionary, Marathi and English. 2nd edition, revised and enlarged. Bombay: Bombay Education Society's press. http://dsal.uchicago.edu/dictionaries/molesworth/ (accessed online 29 June 2011)

Nedjalkov, Vladimir P. & Sergej Je. Jaxontov. 1988. The typology of resultative constructions. In Vladimir P. Nedjalkov (ed.), *Typology of resultative constructions*, 3–62. Amsterdam: John Benjamins.

Nordhoff, Sebastian. 2011. Having come to be a copula in Sri Lanka Malay: An unusual grammaticalization path. *Folia Linguistica* 45 (1): 103–126.

Pardeshi, Prashant. 2000. The passive and related constructions in Marathi. In Rajendra Singh, Probal Dasgupta & K. P. Mohanan (eds.), *The Yearbook of South Asian Languages and Linguistics*, 147–172. Berlin: Mouton de Gruyter.

Perry, John R. 2005. *A Tajik Persian Reference Grammar*. Leiden: Brill.

Pountain, Christopher. 1984. How 'become' became in Castilian. In Richard A. Cardwell (ed.), *Essays in Honour of Robert Brian Tate from his Colleagues and Pupils*, 101–111. Nottingham: University of Nottingham.

Ramat, Paolo. 1998. Typological comparison and linguistic areas: some introductory remarks. *Language Sciences* 20 (3): 227–240.

Riehl, Claudia Maria. 2001. Zur Grammatikalisierung der deutschen *werden*-Periphrasen (vom Germanischen zum Frühneuhochdeutschen). In Birgit Igla & Thomas Stolz (eds.), *"Was ich noch sagen wollte..." – A multilingual Festschrift for Norbert Boretzky on occasion of his 65th birthday*, 469–487. Berlin: Akademie Verlag.

Rohlfs, Gerhard. 1954. *Historische Grammatik der italienischen Sprache und ihrer Mundarten*, Band III, *Syntax und Wortbildung*. Bern: Francke.

Russ, Charles V. J. 2002. *Die Mundart von Bosco Gurin. Eine synchronische und diachronische Untersuchung*. Zeitschrift für Dialektologie und Linguistik Beiheft 120. Stuttgart: Steiner.

Schweizer, Bruno. 2008. *Zimbrische Gesamtgrammatik. Vergleichende Darstellung der zimbrischen Dialekte*. Zeitschrift für Dialektologie und Linguistik Beiheft 132. Stuttgart: Steiner.

Siewierska, Anna. 1984. *The Passive. A comparative linguistic analysis*. London: Croom Helm.

Söhrman, Ingmar & Kåre Nilsson. 2008. Predicative expressions of transition in Portuguese and Spanish. In Folke Josephson & Ingmar Söhrman (eds.), *Interdependence of diachronic and synchronic analyses*, 167–184. Amsterdam: John Benjamins.

Squartini, Mario. 1999. Voice clashing with aspect: the case of Italian Passives. *Rivista di Linguistica* 11 (2): 341–365.

Squartini, Mario. 2003. La grammaticalizzazione di <venire + participio> in italiano: anticausativo o risultativo? In Claus D. Pusch & Andreas Wesch (eds.), *Verbalperiphrasen in den (ibero-)romanischen Sprachen*, 23–34. Hamburg: Buske.

Tavoni, Mirko. 1992. *Il Quattrocento*. [Storia della Lingua Italiana]. Bologna: Il Mulino.

Thackston, Wheeler M. 2006. *Kurmanji Kurdish. A reference grammar with selected readings*. Manuscript. Harvard University.

Tyroller, Hans. 2003. *Grammatische Beschreibung des Zimbrischen in Lusern*. Zeitschrift für Dialektologie und Linguistik Beiheft 111. Stuttgart: Steiner.

Vogel, Petra Maria. 2006. *Das unpersönliche Passiv. Eine funktionale Untersuchung unter besonderer Berücksichtigung des Deutschen und seiner historischen Entwicklung*. Berlin: Mouton de Gruyter.

Wälchli, Bernhard. 1996. Letto-livisches und Livo-lettisches. Eine Studie zur Bedeutungskonvergenz im nordosteuropäischen Kontaktraum. Lizentiatsarbeit in slavischer und baltischer Philologie. Universität Zürich.

Wali, Kashi & Omkar N. Koul. 1997. *Kashmiri. A cognitive-descriptive grammar*. London: Routledge.

Wiemer, Björn. 2004. The evolution of passives as grammatical constructions in Northern Slavic and Baltic languages. In Walter Bisang, Nikolaus P. Himmelmann & Björn Wiemer (eds.), *What makes grammaticalization? A look from its fringes and components*, 271–331. Berlin: Mouton de Gruyter.

Wiesinger, Peter. 1989. Zum passivbildung mit kommen im Bairischen. In Wolfgang Putschke, Werner Veith, Peter Wiesinger (Hrsg.), *Dialektgeographie und Dialektologie. Günter Bellmann zum 60. Geburtstag von seinen Schülern und Freunden*, 256–268. Marburg: Elwert.

Yadav, Ramawatar. 1996. *A reference grammar of Maithili*. Berlin: Mouton de Gruyter.

Zinsli, Paul. 1970. *Walser Volkstum*. Frauenfeld: Huber.

Zürrer, Peter. 1982. *Wörterbuch der Mundart von Gressoney*. Frauenfeld: Huber.

Egle Mocciaro
Passive in motion: the Early Italian auxiliary *andare* ('to go')

1 Introduction

In Italian the analytic (or periphrastic) passive is formed with an auxiliary plus the past participle of a (transitive) verb; although the canonical auxiliary is *essere* 'to be' which may occur in all passive contexts, as in (1), the deictic motion verbs *venire* 'to come' and *andare* 'to go' may perform the same function,[1] as in (2) and (3):

(1)   *Il*   *dipinto*   *fu*   *distrutto*   (*dai*   *Lanzichenecchi*).
      ART painting be:PST.3SG destroy:PST.PTCP.SG   (by   Lanzichenecchi)
      'The painting was destroyed (by Lanzichenecchi).'

(2)   *Il*   *dipinto*   *venne*   *distrutto*   (*dai*   *Lanzichenecchi*).
      ART painting come:PST.3SG destroy:PST.PTCP.SG   (by   Lanzichenecchi)
      'The painting was destroyed (by Lanzichenecchi).'

(3)   *Il*   *dipinto*   *andò*   *distrutto*   (**dai*   *Lanzichenecchi*).
      ART painting go:PST.3SG destroy:PST.PTCP.SG   (by   Lanzichenecchi)
      'The painting was/got destroyed.'

Compared to *essere*, which is basically a stative predicate, motion verbs add a dynamic (thus, aspectual) component to the passive meaning, that is, they emphasize the process leading to the resultant state denoted by the past participle (see Squartini 1999). In general terms, the processual value appears to be metaphorically derived from the basic spatial meaning of the motion verbs, but this semantic characterization is not enough to explain the specific conditions of use of the motion auxiliaries. Apart from the common processual characterization, *venire* and *andare* show in fact quite a different distribution. While *essere* and *venire* are interchangeable in many contexts (see Giacalone Ramat and Sansò, this volume), the selection of *andare* is subjected to numerous restrictions

---

[1] See Bourdin (2008, this volume) on the grammaticalisation of motion verbs into passive auxiliaries in Indo-European (especially Indo-Aryan, Indo-Iranian, and Romance), as well as not Indo-European languages.

involving both the lexical and the morpho-syntactic levels. *Andare* + past participle expresses an unambiguous pure passive meaning when occurring in a perfective past tense as in (3), whereas it more likely conveys an additional deontic sense of impersonal obligation when used in an imperfective tense, as in (4):

(4) *I   documenti   vanno   distrutti.*
     ART documents go:PRS.3PL destroy:PST.PTCP.PL
     'The documents should be destroyed.'

A further constraint on the pure passive reading is represented by the semantics of the past participle, typically expressing a negative value of 'loss' or 'destruction' (or 'consumption' in terms of Bertinetto 1991: 150). *Distrutto* 'destroyed' in (3) is a clear example of this value; other participles belonging to the same semantic area are *perduto* 'lost', *disperso* 'dispersed', *sprecato* 'wasted', *abbattuto* 'pulled down, shot down'. The construction may also occur with participles which, although not expressing a negative value inherently, share with the former group the basic idea of 'separation or deviation from an origin', such as *venduto* 'sold' and *speso* 'spent' (where the origin is a possessor), as in (5) and (6) respectively:

(5) *I   libri   più   preziosi   de-lla collezione andarono*
     ART books more precious.PL of-the collection go:PST.3PL
     venduti.
     sell:PST.PTCP.PL
     'The most precious books of the collection were sold.'   (from Bertinetto 1991: 151)

(6) *Tutti i   suoi soldi   andarono spesi   in profumi*
     all   the his   money go:PST.3PL spend:PST.PTCP.PL in perfumes
     e   gingilli.
     and   trinkets
     'All his money was spent on perfumes and trinkets.'

The examples (5) and (6) are unequivocally associated with a negative evaluation of the event, namely an idea of 'loss, waste', which may or may not be reinforced by adverbs such as *sfortunatamente* 'unfortunately', *stupidamente* 'foolishly', *inutilmente* 'in vain', etc. or other locutions emphasizing the negative nature of the event. This situation clearly suggests that the negative value holds for the construction as a whole, rather than for the past participles only, and at the same time – as I will try to show in due course– it indicates that the semantics of *andare* plays a crucial role in determining the general sense of the passive sentence (Rocchetti 1982; Giacalone Ramat 2000).[2]

The negative value of the construction is moreover conceived of as non-intentional and the impossibility of expressing the agent, as it is shown in (3), reinforces this semantic nuance; moreover, apart from the lack of a *by*-phrase,[3] the construction seems to be much more compatible with adverbs denoting the accidental character of the event, such as *erroneamente* 'by mistake', *inavvertitamente* 'inadvertently', rather than with adverbs bringing about intentionality/agentivity, such as *intenzionalmente* 'on purpose', *accuratamente/attentamente* 'carefully', etc.

The strong restrictions on the passive reading which *andare* + past participle exhibits require a more fine-grained semantic analysis of the source element from which the passive meaning arose, as well as the contexts in which the construction started its process of grammaticalization. A survey of Early Italian (13th–15th centuries) in fact shows that the passive construction is not originally associated with a negative value, occasionally allowing the presence of agentive prepositional phrases. The conditions governing the use of the construction in Early and in Contemporary Italian have not escaped the attention of specialists; however, the origin of the construction has never been analysed in detail.[4]

---

2 I am grateful to an anonymous reviewer for pointing out that the value of 'loss' is not evident for a verb as *spendere* 'to spend (money)'. At least to my knowledge, verbs such as *spendere* 'to spend' and *vendere* 'to sell' are generically classified within the semantically defined array of main verbs (in the past participle form) the passive construction occurs with (see Bertinetto 1991 inter al.). Rocchetti (1982; see also Giacalone Ramat 2000 and Bourdin, this volume) highlights the strong affinity between the semantics of *andare* and the negative value of the past participles; however, he does not explicitly discuss the specific negative potential associated with events of 'spending' and 'selling', which are *per se* neutral in this respect.

3 As an anonymous reviewer correctly observes, the lack of a syntactic agent does not necessarily indicate unintentionality. Many languages permit only agentless passives and the realization of the agent is variable from one construction to another even in languages which do admit agentive phrases (Keenan and Dryer 2007: 330–332). As far as motion auxiliaries are concerned, Romanian *come*-passive does not allow the encoding of the agent (see Dragomirescu and Nicolae, this volume). In Italian, there is another passive construction which does not encode the agent, that is, the *si*-passive (*si vendono molto libri* 'many books are sold'), in which the passive meaning is overtly conveyed by the marker *si*; however, this construction does imply the existence of an external agent (a generic agent which sells many books).

4 Especially in the descriptive accounts (see Rohlfs 1949; Herczeg 1966; Lo Cascio 1968 inter al.). A significant theoretical contribution is made by Rocchetti (1982), whose attention, however, is only focused on contemporary Italian. A fundamental description of *andare* + past participle in Early Italian is provided by Kontzi (1958) and Bertuccelli Papi (1980). More recently, a serious attempt of diachronic explanation is provided by Giacalone Ramat (2000); however, since her main concern is the origin of the modal value, the analysis of the passive meaning only constitutes the background of argumentation.

More in general, although motion verbs as source domain for the passive voice are documented in a number of languages, the grammaticalization process leading to this function has received scant attention in the relevant literature (see Bourdin 2008). Drawing upon the insights of Cognitive Grammar (Langacker 1987) and the findings of the theory of grammaticalization (Heine 1993; Hopper and Traugott 2003), this paper aims at contributing to the debate on this issue, providing a comprehensive description of the process leading to the grammaticalization of *andare* + past participle as a passive construction in Early Italian and to the increasing restrictions governing its usage over time.

The paper is organized as follows: in Section 2 a semantic analysis of motion verbs will be provided, focusing on the components of orientation and deixis, which will be claimed to constitute the basis on which grammatical meanings arose; Section 3 highlights the contextual coordinates and the metaphorical-metonymical shifts determining the development in Early Italian of an intransitive resultative construction and, on the basis of this, a passive reinterpretation; a detailed description of the passive contexts is provided in Section 4; Section 4.1 is concerned with the diachronic development of the passive construction and with the increasing restrictions in its range of usage; an explanation is proposed in terms of retraction (Haspelmath 2004) and semantic specialization, also induced by the competition with the new modal nuance associated with the construction (see Giacalone Ramat 2000 and Bourdin, this volume). Rather than a conclusion, Section 5 represents an attempt to interpret the role of the passive construction with *andare* within the domain of passive voice in Italian.

2 The semantics of directional motion verbs: between deixis and orientation

Motion verbs may be characterized in terms of *orientation* with respect to the (non-subjective) coordinates of the directional motion, that is, depending on the phase they focus on within the schema Source-Path-Goal. In Italian, *andare* 'to go' and *venire* 'to come' show a clear complementary distribution, namely 'to go' focuses on the starting point of the movement, i.e. it is Source-oriented, whereas 'to come' focuses on the end-point, i.e. it is Goal-oriented (Fillmore 1975: 52–53; Taylor 1988: 496). This difference is represented in Figure 1, where E (representing a moveable entity) is associated with the Source in a) and with the Goal in b).

A classic example of the differences in focusing has been proposed by Fillmore (1975: 52) for English. In a sentence as *he came home around midnight* the adverbial item *around midnight* unambiguously refers to the final phase of the

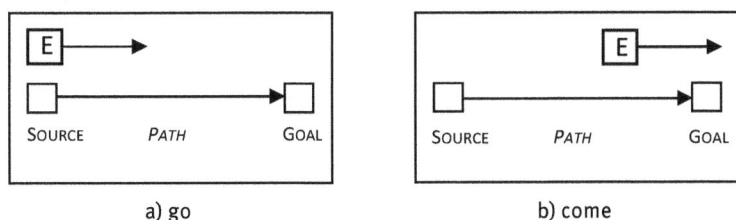

Figure 1. Orientation of motion verbs

motion event (i.e. the arrival at home), whereas in *he went home around midnight*, it indicates the starting point of the movement.

Besides orientation, *andare* and *venire* express a deictic opposition,[5] that is, they represent the directional motion event with respect to the speaker's point of view (deictic centre), namely *venire* (a *ventive* verb) denotes 'movement towards the speaker's location' (e.g. *come here!*, **come there!*) and *andare* (an *itive* verb) prototypically expresses 'movement away from the speaker's location' (e.g. *go away from here!*, *go there!*, **go here!*).

According to Ricca (1993: 29–30, on the basis of Taylor 1988), in Italian the deictic component plays a more significant role compared to the orienting component, as is demonstrated by the fact that when deixis and orientation are in conflict, deixis prevails, such as in the imperative sentence *vieni qui ora!* 'come here now!', where the presence of *venire* is imposed by deixis, whereas the adverb *ora* necessarily refers to the starting point of the movement; or in *vada domani alle 9 alla stazione centrale* 'go tomorrow at 9 am to the central station', where the time reference clearly indicates the endpoint of the movement and the presence of *andare* is interpretable in deictic terms.[6]

---

5 Orientation does not include the couple 'come/go' only, but also involves non-deictic verbs, such as 'to leave', 'to depart', etc., on the one hand, and 'to arrive', 'to reach', etc., on the other. An opposition in terms of orientation describes the opposition of the equivalents of 'come/go' in Latin. Ricca (1993: 117) indicates numerous examples in which *venire* 'come' and *ire* 'go' cannot be interpreted in deictic terms, e.g. *ad iudices veniemus* 'we will go (lit. 'come') to the court' (Terentius, *Phormio* 129), where the presence of *venio* can only be explained in terms of Goal-orientation; *ite foras* '(lit.) go out!' (Plautus, *Persa* 758), where 'out' coincides with speaker's location (i.e. it would be translated as 'come out!') and, hence, the use of *ire* must be interpreted as Source-orientation. In this perspective, the deictic status of Italian *andare* and *venire* represents an innovation, whose beginning is not documented before the 5th century CE.

6 As it refers to the speech act, the imperative mood in the two sentences surely constitutes a suitable environment for deixis to overrun orientation. According to Ricca (1993: 30), the vulnerability of the orienting component is also shown by the selection of the imperfective (progressive) aspect; for instance, in *a mezzanotte stava andando a casa* 'at midnight he was

It is widely recognized that the deictic opposition is not perfectly symmetric; as in other languages in which 'come' and 'go' represent a deictic couple, the ventive verb always constitutes the term marked positively for deixis, whereas the itive is not necessarily linked to the speaker's perspective and allows non-deictic usages (see Langacker 1990: 155; Wilkins and Hill 1995). A sentence as *she came to the park* necessarily implies a deictic point of view, which is located in the end-point of the movement, whereas *she went to the park* does not provide any positive clue about the speaker's location: the source of the movement may or may not coincide with the speaker's location (respectively, *she went from* here *to the park* and *she went from* her home *to the park*), while we only know for sure that the speaker cannot be located in the endpoint. In other words, the deictic opposition mainly concerns the location of the speaker with respect to the endpoint: in this respect, *venire* describes a movement towards the speaker's location, whereas *andare* is characterized negatively as describing a movement towards a point which does not correspond with the speaker's location (Fillmore 1975; Radden 1996 inter al.; see also Bourdin, this volume).[7]

As a consequence, *andare* is always used whenever there is no specific endpoint (e.g. *andare in giro, andare qua e là* 'to go around') or when the endpoint is generic, such as in *adoro andare al cinema* 'I love going to the cinema', where *cinema* does not simply represent a spatial destination, rather evoking additional information about the activities typically carried out in a cinema (i.e. watching a movie); although the presence of the itive verb, such a sentence can be pronounced even if the speaker is actually at the cinema without producing a semantic oddity;[8] that is, the itive verb appears to be the neutral term in the deictic opposition. As a matter of fact, in Italian the semantic network expressed by *andare* comprises both deictic and non-deictic usages and, more relevant to the present analysis, abstract and/or grammatical meanings reflect the complex nature of the basic motion verb in an intriguing fashion.

---

going home' and in *a mezzanotte stava venendo a casa* 'at midnight he was coming home', the adverbial *a mezzanotte* receives the same interpretation, that is, it indicates a temporal point which can be located at any phase of the process.

7 In other words, the itive verb can be analysed as deictic as long as it enters in a relation of opposition with the ventive verb, which in turn is always deictic.

8 The non-deictic value of *andare* in these contexts is also shown by the substitutability with other non-directional verbs, such as *vagare* 'to wander', which is a manner of motion verb.

3 From metaphor to grammar (through context)

The process leading to the grammaticalization of *andare* as passive auxiliary reasonably started from the systematic contiguity of the motion verb with past participles as predicative adjectives. This possibility is commonplace in traditional
descriptions of the construction (see Kontzi 1958; Bertuccelli Papi 1980). While
this perspective can be surely accepted, a more detailed analysis of such syntactic contexts is needed to shed light on the mechanisms underlying the process.
The co-occurrence of *andare* + past participle may give rise to two patterns which
metonymically select different components of the semantics of the motion verb.

In general terms, the abstract meanings of *andare* originate from a metaphorical projection which can be referred to as *fictive motion* in terms of Talmy
(2000); this metaphor attributes autonomous motion capability to concrete
objects, abstract entities, or situations. A widespread use of *andare* is based on
the non-deictic value of motion uniformly proceeding from a Source through a
Path without reaching any Goal. Examples of this type of atelic motion are given
by syntactic contexts in which an adverbial item defines the manner conditions
of the motion, such as in the sentence *la donna andava* a passo spedito/rapida-
mente *lungo la strada* 'the woman went briskly along the road'. This syntactic
context may be metaphorically used to describe abstract situations, such as *le
cose vanno male/bene* 'things are going badly/well'. A clear example of this metaphorical use in Early Italian is in (7):

(7)   *Questa cosa non vuole   **andare**   **a questo modo.***
     this   thing NEG want:PRS.3SG go:PRS.INF at this   way
     'This thing doesn't want to go this way.'
     (Sacchetti, *Trecentonovelle*, 14th cent., 98, p. 217, r. 23)

A second syntactic context which exemplifies the atelic motion through space
consists in the presence of adjectives or past participles in adjectival function
describing the condition of the moving subject, such as in the sentence *la donna
andava* scalza *per le strade* 'the woman went barefoot in the streets'. An Early
Italian example is given in (8):

(8)   *e   s' e'   son   morti, per qual privilegio / **vanno***
     and if   they be:PRS.3PL dead   for what privilege   go:PRS.3PL
     ***scoperti**   de la   grave stola?*
     uncovered of ART heavy stole
     'And if they are dead, by virtue of what privilege they go uncovered of the
     heavy stole?' (Dante Alighieri, *Inferno* 23, 89–90)

This syntactic configuration is frequently used in a metaphorical sense to describe states or conditions referred to the subject, as in (9), where the adjectives *avvisato* 'warned' and *fornito con l'arte sua* '(lit.) provided with his skills' refer to a human subject, and in (10), where the participial form *velata* 'veiled' is referred to an abstract entity, i.e. a science:

(9) *ché   ben sarebbe stato   meglio che 'l   detto ser*
    because well be:COND.PST.3SG better that ART said Mr
    Buonavere non fosse stato   notaio, e   se pur   fu,
    Buonavere NEG be:SBJV.PFV.3SG notary and if actually was
    andare   avvisato   e   fornito   con l'   arte sua,
    go:PRS.INF warn:PTCP.PST and provide:PTCP.PST with ART art his
    come gli altri, che   sono circunspetti, vanno
    as   the others which are   circumspect go:PRS.3PL
    'and it would have been much better if the said Mr. Buonavere hadn't been a notary, and since he actually was, (it would have been much better) to be warned and equipped with his skill, as do go the others, which are circumspect' (Sacchetti, *Trecentonovelle*, 163, p. 404, rr. 7–10)

(10) *e   **va**   più   **velata**   che nulla   scienza,*
    and go:PRS.3SG especially veil:PTCP.PST than no.other science
    in quanto procede   con più sofistici   e   probabili
    since   proceed:PRS.3SG with more sophisticated and probable
    argomenti
    arguments
    'and it goes more veiled than any other science, since it proceeds by means of more sophisticated and probable arguments'
    (Dante Alighieri, *Convivio*, II, 13, p. 124, rr. 9–15).

In these contexts, the subject is metaphorically construed as "going" along a uniform and uninterrupted Path in unchanged conditions. In other words, *andare* emphasizes the continuous character of the states associated with the subject. Compared to the expression of states by means of *essere* (e.g. *he is warned*), *andare* adds a dynamic component of duration (i.e. 'to continue to be in a state', see Kontzi 1958).[9] The development of this aspectual function associated

---

9 Needless to say, *duration* metaphorically expresses a temporal value; this value is only inferential in the concrete configuration of a Path, which is necessarily travelled within a span of time. The metaphorical shift from concrete to abstract motion metonymically selects this secondary, inferential meaning.

with the motion verb clearly signals a process of grammaticalization, which can be described on the basis of Heine (1993: 52–55): 1) the spatial meaning of *andare* is still fully accessible; however, the metaphorical transfer cancels the restrictions in selecting the subject, which is no longer limited to human referents; 2) *andare* is systematically associated with a non-finite verbal form, which constitutes its complement nucleus (Motion Verb$_{main v}$+ State$_{complement}$); 3) the syntactic sequence 'V+complement' is characterized by subject identity (i.e. 'X *goes* + (X) -*ed*'); 4) in this syntactic context, *andare* developed a new grammatical (aspectual) nuance; 5) finally, *andare* appears to occur only in imperfective tenses, i.e. it reduces its temporal-aspectual distinctions.[10]

The semantic properties just described and, in particular, the unchanged character of the state denoted by the past participle, do not permit to consider the construction as the direct forerunner of the passive meaning. A further step should be reconstructed, which contributed a resultative component. In general terms, this shift is not surprising, as motion verbs as source domain for the resultative meaning are well documented cross-linguistically (see Heine and Kuteva 2002: 74, 156). The reinterpretation of the construction must have been favoured by the frequency of the contexts in which *andare* co-occurs with transitive past participles, which inherently denote resulting states. The most immediate and obvious effect of this semantic configuration is a telic interpretation of *andare*: the resulting state expressed by the past participle is viewed as reached through motion and, hence, as representing the Goal of the motion (in accordance with the metaphor CHANGE OF STATE IS CHANGE OF LOCATION as formulated in Lakoff 1987). We are dealing with a context-induced reinterpretation (Heine, Claudi, and Hünnemeyer 1991), which can be represented as in Figure 2:

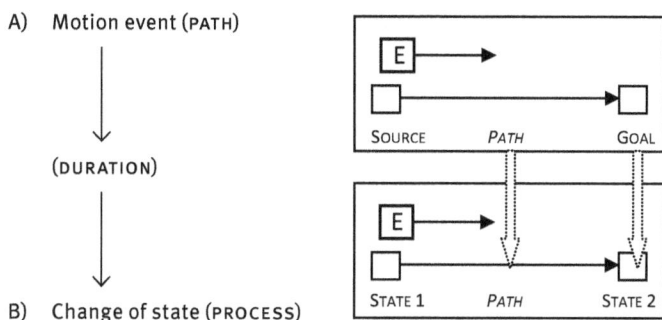

Figure 2. Change of state is change of location

---

10 Heine (1993: 60–61) indicates these properties for the Stage C of grammaticalization, which comprises, among other cases, also English aspectualizers, such as *start* and *stop*.

Clear examples of the resultative meaning of *andare* + past participle are given in (11) and (12):

(11)   *Guai, quanta   ienti foi   meccïata, / ke   tutta la*
       Woe how.many people be:PST.PFV.3SG kill:PST.PTCP that entire ART
       *terra **gia**   **ensanguinentata!***
       earth go.PST.IPFV.3SG cover.with.blood.PST.PTCP
       'Woe how many people have been killed, for the entire earth became covered with blood!' (*Elegia giudeo-italiana*, vv. 25–26, 13th century, from Southern-Central Italy)

(12)   *Se di queste due cose   voi mi   darete   intera speranza,*
       if of these two things you to.me give:FUT.2PL entire hope
       *senza niun dubbio n'   **andrò**   **consolato.***
       without no   doubt from.this go:FUT.1PL console:PST.PTCP
       'If for these two things you will give me full hope, without a doubt I would be consoled for this.' (Boccaccio, *Decameron*, II. nov. 7, p. 134, 22–24)

As in (9) and (10), the presence of *andare* provides the event with a dynamic component: while *essere* expresses a (resulting) state as a location (i.e. 'he *is* dead', according to the metaphor STATES ARE LOCATIONS), *andare* emphasizes the processual character of the event leading to the result (lit. 'to go to be -*ed*'). It should be stressed that, in the contextual reinterpretation, both the orienting and the deictic components are at work. On the one hand, the Source-orientation provides the construction with a strong inchoative and/or ingressive value, which focuses on the initial phase of the change of state; in other words, the movement towards the resulting state is configured as an (unintentional) departure (*diversion*, in terms of Johnson 1987: 45–46; see Radden 1996: 447–450) from a preexisting state of affairs. On the other hand, the endpoint of the movement, that is, the resulting state does not coincide with the speaker's point of view (see also Bourdin, this volume).[11] The inclusion of the deictic perspective in the construal of the change of state – a process inherently non-deictic – is particularly evident

---

11 It should be noted that in Early Italian a (dynamic) change of state meaning is also expressed by *venire* 'to come' + past participle (see Giacalone Ramat and Sansò, this volume). As already pointed out in Section 2, the deictic opposition between verbs meaning 'come' and 'go' concerns the presence or absence of the speaker at the endpoint of the movement, namely: *Movement towards a point (point=Speaker) (COME)* vs. *Movement towards a point (point=not Speaker) (GO)*. The movement towards a point (which needs to be interpreted with respect to the speaker, positively or negatively) characterizes both 'come' and 'go' and justifies their common development in a number of languages (Heine and Kuteva 2002: 74, 156).

in (12), where the subject of the change of state is encoded in the 1st person and, thus, fully corresponds to the speaker;[12] the sentence can be paraphrased as 'I will go away from my preexisting state (=here) moving towards a new state (=non-here)'. In contexts not including the speech act participants, the speaker (or, rather, the narrator) is configured as an abstract observer (see Lindner 1983), who metaphorically assumes the point of view of the moveable/changing entity described; this is the case in (11), where the state 'covered with blood' represents a deviation from the normal state of a street.

The resultative value of *andare* + past participle appears to be quite grammaticalized: 1) the basic motion value of *andare* is no longer fully analytically accessible and univocally denotes a grammatical value of processuality; 2) a categorical constraint is represented by the logical impossibility of imperative forms (e.g. *va' consolato!* 'go consoled!'); 3) the construction expresses a high degree of cohesion (i.e. the past participle is an obligatory component and, moreover, it cannot be syntactically separated from the main verb).

As Figure 3 (stage A) on page 56 shows, the resultative construction expresses an intransitive change of state (namely, unaccusative), involving one participant only (E), which is non-intentional and affected by the event (state 1→state 2).[13] However, the inherent passive orientation of the transitive past participles (Haspelmath 1990, 1994) must have had favoured a passive reanalysis, mainly consisting in the recovery of possible agentive implication (A), as represented in Figure 3 (stage B).

The presence of an (implied) agent produces a radical reorganization of the argumental structure. First, the (non-intentional, affected) subject of the intransitive event is reinterpreted as the (non-intentional, affected) second participant of a transitive event, that is, as a patient (which covers the syntactic role of a subject in the passive sentence). Secondly, both the agent and the patient are arguments of the transitive past participle, while *andare* has lost its argumental structure and only conveys temporal, aspectual, and modal information (TAM) information. In other words, we are dealing with a morpho-syntactic

---

12 The grammaticality of 'consoled' in (12) weakens a traditional account according to which changes of states expressed by 'to go' are necessarily associated with a negative evaluation (see Clark 1974). Cross-linguistic evidence shows that this association, rather than being universal, represents a tendency; see Radden (1996: 433) who indicates the usage of 'to go' in denoting positive change of states in Swedish. More in the spirit of Lindner (1983), the negative evaluation is only probable: the state of the subject before undergoing the change of state is considered to be normal, and in an egocentric worldview normal states are typically associated with a positive evaluation.
13 A fundamental discussion on passive auxiliaries deriving from inactive (that is, non-agentive) verbs is in Haspelmath (1990). See also Dragomirescu and Nicolae (this volume).

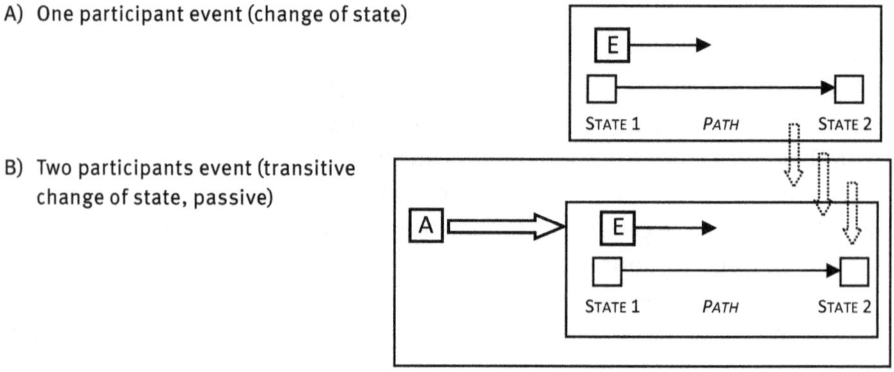

A) One participant event (change of state)

B) Two participants event (transitive change of state, passive)

Figure 2. Shift from CHANGE OF STATE to PASSIVE MEANING

reconfiguration which produces a new conventionalized verbal segment, as represented in the following schema:

Motion Verb$_{main\,v}$ + Past Participle$_{complement}$

↓   ↓

Aux (TAM).........Past Participle (V)

Schema 1. Auxiliarization of *andare*

As we will see in the next section, the auxiliary partially retains its basic semantics – a phenomenon which is not unexpected in the process of auxiliarization (Hopper and Traugott 2003).

It should be noted that the actual existence of this shift in *andare* + past participle is not generally accepted in the relevant literature; while some authors recognize the passive value of the construction (e.g. Giacalone Ramat 2000), others tend to exclude it from the domain of the passive, the main argument being the lack of a syntactic agent (e.g. Salvi 2010). In Section 4 Early Italian data will be discussed, arguing for the passive nature of the construction.

4 *Andare* as a passive auxiliary in Early Italian

As for its geographic distribution, the passive with *andare* appears to be limited to the Tuscan area only, in Old Italian. The first clear attestations date back to the 14th century, but the occurrences are few in number throughout the 15th century.[14] However, despite this very low quantitative significance, they exhibit an unambiguous passive value, as the analysis of the semantic and morphosyntactic properties clearly show.

As far as the lexical semantics of the past participles is concerned, the construction does not show any preference for negative events of 'loss' or 'destruction', as in Contemporary Italian. In general, it is associated with telic verbs, especially non-durative ones (achievements),[15] such as *eletto* 'elected' and *nominato* 'nominated' in (13):

(13) *Et   se 'l   detto notaio in alcuno   de'   detti*
      and if ART said notary in someone of.the said

      office fusse   o vero per alcuno de'   predetti
      offices be:SBJV.IPFV.3SG or   for someone of.the above-mentioned

      andasse   electo   o vero nominato   [...]
      go:SBJV.IPFV.3SG elect:PST.PTCP or   nominate:PST.PTCP

      sia   punito   et condennato   per lo   sindaco
      be:SBJV.PRS.3SG punish:PST.PTCP and condemn:PST.PTCP for ART mayor

      del   comune di Siena.
      of.the city   of Siena

      'And if said notary should occupy one of the said offices or be elected or nominated for one of those, let him be punished and condemned by the Mayor of the city of Siena.'
      (*Stat. sen* 1309–10 Gangalandi, dist. 6a, p. B52163, rr. 13–16).

The presence of durative processes, however, is not excluded, as in the case of the active accomplishment *calcata* 'trodden' in (14):

---

14 Giacalone Ramat and Sansò (this volume) indicate a similar dating for the first, sporadic occurrences of the passive with *venire* 'to come' (Section 2.1, fn. 4). Both passive constructions involving motion verbs are, in fact, Italo-Romance innovations without Latin forerunners (see also Dragomirescu and Nicolae, this volume, on the Romanian passive with *veni*). In the perspective adopted here, this fact is not surprising, as the fundamental semantic component from which the passive meaning arises (through the change of state meaning) is deixis, which is a value not yet fully developed in Latin motion verbs (Ricca 1993).
15 I refer to the classification of verbs in terms of Aktionsart, as formulated in Vendler (1967), Van Valin and La Polla (1997) and, for Italian, Bertinetto (1991).

(14) *la larga strada che mena l' anime a l' inferno*
ART broad street REL lead:PRS.3SG ART souls to ART hell
andò *sì* ***calcata [...]*** *che non si ricorda*
go:PST.PFV.3SG so tread:PST.PTCP that NEG IMPS remember:PRS.3SG
mai che [...] quella strada così ***calcata*** ***andasse***
never that that street so tread:PST.PTCP go:SBJV.IPFV.3SG
'the broad street leading souls to hell has been so trodden that no one ever
remembers that it has been trodden so.'
(Giamboni, *Vizi e virtudi*, 1292, 59, p. 97, rr. 19–22, p. 98, rr. 1–2).

As for the temporal-aspectual properties, the construction selects both perfective and imperfective tenses, as in (15) and (16) respectively:

(15) *Onde il castello s'arrendè a patti, salve le*
hence ART castle surrender:PST.PFV.3SG to.ART pacts safe ART
persone: i quali non furono loro attesi,
persons REL NEG be:PST.PFV.3PL to.them respect:PST.PTCP
perché i Pistolesi ***andarono*** ***presi.***
because ART people.of.Pistoia go:PST.PFV.3PL take:PST.PTCP
'Hence the castle surrendered to the pacts (according to which people
should be left unharmed) which weren't respected, since the people of
Pistoia were captured.'
(Compagni, *Cronica*, 1310–1312, 2.27, p. 176, rr. 33–34).

(16) *fu adiudicato a-lle bestie, a qual morte*
be:PST.PFV.3SG judge:PST.PTCP to.ART beasts to REL death
gli sceleratissimi ***ivano*** ***condennati***
ART wicked go:PST.IPFV.3PL condemn:PST.PTCP
'he was sentenced to the beasts, a death to which black people were condemned'
(Alberti, *Libri della famiglia*, 4.39).

It has been observed that while perfective tenses unequivocally express passive meaning, the selection of the imperfective aspect may sometimes produce semantic ambiguity (see Bertuccelli Papi 1980). For instance in (16), *ivano condennati* (lit. 'went condemned') does not exclude a 'Verb+complement' reading; however, the example more likely conveys a passive sense, which implies the existence of an external agent responsible for the action of 'condemning' (this reading is favoured by the contextual presence of the passive *fu adiudicato* 'he was judged').

More in general, the lack of a syntactic agent does not necessarily attest to a non-agentive meaning and, in a few cases, the agent in fact is overtly encoded by means of a prepositional phrase, as in (17) and (18):

(17) *E* **andata=gli** *la elezione* **confirmata** *da-l* **papa,**
and go:PST.PTCP=to.him ART election confirm:PST.PTCP by-ART Pope
costui si mostrò di non la volere.
this show:PST.PFV.3SG of NEG it want:PRS.INF .
'And once the election was confirmed to him by the Pope, he proved not to want it.'
(Sacchetti, *Trecentonovelle*, 149, p. 345, rr. 14–15).

(18) *E lle lbr. 62 s. 2 d. 9 a fior. per spese di più*
and ART libra [...] per florin for expenses in.excess
andate **fatte** *fuori di Firenze* **per**
go:PST.PTCP make:PST.PTCP out of Florence through
compangni e fattori *per bisongne di compangnia.*
cohorts and farmers for necessities of company
'And 62 libra, s. 2 d.9 per florin for the expenses in excess made outside of Florence by cohorts and farmers for the necessities of the company.'
(*Libri Peruzzi*, 1335–1346, p. 181, rr. 41–42).

An agentive reading is unequivocally implied also in the more frequent cases in which the agent does not receive grammatical encoding, as in (13) to (16): if a notary is elected, an agent responsible for the election must be supposed; analogously, if a street is trodden, there must be someone who performs this action, and so forth. Rather, if we analyse the wider contexts of occurrence, a characteristic clearly emerges which is common to all the examples, namely a general negative connotation of the conditions in which the passive event occurs: in (13), the election of the notary represents a negative event which must be punished; in (14), the street which is trodden is the one leading to hell; in (15), the capture of the people of Pistoia is the consequence of a rejected pact; in (16), it is the lexical semantics of the participle which inherently expresses a negative value (an act of condemning); in (17), the confirmation of the election is negatively evaluated by the subject of the main sentence, who in fact refuses it; finally, (18) describes an event of 'spending (money)', which is represented as 'exceeding' (*di più* 'in excess'), that is, deviating from the original expectation. The negative connotation is likely to foreshadow the future specialization of the construction in denoting events of 'loss' or 'destruction'. If this analysis is correct, the systematic lack of an overt agent can be more easily explained: the focus of attention is on the negative characterization of the event, which somehow deviates from an expectation or a positive evaluation; hence, the agent is quite insignificant and is in fact defocused.[16]

4.1 Diachronic developments

Rather than expanding to more frequent contexts of occurrence, the construction remains sporadic in the later centuries. In Contemporary Italian, the construction conveys a pure passive meaning only with a restricted inventory of telic and non-durative verbs denoting some kind of loss or destruction, e.g. 'to lose', 'to destroy', 'to forget' etc. Moreover, *andare* is used in quasi-idiomatic expressions, such as *l'asta andò deserta* 'the auction went empty' (see Bertinetto 1991). We are dealing with a semantic specialization signalling not only a stop in the process of grammaticalization, but also a retraction with respect to the previous range of uses (Haspelmath 2004). First, the general negative connotation, already noted in Early Italian, develops into selectional restriction relating to the lexical semantics of the past participles. This selection can be analysed on the basis of two patterns: a) in some cases, the past participle expresses a transitive but not inherently intentional (agentive) meaning, e.g. 'losing', 'mislaying', etc., as in (19); b) the past participle of an inherently agentive verb (e.g. 'to destroy', 'to burn (transitive)', 'to spend' etc.) is represented as the accidental result of the action exerted by natural forces which human beings are forced to suffer, as 'the earthquake' in (20), or, alternatively, as the indirect consequence of human actions performed by unspecified agents (e.g. war, bombing, landing operation, etc.), as in (21):

(19) *I   documenti   andarono   smarriti.*
     ART documents go.PST.3PL mislay.PST.PTCP.PL
     'The documents were mislaid'

(20) *I   documenti   andarono   persi*   *(durante / a causa*
     ART documents go:PST.PFV.3PL mislay:PST.PTCP.PL (during / due
     de-l   terremoto).
     to-ART earthquake)
     'The documents were mislaid (during/due to the earthquake).'

---

16 It should be noted that *andare* + past participle is not the only passive construction which only rarely admits the expression of the agent in Early Italian (see Sansò 2011), while banning it in Contemporary Italian: in this respect, the *si*-passive behaves in the same way (see fn. 3).

(21) *I   documenti   andarono   distrutti*   *(durante / a causa*
      ART documents go:PST.PFV.3PL destroy.PST.PTCP.PL (during / due
      de-i   bombardamenti).
      to-ART bombing)
      'The documents were destroyed (during/due to the bombing).'

In both cases, no direct agentive responsibility is in focus and the primal events, be they natural as in (20) or human as in (21), are encoded as causes ('due to') or by means of temporal adverbial phrases providing the contextual frame of the resulting event.[17]

Especially the possible presence of past participles of agentive verbs shows that the non-intentional characterization is more a matter of construal than an inherent property of the event. This characterization constitutes the main function of *andare* + past participle in Contemporary Italian and sharply differentiates it from the passives with *essere* and *venire*. It should be noted that the constructions with *essere* and *venire* do not exclude in principle a non-intentional representation of the passive event, as the presence of temporal adverbs in (22) and (23) shows:

(22) *La   chiesa venne   distrutta   durante / da*
      ART church come:PST.PFV.3SG destroy:PST.PTCP.SG during / by
      un incendio.
      a   fire
      'The church was destroyed during/by a fire.'

(23) *La   città di Varsavia fu   distrutta   durante*
      ART city of Warsaw be:PST.PFV.3SG destroy.PST.PTCP.SG during
      la   guerra / da-lla guerra.
      ART war   / by-ART war
      'The city of Warsaw was destroyed during the war / by the war.'

---

17 Sometimes, the construction does not express telic events of loss or destruction, e.g. 'to stitch' in *La fodera andò cucita per sbaglio/inavvertitamente assieme al tessuto* 'the lining was stitched together with the fabric by mistake/inadvertently' (Bertinetto 1991: 151). However, also in this case the construction conveys a non-intentional meaning signalled by the adverbial items 'by mistake' or 'inadvertently'; although an individual human participation is surely implied (there must be *someone* who has committed a mistake in stitching the lining), 'stitched' represents an accidental result, rather than the effect of an intentional action and, thus, the human participant does not represent an agent.

This situation is fully consistent with one of the main functions of the passive constructions, that is, to render the agent marginal (see Shibatani 1985; Givón 1990; Langacker 1991; Sansò 2003, 2006, inter al.). However, the agentive representation is always possible when *essere/venire* are selected[18] and, in this case, human agents, actions, and natural forces are treated in an analogous fashion, that is, they are encoded by means of a prepositional phrase introduced by *da* (*da un incendio, dalla guerra*).

A second property concerns the temporal-aspectual selection, which shows a strong preference for the perfective domain. This tendency, however, does not represent a real restriction, as the presence of imperfective tenses does not exclude in principle a pure passive reading, as in (24):

(24) *I   documenti cartacei vanno   / andavao   facilmente*
      ART documents paper   go:3PL   go:PST.IPFV.3PL easily
      distrutti   / persi   (perché   deperibili).
      destroy:PST.PTCP.PL   lose:PST.PTCP.PL (because perishable)
      'Paper documents are/were easily destroyed/lost (because perishable).'

Nevertheless, imperfectivity more likely contributes an additional deontic sense of 'impersonal necessity', as in (25):[19]

(25) *I   documenti vanno / andavao   distrutti*
      ART documents go:3PL   go:PST.IPFV.3PL destroy:PST.PTCP.PL
      (perché   compromettenti).
      (because compromising)
      'The documents should be/were to be destroyed (because compromising).'

The imperfective construction exemplified in (25) conveys a rhetorical value of attenuation, in which a certain result is proposed as an inevitable necessity, rather than as an obligation addressed to a specific agent (see Rocchetti 1985; Bertinetto 1991: 150; Giacalone Ramat 2000: 131). This value justifies both the

---

18 Also in the case of non-intentional past participles: a sentence as *il libro fu smarrito da Giovanni* 'the book was mislaid by Giovanni' is fully grammatical, although a non-agentive passive or a *si*-passive would be a more plausible choice, e.g. *il libro si smarrì durante il trasloco* 'the book went/was lost during the removal'.

19 Depending on the context, the possibility of a pure passive or a modal-passive interpretation may create ambiguity of reading in the imperfective tenses, as in the case of the frequently mentioned sentence: *vorrei avere tutti i soldi che vanno spesi per le Olimpiadi* 'I would like to have all the money that is spent on the Olympic games/that has to be spent on the Olympic games' (Peruzzi 1959: 98; English translation from Giacalone Ramat 2000: 131).

strong preference for the 3rd person and, consistent with the pure passive, the absence of a syntactic agent (**da lui* 'by him'). Differently from the pure passive, however, the modal-passive construction does not show any restriction on the lexical semantics of the past participles, and it rather exhibits a high degree of generalization, as the example in (26) shows:

(26) *Il   fenomeno   va   analizzato   in maggiore dettaglio.*
     ART phenomenon go:PRS.3SG analyse:PST.PTCP in greater   detail
     'The phenomenon should be analysed in greater detail.'

Moreover, the modal-passive construction does not convey an unintentional value, as the contrast between (24) and (25)–(26) shows: while in the pure passive sentence in (24) both an agentive ('destroyed') and a non-agentive ('lost') past participle may be selected, the modal-passive sentences in (25) and (26) only allow agentive predicates ('destroy' and 'analyse', respectively). The modal-passive construction in fact expresses 'agent-oriented modality' (in the sense of Bybee, Perkins, and Pagliuca 1994) and, in this perspective, the omission of the agent simply reinforces the impersonal character of the obligation.[20]

The deontic value associated with the passive construction represents a secondary development, not attested in Italian before the 16th century. Giacalone Ramat (2000: 135) individuates the origin of the modal value in "locative expressions which realize the grammatical role of Goal of the motion verb", as in *e segnatamente lavorava sopra le statue che andavano a detta sepoltura* 'and precisely he was working on the statues that had to be located (lit. went) on that gravestone' (Vasari, *Vite*, G. 6 M. Buon. 66.20). This hypothesis suggests that the pure passive construction and the modal one are based on different paths of grammaticalization, namely "the passive reading would be related to *andare* as atelic verb with no explicit goal (as in *vassene il tempo...* 'time goes') [...]. On the contrary, the modal reading seems to presuppose for *andare* the idea of movement towards a goal" (Giacalone Ramat 2000: 132). Though attractive, Giacalone Ramat's analysis underrates some circumstances: 1) when the modal value arises, the passive construction already exists; 2) the deictic component on which the passive meaning (and, before that, the change of state meaning) is based implies the existence of a Goal, namely the resulting state expressed by the past participle (see also Bourdin, this volume); 3) the new

---

20 Though marginal, the overt expression of a generic and non-referential agent is still possible by means of a complex prepositional phrase introduced by *da parte di* 'on the part of', as in *questo problema va affrontato da parte di tutti* 'this problem should be addressed by all' (Bertinetto 1991: 150).

modal construction is basically a passive construction endowed with a modal nuance.[21] As a consequence, rather than originating in non-passive contexts (as suggested by Giacalone Ramat), the modal value should be better considered as an internal development of the passive construction (although I agree that the locative expressions indicated by Giacalone Ramat may have played a role in the semantic reinterpretation of the construction).[22] This development can be interpreted as a focus shift from 'result reached through a path' (passive orientation) to 'movement towards a result which is not yet reached and, for metonymical contiguity, should be reached' (future orientation > deontic reading).

In this respect, *andare* seems to profile the phase immediately preceding the passive change of state denoted by the participle, thus showing its inherent processual and Source-oriented characterization[23]; on the other hand, the deictic component of 'movement not towards the speaker's point of view' seems to be lost, as the absence of the negative value suggests. The exact semantic structure of the modal-passive construction in Contemporary Italian is, however, beyond the scope of the present work; it will be analysed in further detail at another time and place.

5 Towards a conclusion

Compared to the productivity of the deontic construction (and perhaps because of the competition with this productive construction), the pure passive retracts towards a situation of further marginality and obsolescence, which is especially manifested in the lexical selection of the participles and in the aspectual properties. The construction, however, keeps intact its passive value, which is now characterized by a strong semantic specialization. Induced by the new contexts of occurrence (but already foreshadowed in Early Italian), this specialization

---

21 Bourdin (this volume) describes the modal behaviour of the passive auxiliary 'go' in some Indo-Iranian languages. Interestingly, Dragomirescu and Nicolae indicate the same semantic component in the Romanian passive with *veni* 'to come'. The cross-linguistically frequent association of the modal (necessive) nuance to motion passive constructions suggests that there must be a deeper link between these two semantic domains, as pointed out in Bourdin's paper.
22 It is worth noting that the locative expressions coexist beside the modal construction also in Contemporary Italian, as in *i pantaloni vanno nel terzo cassetto, le camicie nel secondo* 'trousers have to be placed in the third drawer, shirts in the second'.
23 Note that the presence of a time reference neutralizes this characterization, as in *le camicie di lino vanno indossate in estate* 'the linen shirts should be worn in summer' or in *la campana va suonata alle 7 in punto* 'the bell should be rung at 7 o' clock', where *andare* indicates the moment in which the event is brought about, rather than the process leading to it.

is fully consistent with the basic meaning of *andare*; that is, the construction expresses diversion from a pre-existing state of affairs, which is construed as unexpected, not controlled, and directed not towards the speaker's point of view. In other words, although we are still dealing with a hetero-induced change of state affecting the patient of a transitive event (in the scalar sense of Hopper and Thompson 1980), the existence of an agentive responsibility is radically defocused.

In this perspective, *andare* + past participle can be legitimately ranked within the functional domain of the agent-defocusing, alongside the other passive constructions, as is represented in the schema in 2:

ITALIAN PASSIVE CONSTRUCTIONS			
TYPE	analytic passive with *essere*/*venire*	*si*-passive	analytic passive with *andare*
FEATURES[24]	affected patient	affected patient	affected patient
	hetero-induced change of state	hetero-induced change of state	hetero-induced change of state
	expressed or implied agent (intentional, specific or generic)	implied agent (intentional, generic)	not implied agent (unintentional cause or force)
DEGREE OF AGENT DEFOCUSING	– .... +		

Schema 2. Agent-defocusing continuum in passive constructions

The schema in 2 shows that the defocusing of the agentive responsibility is a continuous notion, rather than an inherent property of the passive sentences. More in detail, the analytic passive with *essere*/*venire* may optionally encode the defocused participant by means of a *by*-phrase, referred to specific (e.g. 'John') as well as generic or indefinite referents (e.g. 'the people' or 'someone'); when it does not receive a grammatical encoding, the agent remains implied in the semantics of the sentence. The *si*-passive cannot overtly express the agent, although the existence of an agentive responsibility constitutes a strong implication of the sentence and is referred to a generic or indefinite participant, as in *in Italia si leggono molti libri* 'in Italy people read many books/many books

---

24 This description does not comprise other fundamental features, such as the pragmatic role of the patient which is differently focused in the various passive constructions (see Sansò 2003 for the difference between analytic passive and *si*-passive in Italian).

are read'. Finally, the passive with *andare* is selected when the attention is only focused on the (negative) result of an event affecting a patient, while the existence of an agentive responsibility is radically obscured (because it is unknown or irrelevant, or because of pragmatic needs, when the speaker wants to conceal the responsibility of a negative event). This highly specific semantics, which the other Italian passives cannot express, justifies the persistence of the construction with *andare*, in spite of its peripheral and scarcely productive character.

Abbreviations

COND   conditional mood
IMPS   impersonal
PTCP   participle
SBJV   subjunctive

Textual sources

OVI   *Opera del Vocabolario Italiano*, <http://gattoweb.ovi.cnr.it/ >
LIZ 3.0   *Letteratura italiana Zanichelli*, CD-Rom. Bologna: Zanichelli, 1997.

References

Bertinetto, Pier Marco. 1991. Il verbo. In Lorenzo Renzi & Giampaolo Salvi (eds.), *Grande grammatica italiana di consultazione*, Volume 2, 13–161. Bologna: Il Mulino.

Bertuccelli Papi, Marcella. 1980. *Studi sulla diatesi passiva in testi italiani antichi*. Pisa: Pacini.

Bourdin, Philip. 2008. What, if anything, counts as a grammaticalization pathway? The case of so-called ventive and itive passives. Paper presented at the International Conference *New Reflections on Grammaticalization 4 (NRG 4)*, 16–19. University of Leuven, July.

Bybee, Joan, Revere Perkins & William Pagliuca. 1994. *The evolution of grammar: tense, aspect, and modality in the languages of the world*. Chicago & London: The University of Chicago Press.

Clark, Eve V. 1974. Normal states and evalutative viewpoints. *Language* 50: 316–331.

Fillmore, Charles S. 1975. *Santa Cruz lectures on deixis 1971*. Bloomington, Ind.: Indiana University Linguistics Club.

Giacalone Ramat, Anna. 2000. On some grammaticalization patterns for auxiliaries. In John Charles Smith & Delia Bentley (eds.), *Historical Linguistics 1995*, 125–154. Amsterdam & Philadelphia: John Benjamins.

Givón, Talmy. 1990. *Syntax: A Functional-Typological Introduction*, Volume 2. Amsterdam & Philadelphia: John Benjamins.

Haspelmath, Martin. 1990. The grammaticization of passive morphology. *Studies in Language* 14 (1): 25–71.

Haspelmath, Martin. 1994. Passive participles across languages. In Barbara Fox & Paul J. Hopper (eds.), *Voice: Form and Function*, 151–177. (Typological Studies in Language 27.) Amsterdam & Philadelphia: John Benjamins.

Haspelmath, Martin. 2004. On directionality in language change with particular reference to grammaticalization. In Olga Fischer, Muriel Norde & Harry Perridon (eds.), *Up and down the cline. The nature of grammaticalization,* 17–44. (Typological Studies in Language 59.) Amsterdam & Philadelphia: John Benjamins.

Heine, Bernd. 1993. *Auxiliaries. Cognitive forces and grammaticalization*. Oxford: Oxford University Press.

Heine, Bernd, Ulrike Claudi & Friederike Hünnemeyer. 1991. *Grammaticalization. A conceptual framework*. Chicago & London: University of Chicago Press.

Heine, Bernd & Tania Kuteva. 2002. *World Lexicon of Grammaticalization*. Cambridge: Cambridge University Press.

Herczeg, Giulio. 1966. La locuzione perifrastica *andare* + participio passato. *Lingua nostra* 27: 58–64.

Hopper, Paul J. & Sandra A. Thompson. 1980. Transitivity in Grammar and Discourse. *Language* 56: 251–299.

Hopper, Paul J. & Elizabeth Closs Traugott. 2003. *Grammaticalization*, 2nd edn. Cambridge: Cambridge University Press.

Johnson, Mark. 1987. *The body in the mind: the bodily basis of meaning*. Chicago & London: University of Chicago Press.

Keenan, Edward L. & Matthew S. Dryer. 2007. Passive in the world's languages. In Timothy Schopen (ed.), *Language typology and syntactic description. Volume I. Clause Structure*, 325–361. Cambridge: Cambridge University Press.

Kontzi, Reinhold. 1958. *Der Ausdruck der Passividee im älteren Italienischen*. Tübingen: M. Niemeyer.

Lakoff, George. 1987. *Woman, fire, and dangerous things*. Chicago: Chigago University Press.

Langacker, Ronald. 1987. *Foundations of Cognitive Grammar. Volume 1. Theoretical prerequisites*. Stanford: Stanford University Press.

Langacker, Ronald. 1990. Subjectification. *Cognitive Linguistics* 1 (1): 5–38.

Langacker, Ronald. 1991. *Foundations of Cognitive Grammar. Volume 2. Descriptive applications*. Stanford: Stanford University Press.

Lindner, Susan J. 1983. A lexico-semantic analyses of English verb-particle constructions with up and out. Trier: LAUT.

Lo Cascio, Vincenzo. 1968. Struttura, funzione, valore di *andare* + participio passato. *Lingua e stile* 3: 271–293.

Peruzzi, Emilio. 1959. *Problemi di grammatica italiana*. Torino: ERI.

Radden, Günter. 1996. Motion metaphorized. The case of *coming* and *going*. In Eugene H. Casad (ed.), *Cognitive linguistics in the redwoods. The expansion of a new paradigm in linguistics*, 423–258. (Cognitive Linguistics Research 6.) Berlin & New York: De Gruyter Mouton.

Ricca, Davide. 1993. *I verbi deittici di movimento in Europa: una ricerca interlinguistica*. (Pubblicazioni della Facoltà di Lettere e filosofia dell'Università di Pavia 70.) Firenze: La Nuova Italia.

Rocchetti, Alvaro. 1982. Sémantique de *andare*, verbe plein et auxiliaire en italien; de l'expression du mouvement à la modalité d'obligation. *Modèles linguistiques* 4: 115–133.

Rohlfs, Gerhart. 1949. *Historische Grammatik der italienischen Sprache und ihner Mundarten*. Bern: Francke.

Salvi, Giampaolo. 2010. La realizzazione sintattica della struttura argomentale. In Giampaolo Salvi & Lorenzo Renzi (eds.), *Grammatica dell'italiano antico*, Volume 1, 77–189. Bologna: Il Mulino.

Sansò, Andrea. 2003. *Degrees of Event Elaboration. Passive Constructions in Italian and Spanish*. Milano: Franco Angeli.

Sansò, Andrea. 2006. 'Agent Defocusing' Revisited: Passive and Impersonal Constructions in some European Languages. In Werner Abraham & Larisa Leisiö (eds.), *Passivization and Typology: Form and Function*, 232–273. (Typological Studies in Language). Amsterdam & Philadelphia: John Benjamins.

Sansò, Andrea. 2011. Grammaticalization and prototype effects: A history of the agentive reflexive passive in Italian. *Folia linguistic historica* 32: 219–251.

Shibatani, Masayoshi. 1985. Passives and related constructions. *Language* 61 (4): 821–848.

Squartini, Mario. 1999. Voice clashing with aspect: the case of Italian passives. *Rivista italiana di linguistica* 11 (2): 341–365.

Talmy, Leonard. 2000. *Toward a Cognitive Semantics. Volume 1*. Cambridge, MA: MIT Press.

Taylor, Kenneth A. 1988. We've got you coming and going. *Linguistics and Philosophy* 11. 493–513.

Van Valin, Robert D. & Randy J. La Polla. 1997. *Syntax*. Cambridge: Cambridge University Press.

Vendler, Zeno. 1967. *Linguistics in Philosophy*. Ithaca: Cornell University Press.

Wilkins, David P. & Deborah Hill. 1995. When "go" means "come": questioning the basicness of basic motion verbs. *Cognitive Linguistics* 6 (2–3): 209–259.

Adina Dragomirescu and Alexandru Nicolae

The multiple grammaticalization of Romanian *veni* 'come'. Focusing on the passive construction

1 Introduction[1]

In Romanian, as in many other languages, the verb 'come' (Rom. *veni*) is polysemous, having multiple (related) meanings as well as various grammatical values. It is used as a passive auxiliary (1) and as a copula (2) in spoken contemporary Romanian, and as an inceptive verb (3) in standard Romanian.

(1) *Casa   aceea   **vine**   aşezată   aici.*
     house.DEF that.F.SG comes placed.PPLE.F.SG here
     'The house *is placed / will be placed / should be placed* here.'

(2) *Ion   îmi   **vine**   cumnat.*
     John CL.1.SG.DAT comes brother-in-low
     'John *is* my brother-in-law.'

(3) *Îmi   **vine**   să   plâng.*
     CL.1.SG.DAT (it)comes SUBJ cry.SUBJ.1.SG
     'I *feel like* crying.'

Besides the presence of *veni* itself, these constructions have in common the loss of the genuine semantics of *veni* as a motion verb (with different degrees of semantic bleaching) while preserving an abstract dynamic meaning (see also Squartini 1999, 2003 for It. *venire*; for a different interpretation, see Giacalone Ramat and Sansò, this volume). Additionally, in (1) and (2) *veni* has lost its argument structure. These two properties indicate that *veni* has changed its status

---

1 We would like to thank to Adam Ledgeway (Cambridge), Jenneke van der Wal (Cambridge), Andrea Sansò (Pavia), and Gabriela Pană Dindelegan (Bucharest) who read our paper and made very useful suggestions. We are also indebted to the participants at the workshop "Come and go off the beaten grammaticalization path", organised by Maud Devos and Jenneke van der Wal within the 44th SLE meeting (Logroño, 2011). Remaining errors or inconsistencies are all ours.

(in (1) and (2) more conspicuously), from a lexical verb to a functional / semi-lexical element, a change which corresponds to a widely accepted generative view on grammaticalization, namely the idea that grammaticalization is upward movement on the clausal spine from the lexical area to the functional domain (Roberts and Roussou 2003: 20, 36, 194).

From a typological perspective, in connection with the necessive value of motion verbs (see Bourdin, this volume), it is interesting to mention the existence in Old Romanian of a deontic modal usage of the verb *veni*, which is most probably an effect of Slavic influence:

(4) *Pentr-aceea şerbul   tău   le   ţâne,*
     for   that   slave.DEF your CL.3PL.F.ACC keeps
     *păzându-le   întregi, cum **să**   **vine.***
     preserving=CL.3.PL.F.ACC intact how CL.REFL.ACC comes
     'For this reason, your slave keeps them, preserving them intact, as one should do it.'   (Dosoftei, *Psaltirea*)

Starting from these data (presented in more detail in Section 2), the goal of this paper is to answer the following questions:

(i)   Given that in Romanian there are several verbs expressing the endpoint of motion (*veni, ajunge, sosi* '~ come, arrive'), why is it that *veni*, and not other apparently synonymous verbs, grammaticalized in these constructions? How did the lexical semantics and syntax of *veni* influence this multiple-output grammaticalization?

(ii)   Does the grammaticalization of *veni* represent a shift in meaning (of the type metaphor, metonymy, etc.) and/or an instance of re-analysis (triggered by a specific distributional context)? How important is the (narrow distributional) context in this process? How did the original meaning of *veni* influence the semantics of the *veni*-passive construction?

(iii) Given that some of these constructions are also attested in Latin (with *venire*) and that there are parallel developments in Romance, what is the contribution of the Latin heritage to the existence of this broad range of structures involving Rom. *veni*?

(iv)   Is it the case that language contact may have contributed to the emergence of some of the constructions above?

(v)   Finally, do the Romanian data illustrate a single grammaticalization path (with cascade effects) or do they illustrate independent grammaticalization processes?

In this paper, we will focus on the passive construction. However, we will bring into discussion the other constructions illustrated above when they contribute new evidence for this multiple grammaticalization puzzle.

The paper is structured as follows: in Section 2, we present in more detail the Romanian data for each of the four constructions, focussing on the passive construction, which appears in three different varieties of Romanian; in Section 3, we answer the questions above, analyzing the possible factors that have led to the grammaticalization of *veni*. In Section 4, we briefly summarize the results of our research on Romanian *veni* and their contribution to the grammaticalization of motion verbs in general.

2 The Romanian data

As shown in the introduction, in Romanian the verb *veni* 'come' grammaticalized in at least three different constructions. In this section, we will present in detail the *veni*-passive and we will offer more data for the other patterns.

2.1 Romanian *veni* as a passive auxiliary

Alongside the typical passive constructions with the auxiliary *fi* 'be' (5a) and with the *se*-reflexive passive (5b), in Romanian there is a passive construction in which *veni* ('come') is used as an auxiliary verb (mentioned in Iordan 1950; Manoliu 1971; *Tratat* 1984: 181; Pană Dindelegan 2003, 2008b). This *veni*-passive construction occurs in two different styles: (i) it occurs in the popular, oral language ((1), (6a)), and (ii) it occurs in written, high-style texts, an instance where it is considered to be a loan translation from Italian (6b). This structure also exists in the Istro-Romanian dialect / language, where it was claimed to be the outcome of direct contact with Italian (6c) (see Section 2.1.3 for details).

(5)   a. *Copiii*   **sunt lăudaţi** *de părinţi.*
         children.DEF   are   praised   by parents
         'Children are praised by their parents.'

      b. *Se*   **cumpără** *multe cadouri de Crăciun.*
         CL.REFL.PASS buys   many   gifts   on Christmas
         'One buys many gifts for Christmas.'

(6)   a. *Celălalt   bec   vine   slăbit.*   (in Iordan 1950: 277)
         the.other bulb comes loosened
         'The other bulb *must be loosened.*'

      b. *[...] construzione sau alcătuire care   dă Greci   vine*
         construction or   making   which by Greeks comes
         ***numită*   *sintaxis**
         name.PPLE.F.SG syntax
         '[...] construction or making which *was / is named* syntax by the Greeks'
         (Ienache Văcărescu, *Gramatica*, 1787) – cf. It. *viene chiamata*

      c. *váca   virít-a   utíse*   (in *Tratat* 1984: 577)
         cow.DEF come-has killed
         'the cow *was killed*'

We will next discuss in turn these contexts, which are of a great stylistic and dialectal diversity.

2.1.1 The *veni*-passive in the popular, oral language

The existence of a passive construction which uses the auxiliary *veni* instead of *fi* ('be') in some areas of Romania (the south-eastern area of Buzău, and the southern area of Oltenia) has been noticed by Iordan (1950: 277–279), who mentions a few examples from spoken Daco-Romanian (the main dialect of Romanian), given in (7). The *veni*-passive is also attested in literary writings of folkloric inspiration (8). However, the pattern is not present in the Old Romanian corpus that we have surveyed, most probably because the old texts generally belong to the literary, written register.

(7)   a. *Cratiţa   în care   se   coace cozonacul **vine***
         pan.DEF in which CL.REFL.PASS bakes cake.DEF comes
         ***unsă*   *cu   unt   sau cu   grăsime, ca să   nu**
         smear.PPLE.F.SG with butter or   with lard   so that not
         se   lipească de ea cozonacul.
         CL.REFL.ACC stick   of it cake.DEF
         'The pan in which the pound cake is baked *has to / must / ought to be / is smeared* with butter or lard so that the pound cake does not stick to it.'

      b. *Partea   asta   a   feţei de masă   **vine   festonată.***
         part.DEF this GEN tablecloth.DEF.GEN comes hem.PPLE.F.SG
         'This part of the tablecloth *must / should / would have to be hemmed.*'

    c. *Firul*   **vine**   **bătut**   *la margine.*
       thread.DEF   comes   beat.PPLE.M.SG   at   edge
       'The tread *should be sewn* at the edge.'

    d. *Grinda*   *aceea*   **vine**   **aşezată**   *aici.*
       beam.DEF   that   comes   place.PPLE.F.SG   here
       'That beam *should be placed* here.'

(8)   a. *În coaja*   *prăjinei*   **vin**   **însemnate,**   *deosebit de*
       in bark.DEF   pole.DEF.GEN   come   recorded.PPLE.F.PL   different from
       numărul   *oilor,*   *găleţile...*   *ce*   *le*
       number.DEF   sheep.DEF.GEN   buckets.DEF   which   CL.F.3PL.ACC
       ia   *de la stână*   *fiecare propritar.*
       takes   from   sheepfold   each   owner
       'On the edge of the pole, the buckets that each owner takes from the
       sheepfold *are recorded*, differently from the number of sheep.'
                                                     (Păcală, in DLR, s.v. *veni*)

     b. *Peste temeiuri*   **vin**   **culcate,**   *pe axele de lungime,*
       over   foundation   come   placed.PPLE.F.PL   on   axes   of   length
       bârnele   *de brad.*
       beams.DEF   of   fir
       'The beams of fir *should be / are placed* over the foundation, on the
       length axes.'   (Păcală, in DLR, s.v. *veni*)

From a Romance perspective, the existence of the 'come'-passive has been argued to follow from semantic considerations. Manoliu (1971: 204), Posner (1994: 180), and Iliescu (2003: 3274) have shown that, as passive auxiliaries, motion verbs (and especially the descendants of Lat. *venire*) in languages like Italian, Spanish, Old French, Rheto-Romance, Romanian, etc. (see also Bourdin and Giacalone Ramat and Sansò, this volume) have the advantage of maintaining the process meaning of the event, contributing a dynamic and, sometimes, durative overtone to the event, contrasting thus with the 'be'-passive, which has a static, resultative value.

    Iordan (1950: 278) has shown that the Romanian *veni*-passive is not the equivalent of a prototypical *fi*-passive, but a periphrastic equivalent of the reflexive passive (cf. (5b)). Indeed, all the constructions in (7) and (8) may be approximately rephrased with the reflexive passive, rather than with the *fi*-passive. However, what distinguishes the reflexive passive (9) from the *veni*-passive ((7)–(8)) is that the former essentially expresses habituality (with its deontic meaning being a natural extension of the iterated, habitual one), while the latter mainly has a weak deontic meaning (i.e. necessity). The substitution with the canonical *fi*-passive is possible (*este unsă* 'is smeared'), but the resulting construction looses the modal meaning contributed by *veni*. Furthermore, a property which brings the *veni*-passive closer to the reflexive passive is that they are less felicitous with 'by'-phases than *fi*-passives.

(9)   a. *se*   *unge*
         CL.REFL.PASS smears
         'one smears it'

      b. *se*   *festonează*
         CL.REFL.PASS hems
         'one hems it'

      c. *se*   *bate*
         CL.REFL.PASS beats (sews)
         'one sews it'

      d. *se*   *aşază*
         CL.REFL.PASS places
         'one places it'

      e. *se*   *însemnează*
         CL.REFL.PASS records
         'one records it'

      f. *se*   *culcă*
         CL.REFL.PASS place
         'one places it'

The analysis of the examples, on the one hand, and the fact that Iordan establishes a link between the reflexive passive (and not the prototypical *be*-passive) and the *veni*-passive, on the other hand, are cues for the semantic interpretation of the latter.

(i) In contrast with the *fi*-passive, which has a neutral, non-modal interpretation, the *veni*-passive incorporates a weak deontic or iterative value: *vine unsă* (comes smeared) as well as *se unge* (CL.REFL.PASS smears) do not mean 'it is smeared', but 'it must be smeared' or 'typically, one smears it'. Thus, the difference between the *veni*-passive and the reflexive passive (10a-b), on the one hand, and the *be*-passive (10c), on the other hand, is shown by constructions in which a non-iterative / non-generic reading cannot be imposed, and the former are infelicitous.

(10) a. *Astăzi, copilul   **vine   lăudat**   (de părinți).
today   child.DEF comes praised.PPLE.M.SG by parents

b. ??Astăzi, copilul   **se**   **laudă** (de părinți).
today   child.DEF CL.REFL.PASS praise by parents

c. Astăzi, copilul   **este lăudat**   (de părinți).
today   child.DEF is   praised.PPLE.M.SG by parents
'Today, the child is praised by his / her parents.'

d. *Rezultatul **vine   știut**
result.DEF   comes known

e. Rezultatul **se**   **știe.**
result.DEF   CL.REFL.PASS know
'The result is known.'

It is worth mentioning that there is also a very important aspectual difference between the *veni*-passive and the reflexive passive: the *veni*-passive is felicitous only with accomplishments (e.g. (7a)) and, marginally, with achievements (e.g. (7b)), being excluded from combinations with states (10d), while the reflexive passive occurs with accomplishments (9a), achievements (9e), as well as with states (10e) (activities must be set aside, as non-derived activities are mainly intransitive and do not play any role in the discussion regarding passive constructions). The fact that the *veni*-passive is compatible only with certain aspectual classes of verbs shows that this passive structure is primarily a modal one, as stative predicates are incompatible with (weak) necessity (i.e. deontic) usages. By contrast, the compatibility of the *se*-passive with a larger array of aspectual classes proves that the *se*-structure has also non-modal usages.

(ii) In all of Iordan's examples, the *veni*-passive is not accompanied by an agent phrase; the *veni*-passive, similarly to the reflexive passive, involves the demotion of the agent, which is in line with the generic reading of the structures; out of the examples above ((7)–(8)), (7d) is the only one which is ambiguous between a generic / weak modal reading and an episodic / punctual reading, and this is most probably the effect of the presence of deictic elements in the clause (*aceea* 'that', *aici* 'here').

(iii) As noticed by Bourdin (this volume), this type of *veni*-passive seems to be used in instructions related to cooking and handiwork and it occurs only in the 3rd person, a fact which suggest that this construction is covertly impersonal, as the one with *andare* in Italian.

In conclusion, the distinctive modal and aspectual contribution brought about by the auxiliary *veni*, presented in Section 3.2. below, has supplemented the Romanian passive domain with a dynamic passive construction (similar to other Romance dynamic passive constructions, and, in certain respects, to the English *get*-passive).

2.1.2 The *veni*-passive in old translated texts and in literary texts

In the Old Romanian corpus, the *veni*-passive occurs for the first time in non-ambiguous contexts in *Foletul novel*, a text from the period 1693–1704, translated by an Italian from the royal court of Constantin Brâncoveanu (Mareş 1993: 121). In *Foletul novel*, the occurrence of the *veni*-passive, which clearly copies an Italian structure, is far from being accidental, given its 28 occurrences, some of which are given below:

(11) a. *Nişte corăbii neguţătoreşti, den partea ei*   **vin**
          some ships   commercial   from part.DEF her(GEN) come
          arse (p. 7)
          burn.PPLE.F.PL
          'Some commercial ships from her part *are burned*'

    b. *Nesaţiul   unui lup* **vine   stricat**   *de un chibzuit*
          hunger.DEF a.GEN wolf comes spoil.PPLE.M.SG by a   wise
          cioban. (p. 35)
          shepherd
          'The hunger of a wolf *is spoiled* by a wise shepherd.'

    c. *Aşteptarea ceii   curţi* **vine înşălată**   *de un*
          waiting.DEF that.GEN court comes deceive.PPLE.F.SG by a
          deşărt glas (p. 40)
          fake   voice
          'The expectations of that royal court *are deceived* by a fake voice'

    d. *Un obrazu   ostaş* **vine răsplătit**   *cu*
          a   honourable soldier comes rewarded.PPLE.M.SG with
          haină de prucurator (p. 41)
          cloth of prosecutor
          'An honourable soldier *is rewarded* with a prosecutor job'

e. [... *robi...*] *pentru că unii* **vinu închişi** *în temniţă,*
slaves   for   that some come close.PPLE.M.PL in dungeon
alţii **vin tăiaţ** (p. 94)
others come stabbed.PPLE.M.PL
'because some of them (=the slaves) *are locked* in the dungeon, while others *are stabbed*'

f. **Vine descoperită** *o începătură de hicleşug,*
comes disclose.PPLE.F.SG a beginning of fraud
de un nărod prost, înpotriva unor ministri (p. 100)
by a crowd stupid against some ministers
'The beginning of a fraud *is disclosed* by a group of commoners, against some ministers'

g. *De iute vănt* **vine răsipit** *un pălcu de corabii* (p. 108)
by fast wind comes scatter.PPLE.M.SG a group of ships
'A group of ships *is scattered* by a fast wind'

h. *naltă cetate, de cumbarale, tunuri,* **sărutată vine** (p. 135)
tall fortress by shells cannons kiss.PPLE.F.SG comes
'a tall fortress *is kissed* (= harmed) by shells and cannons'

In Ienache Văcărescu's *Grammar* [1797], there is only one occurrence of the *veni*-passive (6b) (repeated below), which may be a consequence of the fact that the author had Italian sources, as also shown by the terminology he uses.

(6b) *construzione sau alcătuire care dă Greci* **vine numită**
construction or making which by Greeks comes name.PPLE.F.SG
sintaxis
syntax
'[...] construction or making which *was / is named* syntax by the Greeks'
(Ienache Văcărescu, *Gramatica,* 1787)

The phrase *vine numită* (comes named) in this example has the meaning of a regular passive, *este numită* ('is called'), and represents a translation of Italian *viene chiamata* (Iordan 1950: 278).

In a later period (centuries 19–20), in other high-style, literary (mainly academic) texts, there appear passive structures with *veni*. Interestingly, all the authors of these texts were speakers of Italian:

(12) a. *Câteva articlii de lege votaţi sub Carol abia acuma*
a.few articles of law voted under Carol just now
venirā sancţionaţi *şi se*
came.SIMPLE.PRF sanction.PPLE.M.PL and CL.REFL.PASS
codificară cu formalităţile usitate.
ratify with formalities usual
'A few articles of law voted in Carol's period *were* just now *amended*
and ratified according to the usual formalities.'

(Bariţiu, in DLR, s.v. *veni*)

   b. *Ciocul* [*cârligului*]... *este aici relativ mare*
tip.DEF [hook.DEF.GEN] is here relatively big
şi **vine aşezat** *ca la pripoane.*
and comes placed.PPLE.M.SG as at tethers
'The tip of the hook is relatively big here and *is placed* as at the tethers.'

(Antipa, in DLR, s.v. *veni*)

   c. [Numele] „*Râpile*" **vine** *pentru întâia oară*
[the name] *Râpile* comes for first time
pomenit *în documente.*
mentioned.PPLE.M.SG in documents
'The name Râpile *is mentioned* for the first time in the documents.'

(Ghibănescu, in DLR, s.v. *veni*)

The *veni*-passive from original or translated literary texts is not equivalent to the *veni*-passive from the popular, oral language. The *veni*-passive in (6b), (11) and (12) has the following characteristics:

(i)   it is equivalent to the prototypical *fi*-passive (*fi* + past participle) and does not display supplementary (root) modal values;

(ii) in many cases, contrasting with the structure from the popular, oral language, it is accompanied by an agent phrase, specified as [+human]: *dă Greci* 'by the Greeks' in (6b), *de un chibzuit cioban* 'by a wise shepherd' in (11b), *de un nărod prost* 'by a group of commoners' (11f) or as [−human]: *de un deşărt glas* 'by a fake voice' in (11c), *de iute vănt* 'by a fast wind' (11g), *de cumbarale, tunuri* 'by shells and cannons' (11h);

(iii) in contrast with the *veni*-passive found in the spoken language, the examples in this section are not subject to a generic reading;

(iv) all the examples in (6b), (11) and (12) involve a simplex paradigm (*vine* 'comes' + past participle), and not a compound paradigm (*a venit* 'has come' + past participle), in line with what is found in Italian (Adam Ledgeway, *p.c.*).

2.1.3 The *veni*-passive in the Istro-Romanian variety

The *veni*-passive is also attested in the Istro-Romanian dialect / language. Timotin (2000: 487) has shown that, regionally, the verbs *veni* ('come') and *rămâne* ('remain') are used instead of the passive auxiliary. Her observation is based on the data collected by the dialectologist Matteo Bartoli: he noted that the passive form of the verb *ucide* ('kill') in Jeiǎni (an Istro-Romanian village from Croatia) is a periphrastic construction in which *veni* is used as a passive auxiliary (13a); similarly, in Noselo (an Istro-Romanian village from the Istrian Peninsula in Croatia), the verb *rămâne* ('remain') is used as a passive auxiliary (13b). Both *veni* and *rămâne* are motion / location verbs. Yet another *veni*-passive form has been attested in a 1982 recording from Jeiǎni (13c).

(13) a. *ie **vire   ucis***
        he comes killed
        'he was killed'

  b. *ie **ramas-a   ucis***
        he remain-has killed
        'he was killed'

  c. *néca víre **càşu yust***   (in Sârbu and Frăţilă 1998: 66)
        SUBJ come whey clogged
        '(so that) the whey is / gets clogged'

Although similar constructions are possible in Italian (Adam Ledgeway, *p.c.*: *è rimasto ucciso* 'he was killed ~ he ended up dead', for (13b)), according to the above quoted authors, these two villages have not been in direct contact with the Italian language, given their geographical placement; and thus, it is hard to consider that the existence of these constructions is the result of direct Italian influence. Timotin (2000: 488) claims that the range of the *veni*-passive structures was more extended prior to the dialectal investigations from which the examples in (13) are drawn. The *veni*-passive is also attested in the southern part of the Istro-Romanian speaking region (example (6c)), a territory which has been under Italian linguistic influence.

Putting these facts together, one may draw the following conclusions: even though Italian might have been one of the sources of the *veni*-passive in Istro-Romanian, this foreign influence cannot be entirely responsible for the existence of this periphrastic construction, since it is also attested in areas not influenced by Italian. Although the examples above (13) are very short, they seem to resemble the *veni*-passive structure from popular, oral Daco-Romanian, not the one from literary texts, which most probably copies the Italian model.

2.1.4 Summary

In conclusion, the existence of various (unrelated) passive *veni*-patterns in different varieties of Romanian indicates the natural predisposition of this verb to grammaticalize as a passive auxiliary.

As for the distribution of the constructions surveyed in this section, the following comments can be made. The structure found in popular, spoken Romanian is still productive (for instance, see the examples in (27) below, which are attestations from the internet). The loan translation from Italian is abundantly attested in *Foletul novel*, a translation highly influenced by its Italian source, and then only sporadically found in few texts from the 19th century and (the beginning of the) 20th century; this structure has not entered the mainstream language, as there is virtually no trace of its presence in present-day Romanian. As for the situation in the Istro-Romanian variety, the data presented above are the only available ones, and no other conclusions may be drawn until more data become available.

2.2 The other patterns illustrating the grammaticalization of *veni* ('come')

Even if we do not discuss in detail the other two patterns in which *veni* grammaticalized, we still need to briefly look at some additional data in order to show that these constructions are far from being accidental in Romanian.

Additionally, the last part of this section presents the usage of *veni* as a full deontic modal verb, a construction in which *veni* is not a grammaticalized (i.e. functional / semi-lexical) verb.

2.2.1 Romanian *veni* as a copula

Of the constructions discussed in this paper, the use of *veni* as a copula seems to be the oldest and the most unusual from a cross-linguistic perspective (it is attested in Italian and Italian dialects in structures similar to (14) and (15), but not in structures like (16) – Adam Ledgeway, *p.c.* –, and it has also been discussed by Nordhoff (2011) for Sri Lanka Malay). In the contemporary language, the *veni*-copula structures are typical of the spoken, popular language. Many of the *veni*-constructions, frequent and diversified especially in the southern area of Romania (Iulia Mărgărit, *p.c.*), may be accounted for by regular grammaticalization mechanisms. Others, however, remain enigmatic.

There are several patterns where *veni* functions as a bona fide copula in parallel with the regular *fi* ('be') copula.

In the *Treatise of Romanian Dialectology*, in the chapter devoted to the Wallachian subdialect (*Tratat* 1984: 181) there are mentioned, besides the passive structures, constructions where *veni* functions as a copula, being followed by an adjective ((14a), (14b)), or by a bare noun (14c). In contrast with the "neutral" *fi*-copular structure, the *veni*-construction contributes a [+change of state] feature to the verbal event. *Veni* is thus the equivalent of the verb *deveni* ('become'), which is typical of the (modern) standard language.

(14) a. *Atuncea-l   scoate   când   să   coace şi...* **vine**
       then-CL.M.3SG.ACC pulls.out when CL.REFL.ACC bakes and comes
       dulce, ... dă o dulceaţă.
       sweet ... of a sweetness
       'And then, (s)he pulls it out, when it is baked, and it *becomes sweet,*
       being of a great sweetness.'   (TDM, I 780)

   b. *Pui   un pumn   dă tărâţe ca să   vie   dulce.*
      (you)put a handful of bran   so that.SUBJ comes.SUBJ sweet
      'You put a handful of bran in order for it to *become sweet*.' (TDM, I 772)

   c. *O   trecut   multă vreme pân' o   vint   copilu*
      has passed much time   until has came child.DEF
      ficior   mare de-o   fost de-nsurat.
      lad.DEF big   so-that.has been SUP-married.SUP
      'It has passed a lot of time until the child *became a big lad*, ready to get
      married.'   (DR, in DLR, s.v. *veni*)

Another construction in which *veni* has a copulative value is illustrated by examples like (15), where, in opposition to the structure discussed above, *veni* is synonymous with *fi* ('be'), and denotes a state, not a change of state:

(15) a. *Am   scos   extracturi letineşti dupe   toate scrisorile...,*
        (I)have extracted quotes   Latin   out.of all   letters.DEF
        ca să   vezi   pricina   acestui lucru cum **vine.**
        so that.SUBJ (you)see.SUBJ cause.DEF this.GEN thing how comes
        'I have written down Latin quotes from all the letters for you to see
        what *the cause of this thing is*.'
        (Bul. Com. Ist., in DLR, s.v. *veni*)

b. *Că   vor   lucra cum s-au   zis deasupra...*
   that (they)will work how CL.REFL.PASS=has said above
   tot una vine, lăsați-i   și   așa,   să   lucreze.
   also one comes let-CL.3PL.M.ACC also like this SUBJ (they)work.SUBJ
   'That they will work as stated above, it *is the same thing*; let the work
   like this.'   (Petrovici, in DLR, s.v. *veni*)

c. *Drept   cam   ciudat   vine.*
   certainly rather strange comes
   'Certainly, *it is rather strange*.'   (Alexandrescu, in DLR, s.v. *veni*)

d. *Vedeți, frații   miei, cum munca preceapere vine*
   (you)see brothers.DEF mine how labour skill   come
   bogatului.
   rich.man.DEF.DAT
   'You see, my brothers, that labour *means / is skilfulness* for the rich man.'
                                         (Coresi, *Evanghelie cu învățătură*)

e. *[părul]   la înpletit vine   foarte urât*
   hair.DEF at braid comes very ugly
   'when braided, the hair *is very ugly*'   (*Studii și documente*)

Yet another construction with copular *veni* is illustrated by the examples in (16),
where its subjective predicative complement[2] is a relational noun (i.e. a kinship
or occupation noun). In contrast with examples like (14), but like the examples in
(15), copular *veni* has a static value in these structures (Pană Dindelegan 2008a:
285):

(16) a. *Ion vine văr   lui   Gheorghe.*
         John comes cousin DAT George
         'John *is George's cousin*.'

      b. *Ea îmi   vine   soră*
         she CL.1.SG.DAT comes sister
         'She *is my sister*'

The pattern in which the subjective predicative complement of *veni* is a kinship
noun is attested rather late, in the 20th century:

---

2 The concept "subject predicative complement" denotes the predicative of a copula verb in
English traditional terminology (cf. Huddleston and Pullum 2005: 76).

(17) a. *Deşi*   *îi*   ***veneam*** *nepot* *de veri*   *primari,*
          although CL.3.SG.M.DAT came   nephew of cousins primary
          nu-l   *cunoşteam nici*   *din vedere.*
          not-CL.3.SG.M.ACC knew   neither of sight
          'Although I *was his nephew* (out) of a first degree cousinship, I didn't
          even know what he looked like.'   (M. I. Caragiale, in DLR, s.v. *veni*)

   b. *[Prietenii]* *ofiţerului*   ***veneau,*** *cum* *s-ar*   *zice,*
       friends.DEF officer.DEF.GEN came   how CL.REFL.PASS=would say
       cumetri   *cu*   *alde Ciupitu cârciumarul.*
       godfathers with (the) Ciupitu publican.DEF
       'The friends of the officer were, as one would say, the godfathers of
       Ciupitu the publican.'   (Camil Petrescu, in DLR, s.v. *veni*)

   c. *[Tânărul]*   *e student. Ne*   ***vine*** *cam*   *rudă.*
       young-man.DEF is student. CL.1.PL.DAT come approximately relative
       'The young man is a student. He *is a sort of relative of ours*.'
                                            (Călinescu, in DLR, s.v. *veni*)

2.2.2 Romanian *veni* as an inceptive verb

Romanian *veni* is also found in partially grammaticalized structures where it
(still) has argumental structure, but has undergone severe semantic bleaching.
Interestingly, we can trace back the evolution of this structure from Old Romanian to Modern Romanian. As with other *veni*-structures, the inceptive structure
is also attested in Italian (Adam Ledgeway, *p.c.*: *mi viene da ridere quando sono
ubriaco* 'I feel like laughing when I am drunk').
    The inceptive value is attested since the earliest Romanian texts. In the
first stages, the complement of *veni* was a mere nominal phrase (18a, b). In an
intermediate stage, this complement was expressed by psych-nouns like *toană*
'mood', *chef* 'mood', *nebuneală* 'madness' (18c, d). Finally, more recently, the
verb *veni* can take a subjunctive complement (as in (3), repeated below).

(18) a. *De greşaşte omul,*   *nu-i*   ***vine*** *luiş* [...] *foamea.*
          if errs   human.DEF not=CL.3SG.DAT come him.DAT hunger.DEF
          'If humans make mistakes they *don't get hungry* (as they would nor-
          mally do).'   (Coresi, in DLR, s.v. *veni*)

b. *Când de multul   vin   se   îmbeată,*
   when of much.DEF wine CL.REFL.ACC get-drunk
   *atunci **vine**   râsul.*
   then   comes laughter.DEF
   'When one gets drunk, one *starts to laugh*.' (Bojincă, in DLR, s.v. *veni*)

c. *Iar   i-o   **venit** toana   nebuniei.*
   again CL.3SG.DAT=have come mood.DEF madness.DEF.GEN
   'He *has started acting* mad again.'   (Alecsandri, in DLR; s.v. *veni*)

d. *Dacă-i   **vine**   aşa o nebuneală sergentului*
   if=CL.3SG.DAT comes such a madness   sergeant.DEF.DAT
   să   spuie   că   el e stăpânul   averii...
   SUBJ say.SUBJ that he is owner.DEF wealth.DEF.GEN
   'If the sergeant *starts acting* crazy by saying that he is the owner of the
   wealth...'   (Caragiale, in DLR, s.v. *veni*)

(3) *Îmi   **vine**   să   plâng.*
     CL.1.SG.DAT (it)comes SUBJ cry.SUBJ.1.SG
     'I *feel like crying*.'

2.2.3 Romanian *veni* as a deontic modal verb

This value of *veni* (obligatorily preceded by a reflexive marker), mentioned in
the introduction (ex. (4)) for Old Romanian, was lost in the transition to Modern
Romanian. The fact that Romanian modal verbs are not fully grammaticalized[3]
(as they are, for instance, in English), corroborated with the replacement of *veni*
by *cuveni* (< Lat. *convenio* 'to be one's due; to be fitting that') as a modal verb
led to the fact that this value did not persist and grammaticalize in Romanian.
However, the existence of this value at some point in the history of Romanian
is important from a typological perspective, and we may speculate that it also
counts for explaining the modal value acquired by *veni* as a passive auxiliary.

The development of this modal value was most probably influenced by old
translations from Slavonic. *Veni* surfaced with this value mainly in religious
texts, which have been substantially influenced by the Slavic model. This is why
veni was used instead of *cuveni*, the regular impersonal verb which has been used
to express the deontic value in Old Romanian and in Modern Romanian as well.

---

3 For instance, they still have lexical usages, they preserve the ability to select a complement
clause, they have a rather large c-selection domain, selecting both finite and non-finite clauses, etc. (see Zafiu 2013, for a comprehensive survey).

(19) a. *[Oile] ceale reale* **se** **veniia** *lui Laban.*
      sheep those bad.PL CL.REFL.ACC come.IMPF DAT Laban
      'Those bad sheep were Laban's due.'   (PO, in DLR, s.v. *veni*)

   b. *Părinte,* *dă-mi*   *ce* *mi*   **să**   **vine.**
      father.VOC give=CL.1SG.DAT what CL.1SG.DAT CL.REFL.ACC come
      'Father, give me what is due to me.'   (Varlaam, in DLR, s.v. *veni*)

   c. *Jumătatea de roada*   *cea de lemn... mi*   **să**   **vine**
      half.DEF   of harvest DEF of wood CL.1SG.DAT CL.REFL.ACC come
      mie   *a*   *lua.*
      me.DAT INF take.INF
      'A half of the wood harvest is due to me (to be given to me).'
                               (Biblia 1688, in DLR, s.v. *veni*)

   d. *M-am*   *lăpădat*   *de tot ce*
      CL.REFL.1SG.ACC=(I)have abandoned of all what
      s-ar   *fi putut* **veni** *mie*   *prin*   *tot dreptul.*
      CL.REFL.ACC=would be could come me.DAT through all right.DEF
      'I abandoned all that was due to me by all rights.'
                           (Cantacuzino, in DLR, s.v. *veni*)

In all these contexts, *veni* was subsequently replaced by *cuveni* in the transition to the modern language.

3 Accounting for the grammaticalization paths

The aim of this section is to answer, in turn, the questions raised at the beginning of the paper, by examining the factors that led to the rise of each pattern. As in the previous section, we will grant more attention to the passive construction.

3.1 Why *veni* was chosen: semantic and syntactic explanations

Recall the first question raised in the introduction:

(i)   Given that in Romanian there are several verbs expressing the final point of motion (*veni, ajunge, sosi* '~ come, arrive'), why is it that *veni* (and not other near-synonymous verbs) grammaticalized in these constructions? How did the lexical semantics and syntax of *veni* influence this multiple-output grammaticalization?

It is well known that motion verbs are frequently engaged in grammaticalization processes (Heine and Kuteva 2002: 69, 73, 74, 78; Stolova 2005: 197; Nicolle 2007: 48; among many others). But *not all* motion verbs grammaticalize. What makes a motion verb *a good candidate* for grammaticalization?

The three Romanian verbs expressing motion towards the speaker's deictic centre are *veni, ajunge* and *sosi,* which are interchangeable in most contexts when used with the genuine motion meaning; they contrast as to how they relate to the deictic centre. Deictic motion verbs, which incorporate the path of motion, are good candidates for becoming functional verbs (Nicolle 2007: 47). However, of these three verbs, as we have seen, only *veni* has undergone a multiple grammaticalization process; *ajunge* only grammaticalized as a copula verb, by a well-known metaphorical semantic change: change of location (the genuine meaning (20a)) to change of state (copula (20b)); the verb *sosi* has only lexical usages (20a). Furthermore, in contrast with *veni* and *ajunge,* which are inherited from Latin, *sosi* is a Modern Greek loanword (cf. the etymologies in DA / DLR); it is thus a lexical item which entered Romanian at a later stage. The effect of this historical timing is that *sosi* is the least polysemous of the three verbs under discussion, and that it has only lexical values.

(20) a. *Ion* **ajunge / soseşte** *acasă*
      'John arrives   home'

    b. *Bisericile*   *Domnului*   **ajunseseră**   *grajduri*
       church.DEF   God.DEF.GEN   arrive.PLUPERF   stables
       pentru caii   *păgânilor.*
       for   horses.DEF pagans.DEF.GEN
       'God's churches had become stables for the pagans' horses.'
                                                (Ispirescu, in DA, s.v. *ajunge*)

The choice of *veni* over *ajunge* and *sosi* is the combined effect of the lexical semantics and syntax of *veni.*

From a semantic point of view, the verb *veni* is the most polysemous of the three verbs discussed. This is true not only for Modern / Contemporary Romanian, but also for Old Romanian (for example, in DA / DLR, the thesaurus dictionary of the Romanian language, there are 44 pages dedicated to *veni,* 4 pages dedicated to *ajunge,* and 2 pages to *sosi*). Similarly to other motion verbs that grammaticalized in various languages (Fr. *aller,* Engl. *go*), *veni* is highly polysemous so it displays a high degree of semantic complexity, a fact which favoured its grammaticalization (Bybee 1993: 153; Bybee, Perkins, and Pagliuka 1994: 5).

Syntactically speaking, *veni* is unaccusative in all its occurrences, contrasting with *ajunge* and *sosi,* which also had or still have transitive usages (21). Thus, from this perspective too, *veni* is the best candidate for grammaticalization (at least for grammaticalization as a passive auxiliary).

(21) a. ***Ajunseră*** *cetatea* *Brusa.*   [Old Romanian]
    (they)arrived fortress.DEF(ACC) Brusa
    'They arrived at the fortress of Brusa.'   (Moxa, in DA, s.v. *ajunge*)

  b. *Alergă* *cu* *mare iuțeală ca să* *o* ***sosească.***
    ((s)he)ran with great speed in order to CL.3SG.F.ACC arrive
    '(S)he ran very fast in order to reach her.'   (Gorjan, in DLR, s.v. *sosi*)

  c. *L-**am***   ***ajuns*** *când vira* *la stânga.* [Mod. Rom.]
    CL.3SG.M.ACC=have arrived when (he)turned at left
    'I reached him when he was turning left.'

The fact that the passive structure is the unaccusative structure par excellence, in that it is derived in the syntax (rather than in the lexicon), favours the choice of unaccusative verbs as candidates for grammaticalization as passive auxiliaries. This is also consistent with Haspelmath's (1990: 38) observation that passive auxiliaries typically grammaticalize from non-agentive verbs. This theoretical correlation takes the form of a statistical universal. The most widely spread passive auxiliary is the verb 'be' (English, Spanish, Polish, Finish, Lithuanian, Baluchi, Urdu, Quechua – Siewierska 1984: 126), a verb which is unaccusative in all its occurrences. Furthermore, if we take into consideration the survey in Siewierska (1984: 126), it is easy to notice that most of the verbs which grammaticalized in the world's languages as passive auxiliaries are unaccusative verbs: 'become' (German, Swedish, Polish, Latvian, Kupia, Kolami, Hindi, Nez Perce), 'go' (Bengali, Hindi, Gujarati, Maitil, Ossetian, Italian and Gaelic), 'suffer (~ undergo)' (Vietnamese, Thai, Cambodian, Burmeze, Dravidian Tamil, Kannada); the verb 'come' is also attested as a passive auxiliary in a few languages: Kurdish Kashmiri, Maithil, and Italian (Siewierska 1984: 126); for an extensive inventory of languages in which the 'come'-passive is attested, see Giacalone Ramat and Sansò (this volume). Passive auxiliaries originating in transitive verbs are also attested (*get, receive, eat* Siewierska 1984: 126, *have* – La Fauci and Loporcaro 1989: 162, 180) but to a much more limited extent; the construction in which transitive verbs grammaticalized as passive auxiliaries may correspond to intransitive usages of these verbs (absolute usages, null complement anaphora, etc.).

    Another factor, pertaining to the lexical semantics / syntax interface, is that the *veni*-passive structure is compatible only with accomplishments and achievements, that is, with telic predicates. This can be related to the fact that, in contrast with *ajunge* and *sosi,* lexical *veni* expresses motion towards the speaker's deictic centre, which is interpreted as the endpoint of the action from an aspectual point of view.

3.2 The role of the context and the persistence of the original meaning of *veni*

The second question raised in the introduction is as follows:

(ii) Does the grammaticalization of *veni* represent a change in meaning (of the type metaphor, metonymy, etc.) and/or an instance of re-analysis (triggered by a specific distributional context)? How important is the (narrow distributional) context in this process? How did the original meaning of *veni* influence the semantics of the *veni*-passive construction?

The variety of distributional contexts in which *veni* appears with an inceptive value in the history of Romanian is an indication that the grammaticalization of *veni* as an inceptive verb did not happen in a narrow distributional context (see Section 2.2.2). Rather, it is more plausible to assume that a metaphorical mutation from [change of location] to [change of state] conceptualized as inception (see also Bourdin, this volume), followed by semantic bleaching has led to the (partial) grammaticalization of *veni* as an inceptive aspectual verb (example (3)), a change which is also categorial in nature (lexical > functional / semi-lexical (i.e. aspectual)). Therefore, the usage of *veni* as an inceptive verb originates in a *change in meaning*, and is accompanied by a categorial mutation as well.

By contrast, the grammaticalization of *veni* as a passive auxiliary and as a copula is a good illustration of the idea expressed by Bybee (2004: 146) that "grammaticalization of lexical items takes place within *particular constructions*" with "grammaticalization [being] the creation of new constructions". This type of reasoning, that what is fundamental in the grammaticalization process is the context, has also been employed in the description of the grammaticalization of Engl. *go* as a future auxiliary in the structure *be going to* (Hopper and Traugott 2003: 87; Disney 2009). In what follows, we will show that this explanation carries over to Romanian passive and copular *veni*-structures. The hypothesis we put forth is that the passive structure found in spoken Romanian grammaticalized independently (from the loan translation passive from Italian, discussed in Section 2.1.2) in structures like (22), which have been attested as early as the 16th century (the earliest surviving Romanian writings). It is not clear whether these structures are instances of a *veni*-passive or of a secondary predication biclausal structure, in which both *veni* and the associated past participle are independent predications with individual semantics. This ambiguity (reflected below by double translations) probably persisted for a long period. What deepens the ambiguity is the fact that the *veni*-passive construction matured in the spoken variety, and, thus, there are very few written records which would unveil its evolution.

(22) a. ***Blagoslovit*** ***vine***, în numele Domnului, împăratul
bless.PPLE.M.SG comes in name.DEF God.DEF.GEN emperor.DEF
izraililor.
Israelis.GEN
'The Israeli's emperor *comes and is blessed* in the name of God.'
'*Blessed is* in the name of God the Israeli's emperor.'
(Coresi, Evanghelie cu învățătură)

b. "***Blagoslovită*** ***vine*** împărăție părintelui nostru David,
bless.PPLE.F.SG comes reign father.DEF.GEN our David
în numele Domnului", ce se zice „den Dumnezeu".
in name God.GEN what CL.REFL.IMPERS says of God
'[That's why, rejoicing he said]: «*Blessed comes* the reign of our father David in the name of God», that is, «from God»."
'[That's why, rejoicing he said]: «*Blessed is* the reign of our father David in the name of God», that is, «from God».'
(Coresi, Evanghelie cu învățătură)

Therefore, what appears to be crucial in this case is the combination *veni* + past participle, a narrow distributional context which served as the basis for re-analysis (a similar context favoured the grammaticalization of *andare* as passive auxiliary in Italian – see Mocciaro, this volume). Two supplementary pieces of evidence favour this conclusion. First, a similar explanation is suggested by Vincent (1982: 84, 2012: 429–430) who considers the periphrastic [auxiliary + past participle] constructions (including the passive) in Latin to originate in biclausal constructions. The Old Romanian examples in (22), where *veni* appears next to a past participle, are exactly the same kind of biclausal constructions discussed by Vincent for Latin periphrastic constructions. Second, a type of ambiguity like the one above still persists in Modern Romanian; this will be discussed in greater detail below (see also Giacalone Ramat and Sansò (this volume) for the similar situation in Italian).

Let us now turn to the *veni*-copula of the type illustrated in (16) and (17). We claim that the appearance of this structure is based on factors which are of the same nature as those invoked for the *veni*-passive structure. Iordan (1950: 278) and Pană Dindelegan (2003: 137, 2008b: 136–137) have each put forth explanations essentially based on the replacement of the copula *fi* 'be' by *veni*, on the basis of their synonymy in other contexts.

While this factor, the semantic affinity of *veni* and *fi* 'be' in Romanian, might have contributed to the rise of this structure, we believe that what is crucial in the grammaticalization of this structure is the syntactic context. Namely, throughout the history of Romanian, one finds a recurring combination of *veni* with bare, person-denoting nouns, which have a kind-level denotation, as in (23) below.

(23) a. *Pătraşco-vodă, cela bunul,* **au venit** <u>domn</u> *în sâmbăta*
Pătraşco-vodă that good.DEF has come king in Saturday
Paştilor, 7062.
Easter.GEN, 7062
'Pătraşco-vodă, the good one, *came king* in the Easter Saturday, 7062.'
(*Anonimul cantacuzinesc*)

   b. *Mircea-vodă iar* *au* **venit** <u>domn</u> *al treilea rând.*
Mircea-vodă again has come king the third time
'Mircea-vodă *(be)came again king* for the third time.'
(*Anonimul cantacuzinesc*)

   c. *de va* *voi, să* **vine** <u>dascăl</u> *aici la mine.*
if (he)will wish SUBJ come teacher here at mine
'If he wishes he may *(be)come (a) teacher* here, at my place.'
(*Studii şi documente*)

Notice that in (23) the person-denoting nouns denote an official function / dignity. In the next historical phase (our first attested contexts of this second stage are from the 20th century), kinship nouns denoting an indirect kinship relation (*cumnat* 'brother-in-law', *socru* 'father-in-law', *cuscru* 'father of a son- / daughter-in-law', *văr* 'cousin', etc.) have been attracted into this pattern (see (17) above, and (24a) below). Thus, chronologically, nouns denoting official dignities precede kinship nouns in this pattern. Importantly, nouns denoting a direct kinship relation (*mamă* 'mother', *tată* 'father', *fiu* 'son', *frate* 'brother', *bunic* 'grandfather', etc.) are excluded from the combination with the copula *veni* (24a). This lexical squish is a clear indication that a rudiment of the initial motion semantics has been preserved by *veni* in this structure: namely, the kinship relation expressed by the subjective predicative complement has to be arrived at in an indirect manner; this is a conceptual difference very similar to that expressed by the contrast between *he is here* vs. *he has come here*. Crucially, with direct kinship relations, the copula *fi* 'be' is the only possibility (24b):

(24) a. Îmi   vine văr   / nepot / *tată / *fiu / *bunic.
     CL.1.SG.DAT comes cousin nephew father son grandfather
     'He is my cousin / nephew.'

   b. Îmi   este tată / fiu / bunic   (/ văr   / nepot).
     CL.1.SG.DAT is   father son grandfather cousin nephew
     'He is my father / son / grandfather (/ cousin / nephew).'

Further comments should be made on the behaviour of the *veni*-pasive structure found in spoken Romanian.

Unlike the usual *fi*-passive and the reflexive passive in Romanian, the *veni*-passive has a root modal meaning, most probably derived from its iterative / habitual or generic meaning. The special modal-aspectual values acquired by *veni* in passive structures accounts for the incompatibility of this type of passive construction with the Romanian compound past, which is always perfective (and hence non-dynamic / punctual) from an aspectual point of view.

As announced, in the present tense, a sentence like the following, without an appropriate linguistic context, is systematically ambiguous between a passive reading (25a) and a secondary predicate interpretation (25b) of the [*veni* + past participle] sequence:

(25) *Cartea* **vine** **pusă** *în cutie.*
     book.DEF comes placed in box
     a. 'The book *is (usually) / must be placed* in a box.'   (passive reading)
     b. 'The book *comes (i.e. it arrives)* in the state of being *placed* in a box.'

Interestingly, the tenses of the past display a rather sharply contrasting behaviour. The *compound past* tense, which is strictly perfective in Romanian, only allows for the biclausal, secondary predicate, interpretation of the [*veni* + past participle] sequence, and *veni* retains its change of location lexical meaning (this is the case for Italian too, as Adam Ledgeway, *p.c.*, pointed out to us: *il re è **venuto circondato** da numerosi cortigiani* 'the king arrived surrounded by many courtiers'):

(26) a. [...] *al cincilea cadou **a** venit **aşezat** pe boboci de trandafiri galbeni*
         the fifth   gift has come placed on flowers of roses   yellow
         'the fifth gift *came / arrived placed* on yellow roses'   (internet)

   b. *setul   verde **a** venit **aşezat** într-o cutiuţă de bijuterii   şi*
     set.DEF green has come placed in-a box   of jewelleries and
     m-a   surprins plăcut gestul pentru că astfel   chiar   arăta
     me=has surprised nicely act.DEF because this way indeed look

a   dar.
as gift
'The green set *came placed* in a box of jewelleries and this fact really
surprised me as it indeed looked like a gift.'   (internet)

By contrast, in the *imperfect* tense, which is strictly imperfective, the sequence
[*veni* + past participle] is interpreted as a passive structure, and the lexical
meaning of *veni* is completely eliminated (see Bourdin, this volume, who argues
that "when it comes to the co-encoding of necessity by itive or ventive passives
perfective aspect is cross-linguistically disfavoured"; see also Mocciaro, this
volume, for the differences between perfective and imperfective in Italian passives):

(27) a. *la toate maşinile pe care le-am   meşterit eu,*
         at all   cars.DEF PE which CL.3PL.F.ACC=have fixed   I
         *rulmentul   **venea aşezat** pe furca   aceea, dar la mine părea*
         bearing.DEF came   placed on fork.DEF that   but at me   seemed
         că e exact   invers.
         that is exactly opposite
         'With all the cars I fixed, the bearing *was placed* on that fork, but in my
         case it seemed exactly the opposite.'   (internet)

      b. *e vorba de stratul cel mai de sus al fundaţiei,   cel peste*
         is word of layer   DEF more of up of foundation.GEN CEL over
         *care **venea aşezat** primul rând de cărămidă.*
         which came   placed first roll of brick
         'We are talking about the upper most layer of the foundation, the one
         over which the first layer of bricks *was placed*.'   (internet)

This contrast between (26) and (27) above can also be described as one between
a single predication represented by [*veni* + past participle] in the imperfective
viewpoint versus a multiple predication of this structure in the perfective viewpoint.

In Section 2.1.1, we have insisted on the special modal-aspectual properties of the *veni*-passive. The contrasting behaviour of this structure in the tenses
of the past is in line with its modal-aspectual values in the present tense. The
deontic and iterative values imposed by the *veni* auxiliary on the verbal event
are incompatible with the *perfective* nature of the *compound past* tense. This
is because a deontic (/root) modal base cannot be imposed upon closed events
or, as Hacquard (2009: 280) puts it, "perfective aspect eradicates the modality".

It is well known that structures containing root modal verbs in past perfective events no longer have a modal meaning but a descriptive, reporting meaning, requiring "their complement to hold in the *actual* world, and not merely in some possible world" (Hacquard 2009: 282) (*You have to close the door* [deontic] → *You had to close the door* [descriptive]). Consequently, the only reading available to *veni* with sentences in the perfective aspect is that of a motion verb.

By contrast, sentences in the imperfective viewpoint are "informationally open" (Smith 1991) or, putting it differently, the imperfective viewpoint does not present a closed event, although it allows inferences about its beginning and/ or ending; thus, a modal base may be imposed upon an event in the imperfective viewpoint. Furthermore, "imperfective comes with its own layer of modality, which [...] forces it [= the event] to happen in the worlds provided by the modal element of the imperfective" (Hacquard 2009: 302). The combination of the imperfective viewpoint, which independently contributes a layer of genericity, with the deontic and iterative values of the passive auxiliary *veni* yields a habitual or dispositional reading of the sentences in the imperfect, illustrated in (27).

The special interaction between modality and aspect displayed by Rom. *veni* can thus be added to the topic of impossible modal and auxiliary combinations, which has been pursued in the literature in different guises (e.g., Picallo 1990 and, more recently, Wurmbrand 2003: 184 and Hacquard 2009).

In conclusion, we may characterize the *veni*-passive of the spoken language as follows: in contrast with the regular 'be'-passive, which is static, the *veni*-passive is dynamic; in contrast with the reflexive passive, the *veni*-passive contributes a stronger deontic or iterative value to the verbal event; in the imperfect, the passive auxiliary *veni* yields a habitual, dispositional reading of the verbal event.

The fact that the modal readings are cancelled out by the perfective aspect further demonstrates that the *veni* passive construction is a root modal construction since epistemic modal readings are not overridden by perfective aspect (Hacquard 2009: 279). Furthermore, the different modal meanings, essentially pertaining to root modality, expressed by the *veni*-passive structure verify the idea that distinct modal meanings generate one another (Arigne 2007). Grammatical aspect, which is syntactically superior to root modality (Hacquard 2009: 279, 285; cf. also Butler 2004), plays a crucial role in generating these distinct modal meanings.

3.3 The Latin heritage and the issue of language contact

Consider the third and the forth questions raised in the introduction:

(iii) Given that some of these constructions are also attested in Latin (with *venire*) and that there are parallel developments in Romance, what is the contribution of the Latin heritage to the existence of the wide variety of structures involving Rom. *veni*?

(iv) Is it the case that language contact may have contributed to the emergence of one of the constructions above?

The alleged Latin 'come'-passive is illustrated in the literature by examples like the following:

(28) *Si iumentum de via   **coactum ueniet***   [Latin]
      if cattle   of road forced   will.come
      (*coactus* = past participle of *cogo*)
                           (*Mulomedicina Chironis*, in Bourciez 1956: 268)

Similarly to what is found in Romanian, Bourciez (1956: 268) claims that the Latin 'come'-passive is attested since 400 AD, alongside the regular analytical 'be'-passive; in contrast with the regular passive, this type of passive contributes a [+ dynamic] aspectual value to the event denoted by the verb.

Ernout and Meillet (1959, s.v. *uenio*), who also record the existence of the Latin 'come'-passive, argue that the starting point for this usage has probably been the use of *uenio* in collocations like the one below:

(29) ***uenire**   amatus*
      come.INF loved

Bourciez suggests that the Latin 'come'-passive has been preserved in the area of Italy and Raetia; the author's comments lead to the idea that Italian and some Rhaeto-Romance varieties have developed these structures to a larger extent than Latin.

However, this claim, very often accepted in the literature, seems to be contradicted on two different reasons.

First, as Adams (2013) shows, most of the examples cited in the literature for Latin are simply not passives. (28) is not a passive and does not mean 'if the horse will be forced' and any attempt to associate *coactum* with *ueneit* in this example is simply misguided. The author further shows that the actual meaning of (28) is 'if a horse comes from the road having been pushed too hard' (*cogo* being a technical term meaning 'to force a horse beyond its capacity leading to serious physical harm'), in which *coactum* is a predicative participle modifying *iumentum* and is not associated with *ueniet*, just as in the Romanian examples in (26) above.

The second argument comes from a closer look at the developments in the Romance languages. While the examination of the evolution of the descendants of Latin *venire* is beyond the goals of this paper, it is instructive to mention a few sharp differences between Romanian and Italian which show that Lat. *venire* has taken different paths of evolution in the Romance languages, refuting thus the claim that the 'come'-passive attested in Romance is directly inherited from Latin (see also Giacalone Ramat and Sansò, this volume, who show that the 'come'-passive emerged independently in Italian, and Vincent 1987, 2011 for the emergence of periphrastic constructions involving an auxiliary + a participle in Latin).

Salvi and Renzi (2010: 144) show that, in contrast with Modern Italian, Old Italian always uses *essere* ('be') not *venire* ('come') as a passive auxiliary, a fact which excludes the continuity from Latin of the *venire* passive structure. In Old Italian, in the construction *venire* + participle, *venire* has the meaning 'diventare' (= become):

(30) *E   allora gli cavalieri tutti **vennoro smarriti***
      and then   the knights   all   came   lost
      [diventarono smarriti, si smarirono].
      became   lost   SI lost
      'And then, all the knight were lost.'
                    (*Tavola rotunda*, cap. 93, p. 352, in Salvi and Renzi 2010: 146)

The difference between the three passive auxiliaries of Italian (*essere* 'be', *andare* 'go' and *venire* 'come') is studied by Maiden and Robustelli (2007 [2000]: 282–284). Comparing Maiden and Robustelli's results on the Italian passive auxiliaries with our description of Romanian above, three important facts may be observed:

1. With respect to semantic interpretation, the Romanian *veni*-passive from the spoken language is similar to the Italian *andare*-passive, both types having a dynamic and a deontic modal meaning (compare Rom. (6a) with It. *la lampadina va svitata* 'the bulb is unscrewed' – see also Bourdin, this volume);
2. by contrast, from the perspective of the restrictions on compound forms, the Romanian *veni*-passive is similar to the Italian *venire*-passive, which does not surface as a passive auxiliary in compound forms;
3. on the other hand, the Romanian *veni*-passive from Italian translations resembles syntactically and semantically the *venire*-passive of Italian.

Thus, provided that almost identical values may be expressed with the use of different motion verbs grammaticalized as passive auxiliaries (e.g. It. *andare* and Rom. *veni*), the 'come'-passive constructions attested in the Romance languages are not etymologically inherited from Latin (as Adams (2013) has shown). Rather, their existence in Latin and their re-emergence in the Romance languages is the effect of the recursive (typological) tendency of distinguishing between a static, resultative passive and a dynamic (and sometimes modal) passive (Iliescu 2003: 3274).

Two of the constructions reviewed above in Section 2 appear to be the result of language contact. First, the lexical usage of *veni* as a deontic modal verb (examples (4), (18)) is the result of Slavic influence. Second, the *veni*-passive in Old Romanian texts translated from Italian ((6b), (10), (11)) is the result of indirect language contact (by means of translation). By contrast, the other constructions analysed above (*veni* as a passive auxiliary in the popular, oral language, as copula and as an inceptive verb) have emerged independently in Romanian, although some of them have late Romance correspondents.

On the other hand, the question of language contact reveals a more interesting aspect. What distinguishes the structures resulting from language contact from those emerging independently in Romanian is their status throughout the history of Romanian. The structures resulting from contact have been present in Romanian for a short period of time and in a very limited inventory of texts: the lexical deontic usage of *veni* was present in texts heavily influenced by Slavic translation, and the loan translation passive is well attested in a single text (*Foletul novel*), a translation from Italian, and then sporadically in texts written by bilingual (Romanian-Italian) authors. These constructions have thus not been part of the mainstream usage at any historical moment. By contrast, the structures emerging in Romanian have been uninterruptedly productive throughout the history of Romanian, and they are still preserved in different varieties of the present-day language.

3.4 A multiple grammaticalization path

The final question posed in the introduction is the following:

(v)   Finally, do the Romanian data illustrate a single grammaticalization path (with cascade effects) or do they illustrate independent grammaticalization processes?

Given all the examples analysed above, this last question might sound superfluous, as it is clear that the Romanian data surveyed indicate that what is at play are independent grammaticalization paths, which have started to manifest themselves at different moments in time.

Veni as a **passive auxiliary** has two sources: one is the loan translation from Italian ((6b), (10), (11)), and the other ((1), (7), (8), etc.) is grammaticalization as re-analysis inside Romanian in contexts in which *veni* was followed by a past participle (21).

Veni as a **copula** has different language-internal sources: the latest grammaticalized value (e.g. (2), (23a)) is based on the genuine semantic content of *veni* as a motion verb, with the re-interpretation triggered in a specific grammatical context (22), and conceptualized as a transfer from [change of location] to [marker of an indirect (kinship) relation] (cf. (23)). For the two other copular usages of *veni* it is hard to put forth a plausible grammaticalization scenario because of the following facts: the dynamic copular *veni* (13) is attested only in modern dialectal texts, is specific to the spoken language, and there are no relevant attestations in the older stages of Romanian; by contrast, the static copular *veni* (14) is attested since the earliest Romanian writings and has not changed its usage and values ever since.

Finally, **inceptive** *veni* has been attested since the earliest Romanian texts (17); throughout the history of Romanian it has changed its syntactic (selection) properties: initially, it could only take a nominal phrase as its complement (17); in an intermediary stage, its complement consisted of a [nominal phrase + subjunctive] cluster (17d); finally, the nominal was dropped and *veni* was followed by a subjunctive complement (3). Thus, the grammatical context was also instrumental in the case of this development.

4 Conclusions

In conjunction with the overall goals and research questions of the present volume, the following conclusions may be drawn as to the grammaticalization of the Romanian motion verb *veni* ('come'):

(i) Romanian *veni* fruitfully illustrates the idea that the same lexical item can be simultaneously involved in several grammaticalization processes.

(ii) These grammaticalization processes are based on various mechanisms: both semantic change operations (metaphor, transfer) and narrow distributional factors (i.e. specific contexts of re-analysis) have concurred to yield a multitude of constructions (with specific usages and meanings) in the present-day language.

(iii) Language contact factor can be claimed to be of low importance since the constructions influenced by foreign patterns (two in this case) did not enter the mainstream language and were active only for a short period and in a limited array of texts.

(iv) Although some of the Romanian structures (have been claimed to) have Latin correspondents, their development inside Romanian as well as the fact that they also "emerged" in other Romance languages indicates that they are not etymologically inherited from Latin. What seems to be at play in fact is a typological recurrence factor rather than direct inheritance.

(v) Finally, one may also comment on the specific contribution of *veni* / *come* to problem of the grammaticalization of motion verbs in general.

Veni appears in constructions parallel to *fi* 'be' and supplements the predication with a special semantic value such as [dynamic] / [change of state], [inceptive], [deontic] or [indirect (kinship) relation], which can all be traced back to the genuine motion meaning of *veni* and viewed as resulting from semantic bleaching.

In the competition of more than one verb expressing motion towards the speaker's deictic centre, such as the one between *veni – ajunge – sosi* (~ 'come, arrive'), it is the verb which has the most semantic values and appears only in one syntactic guise (unaccusative), *veni*, which is chosen for grammaticalization as a passive auxiliary. The affinity of *veni* with the passive construction, which is prototypically an unaccusative construction, is straightforward.

Abbreviations

cl	clitic
def	definite (article)
pluperf	pluperfect
pple	participle
subj	subjunctive
sup	supine

Corpora

Coresi, *Carte cu învățătură* (1581), ed. Sextil Pușcariu & Alexie Procopovici, București, Atelierele grafice Socec & Co., 1914.

Cronicari munteni, Ediție îngrijită de Mihail Gregorian, Studiu introductiv de Eugen Stănescu, I, *Stolnicul Constantin Cantacuzino, Anonimul Cantacuzinesc, Radu Popescu*, București, Editura pentru Literatură, 1961.

DA – *Dicționarul limbii române*, tomurile I-II, București, 1913–1948.

DLR – *Dicţionarul limbii române*, serie nouă, tomul XIII, partea I, litera V, V-veni, Bucureşti, Editura Academiei Române, 1997.
Dosoftei, *Psaltirea în versuri* (1673), ed. N. A. Ursu, Iaşi, Mitropolia Moldovei şi Sucevei, 1974.
Foletul novel. Calendariul lui Constantin Vodă Brâncoveanu, 1693–1704, ed. Emil Vârtosu, Bucureşti, 1942.
Studii şi documente cu privire la istoria romînilor, vol. VIII, *Scrisori de boieri şi negustori olteni şi munteni către casa de negoţ sibiiană Hagi Pop*, publicate cu note genealogice asupra mai multor familii de N. Iorga, Bucureşti: Stelierele grafice Socec & comp.
TDM I, II, III – *Texte dialectale Muntenia*, vol. I–III, ed. Boris Cazacu, Bucureşti, Editura Academiei, 1973–1975–1987.
The electronic database of Old Romanian texts of "Iorgu Iordan - Al. Rosetti" Institute of Linguistics, Bucharest

References

Adams, James. 2013. *Social Variation and the Latin Language*. Cambridge: Cambridge University Press.
Arigne, Viviane. 2007. Grammaticalization, polysemy and iterated modality: the case of *should. CORELA* 1(5)
http://corela.edel.univ-poitiers.fr/index.php?id=343 (accessed 5 May 2012).
Bourciez, Edouard. 1956. *Éléments de linguistique romane. quatrième édition*. Paris: Klincksieck.
Bybee, Joan. 2003. Cognitive processes in grammaticalization. In Michael Thomasello (ed.), *The New Psychology of Language*, volume II, 145–167. New Jersey: Lawrence Erlbaum.
Bybee, Joan, Revere Perkins & William Pagliuka. 1994. *The Evolution of Grammar. Tense, Aspect, and Modality in the Languages of the World*. Chicago, London: The University of Chicago Press.
Butler, Jonny. 2004. *Phase Structure, Phrase Structure, and Quantification*. York: University of York doctoral dissertation.
Disney, Stephen D. 2009. The grammaticalization of "Be going to". *Newcastle Working Papers in Linguistics* 15: 63–81.
Ernout, Alfred & Antoine Meillet. 1959. *Dictionnaire étymologique de la langue latine. Histoire des mots*. Tome II. Paris: Librairie C. Klincksteck.
Hacquard, Valentine. 2009. On the interaction of aspect and modal auxiliaries. *Linguistics and Philosophy* 32: 279–315.
Haspelmath, Martin. 1990. The grammaticalization of passive morphology. *Studies in language* 14: 2572.
Heine, Bernd & Tania Kuteva. 2002. *World Lexicon of Grammaticalization*. Cambridge: Cambridge University Press.
Hopper, Paul J. & Elizabeth C. Traugott. 2003. *Grammaticalization,* 3rd edition. Cambridge: Cambridge University Press.
Huddleston, Rodney & Geoffrey K. Pullum. 2005. *A Student's Introduction to English Grammar*. Cambridge: Cambridge University Press.
Iliescu, Maria. 2003. Phénomènes de convergence et de divergence dans la Romania: morphosyntaxe et syntaxe. In Gerhard Ernst, Martin-Dietrich Gleßgen, Christian Schmitt & Wolfgang Schweickard (eds.), *Romanische Sprachgeschichte / Histoire linguistique de la Romania*, vol. 3, 3266–3281. Berlin & New York: Mouton de Gruyter.
Iordan, Iorgu. 1950. Note sintactice. *Studii şi cercetări lingvistice I*, no. 2. 269–279.

La Fauci, Nunzio & Michele Loporcaro. 1989. Passifs, avencements de l'objet indirect et formes verbales périphrastiques dans le dialecte d'Altamura (Pouilles). *Rivista di linguistica* 1 (1): 161–196.

Maiden, Martin, Cecilia Robustelli. 2007 [2000]. *A Reference Grammar of Modern Italian*, second edition. London: Hodder Arnold.

Manoliu, Maria. 1971. *Gramatica comparată a limbilor romanice*. București: Editura Didactică și Pedagogică.

Mareș, Alexandru. 1993. Cine a fost Ioan Romanul, alias Frâncul. II. *Limba română* 3. 117–122.

Nicolle, Steve. 2007. The grammaticalization of tense markers: a pragmatic reanalysis. *Cahiers Cronos* 17: 47–65.

Nordhoff, Sebastian. 2011. Having *come* to be a copula in Sri Lanka Malay – an unusual grammaticalization path. *Folia Linguistica* 45 (1): 103–126.

Pană Dindelegan, Gabriela. 2003. Note asupra pasivului. In *Elemente de gramatică. Dificultăți, controverse, noi interpretări*, 133–139. București: Humanitas Educațional.

Pană Dindelegan, Gabriela. 2008a. Numele predicativ. In *Gramatica limbii române*, vol. 2, 267–295. București: Editura Academiei Române.

Pană Dindelegan, Gabriela. 2008b. Construcții pasive și construcții impersonale. In *Gramatica limbii române*, vol. 2, 133–144. București: Editura Academiei Române.

Picallo, Carme M. 1990. Modal verbs in Catalan. *Natural Language and Linguistic Theory* 8: 285–312.

Posner, Rebecca. 1994. *The Romance Languages*. Cambridge: Cambridge University Press.

Roberts, Ian & Anna Roussou. 2003. *Syntactic Change. A Minimalist Approach to Grammaticalization*. Cambridge: Cambridge University Press.

Rusu, Valeriu (ed.). 1984. *Tratat de dialectologie românească*. Craiova: Scrisul Românesc.

Salvi, Giampaolo & Lorenzo Renzi. 2010. *Grammatica dell'italiano antico*, vol. 1. Bologna: Il Mulino.

Sârbu, R., V. Frățilă. 1998. *Dialectul istroromân*. Timișoara: Amacord.

Squartini, Mario. 1999. Voice clashing with Aspect: the case of Italian passives. *Rivista di linguistica* 11: 341–365.

Squartini, Mario. 2003. La grammaticalizzazione di <venire + participio> in Italiano: anticausativo o risultativo. In Claus D. Pusch & Andreas Wesch (eds.), *Verbalperiphrasen in den (Ibero-)romanischen Sprachen*, 23–34. Hamburg: Helmut Buske Verlag.

Siewierska, Anna. 1984. *The passive. A Comparative Linguistic Analysis,* London, Sydney, Dover, New Hampshire: Croom Helm.

Smith, Carlota S. 1991. *The Parameter of Aspect*. Dordrecht: Kluwer.

Stolova, Natalya I. 2005. Expressing time through space: a comparative diachronic perspective on Romance periphrastic past and future. In Martine Coene & Liliane Tasmowski (eds.), *On Space and Time in Language*, 193–207. Cluj-Napoca: Clusium.

Timotin, Emanuela. 2000. Modalități de exprimare a pasivului în dialectele românești sud-dunărene. *Studii și cercetări lingvistice* 2: 481–490.

Vincent, Nigel. 2011. Non-finite forms, periphrases, and Autonomous Morphology in Latin and Romance. In Martin Maiden, John Charles Smith, Maria Goldbach & Marc-Olivier Hinzelin (eds.), *Morphological Autonomy. Perspectives from Romance Inflectional Morphology,* 417–435. Oxford: Oxford University Press.

Wurmbrand, Susanne. 2003. *Infinitives. Restructuring and Clause Structure*. Berlin & New York: Mouton de Gruyter.

Zafiu, Rodica. 2013. Modality and evidentiality. In Gabriela Pană Dindelegan (ed.), *The Grammar of Romanian*, 575–584. Oxford: Oxford University Press.

Mood and modality

Philippe Bourdin
When *come* and *go* go necessive

The topic of this paper is a set of pathways that have been sparsely documented in the literature on the grammaticalization routes taken by 'come' and 'go' crosslinguistically — or, more precisely, taken by verbs commonly, though not unproblematically, assumed to be "equivalent" to English *come* and *go*. Yet it is not the case, as I propose to show, that the pathways leading from directional deixis to necessive modality have been infrequently travelled, at least across Indo-European.

The first part will address methodological preliminaries: I will discuss some of the issues involved in considering directional deixis as a putative crosslinguistic category as well as some of the ways in which the notional constellation subsumed by necessive modality can be defined and subdivided. The second part will deal with the necessive interpretation that attaches to certain ventive- and itive-marked futures. The third and most copious part of the paper will address grammaticalization pathways where futurity plays no part: some, attested in Indo-Aryan and Romance languages, involve verbs of 'coming' or 'going' co-encoding passive voice and necessive modality; others, attested in a number of Circum-Baltic languages as well as in two Celtic languages, feature ventive verbs having gone more or less directly necessive.

1 Directional deixis and necessive modality in typological perspective

1.1 The crosslinguistic reality and status of directional deixis

Motion in space is one of the most basic activities that constitute the human experience. It is therefore hardly surprising that languages should possess a number of markers dedicated to encoding it: these are typically verbs, but adverbs may be marshalled for that purpose as well as bound or semi-bound morphemes. Languages may, minimally, have a verb glossed 'move'. However, they usually encode motion in a more fine-grained fashion: English, for instance, has both verbs that specify manner of motion (e.g. *swim* or *walk*) and verbs that specify the direction of the motion event with respect to specific spatial coordinates (e.g.

ascend and *enter*).[1] Not infrequently, languages choose the *deictic centre* (DC) as a favoured coordinate: it is this reality that is captured by the concept of *directional deixis* (DD).

I will assume in what follows that the DC is a variable ranging over a set of locations. In a one-on-one dialogue or a 1st person narrative this set includes the place where the speaker is at speech time and potentially any or all "projections" thereof. As a working hypothesis, typical candidates to the status of "projection" are the location of the addressee at speech time, the location of either speech participant at event time, or the "base" (i.e. place of residence) of either speech participant (Fillmore 1975 [1971]). In situations where two candidates are in competition, there are language-specific rules that determine whether one needs to prevail rather than the other.

A straightforward definition of DD might go something like this: directional deictics are just those lexical or grammatical units which, in a given language, are *primarily* dedicated to encoding motion in relation to the DC and a language that implements DD is one that possesses at least one such unit. This definition of directional deictics is certainly satisfied by *hither* in Middle and Early Modern English or *sjuda*, 'towards here', in Russian, though not by *towards here* in Modern English as it is not a lexical unit; whether it is satisfied by *come* is difficult to ascertain in the absence of clear criteria for determining what the *primary* meaning of a polysemous verb like *come* is. By this definition, Modern English may be, or may not be, a language that implements DD and this presumably is true also of a great many languages.

Such, however, is not the way DD is usually understood; or rather, since the expression "directional deixis" is infrequently used, this is not exactly what typologists mean when they talk about "verbs of coming" and "verbs of going", or about "ventive vs. itive (or andative)" verbs, or about "verbs of deictic motion". While some linguists — e.g. Ricca (1993) and Wilkins and Hill (1995) — have called into question the unitary, let alone universal, nature of DD as a cross-linguistic category, typologists continue by and large to operate on the implicit assumption that it is permissible to make generalizations about the behaviour of the verbs at issue. One problem is that motion in relation to the DC is routinely handled, in language after language, by markers that are not verbs: the German prefixes *her* and *hin* are a case in point.[2] Another problem is that at best only lip

---

1 I will purposely leave aside the important issue of what it means exactly for a motion event to be "directed" *with respect* to a given coordinate. That the notion of "goal" of motion is problematic has been shown by Wilkins and Hill (1995).
2 Even a study as subtle and insightful as that provided by Ricca (1993) overlooks those prefixes and their interplay with *kommen* 'come' and *gehen* 'go'.

service is paid to the considerable range of variation, especially with respect to deictic robustness, exhibited by the verbs at issue across languages.

The second problem cannot be overcome unless empirical studies, especially those addressing grammaticalization pathways, pay close and systematic attention to the semantic properties and pragmatic behaviour of the markers in individual languages, whether they be verbal or non-verbal; this would require going well beyond the descriptors provided in dictionaries and reference grammars, which often reduce to little more than 'come' and 'go' glosses. From a more theoretical perspective, we need to sharpen our understanding of DD as a "comparative concept" (Haspelmath 2010: 665).[3] This requires working towards defining the cluster of properties that ultimately may, or may not, legitimize continuing with current typological practice. I will confine myself here to setting down six principles, or rather general observations, that might provide the framework for such an endeavour, each of which would require considerable elaboration.

(1) DD is unlikely to be a universal category.

(2) DD need not be implemented, in a given language, by a pair of markers. For instance, a language may have a ventive affix without a corresponding itive, or (though more rarely) the other way round; or, as is the case in many Oceanic languages, we may find a three-way DD system aligned on person deixis. More idiosyncratic arrangements, however, are not hard to find.

(3) DD is frequently implemented by overtly grammatical markers. Countless languages use closed-class items (e.g. affixes, clitics, auxiliaries, etc.) to impart deictic directionality to the motion event "associated" with the situation denoted by the predicate. Besides, it is not uncommon for those items to co-encode such typically grammatical categories as tense, aspect, mood, or person.

(4) Even when DD is implemented by open-class items, such as verbs, these tend to exhibit properties that flag them as members of a small, tightly knit group within a paradigm which is otherwise unimpeachably lexical. Thus, in language after language putative ventive and itive verbs rank among the dozen or so verbs with the highest token frequency, they typically display extensive morphological irregularity (e.g. suppletion), and they are also the

---

3 "Comparative concepts are concepts created by comparative linguists for the specific purpose of crosslinguistic comparison. Unlike descriptive categories, they are not part of particular language systems and are not needed by descriptive linguists or by speakers."

verbs most susceptible to serialization (Foley and Olson 1985: 41). Many languages assign a special structural status to the encoding of DD as against other types of directionality (Lamarre 2008: 75). Crucially, DD is not infrequently subject to obligatory specification: in Korean, a motion event like 'Kim climbed down the tree' cannot typically be described without compounding 'descend' with 'come' (Chai-Song 1985: 86–87).

Arguably, these are all tell-tale signs that even when structurally they belong to open-class paradigms, markers of DD have a *latent grammatical status*. This is consonant with the following observation, made by von Fintel (1995: 184): "[...] most examples [of grammaticalization] I have seen start with a source item that is already fairly abstract and belongs to a special semantic field. It seems to me that source items already have a "logical" meaning. They may all belong to the intermediate category discussed above." The "intermediate category" von Fintel is referring to is comprised of items that combine two properties: they have both a "lexical syntax" and a "logical meaning". I would hypothesize that this is an all-important feature with respect to the grammaticalization of some of the constructions into which verbal exponents of DD enter: these are ontologically primed for what is always, in a sense, *second-stage grammaticalization*. By "second-stage grammaticalization" I am referring to the italicized portion in the well-known definition proposed by Kuriłowicz (1975 [1965]: 52): "Grammaticalization consists in the increase of the range of a morpheme advancing from a lexical to a grammatical or *from a less grammatical to a more grammatical status*" [emphasis mine, Ph. B.].

It is for that matter inconceivable that first-stage grammaticalization *stricto sensu* would have any reality at all if one adheres to a strict Aristotelian conception of change: "The point is that change is not catastrophic. It is not the case that A which is sheerly not-B suddenly becomes B. Consider A more carefully and you will find some of the conditions of B-ness already present; if it were not so, A would never become B." (Ross 1949: 177).

(5) It turns out, time and again, that what languages implementing DD "pay attention" to is the positioning of the goal of motion (G) in regard to the deictic centre, rather than the positioning of its source (S). It may be claimed, on the basis of this recurrent observation, that the feature of goal-orientedness is intrinsic to DD — which claim has a strong version and a weaker one. The strong version would be falsified if there turned out to be a language possessing, possibly among other DD verbs, one (S1) glossed 'move away from a starting position identified with the DC' and another (S2) glossed 'move away from a starting position other than the DC'. A weak version of

the claim holds that there is no language where DD is implemented by such verbs as S1 and S2 without also being implemented by G1, 'move towards a location identified with the DC', and G2, 'move towards a location other than the DC'.

Whether goal-orientedness is a universal feature of DD systems is a question that raises a host of empirical issues.[4] From a theoretical point of view, Bourdin (1997: 206) has suggested that it is a specific instantiation of the so-called "goal bias" or "allative bias", whereby "people have a Goal biased perspective on events that makes them more likely to encode Goal states than Source states" (Lakusta and Landau 2005: 30).[5]

While both ventive and itive markers are goal-oriented, ventives instantiate an even greater asymmetry between goal and source than itives do. This is because added to the irrelevance of the source with respect to the DC is the identification of the goal itself with the DC. I would venture the claim that itives exhibit *degree-1 goal-orientedness* and ventives *degree-2*.

The goal-orientedness of DD markers plays a crucial role, it will be argued below, in their grammaticalization into exponents of necessive modality.

(6) Languages tend to conflate the encoding of DD and that of the salient phases of the motion event at issue, i.e. its starting-point and its endpoint. There is a synchronic dimension to this conflation: for instance, a marker interpreted as ventive in some contexts will typically be used non-deictically, in other contexts, to refer to arrival at the goal (e.g. *koma* in Icelandic; see Bourdin 1999: 194–195). There is also a diachronic dimension to the conflation: for instance, Ricca (1993) traces in detail the diachronic changes undergone by *venire* in Latin and the evolution from *qiman* in Gothic to *come* in Modern English; he shows that in both cases the shift, simply put, is from a verb that essentially denotes arrival at any location whatsoever to one whose primary function is to identify the goal with the DC.

---

4 Highly relevant to a discussion of these issues is how one goes about delimiting the criteria to be used in determining whether a system of directional markers qualifies as a DD system or not. For example, if a relatively loose definition of DD is adopted, then the strong version of the claim of goal-orientedness is quite possibly falsified by the facts of Czech (Filip 2003: 77).

5 The goal-bias hypothesis has been discussed in recent years by linguists (e.g. Ikegami 1987, Bourdin 1997, Filip 2003, Nam 2004, Stefanowitsch and Rhode 2004, Verspoor, Dirven and Radden 2004, Markovskaya 2006, Gehrke 2008a and 2008b, and several of the papers in Kopecka and Narasimhan 2012), while being researched also by psycholinguists, developmental psychologists and cognitive scientists (e.g. Lakusta 2005, Lakusta and Landau 2005, Regier and Zheng 2007, Papafragou 2010, Lakusta and Landau 2012).

The intertwining of deicticity and phase-saliency is negotiated in ways that are both subtle and variable from one language to the next and to which glosses such as 'depart' and 'arrive' are far from giving full justice (for English *come* and *go*, see Taylor 1988). The crosslinguistic analysis that has been conducted by Wälchli and Cysouw (2012: 700) in the semantic map framework ends on a note at once cautious and upbeat: "The amount of diversity to be accounted for is high [...] However, at the same time there is a high amount of regularity." This tension between relative variability and relative invariance is, of course, an intrinsic feature of putative crosslinguistic categories. The practical reality, though, is that the evidence available to the typologist is often woefully insufficient for a reasonably precise assessment of the extent to which a given marker encodes DD vs. phase-saliency.

Given this state of affairs, I will try, in what follows, to be mindful at all times that there are probably no two languages that implement DD in quite the same way. I will also assume that the non-deictic functions of a given marker may be so predominant as to preclude its being categorized as a marker of DD proper.

1.2 Necessive modality

As Lyons (1977: 787) puts it, "necessity and possibility are the two central notions of traditional modal logic". They are instantiated within each of several distinct modal categories and a great many proposals have been made by both linguists and philosophers as to what these categories are. For instance, von Fintel (2006: 2) distinguishes epistemic, deontic, bouletic, circumstantial and teleological modalities. In the linguistic literature, epistemic modality is usually the odd man out. One overarching reason for this is that epistemic necessity or possibility involves a judgement as to the standing of a given proposition with respect to truth, whereas the "other" modalities are concerned, broadly speaking, with the desirability or appropriateness of a given action.[6] I will have no more to say about epistemic necessity, except this: all of the markers that will be dealt with in this paper are specialized in the encoding of non-epistemic necessity, to the exclusion of epistemic necessity. This is quite striking when one considers that out of a

---

6 For a thought-provoking discussion of the relationship between epistemic and non-epistemic modality, see Chilton (2010). With respect to necessive modality, Chilton's thesis, *pace* the view commonly held by linguists, is that "deontic meanings appear to presuppose epistemic ones" (*ibid.*: 193).

sample of 207 languages in the *World Atlas of Language Structures* (Haspelmath et al. 2005: 310–313), 36 display overlap of the marking of epistemic possibility and necessity with that of non-epistemic possibility *and* necessity, while in 66 languages overlap is limited to *either* possibility *or* necessity. The overlap is by far the greatest in Standard Average European languages.[7] Significantly, this is a grouping to which many of the languages we will be looking at below happen to belong.

Somewhat more controversial than the epistemic/non-epistemic dichotomy is the classification of non-epistemic modalities. Von Fintel's proposal is based on distinctions that are philosophically important. Whether such distinctions or those made by other philosophers are linguistically relevant, however, depends (a) on the modal system of the specific language being described and (b) on the formal and semantic criteria that are used for making this sort of decision.

The typology proposed by Van der Auwera and Plungian (1998) has been influential in recent studies on modality because it is meant to mesh with observable patterns of polyfunctionality and attested diachronic tendencies across a spectrum of languages. It is based on the insight that non-epistemic modality is fundamentally "participant"-oriented to the extent that it involves the agency of a participant in the modalized situation who, in the case of necessity, is the target of a requirement. If the requirement originates in her own internal state, Van der Auwera and Plungian talk about participant-internal necessity, as in *Jill's tired, she needs to rest*. If the source of the requirement is an outside force, we are dealing with participant-external necessity, of which there are a deontic variant and a non-deontic[8] variant. As I understand it, the term "deontic" covers all instances where the outside force is ultimately human, whether it be the speaker directly (*You must tidy up your room*) or a set of rules enforced by a social group and mediated in varying degrees by the speaker (*Motorists are to wear seat belts at all times*). Non-deontic necessity takes care of instances where the requirement is imposed by some law of nature or circumstance independent from human volition (*The rodeo had to be cancelled because of heavy snowfall*). It corresponds to that subspecies of "dynamic" necessity (Palmer 1979: 23; 36–37) which is dubbed "situational" by Nuyts (2006: 4) and which he characterizes as "a necessity/inevitability inherent in the situation described in the clause as a whole".

---

7 See Van der Auwera et al. (2005: 247; 256), quoted by Narrog (2010: 396).

8 Van der Auwera and Plungian do not actually use the term "non-deontic". In their typology, "deontic" modality has a special status, but participant-external modality that is not deontic does not.

No particular taxonomy can be expected to capture exactly the division of labour between the modal markers of a given language. The problem of categorization is compounded by the reality that the descriptive sources available to typologists usually offer, at best, a loose characterization of the semantics of individual modal markers.[9] For these reasons I will refrain from specifying the particular type of non-epistemic modality instantiated by any given marker except when it seems feasible and safe to do so.

An important distinction which is relevant to some of the markers discussed in this paper is that between strong and weak necessity. Von Fintel and Iatridou (2008: 117) illustrate the distinction by means of the following acceptability contrast (borrowed from Copley 2006):

(1)　a)　*You **ought** (weak) to wash your hands—in fact, you **have** (strong) to.*
　　　b)　*??You **have** (strong) to wash your hands—in fact, you **ought** (weak) to.*

(1a) is acceptable because *You ought to wash your hand* implicates *You don't have to wash your hands* (as per Grice's Quantity maxim) and it is permissible to cancel an implicature, which is exactly what the sentence *in fact, you have to* does. (1b) is unacceptable because there is simply no implicature that the sentence *in fact, you ought to* can possibly cancel. According to von Fintel and Iatridou (2008: 119), a weak necessity modal such as *ought (to)* implies that the course of action "is better than all alternatives", whereas a strong necessity modal such as *must* or *have (to)* "picks out the only candidate". This would explain another acceptability contrast adduced by von Fintel and Iatridou (2008: 127):

(2)　a)　*?According to the law, people convicted of stealing **ought** to go to prison.*
　　　b)　*You **ought** to do the dishes.*

A law, by definition, fits to a given crime a specific penalty rather than a "preferred" one. On the other hand, one can imagine a situation where doing the dishes could be construed as the most appropriate course of action in comparison to other courses of action that are not so highly valued, such as watching a soccer game on television.

Von Fintel and Iatridou (2008: 126) point out that in languages as diverse as Modern Greek, French, or Hungarian, weak necessity is typically encoded by attaching "counterfactual morphology" to a modal that otherwise marks strong necessity: a case in point is the French weak necessive *tu devrais*, 'you ought to',

---

9 On the pitfalls of crosslinguistic comparison in the area of necessive modality, see Myhill and Smith (1995).

which is the so-called "conditional" form of the strong necessive *tu dois*, 'you must'. Deontic strength can also be lexicalized: *it is fitting (that)* in English and *il convient (de)* in French involve social norms or standards of expediency which do not have the degree of stringency that laws and regulations possess, so that failure to observe such "conventions" or "proprieties" does not trigger the same sort of penalties as offending against laws enforced by the police and the courts. As will be shown below, there are languages in which DD verbs play a role in the encoding of propriety or appropriateness.

2 From deictic goal-orientedness to necessity via futurity

As has been noted by Bybee, Perkins and Pagliuca (1994: 268–269), Giacalone Ramat (2000: 132) and Heine and Kuteva (2002: 75–78; 161–163), among others, it is the feature of goal-orientedness, or allativity, that motivates the grammaticalization of verbs of coming and going worldwide into future and prospective markers: as long as the motion is in progress, the goal is logically construed as being situated in the future. The motivation is in the final analysis of a metaphorical nature, as it involves a shift from a location situated in space to a state of affairs situated in time.

Modal verbs are another major source of future and prospective markers crosslinguistically and the reason for this is fundamentally ontological. What is past is passed and wanting to engineer at time t_i a state of affairs situated before t_i is therefore not an option. In other words, volitional modality is ontologically non-retrospective. So is non-epistemic necessity, at least of the deontic or obligative kind: to say at t_i that someone is obliged to bring about a given state of affairs hardly makes sense if it is situated before t_i (De Haan 2006: 50; also Chilton 2010: 205). As a result, the step from encoding either volition or necessity to encoding futurity is a logical one. It is indeed routinely taken by languages, as is illustrated for instance by the destiny of Old English *willan* and *sculan*.

In the languages examined below, however, the road that has been taken would appear to have been in the opposite direction, i.e. from futurity to necessity.

2.1 Dehu

The following sentences feature the motion verb *tro* and give a rough idea of its semantics:

(3) Dehu (Austronesian, Remote Oceanic; New Caledonia)

  a) *eni   a   **tro**   (e) Drehu*
     1SG TENSE **move** (to) Lifou
     'I'm going to Lifou.'   (Moyse-Faurie 1983: 76)

  b) *eni   a   pi   **tro***
     1SG TENSE feel_like **move**
     'I feel like leaving.'   (Moyse-Faurie 1983: 103)

  c) *angeic a   **tro**   the-ng*
     3SG   TENSE **move** at_the_house-POSS.1SG
     'He is coming to my home.'   (Moyse-Faurie 1983: 172)

I will assume that *tro* is a bare motion verb, i.e. a verb that denotes motion in space stripped of any specification involving directionality or manner of motion. As a result, how bare motion verbs are to be interpreted is solely induced by context or situation of utterance. Whether it is permissible to lump them together with DD verbs, especially when analyzing their susceptibility to grammaticalization, is an issue to which I return presently.

   With respect to tense and aspect as well as constituent order, Dehu has three types of sentences, the first one of which need not concern us here.

   Type II sentences feature a tense marker, realized by *a*, which is compatible with adverbials referring to the past, the present or the future. As is shown in (3) above, constituent order is basically SVO. Sentence (4) instantiates an important subtype within Type II:

(4) Dehu

  tro   *angeic a   humuth   la   puaka*
  FUT[<move] 3SG   TENSE kill.TR.DEF DEF pig
  'He will kill the pig.'   (Moyse-Faurie 1983: 90)

It would appear that *a* here joins forces with *tro* to form a discontinuous marker of future tense. The constituent order is < *tro* + SVO >. The semantics of *lapa* suggests that in (5) future *tro* has lost its motional moorings, which is to be expected from verbs of motion having undergone grammaticalization:

(5) Dehu

> *maine* **tro**   *epun a*   *lapa ecelë...*
> if   **FUT[<move]** 2PL   TENSE stay   here
> 'If you stay here...'   (Moyse-Faurie 1983: 194)

Type III sentences, in which constituent order is almost systematically VOS, feature one of four distinct TAM markers. Among these is *troa*, which is made up of the verb *tro* and the tense marker *a* and which encodes necessive modality:

(6) Dehu

> **tro-a**   *xen*   *la   koko hnen la   itre nekönatr*
> **NEC[<move-TENSE]** eat.TR.DEF DEF   yam AGT   DEF PL   child
> 'The children must eat the yam.'   (Moyse-Faurie 1983: 159)

Given that both *tro* and *a* exist as independent elements, it is reasonable to assume, on grounds of plausible morphosyntactic change, that deontic *troa* is derived from discontinuous *tro...a* rather than the other way around. In other words, future-marking *tro* has attracted *a* to its clause-initial position and coalesced with it. However, the change of constituent order from SVO to VOS would suggest that *tro* has not just attracted the tense marker, but in fact the whole VP.[10]

If the above scenario is correct, two distinct questions arise.

The first has to do with the status of *tro* vis-à-vis directional deixis. It is not just verbs of motion that are supposed to grammaticalize into future markers, but verbs that encode motion towards the DC or to a location distinct from the DC. If indeed *tro* is a bare motion verb, it clearly does not fit this description. Yet it appears to have taken a diachronic route that is frequently travelled by ventive and itive verbs. In order to try and account for this paradox, I will make two assumptions. First, there appears to be no verb in Dehu that has the encoding of DD as its primary function. Second, in the absence of any such verb, it is up to the "next best" verb, i.e. *tro*, to follow the grammaticalization pathway that is open to a "true" ventive or itive verb in languages possessing such verbs. The *"next-best-tool" principle* that I assume is operating here is congruent with the notion that languages are problem-solving mechanisms and that they have to do the best job they can with the resources available, even when these are not "optimal".

---

10 Topicalization of the agent NP has the effect of coercing *troa* into clause-medial position, in which case constituent order is SVO (Moyse-Faurie 1983: 159). This is evidence that VOS order is contingent on *troa* being in clause-initial position.

The other question raised by the scenario above has to do with sequentiality along the grammaticalization pathway. What we presumably have in Dehu is a future marker that has grammaticalized into a necessive marker (while continuing to function also as a future marker). Usually, the pathway runs in the opposite direction, as has been documented by, among many other authors, Ultan (1978: 112–113). Fleischman (1982: 24), however, observes that futures originating from modals may in turn evolve into modals: "Specifically, the diachronic relationship of modality to futurity tends to operate in both directions, i.e. futures evolve from modals and are also likely to be put to modal uses. In both of these 'dynamic' situations, obligative, volitional, and hypothetical-dubitative modalities occur with relatively high frequency." What she may have in mind is such phenomena as deontic/jussive uses of *will* in English (e.g. *And then, you will write a list of the medical supplies you need. You will list everything from medicines to equipment to furniture.*[11]). That such uses are very much situation-bound seems clear and Huddleston and Pullum (2002: 194) view them as implicatures: "if I predict your agentive actions (or someone else's) in a context where I have the authority to require them, I will be understood as tacitly invoking that authority." These uses, in fact, instantiate a subtype of what Huddleston and Pullum (2002: 941) elsewhere dub "indirect directives", i.e. "non-imperative directives".[12]

It may well be that this is the pragmatic mechanism that underlies the emergence of necessive *troa* in Dehu. It would seem, however, that in this case the development of the necessive sense has gone further than the implicature stage, to the extent that its manifestation does not appear to be tied to context and situation. Examples such as (7) are suggestive in this regard:

---

11 *New England Review*, 28: 3 (*COCA*).
12 The extent to which deontic necessity should be distinguished from imperative mood constitutes a difficult issue for scholars of modality and speech acts: see Palmer (1986: 29–30). Interestingly, itive and ventive verbs are crosslinguistically prone to grammaticalizing into imperative and hortative markers: see Mauri and Sansò (this volume). Following Lyons (1977: 835), Timberlake (2007: 320) argues that imperatives and obligative modals both involve a "so-be-it": "In the imperative, the speaker precipitously declares 'so-be-it'; the obligation comes out of the blue and is imposed on the addressee. In lexical verbs that express obligation — verbs such as *ought, must, should, behoove* — the obligation is normally a static obligation, always applicable when a relevant occasion arises... The actual speaker, instead of imposing the 'so-be-it', speaks on behalf of a higher speaker or, it might be better to say, on behalf of all speakers. Authority becomes impersonal, generalized." I will come back below to the affinity of deontic necessity with impersonal constructions.

(7) Dehu

> ***tro-a***   *xom la ka*   *u*
> **NEC[<move-TENSE]** take this STATIVE do_what
> 'What must we take?'   (Moyse-Faurie 1983: 191)

Another important piece of evidence is provided by the following examples, where *troa* functions as a complementizer:

(8) Dehu

> a) *joxu a*   *upi*   *easë*   ***tro-a***   ***tro***
> chief TENSE order.TR 1PL.INCL **NEC.COMP[<move-TENSE]** move
> 'The chief is ordering us to leave.'

> b) *önii angeic* ***tro-a***   *angeic a*   *traqa elany*
> say 3SG   **COMP[<move-TENSE]** 3SG   TENSE arrive tomorrow
> 'He says he will come tomorrow.'   (Moyse-Faurie 1983: 181–182)

There is every reason to believe that we are dealing with a third stage in the grammaticalization of *tro*, whereby the obligation marker is reinterpreted, when the syntactic environment warrants it, as a complementizer. Sentences such as (8a) point to a possible explanation as to why *troa* underwent this further transformation. Initially, it is likely to have functioned as a deontic/jussive-mood-marker-cum-subordinator, redundantly flagging the embedded clause as the expression of an obligation. Subsequently the deontic meaning faded, which allowed the functional range of the marker to extend to the point where it was able to function as a run-of-the-mill complementizer, as in (8b). Its initial position in the clause rendered this possible, as complementizers in Dehu would appear to be clause-initial. Also, the SVO order in the complement clause (8b) suggests that the reanalysis of *troa* as a straightforward complementizer was not syntactically innocuous: it quite simply lost the ability to trigger VOS word order.

All four incarnations of *tro* — i.e. verb of motion, future tense marker, necessive marker and complementizer — coexist synchronically within the grammatical system of Dehu. Sentence (8a) is illustrative in this regard, where the coexistence is of a syntagmatic nature.

Nengone, which is the language most closely related to Dehu genetically and geographically, has a non-deictic motion verb, *co*, that would appear to have followed a pathway analogous, to some extent, to that taken by *tro* in Dehu (Tryon and Dubois 1969: 96–97; 200). According to Moyse-Faurie (2010: 303), however, the shape of the verb and the coexistence of an indigenous verb of 'going' (*hue*) suggest that Nengone has borrowed *tro* directly and subjected it to a sound change. The following examples instantiate the use of *co* as a future marker and as a necessive, respectively:

(9)   Nengone (Austronesian, Remote Oceanic; New Caledonia)

   a) *inu **co**   hue i Numea*
      1SG **FUT[<move]** go   to N.
      'I will go to Nouméa.'   (Moyse-Faurie 2010: 303)

   b) ***co**   yeil   ore nodei woc ri toto*
      NEC[<move] clear_of_weeds ART PL   weed in field
      'The field needs to be cleared of weeds.'   (Moyse-Faurie 2010: 304)

As its cognate in Dehu, *co* also functions as a complementizer (Moyse-Faurie 2010: 304).

2.2 Kru languages

The grammaticalization of DD verbs into future markers is ubiquitous among Kru languages. The following examples give a rough illustration of the diachronic process involved:

(10) Tchien Krahn (Niger-Congo, Volta-Congo, Kru; Côte d'Ivoire)

   ɔ **gi**   tɔ̃ dḛ̀ nā
   he **come** salt buy NMLZ
   'He comes (in order) to buy salt.'   (Marchese 1986: 121)

(11) Kuwaa (Niger-Congo, Volta-Congo, Kru; Côte d'Ivoire)

   ɔ́ **mí**   tulubɔ́   mú ma
   he **FUT[<go.IPFV]** Monrovia go NMLZ
   'He'll go to Monrovia.'   (Marchese 1986: 122)

(12) Krahn (Niger-Congo, Volta-Congo, Kru; Côte d'Ivoire)

   junu-a   **mu**   *duba glae*
   dew-IPFV **FUT[<go]** fall   tomorrow
   'Dew will fall tomorrow.'   (Marchese 1986: 100)

In (10), the ventive verb *gi* is used as a straightforward verb of motion governing an embedded clause referring to the purpose of the motion event. Reinterpretation of the itive verb as a future marker has taken place in both (11) and (12). In (11), no syntactic restructuring has taken place: the nominalizer is still present. In (12), it has disappeared.

Some of these markers have taken on an added modal meaning. It would appear that we are dealing with an invited inference, a sort of opportunistic extension; also, the evidence available suggests that full-fledged reinterpretation as a necessive marker is rare. In addition, this further stage in the semantic reshaping of the markers has not been accompanied by quite the degree of syntactic restructuring that has taken place in Dehu.

In Dadjriwalé, the verb 'come' is first and foremost a future tense marker; the abilitative and necessive meanings are, so to speak, functional outgrowths:

(13)   Dadjriwalé (dial. of Godié, Niger-Congo, Volta-Congo, Kru; Côte d'Ivoire)

       *Sìkà **jī***   *dű*   *mɔ̄*
       S.   **FUT[<come]** village go
       'Sika will go to the village.'
       Or: 'He is able to go.'
       Or: 'He must go.'   (Godé 2008: 220)

In Lakota Dida, on the other hand, the verb 'come' may function as a future tense marker, as in (14a) or as a full-fledged necessive marker, as in (14b):

(14)   Lakota Dida (Niger-Congo, Volta-Congo, Kru; Côte d'Ivoire)

    a) *Kúdu **yi***   *ziki*   *sáká li*
       K.   **FUT[<come]** tomorrow rice   eat
       'Kudu will eat rice tomorrow.'   (Marchese 1986: 211)

    b) *ɔ́*   **yi**   *wa sáká ɓlu*
       she.NEG **NEC[<come]** PST rice   pound
       'She shouldn't have pounded rice.'   (Marchese 1986: 211)

Example (14b) is especially interesting as it features a counterfactual deontic, with counterfactuality being supported by the past tense.

3 From deictic goal-orientedness to necessity, absent futurity

The previous section has addressed grammaticalization pathways for which the basic motivation is the link, metaphorical in nature, between goal-orientedness, as a defining feature of DD markers, and futurity. This section deals with phenomena where futurity plays no discernible role. This is not to say, however, that the feature of goal-orientedness is irrelevant, quite the contrary. The conceptual link between goal-orientedness and necessive (or for that matter volitional) modality is just as straightforward as that between goal-orientedness and futurity, but it is essentially of a metonymic nature: moving towards a goal is an activity that people typically do not engage in unless they need to (and/or want to).

This, ultimately, is the logic underlying the two broad sets of pathways to be described below. These, however, would not have been followed unless extra triggers had come into play, of a syntactic and semantic nature.

3.1 The encoding of necessity by DD-derived markers of passive voice

3.1.1 Some thoughts on "ventive" and "itive" passives

Following work by Keenan and Dryer (2007), among others, I am assuming that a construction B is passive when it stands in contrast with a construction A such that A and B usually have the same truth-value and B is typically characterized by a diminished valency as well as by some extra marker which may be a morpheme or some more substantial structure of a periphrastic nature. In the B construction the Agent nominal is deleted or is in a syntactically oblique position and the Patient or Undergoer nominal, if there is one, is in subject position. Finally, and ideally, the class of verbs susceptible to the alternation between the A type of construction and the B type is open-ended.

When the extra marker which characterizes passive voice is of a periphrastic nature, the lexical verb is usually in a non-finite form and it combines with an "auxiliary" verb which typically handles the encoding of such grammatical functions as tense, aspect, mood and person/number. As shown in Bourdin (2008 and 2009), the grammaticalization of deictic motion verbs into passive auxiliaries is widespread among Indo-European languages, especially in Indo-Aryan, Iranian and Romance.[13] It is also attested in a number of languages

---

13 The itive marker of passive voice in such languages as Scottish Gaelic and Tajiki does not conform with what is usually understood by the auxiliation template. I will not pursue this discussion, which hinges on how the category of auxiliary is defined.

outside Indo-European, such as Neo-Aramaic (Afro-Asiatic; Iraq) and Hayu (Sino-Tibetan; Nepal).

Why is it that some languages recruit verbs of coming and going as passive auxiliaries? Before answering this question, I believe it is necessary to make a fundamental distinction between two major types of grammaticalization.

Much has been written about what I would call the "easy", or "nice", grammaticalization pathways. By this I mean the diachronic processes whereby an overtly[14] lexical item shifts from one referential domain to a different referential domain and in so doing becomes part of the functional inventory of the language. An obvious instance of this type of grammaticalization is the development of verbs of volition or obligation into future auxiliaries. There is, to be sure, grammaticalization involved, because the markers at issue typically join the ranks of closed-class items and in so doing undergo morphosyntactic recategorization and, sometimes, some loss of phonological substance. Semantically, however, the target domain is neither more nor less referential than the source domain. There is clear evidence of this in the fact that the target domain can be handled in straightforward fashion by items that fully belong in the lexicon. When it comes to referring to the future, for example, *bona fide* lexical expressions such as *tomorrow* or *next year* can do the job just as well as tense affixes or auxiliaries, and for that matter with greater referential accuracy. Crucially, the shift from the source domain to the target domain involves processes of a metonymic or metaphorical nature: the literature on these is plentiful.

For an overtly lexical item such as 'come' or 'go' to become an exponent of voice is to sustain a process which I propose to call *"deep" grammaticalization*, as it is fundamentally different from the *"shallow" grammaticalization* I have just discussed. This is because, in contradistinction to functional domains such as modality, tense-aspect, person or number, the domain of voice has only a tenuous connection to the world outside language. One of the few connections that might conceivably be invoked is the feature of affectedness, which is claimed by Shibatani (1985: 840) to be "an integral semantic property of the prototypical passive." However, affectedness of the Patient goes only so far when it comes to defining passive voice. At its core, voice has to do with the manipulation of argument structure: there are just no lexical resources that can conceivably be deployed in a transparent and straightforward fashion to carry out this reshuffling of the morphosyntactic cards.

Because the grammaticalization of 'come' and 'go' into passive auxiliaries involves an almost complete break from the referential domain, the semantic

---

14 "Overtly" points to the caveat discussed above with respect to the "latently" grammatical status of the items that undergo grammaticalization.

impetus for it is distinctly more elusive than the metaphorical or metonymic processes which are commonly assumed to be at work when 'go' and 'come' are reanalyzed as, say, future tense markers. Though to my knowledge no explanatory routes have so far been systematically pursued in the literature, there are two that suggest themselves: (a) arguably, 'come' and 'go' are almost as basic, in cognitive terms, as 'be' and 'become', which are the most common auxiliaries of passive voice, and (b) 'change of location in space' qualifies, possibly, as an ontological variant of 'change of state'. Such explanations, however, are lacking in specificity and, crucially, they fail to take into account the feature of deicticity as well as that of goal-orientedness which I am assuming are intrinsic to the semantics of DD verbs.

I will make the claim that an explanation in terms of language-internal iconicity is warranted. Let us assume, in the spirit – if not the letter – of work by Kuno on the role of empathy in syntax (e.g. Kuno 1978 and 1987), that speakers tend to identify with Agents rather than Patients and with Topics rather than Non-topics, where "identification" involves no more than the adoption of the same vantage point. In prototypical active sentences the Agent is also the Topic, which means that only one vantage point is activated. Not so in prototypical passive sentences, as these involve a decoupling of Agent and Topic and therefore two distinct nominals vying for the status of vantage point. Let us make the further uncontroversial assumption that both in active and passive sentences, transitivity involves "kinesis" from the Agent nominal, which refers to the initiator of the activity, to the Patient nominal (Hopper and Thompson 1980: 251–252). In prototypical passive sentences, the Patient nominal happens to be the Topic. It follows that if the status of vantage point is assigned to the Topic, the (abstract) speaker identifies with the endpoint of the vector representing transitive kinesis: what we get is a ventive configuration. If the status of vantage point is assigned to the Agent, the (abstract) speaker identifies with the starting-point of the vector; what we get then is an itive configuration, as all this configuration requires is for the speaker to "situate" herself at some location distinct from the goal of the motion event:

Table 1. The iconic logic underlying ventive and itive passives

	Topic (Patient) ⟵———— Agent	
ventive passives	vantage point	
itive passives		vantage point

The "speaker" here is an abstraction of convenience, because in actual fact the choice between the two available vantage points is entrenched in the grammatical system of the language and not at all left to the whim of "real" individual speakers. There is nothing, for that matter, to prevent a language from allowing either option: as we will see presently, Italian has both a ventive passive and an itive passive.

3.1.2 A survey of ventive and itive passives co-encoding necessive modality

It turns out that a small number of ventive and itive passives function as exponents of necessive modality. Before attempting to determine the motivation for this, I will review the constructions at issue.

Naturally, the question arises, as it always should when the grammaticalization pathways followed by putative DD markers are being considered, what exactly the original semantics of each individual marker is and in particular how robust its deicticity is. I am aware of two detailed descriptions that are relevant with regard to the languages surveyed in this section, which all belong to either the Romance or Indo-Aryan branch of the Indo-European phylum. Ricca (1993: 79–82; 92) shows that Italian belongs to a cluster of languages possessing what he calls a "fully deictic" set of DD verbs. The description provided by Sinha (1972) suggests that Hindi probably belongs to that cluster, too, or at the very least to the cluster of languages having, in Ricca's terminology, a "predominantly deictic" set of DD verbs. Although I was unable to find works dealing with this topic for the other languages in this section, I will assume, pending further examination, that they belong to either of the aforementioned clusters.

3.1.2.1 Italian
Italian has a ventive passive, illustrated by (15a), and an itive passive, illustrated by (15b):[15]

(15)   Italian (Indo-European, Romance)

    a) *la*   *finestra* **viene**   *chius-a*
        DEF.FSG window **PASS[<come]**.PRS.3SG close.**PST.PTCP**-FSG
        'The window is being closed.'
          * 'The window needs to be closed.'   (A. L. and G. Lepschy 1981: 137)

---

15 See also Giacalone Ramat and Sansò (this volume).

b) *la*   *finestra* **va**   **chius**-*a*
DEF.FSG   window   **NEC.PASS[<go].**PRS.3SG   close.**PST.PTCP**-FSG
'The window needs to be closed.'
* 'The window is being closed.'   (A. L. and G. Lepschy 1981: 137)

The semantic contrast between the two is clearly of a modal nature: the <*venire + V-ato*> construction is a "pure" or "bare" passive (where -*ato* is the regular ending encoding the past participle in the masculine singular), while in the <*andare + V-ato*> construction *andare* coerces a necessive interpretation. There are, however, ten verbs or so in the language that elude this coercion, thereby licensing <*andare + V-ato*> being interpreted as either a bare passive or as a passive-necessive. Thus the following sentence is ambiguous:

(16)   Italian

     vorre-i   *av-ere*   *tutt-i*   *i*   *sold-i*   *che*
     want.COND.PRS-1SG   have-INF   all-MPL   DEF.MPL   penny-PL   REL
     vanno   **spes**-*i*   *per le*   *Olimpiadi*
     PASS[<go].PRS.3PL   spend.**PST.PTCP**-MPL   for   DEF.FPL   Olympics.PL
     'I would like to have all the money that's being spent for the Olympics.' Or:
     'I would like to have all the money that needs to be spent for the Olympics.'
                                                      (Rocchetti 1982: 116)

The verbs in question refer to loss (and related processes such as the wasting of money), disappearance or destruction. As suggested by Rocchetti (1982: 124) and Giacalone Ramat (2000: 132), this particular affinity is consonant, ultimately, with the deictic value of *andare*: if the deictic centre is construed as "a NORMAL state of being" (Clark 1974: 316), then the act of moving to a place distinct from it will by inference be evaluated negatively.[16]

The passive-necessive use of the <*andare + V-ato*> construction differs from the bare passive use on two counts. On the one hand, it is lexically unconstrained. On the other, it is subject to strict aspectual restrictions: specifically, it is incompatible with the simple past and with compound tenses (Giacalone Ramat 2000: 127).

Sentences such as the following are accordingly rendered uninterpretable by a conspiracy involving the lexical constraint on the bare passive reading of the construction (*lavare* is not a verb of loss or destruction) and the aspectual

---

16 This hypothesis is discussed by Ricca (1993: 43–45), Radden (1996), Bourdin (2003) and Mocciaro (this volume).

constraints on the passive-necessive reading (*andare* is in the "passato pros-simo", a compound tense):

(17) Italian

*il	*pavimento*	*è*	***and*-*at-o***	*lav-**at**-o*
DEF.MSG	floor	be.PRS.3SG	**go**-PST.PTCP-MSG	wash-**PST.PTCP**-MSG

(Bentley 2006: 346)

There is no ban, however, on passive-necessive *andare* being in the future or the conditional, for instance:

(18) Italian

è *possibile (ma **andr**-ebbe* *verific-**at**-o*
be.PRS.3SG possible but **NEC.PASS[<go]**-COND.3SG verify-**PST.PTCP**-MSG
con *tutt'altr-a* *mole di dat-i)* *che* *emerg-a* *in*
with all_other-FSG size of data-PL COMP emerge-PRS.3SG in
quest-i *fras-i ...*
this-MPL sentence-PL
'It is possible (but it would need to be verified with a much larger data-base) that there emerges in these sentences...'   (Ricca 1993: 88)

A number of further observations may be made that will contribute to a more precise understanding of the passive-necessive construction.

   Although there is no hard and fast prohibition on the person of the syntactic subject, it is overwhelmingly in the 3rd person. Rocchetti (1982: 122) links this fact with the "impersonal" nature of obligation as a modality: "même lorsque je dis *tu dois faire*, j'exprime en réalité une obligation d'ordre impersonnel ou traitée comme telle. S'il n'en était pas ainsi, je dirais « *je veux (il veut, nous voulons, ils veulent)* que tu fasses ». Dans *tu dois faire*, *tu* n'est que le point d'application de la notion impersonnelle d'obligation."[17] Rocchetti is on to something and it is no accident that in Italian impersonal constructions are favoured when it comes to encoding deontic modality: besides <*andare + V-ato*>, which according to Lo Cascio (1968: 287) belongs to the "impersonal type", Cornillie et al. (2009: 117–118) mention constructions with *bisogna, occorre* and *conviene*. This affinity

---

17 "Even when I say *you must do*, what I am expressing in actual fact is an obligation of an im-personal nature or treated as such. If that were not the case, I would say: "*I want (he wants, we want, they want)* you to do". In *you must do*, *you* is but the point of incidence of the impersonal modality of obligation."

with impersonality is, as we will see in greater detail below, a recurrent feature of necessive modals in many Indo-European languages.

Giacalone Ramat (2000: 134–137) endorses the traditional view that the passive-necessive use of <*andare* + *V-ato*> is unattested before the 16th century, whereas there are examples going back to the 14th century of the construction being used as a bare passive, though at that initial stage neither the stringent lexical constraint nor the prohibition on an Agent *da*-phrase that apply in contemporary Italian were in effect (see also Mocciaro, this volume). She does not subscribe to the view, however, that these two developments are sequentially ordered, i.e. that the passive-necessive use represented an extension of the bare passive use. She hypothesizes, rather, that the passive-necessive interpretation originates in a construction of the type <*andare a NP*>, where *a NP* refers to the role or location to which an inanimate object is destined or for which it is meant:

(19) 16th cent. Italian

> *e segnatamente lavor-av-a   sopra le   statu-e   che*
> and precisely   work-PST.IPFV-3SG over   DEF.FPL statue-PL REL
> **and**-*av-ano   a   dett-a   sepoltura*
> **go**-PST.IPFV-3PL **to** aforesaid-FSG gravestone
> 'and precisely he was working on the statues that had to be located (lit. went) on that gravestone.'
> (G. Vasari, *Vite (Michelangelo Buonarroti)*, 66.20; quoted by Giacalone Ramat (2000: 135))

This scenario accords well with the type of necessity that the construction frequently encodes in contemporary Italian, i.e. convenience, suitability or propriety:

(20) Present-day Italian

> *le   gonn-e **vanno**   port-at-e   lungh-e*
> DEF.FPL skirt-PL **NEC.PASS[<go].PRS.3PL** wear-PST.PTCP-FPL long-FPL
> *quest'anno*
> this_year
> 'Skirts are (to be) worn long this year.'
> Or: 'Long skirts are in fashion this year.'   (Rocchetti 1982: 122)

Both Rocchetti and Giacalone Ramat attempt to identify the semantic motivation for the reanalysis *andare* has undergone.

Rocchetti's account is formulated in terms of Guillaume's "psychomechanic" theory of language. In essence, the process of grammaticalization has gone through five successive stages, each of which corresponds to a specific "interception" of the cognitive process that underlies auxiliation. The use of *andare* as an exponent of necessive modality represents the final stage. At this point all *andare* does is situate the observer at the point where the "verbal idea" expressed by the lexical verb is yet to be accomplished. This would explain why the construction is disallowed when *andare* is aspectually perfective.

Giacalone Ramat (2000: 132) also underscores the prospective, or "future-projecting"[18], import of the construction and attributes it to the fundamental goal-orientedness of *andare*: "...the modal reading seems to presuppose for *andare* the idea of movement towards a goal. The shift from physical movement to the world of deontic obligation seems quite natural, since moving towards a goal implies that the goal has not yet been attained, but that the intention to attain it exists." She goes on to hypothesize that this "metaphorical extension" is "perfectly in line" with the grammaticalization of itive verbs into future markers.

While not as detailed, Giacalone Ramat's explanation in terms of goal-orientedness is better able to explain why in other languages verbs of coming can also evolve into passive auxiliaries co-encoding necessity, a topic to which I return presently. In fact, this development would seem to be precluded by the way in which Rocchetti (1982: 125) contrasts the semantics of *andare* with that of *venire*. This being said, neither linguist contemplates the possibility that there might conceivably be a link between passive voice and modality, specifically necessive modality. Giacalone-Ramat, as we have seen, actually downplays such a possibility on grounds of diachronic plausibility.

3.1.2.2 Romanian

As shown by Dragomirescu and Nicolae (this volume), several varieties of Romanian use ventive *veni* as a passive auxiliary. In colloquial usage, and singularly it seems in instructions having to do with cooking or handiwork, the construction may receive a prescriptive interpretation:

(21) Romanian (Indo-European, Romance, Eastern)

aici	*ar*	**veni**	*bătu-t*	*un*	*cui*
here	COND.3SG	**NEC.PASS[<come].INF**	strike-**PST.PTCP**.MSG	INDF.MSG	nail

'A nail ought to be driven here.' (Irimia 1976: 153–154)

---

18 Sansò and Mauri, "Go and come as sources of directive constructions" (this volume).

Necessity is not as robust a component of the ventive passive of Romanian as was the case with <*andare V-ato*> in Italian: firstly, because the construction can be vague as to whether a necessive reading is called for or what Dragomirescu and Nicolae call "a habitual, dispositional reading"; secondly, because a "pure" passive interpretation is often a possibility; thirdly, because this tends to be the only possibility in the written language.

All the examples provided by Dragomirescu and Nicolae are in the third person, which suggests that the construction is covertly impersonal, as is <*andare V-ato*> in Italian.

3.1.2.3 Indo-Aryan languages

The encoding of passive voice by an auxiliary derived from an itive verb and, though more rarely, from a ventive verb is a salient feature of Indo-Aryan languages, as is the co-encoding of passive voice and modality. Though it is not uncommon for necessive modality to be at play, abilitative modality is probably more frequent.[19] Often, both types are represented in one and the same language, as for instance in Marathi:

(22) Marathi (Indo-European, Indo-Aryan, Southern zone)

a) *Ra:m-kaḍu:n pustak*   ***wa:tsla***   ***gela***   *na:hi:*
R.-by   book[NSG]   read.**PFV**.3NSG   **PASS[<go]**.PST.3NSG   NEG
(lit.) 'The book did not go read by Ram.'
'Ram was unable to read the book.'   (Pandharipande 1997: 396–397)

b) *a:dzobã:nśi:*   *asa*   ***bolla***   ***dza:t***   *na:hi:*
grandfather.DAT   like_this   talk.**PFV**.3NSG   **PASS[<go]**.PRS.3NSG   NEG
(lit.) 'It does not go talked like this with grandfathers.'
'One should not talk like this with grandfathers.'
(Pandharipande 1997: 396–397)

As well, the licensing of a modal interpretation typically requires certain syntactic conditions to be met, which vary to some extent from language to language. These have to do, in particular, with the presence or absence of a negative marker and with the overt presence of an Agent phrase or else its suppression. By and large, in Western Indo-Aryan abilitative modality favours or requires the presence of an Agent phrase, while necessive modality tends to coerce suppression of the Agent (Khokhlova 2012).

---

19 Pandharipande (1997: 396) mentions Hindi, Kashmiri, Nepali, Punjabi as well as Marathi.

As far as Marathi goes, Pandharipande (1997: 397) observes that the prescriptive use of the itive passive is subject to three distinct constraints: besides requiring suppression of an overt Agent phrase, it is ruled out unless the auxiliary is in the third person and in the imperfective present tense. This entails, for instance, that (22a) cannot mean 'It was not necessary for Ram to read the book'.

In Hindi, the absence of negation in the following sentence precludes a modal interpretation, according to Davison (1982: 160):[20]

(23) Hindi (Indo-European, Indo-Aryan, Central zone)

> *diva:lii-par*   *ghar-ghar-mẽ*   *di:p*   *jala:-e*
> Diwali.OBL.SG-on house-house.OBL.SG-in lamp.PL light.**PFV.PTCP**-MPL
> *ja:t-e*   *haĩ:*
> **PASS[<go]**.IPFV.PTCP-MPL be.PRS.3PL
> 'On Diwali, lamps are lit in every house.'
> *'On Diwali, lamps can be lit in every house.'
> *'On Diwali, lamps should be lit in every house.'   (Davison 1982: 160)

Tense and aspect are also relevant factors in Hindi, as is the prohibition of an overt Agent phrase. Thus, Montaut (1991: 130) claims that the use of the (present) imperfective in (24a) licenses a necessive interpretation, while (24b), with the auxiliary in the (past) perfective, is difficult to interpret:

(24) Hindi

> a) *ais-i:*   *ba:t-õ-par*   *nahĩ:* *hãs-a:*
>   such-FPL thing-OBL.PL-on NEG   laugh.**PFV.PTCP**-MSG
>   *ja:t-a:*
>   **NEC.PASS[<go]**.IPFV.PTCP-MSG[21]
>   'Such things are not to be laughed at.'   (Montaut 1991: 130)

> b) ?*ais-i:*   *ba:t-õ-par*   *nahĩ:* *hãs-a:*
>   such-FPL thing-OBL.PL-on NEG   laugh.**PFV.PTCP**-MSG
>   *gay-a:*
>   **PASS[<go]**.PFV.PTCP-MSG   (Montaut 1991: 130)

---

20 Davison refers to Pandharipande (1978: 160), from whom both the example and the analysis are taken.

21 In negative sentences the tensed 'be' auxiliary is usually omitted, leaving the participle form of the verb unauxiliated.

Similar aspectual strictures are at play, as mentioned above, in Italian. It may well be that when it comes to the co-encoding of necessity by itive or ventive passives, perfective aspect on the auxiliary is crosslinguistically disfavoured.

Hindi allows passivization of both transitive and intransitive verbs and necessive modality is not constrained in this regard, as it is compatible with both types. While the lexical verb is intransitive in (24), it is transitive in (25):

(25) Hindi

> *a:m*   *aise* **kha:-e**   **ja:t-e**   *haĩ*
> mango.PL SO   eat.**PFV.PTCP**-MPL **PASS[<go]**.IPFV.PTCP-MPL be.PRS.3PL
> 'Mangoes are eaten like that.'
> Or: 'One should eat mangoes like that.'   (Montaut 2004: 132)

What is crucial to the topic of this paper, however, is the fact that in at least some Indo-Aryan languages the co-encoding of modality is not tied to any particular marking of passive voice. Thus, necessive modality in Rajasthani can be supported by the synthetic passive as well as by the periphrastic passive involving the itive auxiliary:

(26) Rajasthani (Indo-European, Indo-Aryan, Central zone, macrolanguage)

> a) *phaag-AA*   *yUU nII khel-iij-ai*
>   holy_game-FPL thus NEG play-PASS-PRS.3
>   'Holy games should not be played like that.'   (Khokhlova 2003: 9)

> b) *puuro dhyaan raakh-y-o*   *jaav-ai*   ...
>   full   attention put-**PST.PTCP**-MSG **NEC.PASS[<go]**-PRS.3
>   'Full attention should be paid...'   (Khokhlova 2003: 9)

In discussing the affinity of passive voice with modality, Khokhlova (2003: 7) suggests that the prescriptive interpretation that attaches to a sentence like (26a) is linked, possibly by implicature, with the generic meaning that the passive imparts to the sentence. As is well-known, one of the situations where backgrounding or suppression of the Agent makes most sense is when its referent is diffuse and this is certainly a common feature of statements divorced from the speaker's *hic and nunc* such as general prescriptions as well as descriptions of permanent properties or "dispositions". As mentioned above, certain uses of the *veni*-passive in Romanian do lend themselves to a dispositional or necessive reading and there is arguably no hard and fast dichotomy between the two interpretations, but rather a modal shading that may be more or less pronounced. The inferential logic invoked by Khokhlova ultimately hinges on the link between descriptive rules and prescriptions: it may well be that the step from talking about how the world is to talking about how it should be, though it is a major one philosophically, is one in fact that people, and languages, routinely take.

This being said, neither the link between passive voice and genericity nor that between genericity and necessary modality is automatic. The following examples provide an illustration of this:

(27)   Hindi

    a) *bacc-õ-ko*   *is*   *tarah* **biga:ɽ-a:**   *nahĩ:*
        child-OBL.PL-DAT   DEM   way   spoil.**PFV.PTCP**-MSG   NEG
        ja:t-a:
        NEC.PASS[<go].IPFV.PTCP-MSG
        'One should not spoil children like this.'   (Davison 1982: 159)

    b) *bacc-õ-ko*   *is*   *tarah*   *nahĩ:*   *biga:ɽt-e:*
        child-OBL.PL-DAT   DEM   way   NEG   spoil.IPFV.PTCP-PL
        'People do not (usually) spoil children like this.'
        *'People should not spoil children like this.'   (Davison 1982: 159)[22]

While the structure of (27b) coerces a generic interpretation, only sentence (27a) can be construed as the expression of a prohibition and it so happens that it involves both a passive construction and negative marking.

3.1.3 One pathway or several?

Rocchetti (1982) and Giacalone Ramat (2000) have offered an account of the *<andare V-ato>* construction of Italian that seeks to identify the cognitive motivation for its particular semantics, specifically for its deontic force. Whether their explanatory models can account for the ventive passive of Romanian or the itive passives of Marathi, Hindi and Rajasthani is doubtful. Rocchetti's account is "local" to the extent that it fits the facts of Italian; however, it would need, at the very least, to undergo a major revision to handle the *veni*-passive of Romanian. Giacalone Ramat's account is also local, though in a different way: while the feature of goal-orientedness could in theory be invoked for both the *andare*-passive of Italian and the *veni*-passive of Romanian, the explanatory route she hypothesizes is too closely tied to the specific diachrony of the Italian construction to be relevant when it comes to the other DD-marked passives discussed

---

22 Davison refers to Pandharipande (1979: 102), from whom the examples are taken.

above. Further, she comes close to denying that the passive morphosyntax of the construction has played any part at all: if she is correct, there is little point in bringing together under the same roof the constructions of Italian, Romanian and Indo-Aryan languages such as Hindi. In other words, the fact that they are all morphosyntactically passive, that they all feature a DD auxiliary *and* that they all co-encode necessive modality is the end-product of processes that share little, if any, commonality — a state of affairs that typically leaves typologists somewhat sceptical.

Khokhlova (2003)'s approach is very different. She claims that the necessive itive-marked passives of Indo-Aryan are necessive by virtue of their being passives, which entails that they do not owe their modal force at all to the semantics of their itive auxiliaries. This is also the tack taken by Montaut (1991: 139), who bases her account of the itive-marked passive of Hindi on the general characterization of passive voice formulated by Shibatani (1985). If the defining property of passive constructions is Agent defocusing, as is claimed by Shibatani, then passive sentences in a "tenseless" present will tend to provide the syntactic clothing most favoured by generic propositions, statements of general truths, and the sort of prescriptive pronouncements which speakers routinely take these propositions and statements to stand for: as Montaut (1991: 139) puts it, "ce qui se fait, sans distinction de temps ni de personne, prend facilement des allures normatives, puis prescriptives [...] Là encore, c'est la valeur fondamentale de déthématisation de l'agent qui a servi de base à cette spécialisation [...] Si on référentialise le procès, par exemple en modifiant le temps et/ou en exprimant un agent, la valeur prescriptive disparaît [...]"[23] This characterization, as we have seen, fits in well with the *veni*-passive of Romanian and with the necessive itive passives of Hindi and Marathi, but not so well with the *<andare V-ato>* construction of Italian: a sentence like *La finestra va chiusa*, after all, is perfectly capable of handling a situational type of necessity, i.e. one anchored in the here-and-now of the speech act.

There are, unquestionably, two formal features that are common to all the DD-marked necessive passives, without exception, that have been discussed above: the ban on perfective past tense and the prohibition of any overt Agent phrase. The second feature is especially noteworthy as it provides, at least in Marathi and Hindi, a crucial diagnostic test for distinguishing necessive from abilitative modality. The fact that the target of obligation is suppressed not only confers a

---

23 "What is done, without distinction of time or person, easily takes on the appearance of a norm, then a prescription... Here again, it is the fundamental value of detopicalization of the Agent that has motivated this specialization... If the process is referentialized, for instance by changing the tense and/or inserting an overt Agent, then the prescriptive force fades away."

latent "impersonality" on the construction, as Rocchetti has shown for Italian, it also has a direct impact on the transitivity of the clause, in the sense of Hopper and Thompson (1980). This is because a reduction in the number of "participants" in the predicative nexus represents a decrease in transitivity, i.e. in what Hopper and Thompson (1980: 251) term "the effectiveness with which an action takes place". Another tell-tale sign of lower transitivity is what they term "mode", by which they mean irrealis, one manifestation of which is precisely the sort of qualification of the state of affairs brought about by necessive modality, among other types of modality: to say that someone is under some obligation to carry out an action does not impart to it the same degree of "effectiveness" as to say that it has taken place or is taking place.[24] Shibatani (1985) has recognized the correlation between passive voice and what he terms potential modality; the correlation with necessive modality is no less motivated, as Montaut (1991) has suggested.

Whether the co-encoding of necessive modality by DD-marked passives is to be described in terms of a unitary pathway is uncertain. What is less uncertain is that in tandem with the aspectual constraint, Agent suppression constitutes a blueprint for the pathway, or pathways, at issue.

3.2 The encoding of necessive modality by unipersonal ventive verbs

The contribution of ventive verbs to the encoding of necessive modality, other than by way of passive marking, is a pervasive phenomenon among the languages spoken in Europe, irrespective of genetic affiliation. There is, however, a sharp division between two groups of languages. In one group, the process of grammaticalization has involved the verbs in and of themselves. Intriguingly, these languages are clustered in the Circum-Baltic area, with two notable exceptions: Scottish Gaelic and Irish. In another group, occupying a wide swath of Southern, Western and Northern Europe, it is not verbs of coming in and of themselves that have grammaticalized into necessive markers, but rather verbs derived from them by prefixation: Ancient Greek *prosēkei* is a case in point, as are *tillkomma* in Swedish, *become* in Old and Middle English, and Romance reflexes of Latin *convenir*.

Space limitations will force me to leave aside the second group of languages, a decision that finds some measure of justification in the fact that necessives derived from a verb of coming by prefixation are arguably the product of a process of lexicalization rather than grammaticalization proper.

---

24 See Chilton (2010: 193), who holds "counterfactuality" and "normativity" to be the two essential and inseparable "components" of deontic modality.

3.2.1 Shared formal features and possible semantic motivations

Two formal features that characterize almost all of the constructions to be discussed or mentioned in this section are their impersonality and the oblique coding of the nominal bearing the role of Agent/Experiencer, i.e. the nominal referring to the individual placed under the obligation to act. These, however, are not properties that are unique to ventive-encoded necessives. As the following examples in Latvian illustrate, they tend to characterize necessives as distinct from other modal constructions:

(28) Latvian (Indo-European, Baltic)

    a) *man   vajag   strādā-t*
       1SG.DAT NEC.PRS3 work-INF
       'I have to work.'   (Forssman 2001: 292)

    b) *vai es   drīkst-u   tev   palīdzē-t ?*
       Q   1SG.NOM be_allowed.PRS-1SG 2SG.DAT help-INF
       'May I help you?'   (Forssman 2001: 294)

    c) *bērns   jau   māk   lasī-t*
       child.NOM.SG already be_able.PRS3 read-INF
       'The child already knows how to read.'   (Forssman 2001: 295)

Masica (1990) has observed that oblique coding of the Agent/Experiencer in "obligational" constructions is relatively common also in a number of Indo-Aryan and Dravidian languages, especially where the degree of compulsion is high. He makes the point that the nominal bears a dual semantic role and that direct case marking (typically the nominative) and oblique case marking (typically the dative) reflect a foregrounding of the Agent role and the Experiencer role, respectively. This may be schematized as follows:

> *John must [John$_{[Agent]}$ solve the problem]*   →   direct case marking
> *John$_{[Experiencer]}$ must [John solve the problem]*   →   oblique case marking

Smit (2006: 133) makes a similar point with respect to case-marking in the necessive constructions of Finnish, while Fortuin (2003: 63–64) notes that integral to the meaning of the dative case in Russian is the notion of "force directed" at the individual that the nominal refers to: the constraint that necessity or obligation represents is arguably a prototypical "force" (see also Fortuin 2005: 44). Not coincidentally, the concept of "force dynamics" plays a crucial role in accounts of deontic modality that have been developed within the framework of Cognitive Grammar (e.g. Radden and Dirven 2007: 243–245).

The formal attributes just described point in straightforward fashion to one possible motivation for the grammaticalization of ventive verbs into necessive markers. The process to be accomplished may be conceptualized as a moving object (Majsak 2005: 212). The starting point of its trajectory is a location distant from the individual and the endpoint, or "receiving end", is the individual himself, the impetus for the motion being the "force" mentioned above. This particular grammaticalization pathway may be said to be *"compulsion-salient"*, as the process to be accomplished is construed as a burden weighing on the individual rather than as an action dictated by some ethical principle. In other words, lack of control on his part is foregrounded and the resulting construction may be expected to encode a non-deontic, or situational, type of necessity, which is impervious to any kind of positive valuation. There are good grounds, I will argue, for assuming that it is this grammaticalization pathway that is instantiated in Russian.

'Come'-derived necessive constructions may be the end-product of a different scenario. The initial trigger this time is the evaluative inference that attaches to ventive markers, whereby motion towards the DC stands, as was mentioned above, for motion towards a state of affairs which is positively valued. As moral precepts and social norms are by their very nature the ultimate template for types of behaviour that are subject to such valuation, it is not illogical that verbs of coming would evolve into markers of deontic necessity. Ventive verbs that follow the *"valuation-salient"* pathway come to encode a form of deontic modality where the individual typically has some measure of control, to the extent that she is free to "meet" the obligation placed upon her or not. The endpoint of this pathway may be expected to be weak necessity, of the sort lexically handled in English by such predicates as *be proper, appropriate* or *fitting*.[25]

Thus, both types of pathway originate in what constitutes the fundamental deictic identity of ventive markers, namely identification of the goal with the DC. What they sanction, however, are two quite distinct storylines flowing from this. The compulsion-salient pathway is a function of ventives exhibiting what I have called above degree-2 goal-orientedness: the goal is "where the action is", to the extent that the individual is immobile and located at the endpoint of the metaphorical trajectory followed by the process that needs to be accomplished. The valuation-salient pathway involves a very different scene: whoever undertakes to accomplish the process is moving towards the deictic centre, therefore in the "right" direction.

---

25 Necessives derived from 'come' by prefixation (e.g. *become, convenir*, etc.) overwhelmingly typify weak necessity.

In some languages, such as Finnish and Estonian, it is unclear which of the compulsion-salient or valuation-salient routes has been taken. In Scottish Gaelic both have been travelled and this, as might be expected, has resulted in two expressions of necessive modality that are distinct formally and semantically.

3.2.2 Scottish Gaelic and Irish

The examples to be found in the entry for *thig* in Mark (2003)'s Gaelic-English dictionary suggest that it satisfies the deicticity criteria on ventive verbs. The following example instantiates one of the two ways in which *thig* contributes to the encoding of necessive modality:

(29) Scottish Gaelic (Indo-European, Celtic)

   thàinig   ***air*** Anna an leabhar a   thoirt   do Mhàiri
   NEC[<come].PST on A.   DEF book   PTCL give.NMLZ to M.
   (lit.) 'It came on Anna to give the book to Màiri.'
   'Anna had to give the book to Màiri.'   (MacAulay 1992: 188)

There are solid syntactic grounds for claiming, as Gillies (1993: 187) does, that *thig* here is subjectless, a type of behaviour of which a small number of predicates are capable. MacAulay (1992: 188) takes a different tack: he suggests that *[thàinig air Anna]*, i.e. the predicate headed by the tensed verb, takes as subject *[an leabhar a thoirt do Mhàiri]*, i.e. the embedded clause which is headed by the nominalized form of the lexical verb (and which, incidentally, features obligatory fronting of the object noun phrase). It may well be that what MacAulay has in mind is the "notional" subject of *thàinig*, rather than its syntactic subject *stricto sensu*. In any event, his analysis fits in well with the cognitive schema underlying the compulsion-salient scenario described above: the process is conceptualized as a burden that literally weighs *upon* the individual placed *under* the obligation to act.

Crucially, the nominal bearing the role of Agent/Experiencer is governed by the preposition *air*, which is "often associated with illness or trouble" (Mark 2003: 22):[26]

---

26 Prepositions are inflected for person, which explains why *air* takes different shapes in the following examples.

(30) Scottish Gaelic

    a) *tha   an   cnatan **orm***
       be.PRS DEF cold   **on.1SG**
       'I have a cold.'   (Mark 2003: 22)

    b) *dé   tha   ceárr **ort?***
       what be.PRS wrong **on.2SG**
       'What's wrong with you?'   (Mark 2003: 22)

In this type of examples the state or process eludes the control of the individual and is viewed as detrimental to her. There is a natural fit between the semantics of *air* and the compulsion-salient nature of the *thig (air)* necessive construction. This is reflected in example (29) above or in example (31) below, both of which involve a non-deontic, value-free type of necessity:

(31) Scottish Gaelic

    thàinig   ***air***   *an eaglais fhàg-ail*   *mus   robh*   *an*
    NEC[<come].PST **on.3SG** DEF church leave-NMLZ before be.DEP.PST DEF
    t-seirbhis   *seachad*
    DEF-service   over
    'He had to leave the church before the service was over.' (Mark 2003: 579)

Though he is not concerned with Scottish Gaelic, Masica (1990: 335) provides an apt description of the dynamics underlying the semantics of *thig* in this type of example: "They [obligational constructions] are indeed parallel to ordinary Dative Subject constructions not only in their datively marked Subject... but also semantically in that the factor of non-volitionality is involved: the obligation in question is somthing [sic] which, like fever, drowsiness, memory, hunger, or spontaneous likes and dislikes, is beyond the hapless Experiencer-Subject's control."

    The following sentences illustrate a very different sort of ventive-marked necessity:

(32) Scottish Gaelic

    thig-*eadh*   ***dhuit***   *a*   *dhean-amh*
    NEC[<come]-COND **to.2SG** 3MSG do-NMLZ
    'It would become you to do it.'
    Or: 'You ought to do it.'   (Dwelly 1971: 947)

(33) Scottish Gaelic

> *chan*   *ann* **dhuinn** *a*   **thig**   *e*   *a*   *bhith*
> COP.NEG.PRS FOC **to.1PL** REL **NEC[<come].**FUT 3SG PTCL be.NMLZ
> *bruidhinn*   *air dìoghaltas*
> speak.NMLZ on vengeance
> (lit.) 'It is not to us that it comes to speak of revenge.'
> 'It does not become us to be speaking of revenge.'[27]   (Mark 2003: 579)

(34) Scottish Gaelic

> *is*   *e*   *a*   *Ghàidhlig a'*   *chainnt*   *a*   **thig**-*ead*   *bhi*
> COP.PRS FOC DEF Gaelic   DEF language REL **NEC[<come]**-COND be
> *anns an*   *dùthaich*
> in   DET country
> 'It is the Gaelic language that ought to be (spoken) in the land.'[28]
> (Robertson 1897–1898: 25)

The construction instantiated here is compatible with various syntactic environments: it is subjectless in (32) and (33), though not in (34). The construction in (34), in fact, has a referential subject, which makes it almost unique among the ventive necessives reviewed in this part of the present paper.

All three sentences encode deontic necessity, which suggests a valuation-salient grammaticalization pathway. This happens to be in line with the semantics of the allative preposition *do*, which governs the Agent/Undergoer phrase when it is overt, as in (32) and (33). The following sentence is illustrative of *do*'s semantics:

(35) Scottish Gaelic

> *tha*   *an ad sin a'* **tigh**-*inn*   **dhut**   *gu math*
> be.PRS DEF hat DEM at **come**-NMLZ **to.2SG** to good
> 'That hat suits you well.'   (Mark 2003: 579)

In combination with *do*, the verb *thig* encodes propriety and conformity with a standard. This happens to be a notional domain which, as documented by

---

27 *Ann* is morphologically the preposition 'in' inflected for 3rd person masculine. It appears in clefted sentences when the focused constituent is a prepositional phrase.
28 *E* is morphologically the 3rd person masculine form of the personal pronoun. It appears in clefted sentences when the focused constituent is a noun phrase.

Bybee, Perkins, and Pagliuca (1994: 182–183) and Heine and Kuteva (2002: 285–286), is crosslinguistically a source of grammaticalization into deontic modality.

The route that *thig* has presumably followed in order to carry the meaning it does in (32) to (34) may be represented as follows:

evaluative deixis > conformity with a standard > deontic necessity

The type of necessity at issue is usually weak, to the extent that the speaker delivers a recommendation to act "properly", rather than an order.

What is interesting, and singular, about *thig* is that it has followed, if the above hypotheses are correct, both the compulsion-salient and the valuation-salient pathways. While on the surface this was rendered possible by its affinity with either an <*air* NP> or a <*do* NP> complement, I would argue that this affinity itself is a function of what, at a deeper level, constitutes the deictic identity of ventives as described above.

The ventive verb *tar* in Irish exhibits the same behaviour in combination with the preposition *ar* as *thig* does in Scottish Gaelic when it combines with *air*, including the ability to encode non-deontic necessity:

(36)   Irish (Indo-European, Celtic)

   a) ***tháinig***   *an   bas*   ***uirthi***
      come.PST DEF death **on.3FSG**
      'She took fatally ill.'   (*GG-B*: 740)

   b) ***tháinig***   *orainn   imeacht*
      NEC[<come].PST **on.1PL**   leave.NMLZ
      'We had to leave.'   (*GG-B*: 740)

On the other hand, I have found no evidence that the valuation-salient route has been followed by *tar*, even though, just like its Scottish Gaelic counterpart, it can encode the notion of suitability when it combines with the preposition *do* (*GG-B* 1981: 741).

3.2.3 Russian

The construction which is the topic of this section is instantiated by the following authentic example:

(37) Russian (Indo-European, Slavic, East)

emu	**pri-š-l-o-s'**			*tri*	*dnja*
3MSG.DAT	**NEC[<ARRIVING-move.PFV]**-PST-NSG-**REFL**	three	day.GEN.SG		

provesti *v* *peščer-e*
spend.INF in cave-PREP.SG
'[In order to hide from his pursuers] he had to spend three days in a cave.'[29]

(*Pravda*, Jan. 21, 2012[30])

The verb *prišlos'*, as it is used here, raises three main issues: the deicticity, or lack thereof, of the non-reflexive verb from which it proceeds, its morphosyntax and its semantics.

Before addressing these issues, it may be useful to clarify the internal structure of *prišlos'*. It is derived from the verb *idti*, which denotes motion on foot. Verbs of motion in Russian form paradigms that are structured by three interacting dichotomies: unprefixed/prefixed, determinate/indeterminate and perfective/imperfective. The imperfective/perfective dichotomy governs the entire verbal system of Russian: any given verbal notion is in principle encoded by a perfective form and an imperfective form. Based on the working definition proposed by Comrie (1976: 18–24), perfectivity involves viewing the process as a complete whole, from the outside, while imperfectivity involves viewing it "from within". Unprefixed verbs of motion are idiosyncratic in so far as they elude the perfective/imperfective dichotomy (they are imperfective) and are subject instead to the determinate/indeterminate dichotomy, whereby "motion occurring along a single goal-directed trajectory (determinate)" contrasts with "motion not consisting of a single goal-directed trajectory (indeterminate)" (Dickey 2010: 68). Thus, determinate *idti* is paired with indeterminate *xodit'*. Combining these verbs with a prefix such as *pri-* has a lexical effect, in so far as it derives verbs profiling a specific phase of the motion event: for instance, according to standard descriptions, *pri-* is one of two prefixes profiling the attainment of the goal.[31] Combining *idti* and *xodit'* with a prefix also has an aspectual effect: the prefix brings verbs

---

29 Technically, *provesti* is made up of the prefix *pro-* and the lexical verb *vesti*. In this example and those that follow, only prefixed motion verbs are segmented into prefix and lexical verb.

30 http://www.pravda.ru/faith/religions/islam/21–01–2012/1105384-hidjra-1/ (accessed 30 September 2013).

31 For an insightful discussion of the semantics of *pri-*, see Dickey (2010: 96–97), who claims that *pri-* encodes "the actual crossing of the boundary of the landmark" (i.e. the goal), whereas *do-* encodes "the traversal of a trajectory up to the goal". It is this distinction that the ARRIVING gloss used in this paper for the *pri-* prefix is meant to capture, while the REACHING gloss would be more appropriate for *do-*.

of motion in line with the overarching logic of the verbal system by neutralizing the determinate/indeterminate dichotomy and replacing it with the perfective/imperfective contrast.

How the three dichotomies interact is summarized in the table below. Only the forms most relevant to the discussion to follow are provided, namely the infinitive, the present tense in the 3rd person singular and the past tense in the neuter singular.

Table 2. A synopsis of Russian verbs of motion based on *idti/xodit'*

	Determinate	Indeterminate
Unprefixed (imperfective) 'to move (on foot)'	INF: *idti* PRES, 3SG: *idët* PAST, NSG: *šlo*	INF: *xodit'* PRES, 3SG: *xodit* PAST, NSG: *xodilo*

↓   ↓

	Perfective	Imperfective
Prefixed 'to arrive, come (on foot)'	INF: *prijti* PRES, 3SG: *pridët* PAST, NSG: *prišlo*	INF: *prixodit'* PRES, 3SG: *prixodit* PAST, NSG: *prixodilo*

The contrast between *prijti* and *prixodit'* extends to their reflexive counterparts, which are *prijtis'* and *prixodit'sja*, respectively, and are the focus of this section. While some of the examples below feature *prijtis'* and others *prixodit'sja*, I will henceforth, for ease of exposition, use *prijtis'* when referring to both the perfective and imperfective members of the pair.

3.2.3.1 The issue of deicticity

As noted by Grenoble (1991: 255), standard Russian dictionaries provide definitions of the verbs *prijti/prixodit'* that do not make reference to arrival at the DC, but suggest that the verbs are tasked instead with encoding straight phase-saliency. Likewise, Ricca (1993) is insistent that by his criteria the lexical inventory of Russian and that of other Slavic languages as well as Lithuanian do not feature verbs having the encoding of DD as one of their main functions, let alone as their unique function. The discussion will be confined to Russian and I will focus on the encoding of motion events directed towards the DC. Only brief mention will be made of the prefix *po-*, with which *pri-* contrasts.

The crux of Ricca's argumentation is that in those types of situation where "fully deictic" or "predominantly deictic" languages would be most forceful in requiring a ventive verb, Russian typically uses an unprefixed, deictically neutral verb:

(38) Russian

    a) *id-i*   *sjuda!*
        move.DTRM-IMP.2SG to_here
        'Come here!'   (Ricca 1993: 85)

    b) *Ivan id-ët*   *sjuda*
        I.   move.DTRM-PRS.3SG to_here
        'Ivan is coming here.'   (Ricca 1993: 89)

The problem is not limited to the failure of *prijti/prixodit'* to show up in contexts where ventive verbs in other languages would be expected to occur. Ricca also mentions the acceptability of examples such as (39), where *prixodit'* shows up where according to him an itive verb would be expected:

(39) Russian

    on   *pri-xodi-l*   *k nej*   *včera*
    3MSG.NOM ARRIVING-move.IPFV-PST.MSG to 3FSG.DAT yesterday
    'He went to her place yesterday.'   (Ricca 1993: 86)

Ricca's conclusion is that the would-be verbal candidates for the status of directional deictics fail to meet some of the most crucial requirements that DD markers are supposed to satisfy.

I would argue, on the basis of work by Grenoble (1991 and 1998) and Israeli (2002), that Ricca overstates his case.

Grenoble (1991)'s thesis is essentially threefold: (a) the unprefixed verbs *idti* and *xodit'* are deictically neutral; (b) in keeping with the basic semantics of the prefixes *po-* and *pri-*, the selection of *po*-prefixed verbs of motion (e.g. *pojti*) or *pri*-prefixed verbs (e.g. *prijti* and *prixodit'*) is primarily sensitive to which phase of the motion event receives saliency; (c) the selection may also be sensitive to the direction of the event with respect to the DC. Thesis (c) is summarized as follows by Grenoble (1998: 52): "It then follows that the prefix *pri-* is preferred when the goal corresponds with s_0." — where s_0 is either "the speaker's location" or the "addressee's".

Of these three theses, only (a) would appear to be uncontroversial. The strength of Thesis (b) is much more difficult to assess, as it is obviously dependent on the difficult issue of the weight to be given to Thesis (c) (e.g. Israeli 2002: 102). The following examples are illustrative of Thesis (c):

(40) Russian

   a) *ty*   *pr-id-ëš'*   *zavtra*   *v*   *muzej?*
      2SG.NOM ARRIVING-move.PFV-PRS.2SG tomorrow into museum.ACC.SG
      'Are you coming to the museum tomorrow?'   (Israeli 2002: 105)

   b) *ty*   *po-jd-ëš'*   *zavtra*   *v*   *muzej?*
      2SG.NOM DEPARTING-move.PFV-PRS.2SG tomorrow into museum.ACC.SG
      'Are you going to the museum tomorrow?'   (Israeli 2002: 105)

The implication of (40a), according to Israeli, is that the speaker is planning to be at the museum on the day in question; the implication of (40b) is that she is not planning to be there. As well, Israeli (2002: 108) addresses the difference in "viewpoint" signalled by the selection of *prijti* or *pojti* in third-person narratives. She shows that what motivates the use of *prijti* is the fact that the narrator typically adopts as her vantage point the position of whoever is at the endpoint of the motion event. On the assumption that 3rd person narratives have a "projected" DC and that it is the location of the salient character, what this means is that *pri-* functions as a straightforward ventive marker (and *po-* as an itive marker). The Bible, for one, abounds in uses of *prijti* of this type:

(41) Russian

   Avimelex pri-šë-l   *k nemu*   *iz*   *Gerar-a ...*
   A.   ARRIVING-move.PFV-PST.MSG to 3MSG.DAT from G.-GEN.SG
   'Abimelech had come to him from Gerar ...'[32]
                            (Book of Genesis 26:26; *Slovo Žizni*)

In this passage, Isaac, to whom the pronoun *nemu* refers, is the central character. The Book of Genesis provides other pieces of evidence in support of Grenoble (1998: 52)'s Thesis (c). Most tellingly, *prijti* (or *prixodit'*) is frequently attested where versions of the Bible in "fully deictic" languages by Ricca's standards (i.e. Spanish, Portuguese, Italian, Modern Greek, Hungarian and Finnish) typically feature a ventive verb, rather than a verb of arrival: for example, 'Why have you come to me?' (26:27) and 'Where do you come from?' (42:7).[33]

---

32 The English translation here and in what follows is taken from the *New International Version* of the Bible.
33 The following translations have been consulted, all available at http://www.biblegateway. com (accessed 30 September 2013): Gáspár Károli's translation into Hungarian (1590, rev. 2003); for Italian: *La Nuova Diodati* (1991), *Nuova Riveduta* (1994 and 2006 eds.), *Conferenza Episcopale Italiana* (2008); for Portuguese: *João Ferreira de Almeida Atualizada* (1948), *Nova Versão*

Likewise, *prijti* or *prixodit'* is very often the preferred option to refer to a habitual or hypothetical motion event ending at the DC. The Bible offers numerous instances: e.g., in both the *Russian Synodal* and *Slovo Žizni* versions, Exodus 18:15 and 18:16, 2 Samuel 15:4, Luke 6:47, John 6:35 and John 6:45; and in the *Slovo Žizni* version only, Deuteronomy 25:11, 1 Samuel 11:3, 1 Samuel 22:3 and Isaiah 27:5.

From the above observations it seems fair to conclude that *prijti* and *prixodit'* are not insensitive to deixis. Ricca's claim to the contrary is attributable to the cumulative effect of two factors. Firstly, it would appear that it is typically in sentences referring to past or future occurrences or to habitual or hypothetical events that *prijti* and *prixodit'* behave as quasi-DD markers. In utterances tied to the *hic-et-nunc* of one-on-one interaction, on the other hand, deicticity is encoded by non-verbal markers such as *sjuda*, rather than by the verb. Thus, the use of deictically neutral *idi* is routine in injunctions, irrespective of the location of the goal of motion with respect to the DC, and indeed when the goal is the DC *idi sjuda*, *pojdi sjuda* and *pridi sjuda* are all possible.[34] As well, the use of *prijti* and *prixodit'* is precluded in scenarios involving motion in progress (Grenoble, 1991: 260; Rakhilina: 2004, 27–28): the reason for this, however, has to do with tense and aspect constraints on verbs of motion and is therefore extraneous to the issue of deixis *per se*. Secondly, when it comes to conflating the encoding of DD and that of phase-saliency, Russian is certainly more forceful than Romance languages. However, whether it is much more so than German, a "predominantly deictic" language according to Ricca (1993: 82–83), is arguable (Bourdin 1999: 197–199).

Even if we were to deny DD status proper to *prijti* and *prixodit'*, it seems to be beyond dispute that no other verbs in Russian come closer to the ventive prototype than they do. By virtue of the next-best-tool principle, we would therefore expect the grammaticalization pathways typically travelled by ventive verbs in other languages to be open to *prijti* and *prixodit'*. In this regard, it is hardly coincidental that in Majsak's 2005 book, which is written in Russian, the section dealing with those pathways features the verb *prixodit'* as exemplar.

Internacional (2000) and *O Livro* (2000); for Spanish: *Reina-Valera Antigua* (1569, rev. 1602), *Reina-Valera* (1960 and 1995 eds.), *La Biblia de las Américas* (1986), *Dios Habla Hoy* (1996), *Nueva Biblia Latinoamericana de Hoy* (1997), *Nueva Versión Internacional* (1999, and *Castilian* ed. 2005), *Traducción en lenguaje actual* (2000), *Nueva Traducción Viviente* (2010), *La Palabra* (*España* ed. 2010, *La Palabra, Hispanoamérica* ed. 2010), *Reina Valera Contemporánea* (2011) and *Palabra de Dios para Todos* (2012). The Finnish translation consulted is *Vuoden kirkkoraamattu* (1938), available at http://bibledbdata.org/onlinebibles/finnish_1938/ (accessed 30 September 2013) and the Modern Greek translation is *I Agía Grafí—Metáfrasi Néou Kósmou* (1997), available at http://www.watchtower.org/g/bible/index.htm (accessed 30 September 2013).

34 I owe this observation to Sergej Rabenok.

3.2.3.2 *Prijtis'* and *prixodit'sja* as unipersonal reflexives

Formally, perfective *prijtis'* and imperfective *prixodit'sja* conjoin two properties: they are unipersonal, to the extent that they tolerate only 3rd person singular inflection (and the neuter ending in the past tense), and the *-s'/-sja* suffix pegs them as reflexive. While not all impersonal verbs are reflexive in Russian, a distinct subset of them possesses this property: they form the so-called "impersonal reflexive" predicates. As with the other predicates of this type, the nominal playing the role of Agent/Experiencer is in the dative case.

The grouping of impersonal reflexives of which *prijtis'* is a member is defined as follows by Pariser (1982: 41–42, quoted by Gerritsen 1990: 206): "In impersonal constructions, [these verbs] serve to qualify the subject's relationship, attitude, or disposition toward his (potential) participation in the activity (or state) described by the infinitive. These relationships can be realized as: necessity (*prixodit'sja*), capability or possibility (*dovodit'sja, udavat'sja*), desire (*xotet'sja, želat'sja*), patience (*terpet'sja*), futility (*ostavat'sja*), and others."[35] Within this grouping, *prijtis'* belongs to a specific cluster of verbs which are characterized by their opacity (Gerritsen 1990: 201; 205): whereas *Mne xotelos' V_{inf}* ('I felt like V-ing') is semantically close to its non-reflexive counterpart *Ja xotel V_{inf}* ('I wanted to V'), the meaning of *Mne prišlos' V_{inf}* ('I had to V') cannot be inferred from the meaning of *Ja prišël V_{inf}* ('I came to V'). As a result, whatever contribution *-s'/-sja* brings to the meaning of *prijtis'* — its semantic transformative power, so to speak — is, on the face of it, more drastic than it is in the case of such transparent impersonal reflexives as *xotet'sja*. According to Gerritsen (1990: 206), the suffix has an abstract meaning: it refers to the "'force' (fate or circumstance)" responsible for the "necessity" that "comes" to the individual denoted by the nominal in the dative case. It would seem that we are here in the territory of compulsion-saliency.

One problem with attributing this particular semantic function to *-s'/-sja* is that, as Gerritsen (1990: 206) notes, the suffix has not always been there. The following example, from one of Krylov's *Fables*, suggests that the use of *prišlo* where *prišlos'* would be required in contemporary Russian may have been permissible into the first half of the 19th century, at least in the literary language:

---

35 Guiraud-Weber (1984: 214–39) provides an alternative taxonomy. She identifies five notional domains: "timeliness" ("opportunité" in French), "propriety" ("convenance"), "necessity and duty", "possibility and opportunity" ("occasion") and "volition". She notes that the divisions between these domains are fluid and offers as an example the "polysemy" of *mne prixoditsja*, which can mean "I am compelled" or "I have the opportunity" (more on this topic below).

(42)   Early 19th century Russian

tak   dela-t' nečego   :   **pri-š-l-o**
thus do-INF there_is_nothing **NEC[<ARRIVING-move.PFV]**-PST-NSG
pisa-t'   ukaz   …
write-INF sentence.ACC.SG
'There was no help for it: a sentence had to be passed
[Condemning the guilty party to a shameful punishment].'[36]

(I. A. Krylov, "The pike" (1829–30))

Further, other prefixed motion verbs, such as *vyjti*, function to this day as impersonals:

(43)   Contemporary Russian

vy-š-l-o,   *čto*   *on*   *vinovat*
EXITING-move.PFV-PST-NSG COMP 3MSG.NOM guilty.NOM.MSG
'It turned out that he was to blame.'   (*ORD* (vide *vyjti*))

Pending further research, it may be hypothesized that its having undergone reflexivization in the course of its diachronic development makes *prijti* unique among unipersonal verbs of motion derived from *idti* (or *xodit'*).[37] Why reflexivization occurred is a complex issue that limitations of space prevent me from going into.[38] In any event, Gerritsen (1990: 206)'s claim that it was due to "a tendency to avoid homonymy" is arguably lacking in explanatory force.

A further complication is that quite apart from its use as an impersonal, to which I return below, *prijtis'* exhibits considerable semantic plasticity. The *ORD* mentions its use as a copula restricted to predications of kinship ('She's my grandmother') and date attribution ('Easter will fall on April 3 this year') as well as its use to indicate suitability, or more precisely the quality of befitting, or being commensurate with, someone's size or taste:

---

36 I am grateful to Nataša Lenina and Sergej Rabenok for communicating this example to me and for bringing to my attention two other occurrences of necessive *prišlo* in Krylov's *Fables*.
37 This in no way implies that *prijti* is the only *idti/xodit'*-derived verb that can take the reflexive suffix: the *ORD* specifically lists *zajtis'*, *najtis'*, *projtis'*, among others. Whether any of those verbs is capable of exhibiting impersonal behaviour remains to be investigated, however. It is also unclear whether any of them has departed from the referential domain of motion in space as radically as *prijti/prijtis'* has as it evolved into a necessive modal.
38 Besides Gerritsen (1990), the semantic import of reflexivization in Russian has been studied in depth by Israeli (1997), among others.

(44) Present-day Russian

> *pal't-o*   **pri-š-l-o-s'**   *mne*
> coat-NOM.SG[N] **ARRIVING-move.PFV-PST-NSG-REFL** 1SG.DAT
> *po razmer-u*
> by size-DAT.SG
> 'The coat fitted me.'   (*ORD* (vide *prijtis'*))

(45) Present-day Russian (2004)

> *romantik-a*   *i*   *buntarstv-o*   *eë*   *geroin'*
> romance-NOM.SG and rebelliousness-NOM.SG 3FSG.GEN heroine.GEN.PL
> **pri-š-l-i-s'**   *po vkus-u*   *parižsk-oj*
> **ARRIVING-move.PFV-PST-PL-REFL** by taste-DAT.SG Parisian-DAT.SG
> *publik-e*
> public-DAT.SG
> 'The romance and rebelliousness of her heroines were to the taste of the
> Parisian public.'   (*RNC* (vide *prijtis'... po vkusu*))

I will examine below whether or not this particular meaning offers a clue as to
why *prijtis'* has grammaticalized into a necessive modal.

Clearly, it is one thing to list the various uses to which "personal" *prijtis'*
lends itself and quite another to try and delineate its core semantics. Suffice it to
say that there are contexts in which it retains the spatial meaning it has when it
is non-reflexive (Hansen 2001: 198–199) and other contexts in which it points to
more abstract "comings", i.e. the occurrence of events:

(46) Present-day Russian (1965)

> *poezdk-a*   *Ganzelk-i i*   *Zikmund-a* **pri-š-l-a-s'**
> tour-NOM.SG[F] G.-GEN.SG and Z.-GEN.SG **ARRIVING-move.PFV-PST-FSG-REFL**
> *na moment*   *otstavk-i*   *Xruščev-a*
> at moment.ACC.SG resignation-GEN.SG K.-GEN.SG
> (lit.) 'The tour of Hanzel and Zikmund came at the time when Khrushchev
> resigned.'
> 'The tour of Hanzel and Zikmund happened right when Khrushchev
> resigned.'   (*RNC* (vide *prišlas' na moment*))

Much work would be needed to do justice to such issues as the intricate link
between reflexivization and impersonality in Russian as it relates to the semantics of *prijtis'*. Those issues are summarized neatly, if provocatively and contro-

versially, by Israeli (1997: 130): "The presence of -*sja* in *prixodit'sja* and *dostat'sja* is "accidental", for it is irrelevant to the formation of impersonal constructions, which in turn are not semantically related to constructions with the verb *prixodit'* 'to come' and *dostat'* 'to get with difficulty'."

I propose to dispute in the next section the second of these claims. In so doing, I will be implicitly advocating a nuanced approach to what I called above the "semantic transformative power" of -*sja/-s'*.

3.2.3.3 *Prijtis'* and *prixodit'sja* as necessives

As a marker of necessive modality, *prijtis'* belongs in the same semantic group as predicative adjectives such as *dolžen* ('obliged'), the predicative elements *nado* and *nužno* ('it is necessary'), and the verbs *nadležit* ('it is necessary') and *sleduet* ('it is advisable/fitting/necessary'). Formally, *prijtis'* is closest to *nado*, *nužno*, *sleduet* and *nadležit* for two reasons: it cannot take a referential subject and the nominal bearing the role of Agent/Experiencer is in the dative case. However, *prijtis'* has a history and a modal identity that set it apart not only from *dolžen*, but also from *nado* and *nužno*, which together with *dolžen* are standardly described as the core markers of necessive modality.

According to Hansen (2001: 371–394), there is no written record of necessive *prijtis'* before the 18th century, which suggests that it emerged as a modal significantly later than *dolžen*, *nado* and *nužno* did. Hansen, however, makes no mention of the necessive use of the non-reflexive form *prijti*, which may well have predated the use of the reflexive form (see example (42) above).

Necessive *prijtis'* appears in a well-defined syntactic environment, namely <dative nominal ___ infinitive>, though neither the nominal nor the infinitive need be overt. In this environment, impersonal *prijtis'* may also be used, though more rarely according to Guiraud-Weber (1984: 236), in the sense of 'to have the occasion/opportunity':

(47)   Present-day Russian (1965)

> *mne   bol'še uže   nikogda ne **pri-š-l-o-s'***
> 1SG.DAT more   already never   NEG **ARRIVING-move.PFV**-PST-NSG-**REFL**
> *vide-t' ego   i   ne **pr-id-ët-sja** :*
> see-INF 3SG.GEN and NEG **ARRIVING-move.PFV**-PRS.3SG-**REFL**
> (lit.) 'It never came to me to see him again and it will never come...'
> 'I never saw him again and I will never see him again [he was burned in his tank].'   (*RNC* (vide *ne prišlos'*))

It is plausible to relate this usage to the non-impersonal use of *prijtis'* as a verb of occurrence instantiated by (46), which I argued is itself transparently linked with the meaning of *prijti* to denote motion in space. While in (47) the individual denoted by the nominal in the dative is in a sense "at the receiving end" of the occurrence, and is clearly not in full control, there is not the slightest hint of the process representing a constraint or imposition on him. The event, or rather non-event, is attributed to the constraints of circumstance, but an onerous force it need not be.

Not so with necessive *prijtis'*. Grammarians and scholars characterize the necessity encoded by *prijtis'* as being due to "circumstances" ("Umstände") outside the individual's control (Hansen 2001: 199). Dunn and Khairov (2009: 347) talk about "necessity through force of circumstances" and Majsak (2005: 212) about "inevitability" (*neizbežnost'*). Likewise, *prijtis'* is glossed "*to have to* (reluctantly, in response to compelling circumstances)" by Wade and White (2004: 221), while much in the same spirit Wade (2011: 343) characterizes *prijtis'* as "[implying] reluctant acceptance of necessity". The notion of "force" is discussed at some length by Gerritsen (1990: 204–206), who makes the claim, not unproblematic as mentioned above, that it resides in the *-sja/-s'* suffix. That the individual is coerced into action by extraneous circumstances or a "concrete occurrence" (Hansen 2001: 200) rather than being guided by some moral precept or ethical principle is clear enough from examples such as these:

(48) Early 20th cent. Russian

> **pri-*xodi*-t-*sja***   *lga-t'*, *a* *ja*
> **NEC[<ARRIVING-move.IPFV]**-PRS.3SG-**REFL** lie-INF but 1SG.NOM
> *èt-ogo*   *ne* *ljub-lju*
> DEM-GEN.NSG NEG like-PRS.1SG
> 'It's necessary to lie, but I don't like it.'
>   (M. Gor'kij, *Enemies*, 1906; quoted by Guiraud-Weber (1984: 230))

(49) Early 20th cent. Russian (1916)

> *s*   *golod-u*   *umr-u*,   *esli*
> from hunger-GEN.SG die.PRS-1SG if
> **pr-*id*-ët-*sja***   ...
> **NEC[<ARRIVING-move.PFV]**-PRS.3SG-**REFL**
> 'I'll die of starvation, if necessary, [but I will not take a kopeck from you].'
>   (*RNC* (vide *esli pridëtsja*))

Sentences featuring necessive *prijtis'* refer to processes to which no positive valuation attaches, so that compliance with some moral precept is not at issue. This clearly speaks in favour of identifying the grammaticalization pathway as compulsion-salient, rather than as valuation-salient. To make such an assumption, however, runs the risk of circularity unless it is supported by independent evidence; this can only be provided by constructions where the verb *prijtis'* behaves morphosyntactically much as it does when it encodes necessity.

In (44) and (45) above, *prijtis'* is used to denote the quality of being suited to someone's size or taste. As we saw above for Scottish Gaelic, if this type of semantics were to have been the trigger for the grammaticalization of *prijtis'* into a necessive, we would expect it to have followed the valuation-salient, rather than the compulsion-salient, pathway. It is, however, unlikely that sentences (44) and (45) offer a clue as to why *prijtis'* evolved into a necessive marker. This is because, in so far as they feature a referential subject, they depart fundamentally from the syntactic environment required by necessive *prijtis'*.

There is, on the other hand, an impersonal construction that accommodates non-necessive *prijtis'* and that happens to be quite congruent with this specific environment:

(50)   Present-day Russian (1964)

> *v   voenn-ye   god-y   emu*
> in of_the_war-ACC.PL year-ACC.PL 3MSG.DAT
> **pri-š-l-o-s'**   *očen' očen'* **tugo**
> **ARRIVING-move.PFV-PST-NSG-REFL** very very **tightly**
> 'In the war years he had a very, very rough time.'
>
> (*RNC* (vide dative+ *prišlos'*+adv.))

(51)   Present-day Russian (1967)

> *mladš-emu   že   naseleni-ju*
> young-DAT.SG but population-DAT.SG
> **pri-š-l-o-s'**   *xudo*
> **ARRIVING-move.PFV-PST-NSG-REFL** **badly**
> '[At first this did not touch the adults much — they were at work all day.]
> But for the young things were bad.'   (*RNC* (vide dative+ *prišlos'*+adv.))

The environment in which *prijtis'* occurs here is <dative nominal ___ adverb> and *prijtis'* is compulsorily unipersonal, i.e. it requires 3rd person singular inflection (and in the past the neuter ending). Crucially, this morphosyntactic behaviour matches closely that exhibited by necessive *prijtis'*. The adverbs that collocate with *prijtis'* belong to a small and semantically well-defined set: a search in the *RNC* reveals that the most frequent items are *nelegko* ('not lightly', i.e. 'with difficulty'), *tugo* ('tightly', i.e. 'with difficulty'), *nesladko* ('bitterly'), *ploxo* ('badly'), *trudno* ('with difficulty') and *tjaželo* ('heavily', i.e. 'with difficulty'); no occurrences of antonymous adverbs such as *xorošo* ('well'), *prosto* ('simply', 'easily') and *sladko* ('sweetly') have been found.[39] The notional thread common to such adverbs as *tugo*, *xudo* and *ploxo* is unmistakeable: the individual to which the dative nominal refers undergoes a predicament which is outside his control and which he has no option but to bear, no matter how burdensome and detrimental it is. The data suggest that perfective *prijtis'* is usually in the past tense, the predicament being typically associated with an episode in the individual's life.

The negative import of the adverbs has been noted by Hansen (2001: 200) and is explicitly linked by him with the semantics of *prijtis'* as a necessive marker: "Es ergab sich die als negativ bewertete Situation, dass X p, also war X gezwungen zu p."[40] This account is consonant with the assumption that the route taken by *prijtis'* as it evolved into a necessive marker was compulsion-salient.

To sum up, sentences with necessive *prijtis'* describe an individual pressed into action by the force of circumstances outside her control, rather than by the urge to comply with some moral standard. This is strongly suggestive of a compulsion-salient grammaticalization scenario. This assumption is in turn borne out by the affinity of *prijtis'* with a semantic domain featuring the notion of a predicament "weighing" upon the individual and eluding her control; the evidence for this affinity is provided by a construction where *prijtis'* behaves much in the same way morphosyntactically as it does when acting as a necessive marker.

3.2.4 Non-slavic languages in the Circum-Baltic area

In such languages as Latvian, Finnish and Estonian, which are all spoken in countries bordering the Baltic Sea but belong to two distinct phyla, necessive modality can be encoded, among other devices, by a construction involving a ventive verb:

---

39 The search, however, has turned up a few occurrences of *legče* and *polegče*, which are the comparative forms of *legko*, 'lightly': the sentences involved refer to an easing of the hardship befalling the individual, thereby necessarily alluding to the heavy burden that he had carried previously.
40 "It turned out that X p, a situation assessed negatively: therefore X was forced to p.". (X stands for the individual and p for the action to be carried out.)

(52)   Finnish (Uralic, Finnic)

mei-dän **tule**-*e*   *muista-**a**,*   *että*   *synni-llä*
1PL-GEN   **NEC[<come]**.PRS-3SG   remember-**INF1**   COMP   sin.SG-ADESS
leikki-minen   on   *vaara-llis-ta*   *leikki-ä*
play-NMLZ   be.PRS.3SG   danger-ADJLZ-PART   game.SG-PART
'We must remember that playing with sin is a dangerous game.'
(Kangasniemi 1992: 100)

(53)   Estonian (Uralic, Finnic)

mei-l   **tule**-*b*   *töö*   *lõpeta-**da***
1PL-ADESS   **NEC[<come]**-PRS.3SG   job.SG.NOM   finish-**INF1**
'We have to finish the job.'   (Penjam 2006: 167)

(54)   Latvian (Indo-European, Baltic)

mums   **nāk**-*a*-**s**   *aiz-brauk-**t***
1PL.DAT   **NEC[<come]**.PRS-3-**REFL**   away-travel-**INF**
'We have to leave.'   (Mathiassen 1996: 130–131)

The areality of the feature is a topic which obviously also involves Russian and has been addressed, though in somewhat cursory fashion, by Stolz (1991: 79–81) and by Heine and Kuteva (2005: 23–24, 268).

   According to Ricca (1993: 79–80), the Finnish verb *tulla*, 'come', is robustly deictic. The deiticity of *tulema* in Estonian and that of *nākts* in Latvian do not appear to be an issue, either.[41] The constructions involved are strikingly similar. In all three languages, the ventive auxiliary, or semi-auxiliary, is subject to tense/mood marking. When it is expressed, the Agent/Experiencer NP is in an oblique case: the genitive in Finnish,[42] the adessive in Estonian and the dative in Latvian. As well, the constructions are unipersonal, with the verb of coming that is the carrier of necessive modality bearing default third person singular marking. In Latvian, it bears in addition the reflexive 3rd person suffix, a feature it shares with *prijtis'/prixodit'sja* in Russian. In fact, because it is both reflexive and unprefixed Latvian *nākts* is formally in an intermediary position between *prijtis'* and *tulla/tulema*.

---

41 For *tulema* see Saagpakk (1982: 989–990) and for *nākts* Wälchli (2001: 311–312), who indicates that the verb is as deictic as *come* in English.
42 The nominative is possible also, though exceptional when the NP refers to a specific human being (Laitinen and Vilkuna 1993: 45).

3.2.4.1 Finnish

The encoding of necessity by means of a ventive verb cognate with Finnish *tulla* and Estonian *tulema* is a feature of all Finnic languages (Saukkonen 1965: 150–155, quoted by Penjam 2006: 168). That it is attested in Old Finnish has been noted by Smit (2006: 119) and Penjam (2006: 183). However, early attestations may have been semantically distinct from the present-day construction. This is because in early written texts the lexical verb is of the 'receive' type, so that the nominal bearing genitive case is to be interpreted as Beneficiary rather than as Experiencer/Agent:

(55) Old Finnish (c1580)

  ia   *häne-n*   ***tul-e***   *saadha*   *colmannexet*
  and 3M/FSG-GEN **NEC[<come]**-PRS.3SG receive.INF1 a_third.ACC
  'And he shall receive a third [of all fines from that county].'
                              (legal text; quoted by Smit (2006: 133))

Tulla happens to have grammaticalized also into a future marker:

(56) Finnish

  tul-e-n   *osta-**ma-an***   *auto-n*
  FUT[<come]-PRS-1SG buy-**INF3-ILL** car-ACC.SG
  'I'm going to buy a car.'   (Sulkala and Karjalainen 1992: 302)

Contrary to what happens in Kru languages, the ventive necessive and the ventive future are markedly different constructions. The future construction, which may be calqued on Swedish (Dahl 2000: 316), is not unipersonal and the shape of the lexical verb is not the 1st infinitive, but the 3rd infinitive in the illative case — which suggests that the allative/illative component is more muted in the necessive construction than it is in the future construction. However, according to Saukkonen (1965: 150–155, quoted by Penjam 2006: 182) a construction following the pattern in (56), where the verb takes as subject the NP bearing the role of Agent, may have been the precursor of the necessive construction in Finnish and other Finnic languages.[43] This presupposes that at some point a major reanalysis occurred whereby (a) *tulla* could no longer take a referential

---

43 Saukkonen notes that this morphosyntactic pattern is attested to this day, with a necessive interpretation, in some dialects of Livvi-Karelian (Finnic; Russia). Furthermore, Penjam (2006: 186; 188) points to some (limited) evidence suggesting that the semantics of necessive *tulema* in Estonian retains a futurate component.

subject, i.e. it underwent unipersonalization; (b) any NP in a non-oblique case now had to be construed as bearing the role of Undergoer with respect to the lexical verb; (c) the lexical verb switched to a different infinitival form.

3.2.4.2 Estonian

In Estonian, the verb *tulema* governs the 1st infinitive when it is used as a necessive marker, as in (53), repeated here as (57):

(57) Estonian (Uralic, Finnic)

> *mei-l*   **tule-***b*   *töö*   *lõpeta-**da***
> 1PL-ADESS **NEC[<come]**-PRS.3SG job.SG.NOM finish-**INF1**
> 'We have to finish the job.'   (Penjam 2006: 167)

On the other hand, it governs the illative case of the 3rd infinitive when used as a verb of motion:

(58) Estonian

> *et*   *ma olen*   **tul-***nud*   *rahu*   *too-**ma***
> COMP 1SG be.PRS.1SG **come**-PST.PTCP peace.PART bring-**INF3.ILL**
> 'that I have come to bring peace.'
>   (Gospel according to Matthew, 10:34; quoted by Lees (2010: 10))

It is possible that, as seems to be the case also for Finnish, the allative component intrinsic to *tulema* is somehow weakened when it functions as a necessive marker. It should be kept in mind, however, that all impersonal constructions in Estonian, with one exception, involve verbs governing the 1st infinitive and that it is also the 1st infinitive that is used after verbs of wish or volition and also after the purposive subordinator *et* (Tuldava 1994: 126–129). In other words, necessive *tulema* is in good company when it comes to signalling goal-orientedness.

While they are not attested in the oldest texts of Estonian, necessive uses of *tulema* appear as early as 1699 (Penjam 2006: 182). In those early attestations, *tulema* agrees in number with the NP in the nominative that bears the role of Undergoer with respect to the embedded verb in the infinitive, which infinitive has passive orientation:

(59) Old Estonian (1739)

> *wämla-d*   ***tulle*-*wad***   *arwata-**da**   temma   wasto*
> cudgel-PL.NOM NEC[<come]-PRS.3PL regard-INF1 3SG.GEN against
> *körre-ks*
> straw-PL.TRANSL
> 'Cudgels should be regarded as straws by comparison with him, [and he
> laughs at the rattle of the spear].'
>
>   (Book of Job; quoted by Penjam (2006: 173))

Starting in the 19th century, it becomes common for the Undergoer NP to be
encoded in the partitive case and correlatively for *tulema* to undergo unipersonalization:

(60) Present-day Estonian

> ***tule*-*b***   *Tatarimaa-l toot-**a**   vähemalt 500*
> NEC[<come]-PRS.3SG T.-ADESS   produce-INF1 at_least 500
> *miljoni-t*   *tonn-i*   *nafta-t*
> million-PART ton-SG.GEN oil-SG.PART
> '[During the next five years] at least five hundred million tons of oil has to
> be produced in Tatarstan.'   (Penjam 2006: 180)

There are however, to this day, instances where *tulema* remains subject to
number agreement:

(61) Present-day Estonian

> *kari- ja kodu-looma-d*   ***tule*-*vad***   *võistlus-päeva-l*
> cattle- and home-animal-PL.NOM NEC[<come]-PRS.3PL contest-day-SG.ADESS
> *hoid-**a**   köide-tu-lt*   *500 m kaugusel ring-tee-st*
> keep-INF1 tether-PASS.PTCP-ADVLZ 500 m from   ring-road-SG.EL
> 'On the day of the contest livestock and domestic animals are to be kept
> tethered at a distance of 500 m from the speedway...' (Penjam 2006: 181)

Such instances, which stand as exceptions to the unipersonal behaviour of
almost all constructions covered in this part of the paper, are claimed by Penjam
(2006: 181) to be infrequent in the contemporary language, a state of affairs she
attributes to the pressure of normative grammars, which tend to mandate the 3rd
person singular. The effect of such pressure, and possibly the motivation for it,
is to bring the syntax of necessive *tulema* in line with parallel constructions in

both Finnish and Russian. Nevertheless, the mere fact that number agreement remains permissible represents a feature of necessive *tulema* that distinguishes it crucially from those constructions: it would seem that the process of unipersonalization in Estonian remains unfinished.

3.2.4.3 *Tulla* and *tulema* as undifferentiated necessives?

Not only do verbs cognate with *tulla* and *tulema* encode necessity in all Finnic languages, they rank also among the five "most typical modal verbs" that those languages feature (Kehayov and Torn-Lessik, 2009: 367–368). This is an unusual situation, as in most languages where ventive verbs encode necessity their status as modal markers is peripheral.

My research has not turned up for Finnish and Estonian (or for Latvian) the kind of evidence that I have been able to adduce with respect to the semantics of ventive-marked necessives in Scottish Gaelic and Russian. It would seem, in fact, that *tulla* and *tulema* are capable of encoding both deontic obligation and circumstantial necessity or inevitability and that neither type of necessity is predominant. This makes it difficult, at this point, to venture any hypothesis as to which of the constraint-salient or valuation-salient routes has been taken by these verbs or as to whether the distinction has indeed any explanatory value with respect to the constructions of which they are part.

There may well be a correlation between their high frequency and their status as core modals on the one hand and what appears to be their relatively undifferentiated semantic profile on the other hand. In general, necessives enjoying a core status, such as *devoir* in French or *sollen* in German for example, tend to cover a wide semantic spectrum.

4 Concluding thoughts

The time may have come for typologists to grapple with the status of directional deixis as a potential grammatical category in a more systematic fashion than has been the case thus far. Quite apart from its intrinsic significance, it is an issue that is directly relevant to grammaticalization studies. This is because, unless we assume that verbs putatively encoding DD are *covertly grammatical* to start with, it is no easy task to understand why they would grammaticalize crosslinguistically with the kind of exuberance that they exhibit. The widely held assumption that such proclivity is a function of their conceptual basicness is, I would argue, lacking in explanatory force. Some principle, equally fundamental and overarching but at the same time more sharply defined, must be at work here. I have suggested, borrowing from von Fintel (1995), that putative DD verbs are hybrid in nature: they are (mostly) lexical in their morphosyntax and (mostly) grammatical in their semantics. The encoding of passive voice by DD verbs, which is pervasive across Indo-European, and in particular among Indo-Aryan and Romance languages, offers fertile ground for testing this hypothesis. What 'come' and/or 'go' have sustained here is what I propose calling *deep grammaticalization*, a process which standard accounts of grammaticalization are arguably ill-equipped to handle, based as they are on explanatory concepts (metaphor, metonymy, subjectification) that are applicable, rather, to *shallow grammaticalization*. This process is in my view singularly enigmatic unless we hypothesize, as I have tried to show, (a) that the verbs at issue are latently grammatical; (b) that their use iconically reflects the abstract trajectory resulting from the decoupling of Agent and Topic, which is one of the defining features of passive voice.

Not all verbs that would appear to be prime candidates for the status of DD markers are "created equal", in terms of their deictic strength and the extent to which, in particular, they conflate deicticity and phase-saliency. One way of dealing with this problem is to set up stringent criteria that *de facto* exclude a great many candidates (see Ricca 1993; Wilkins and Hill 1995). Another strategy, until recently implicit in much work on the "grammaticalization-of-'come'-and-'go'-verbs", is to downplay differences, and all too often to ignore them, for the sake of making generalizations in the shape of grammaticalization pathways purportedly attested across a number of languages. In my view, this dilemma cannot truly be resolved until a consensus emerges among typologists as to whether or not it is empirically legitimate to bestow upon DD the status enjoyed by grammatical categories that demonstrably possess a reasonable degree of crosslinguistic validity. In the meantime, I think a case can be made for suspending disbelief, which could take the form of viewing DD as a "comparative concept", as outlined by Haspelmath (2010). This, in my view, carries a methodological consequence: I have argued that it would be advisable to state, as systematically and precisely as is feasible, what is known about the semantics of any given marker, and in particular about its deictic robustness, when describing the grammaticalization route(s) it has followed. There is also a more theoretical consequence: unless DD, whether as a category or as a comparative concept, is to be so unconstrained as to lose any substantive content, there needs to be some provision made for the reality that pathways known to be taken by "prototypical" DD verbs are occasionally travelled by adeictic, or weakly deictic, verbs of motion. I have assumed in this paper that there is a *next-best-tool principle* that accounts for this phenomenon. A working hypothesis is that it can only be operative if the language has no verbs of motion coming reasonably close to the

DD prototype — where "prototype" is to be understood, roughly, as Ricca (1993) understands the semantics of ventive and itive verbs in what he calls "fully deictic" languages.

I have attempted to show, within this methodological framework, that the encoding of necessive modality by putative ventive and itive verbs is reasonably well attested crosslinguistically. One major caveat is that they get to go necessive by following different routes. In some languages, the encoding of necessity is a functional offshoot, as the verbs at issue have primarily grammaticalized either into future markers or into markers of passive voice, with their use as necessive markers "piggybacking", so to speak, on either of these two functions. In other languages, a more straightforward pathway would appear to have been followed, whereby verbs of "coming" have evolved into deontic necessives, by way of a *valuation-salient* route, or into markers of circumstantial, value-free coercion, by way of a *compulsion-salient* route. While I have paid some attention, in this regard, to Scottish Gaelic on the one hand and to Finnish and Estonian on the other, I have made a conscious decision to explore in greater detail the Russian verbs *prijtis'* and *prixodit'sja*, in view of the many issues they raise with respect to their morphosyntax and their modal force, not to mention the semantics of the verbs of motion from which they have proceeded.

While they are diverse, the pathways that have been reviewed owe their existence, ultimately, to the feature of goal-orientedness, which there is every reason to believe is one of the design properties of directional deixis. It is plausible to assume that the co-encoding of futurity and necessity by DD markers proceeds from the conjunction of two forces: one is the metaphorical shift from goal in space to goal in time and the other is the future-oriented ontology of deontic modalities such as volition and necessity. In the case of the second broad set of pathways, where futurity is not a mediating factor, the basic impetus is arguably of a metonymic nature, necessity being, along with volition, one of the main well-springs of goal-oriented actions; disparate though they may appear, the pathways at issue are bound together by the morphosyntactic feature of impersonality.

Further, I have made the claim that by virtue of their respective deictic identities, itives exhibit degree-1 goal-orientedness and ventives degree-2. The extra weight imparted to the goal would explain the ability of ventives to take the compulsion-salient route, while their affinity with the valuation-salient route is grounded in the positive valuation that flows from the identification of the goal with the deictic centre.

Quite apart from the many issues left unresolved by this paper, there are at least three areas in need of exploration. One is the quasi-systematic encoding of propriety, a form of weak necessity, by prefixed verbs of "coming" in Ancient

Greek, in Latin and its daughter languages, as well as in several Germanic languages. Another issue is the possibility of "replica grammaticalization" (Heine and Kuteva 2005) that is raised by this very proliferation, as it is raised also, in any event, by those ventive-marked necessives discussed in this paper that clearly are a feature of the Circum-Baltic Sprachbund. Lastly, Majsak (2005: 211–212) has identified a number of languages, among which Quechua, Kashmiri and Turkish, in which verbs roughly equivalent to Russian *prixodit'* have grammaticalized into markers of obligation, need or necessity (*neobxodimost'*): whether the trajectories they have followed instantiate mechanisms in any way similar to those discussed in the third part of this paper will be, hopefully, the topic of a sequel.

Abbreviations

ADESS	adessive
ADJLZ	adjectivalizer
ADVLZ	adverbializer
AGT	agent
DEP	dependent
DTRM	determinate
EL	elative
ILL	illative
NEC	necessive
PREP	prepositional
PTCL	particle
TRANSL	translative

References

Bentley, Delia. 2006. *Split Intransitivity in Italian*. (Empirical Approaches to Language Typology 30). Berlin & New York: Mouton de Gruyter.

Bourdin, Philippe. 1997. On Goal-bias across languages: modal, configurational and orientational parameters. In Bohumil Palek (ed.), *Proceedings of LP'96. Typology, Prototypes, Item Orderings and Universals (Proceedings of the Conference Held in Prague, Aug. 20–22, 1996)*, 185–218. Prague: Charles University Press.

Bourdin, Philippe. 1999. Deixis directionnelle et "acquis cinétique" : de 'venir' à 'arriver', à travers quelques langues. *Travaux linguistiques du CerLiCO*, 12 (La référence – 2 – Statut et processus): 183–203.

Bourdin, Philippe. 2003. On two distinct uses of *go* as a conjoined marker of evaluative modality. In Roberta Facchinetti, Manfred Krug & Frank Palmer (eds.), *Modality in Contemporary English* (Topics in English Linguistics 44), 103–127. Berlin & New York: Mouton de Gruyter.

Bourdin, Philippe. 2008. On ventive and itive passives in Indo-European languages and beyond. Paper presented at *High Desert Linguistics Conference*, University of New Mexico (Albuquerque), Nov. 6–8.

Bourdin, Philippe. 2009. The 'come' and 'go' passives of Indo-Aryan in typological perspective. Paper presented at *31st All-India Conference of Linguists*, University of Hyderabad, Dec. 15–17.

Bybee, Joan, Revere Perkins & William Pagliuca. 1994. *The Evolution of Grammar. Tense, Aspect, and Modality in the Languages of the World*. Chicago & London: The Chicago University Press.

Chai-Song, Hong. 1985. *Syntaxe des verbes de mouvement en coréen contemporain* (Linguisticae Investigationes Supplementa 12). Amsterdam & Philadelphia: John Benjamins.

Chilton, Paul. 2010. The conceptual structure of deontic meaning: a model based on geometrical principles. *Language and Cognition* 2 (2): 191–220.

Clark, Eve V. 1974. Normal states and evaluative viewpoints. *Language* 50 (2): 316–332.

Comrie, Bernard. 1976. *Aspect* (Cambridge Textbooks in Linguistics). Cambridge: Cambridge University Press.

Copley, Bridget. 2006. What should *should* mean? Ms of a paper given at the Workshop "Language under Uncertainty: Modals, Evidentials, and Conditionals", Kyoto University, Jan. 2005. http://copley.free.fr/copley.should.pdf (accessed 1 October 2013)

Cornillie, Bert, Walter De Mulder, Tine Van Hecke & Dieter Vermandere. 2009. Modals in the Romance languages. In Björn Hansen & Ferdinand de Haan (eds.), *Modals in the Languages of Europe. A Reference Work* (Empirical Approaches to Language Typology 44), 107–137. Berlin & New York: Mouton de Gruyter.

Dahl, Östen. 2000. The grammar of future time reference in European languages. In Östen Dahl (ed.), *Tense and Aspect in the Languages of Europe* (Empirical Approaches to Language Typology 20), 309–328. Berlin & New York: Mouton de Gruyter.

Davison, Alice. 1982. On the form and meaning of Hindi passive sentences. *Lingua* 58 (1–2): 149–179.

De Haan, Ferdinand. 2006. Typological approaches to modality. In William Frawley (ed.), *The Expression of Modality* (The Expression of Cognitive Categories 1), 27–69. Berlin & New York: Mouton de Gruyter.

Dickey, Stephen M. 2010. Common Slavic "indeterminate" verbs of motion were really manner-of-motion verbs. In Victoria Hasko & Renee Perelmutter (eds.), *New Approaches to Slavic Verbs of Motion* (Studies in Language Companion Series 115), 67–109. Amsterdam & Philadelphia: John Benjamins.

Dunn, John & Shamil Khairov. 2009. *Modern Russian Grammar* (Routledge Modern Grammars). Abingdon & New York: Routledge.

Dwelly, Edward. 1971. *The Illustrated Gaelic-English Dictionary*, 7th edn (Gairm Publications 38). Glasgow: Gairm.

Filip, Hana. 2003. Prefixes and the delimitation of events. *Journal of Slavic Linguistics* 11 (1): 55–101.

Fillmore, Charles. 1975 [1971]. *Santa Cruz Lectures on Deixis*. Bloomington (Ind.): Indiana University Linguistics Club.

von Fintel, Kai. 1995. The formal semantics of grammaticalization. *Proceedings of NELS* 25 (2): 175–189.

von Fintel, Kai. 2006. Modality and language. In Donald M. Borchert (ed.), *Encyclopedia of Philosophy*, 2nd edn., [Appendix], Detroit: Macmillan Reference.

von Fintel, Kai & Sabine Iatridou. 2008. How to say *ought* in foreign: the composition of weak necessity modals. In Jacqueline Guéron and Jacqueline Lecarme (eds.), *Time and Modality* (Studies in Natural Language and Linguistic Theory 75), 115–141. Dordrecht: Springer.

Fleischman, Suzanne. 1982. *The Future in Thought and Language. Diachronic Evidence from Romance* (Cambridge Studies in Linguistics 36). Cambridge: Cambridge University Press.

Foley, William & Mike Olson. 1985. Clausehood and verb serialization. In Johanna Nichols & Anthony Woodbury (eds.), *Grammar Inside and Outside the Clause: Some Approaches to Theory from the Field*, 17–60. Cambridge: Cambridge University Press.

Forssman, Berthold. 2001. *Lettische Grammatik*. Dettelbach (Germany): Röll.

Fortuin, Egbert. 2003. The conceptual basis of syntactic rules: a semantic motivation for the second dative in Russian. *Lingua* 113: 49–92.

Fortuin, Egbert. 2005. From necessity to possibility: the modal spectrum of the dative-infinitive construction in Russian. In Björn Hansen & Petr Karlík (eds.), *Modality in Slavonic Languages. New Perspectives* (Slavolinguistica 6), 39–60. Munich: Otto Sagner.

Gehrke, Berit. 2008a. Goals and sources are aspectually equal: evidence from Czech and Russian prefixes. *Lingua* 118 (11): 1664–1689.

Gehrke, Berit. 2008b. *Ps in Motion. On the Semantics and Syntax of P Elements and Motion Events*. Utrecht: LOT. http://igitur-archive.library.uu.nl/dissertations/2008–0709–070710/gehrke.pdf (accessed 30 September 2013).

Gerritsen, Nelleke. 1990. *Russian Reflexive Verbs. In Search of Unity in Diversity* (Studies in Slavic and General Linguistics 15). Amsterdam & Atlanta: Rodopi.

Giacalone Ramat, Anna. 2000. On some grammaticalization patterns for auxiliaries. In John Charles Smith & Delia Bentley (eds.), *Historical Linguistics 1995. Selected Papers from the 12th International Conference on Historical Linguistics, Manchester, August 2005 (Vol. 1: General Issues and Non-Germanic Languages)* (Amsterdam Studies in the Theory and History of Linguistic Science. Series IV – Current Issues in Linguistic Theory no. 161), 279–300. Amsterdam & Philadelphia: John Benjamins.

Gillies, William. 1993. Scottish Gaelic. In Martin J. Ball & James Fife (eds.), *The Celtic Languages* (Routledge Language Family Descriptions), 145–227. London & New York: Routledge.

Godé, Victor. 2008. *Le Dadjriwalé : langue kru de la Côte d'Ivoire*. Paris: L'Harmattan.

Grenoble, Lenore. 1991. Deixis, point of view, and the prefixes *po-* and *pri-* in Russian. *Die Welt der Slaven* 36: 254–70.

Grenoble, Lenore. 1998. *Deixis and Information Packaging in Russian Discourse* (Pragmatics & Beyond, New Series. no. 50). Amsterdam & Philadelphia: John Benjamins.

Guiraud-Weber, Marguerite. 1984. *Les Propositions sans nominatif en russe moderne* (Bibliothèque russe de l'Institut d'études slaves 79). Paris: Institut d'études slaves.

Hansen, Björn. 2001. *Das slavische Modalauxiliar. Semantik und Grammatikalisierung im Russischen, Polnischen, Serbischen/Kroatischen und Altkirchenslavischen* (Slavolinguistica 2). Munich: Otto Sagner.

Haspelmath, Martin. 2010. Comparative concepts and descriptive categories in crosslinguistic studies. *Language* 86 (3): 663–687.

Haspelmath, Martin, Matthew S. Dryer, David Gil & Bernard Comrie (eds.). 2005. *The World Atlas of Language Structures*. Oxford: Oxford University Press.

Heine, Bernd & Tania Kuteva. 2002. *World Lexicon of Grammaticalization*. Cambridge: Cambridge University Press.

Heine, Bernd & Tania Kuteva. 2005. *Language Contact and Grammatical Change* (Cambridge Approaches to Language Contact). Cambridge: Cambridge University Press.

Hopper, Paul J. & Sandra A. Thompson. 1980. Transitivity in grammar and discourse. *Language* 56 (2): 251–299.

Huddleston, Rodney & Geoffrey K. Pullum. 2002. *The Cambridge Grammar of the English Language*. Cambridge: Cambridge University Press.

Ikegami, Yoshihiko. 1987. 'Source' vs. 'goal': a case of linguistic dissymmetry. In René Dirven & Günter Radden (eds.), *Concepts of Case* (Studien zur englischen Grammatik 4), 122–146. Tübingen: Günter Narr.

Irimia, Dumitru. 1976. *Structura gramaticală a limbii române. Verbul*. Iaşi (Romania): Junimea.

Israeli, Alina. 1997. *Semantics and Pragmatics of the "Reflexive" Verbs in Russian* (Slavistische Beiträge 349). Munich: Otto Sagner.

Israeli, Alina. 2002. Russian verbs of motion: focus, deixis and viewpoint. *Cahiers Chronos* 10: 97–118.

Kangasniemi, Heikki. 1992. *Modal Expressions in Finnish* (Studia Fennica Linguistica 2). Helsinki: Suomalaisen Kirjallisuuden Seura.

Keenan, Edward L. & Matthew S. Dryer. 2007. Passive in the world's languages. In Timothy Shopen (ed.), *Language Typology and Syntactic Description. Vol 1: Clause Structure*, 2nd edn., 325–361. Cambridge: Cambridge University Press.

Kehayov, Petar & Reeli Torn-Lessik. 2009. Modal verbs in Balto-Finnic. In Björn Hansen & Ferdinand de Haan (eds.), *Modals in the Languages of Europe. A Reference Work* (Empirical Approaches to Language Typology 44), 363–401. Berlin & New York: Mouton de Gruyter.

Khokhlova, L. V. 2003. The distribution of analytic and synthetic passives in Indo-European languages of Western India. In Ritva Laury, Gerald R. McMenamin, Shigeko Okamoto, Vida Samiian & K. V. Subbarao (eds.), *Perspectives in Linguistics. Papers in Honor of P. J. Mistry*, 139–158. New Delhi: Indian Institute of Language Studies. http://www.iaas.msu.ru/pub_on/khokhlova/frisna.pdf (accessed 30 September 2013)

Khokhlova, L. V. 2012. Modal passives in Western New Indo-Aryan languages (Gujarati, Punjabi, Rajasthani). Paper presented at *44th Annual Meeting Societas Linguistica Europaea*, University of Stockholm, 29 Aug. – 1 Sept.

Kopecka, Anna & Bhuvana Narasimhan (eds.). 2012. *Events of Putting and Taking: A Crosslinguistic Perspective* (Typological Studies in Language 100). Amsterdam & Philadelphia: John Benjamins.

Kuno, Susumu. 1978. Subject, theme and the speaker's empathy: a reexamination of relativization phenomena. In Charles N. Li (ed.), *Subject and Topic*, 417–444. New York: Academic Press.

Kuno, Susumu. 1987. *Functional Syntax: Anaphora, Discourse and Empathy*. Chicago: The University of Chicago Press.

Kuriłowicz, Jerzy. 1975 [1965]. The evolution of grammatical categories. In Jerzy Kuriłowicz, *Esquisses linguistiques II* (International Library of General Linguistics 37), 38–54. Munich: W. Fink. First published: *Diogenes* 51: 55–71.

Laitinen, Lea & Maria Vilkuna. 1993. Case marking in necessive constructions and split intransitivity. In Anders Holmberg & Urpo Nikanne (eds.), *Case and Other Functional Categories in Finnish Syntax* (Studies in Generative Grammar 39), 23–48. Berlin & New York: Mouton de Gruyter.

Lakusta, Laura. 2005. Source and goal asymmetry in non-linguistic motion event representations. Ph.D. dissertation, The John Hopkins University, Baltimore (Maryland). http://web.jhu.edu/sebin/s/k/LakustaDissertation.pdf (accessed 30 September 2013).

Lakusta, Laura & Barbara Landau. 2005. Starting at the end: the importance of goals in spatial language. *Cognition* 96: 1–33.

Lakusta, Laura & Barbara Landau. 2012. Language and memory for motion events: origins of the asymmetry between source and goal. *Cognitive Science* 36 (3): 517–544.

Lamarre, Christiane. 2008. The linguistic categorization of deictic direction in Chinese — with reference to Japanese. In D. Xu (ed.), *Space in Languages of China: Cross-linguistic, Synchronic and Diachronic Perspectives*, 69–97. Dordrecht: Springer.

Lees, Aet. 2010. Non-finite verbs and their objects in Finnic. In Yvonne Treis & Rik De Busser (eds.), *Selected Papers from the 2009 Conference of the Australian Linguistic Society*, 1–30. http://www.als.asn.au/proceedings/als2009/lees.pdf (accessed 30 September 2013).

Lepschy, Anna Laura & Giulio. 1981. *La lingua italiana: storia, varietà dell'uso, grammatica*. Milan: Bompiani.

Lo Cascio, Vincenzo. 1968. Struttura, funzione, valore di « andare + participio passato ». *Lingua e stile* 3: 271–93.

Lyons, John. 1977. *Semantics. Vol. 2*. Cambridge: Cambridge University Press.

MacAulay, Donald. 1992. *The Celtic Languages* (Cambridge Language Surveys). Cambridge: Cambridge University Press.

Majsak, Timur. 2005. *Tipologija grammatikalizacii konstrukcij s glagolami dviženija i glagol- ami pozicii*. [Grammaticalization of constructions involving verbs of motion and verbs of posture: A typology] (Studia Philologica). Moskva: Jazyki slavjanskix kul'tur.

Marchese, Lynell. 1986. *Tense/Aspect and the Development of Auxiliaries in Kru Languages* (Summer Institute of Linguistics Publications in Linguistics 78). Dallas: Summer Insti- tute of Linguistics and the University of Texas at Arlington.

Mark, Colin. 2003. *The Gaelic-English Dictionary*. London & New York: Routledge.

Markovskaya, Evgenija. 2006. Goal-source asymmetry and Russian spatial prefixes. In P. Svenonius (ed.), *Nordlyd, Tromsø Working Papers in Linguistics* 33 (2) [Special Issue on Adpositions]: 200–219. Tromsø: University of Tromsø.

Masica, Colin P. 1990. Varied case marking in obligational constructions. In Manindra K. Verma & K. P. Mohanan (eds.), *Experiencer Subjects in South Asian Languages*, 335–342. Stanford: The Center for the Study of Language and Information, Stanford University.

Mathiassen, Terje. 1996. *A Short Grammar of Latvian*. Columbus (Ohio): Slavica.

Montaut, Annie. 1991. *Aspects, voix et diathèses en hindi moderne. Syntaxe, sémantique, énonciation* (Bibliothèque de l'information grammaticale). Leuven & Paris: Peeters.

Montaut, Annie. 2004. *A Grammar of Hindi* (LINCOM Studies in Indo-European Linguistics 02). Munich: Lincom Europa.

Moyse-Faurie, Claire. 1983. *Le Drehu, langue de Lifou (Îles Loyauté). Phonologie – Morpholo- gie – Syntaxe* (Langues et cultures du Pacifique 3). Paris: Société d'études linguistiques et anthropologiques de France.

Moyse-Faurie, Claire. 2010. (Dé)grammaticalisation d'expressions spatiales dans des langues océaniennes. In Injoo Choi-Jonin, Marc Duval & Olivier Soutet (eds.), *Typologie et comparatisme. Hommages offerts à Alain Lemaréchal* (Orbis/Supplementa, Mono- graphs published by the International Center of General Dialectology (Louvain) 28), 295–314. Leuven & Paris & Walpole, MA: Peeters.

Myhill, John & Laura A. Smith. 1995. The discourse and interactive functions of obligation expressions. In Joan Bybee & Suzanne Fleischman (eds.), *Modality in Grammar and Dis- course* (Typological Studies in Language 32), 239–292. Amsterdam & Philadelphia: John Benjamins.

Nam, Seungho. 2004. Goal and source: asymmetry in their syntax and semantics. Paper pre- sented at the Workshop on Event Structure, Leipzig, March 17–19.

Narrog, Heiko. 2010. (Inter)subjectification in the domain of modality and mood – Concepts and cross-linguistic realities. In Kristin Davidse, Lieven Vandelanotte & Hubert Cuyckens (eds.), *Subjectification, Intersubjectification and Grammaticalization* (Topics in English Linguistics 66), 385–429. Berlin & New York: Mouton de Gruyter.

Nuyts, Jan. 2006. Modality: overview and linguistic issues. In William Frawley (ed.), *The Expression of Modality* (The Expression of Cognitive Categories 1), 1–26. Berlin & New York: Mouton de Gruyter.

Palmer, Frank R. 1979. *Modality and the English Modals* (Longman Linguistics Library). London: Longman.

Palmer, Frank R. 1986. *Mood and Modality* (Cambridge Textbooks in Linguistics). Cambridge: Cambridge University Press.

Pandharipande, Rajeshwari. 1978. Exceptions and rule government: the case of the passive rule in Hindi. *Studies in the Linguistic Sciences* 8 (1): 153–73.

Pandharipande, Rajeshwari. 1979. Passive as an optional rule in Hindi, Marathi and Nepali. In B. Kachru (ed.), *South Asian Languages Analysis*, 89–106. Urbana: Dept of Linguistics, University of Illinois.

Pandharipande, Rajeshwari. 1997. *Marathi* (Routledge Descriptive Grammars). London & New York: Routledge.

Papafragou, Anna. 2010. Source-goal asymmetries in motion representation: implications for language production and comprehension. *Cognitive Science* 34: 1064–1092.

Pariser, Jon Richard. 1982. Dative-reflexive constructions in contemporary Russian. Ph.D. dissertation, University of California at Los Angeles.

Penjam, Pille. 2006. Development of the modal function of the verb *tulema* 'come' in written Estonian. *Linguistica Uralica* 42: 167–191.

Radden, Günter. 1996. Motion metaphorized: the case of *coming* and *going*. In Eugene Casad (ed.), *Cognitive Linguistics in the Redwoods: the Expansion of a New Paradigm in Linguistics* (Cognitive Linguistics Research 6), 423–458. Berlin & New York: Mouton de Gruyter.

Radden, Günter & René Dirven. 2007. *Cognitive English Grammar* (Cognitive Linguistics in Practice 2). Amsterdam & Philadelphia: John Benjamins.

Rakhilina, Ekaterina V. 2004. There and back: the case of Russian 'go'. *Glossos* 5: 1–33. http://seelrc.org/glossos/issues/5/rakhilina.pdf (accessed 30 September 2013).

Regier, Terry & Mingyu Zheng. 2007. Attention to endpoints: a cross-linguistic constraint on spatial meaning. *Cognitive Science* 31 (4): 705–719.

Ricca, Davide. 1993. *I verbi deittici di movimento in Europa: una ricerca interlinguistica* (Pubblicazioni della Facoltà di Littere e Filosofia dell'Università di Pavia 70). Florence: La Nuova Italia Editrice.

Robertson, Rev. C. M. 1897–1898. Prize essay on the peculiarities of Gaelic as spoken in the writer's district. *Transactions of the Gaelic Society of Inverness* 22: 4–42.

Rocchetti, Alvaro. 1982. Sémantique de *andare*, verbe plein et auxiliaire en italien: de l'expression du mouvement à la modalité d'obligation. *Modèles linguistiques* 4 (2): 115–133.

Ross, David. 1949. *Aristotle*, 5th edn. London: Methuen.

Saagpakk, Paul, F. (ed.). 1982. *Estonian-English Dictionary*. Tallinn: Koolibri.

Saukkonen, Pauli. 1965. *Itämerensuomalaisten kielten tulosijainfinitiivirakenteiden historiaa I* [History of Constructions with the Allative/Illative Infinitive in Baltic-Finnic Languages] (Suomalais-Ugrilaisen Seuran Toimituksia 137). Helsinki: Suomalais-ugrilainen Seura.

Shibatani, Masayoshi. 1985. Passives and related constructions: a prototype analysis. *Language* 61 (4): 821–848.

Sinha, Anjani Kumar. 1972. On the deictic use of 'coming' and 'going' in Hindi. In Paul M. Peranteau, Judith N. Levi & Gloria C. Phares (eds.), *Papers from the Eighth Regional Meeting of the Chicago Linguistic Society*, 351–358. Chicago: University of Chicago.

Smit, Merlijn de. 2006. *Language Contact and Structural Case. An Old Finnish Case Study* (Acta Universitatis Stockholmiensis. Studia Fennica Stockholmiensia 9). Stockholm: Universitet Stockholms.

Stefanowitsch, Anatol & Ada Rhode. 2004. The goal bias in the encoding of motion events. In Günter Radden & Klaus-Uwe Panther (eds.), *Studies in Linguistic Motivation* (Cognitive Linguistics Research 28), 249–67. Berlin & New York: Mouton de Gruyter.

Stolz, Thomas. 1991. *Sprachbund im Baltikum? Estnisch und Lettisch im Zentrum einer sprachlichen Konvergenzlandschaft* (Bochum-Essener Beiträge zur Sprachwandelforschung 13). Bochum: Universitätsverlag Dr. N. Brockmeyer.

Sulkala, Helena & Merja Karjalainen. 1992. *Finnish* (Routledge Descriptive Grammars). London & New York: Routledge.

Taylor, Kenneth A. 1988. We've got you coming and going. *Linguistics and Philosophy* 11 (4): 493–513.

Timberlake, Alan. 2007. Aspect, tense, mood. In Timothy Shopen (ed.), *Language Typology and Syntactic Description. Vol 3: Grammatical Categories and the Lexicon*, 2nd edn., 280–333. Cambridge: Cambridge University Press.

Tryon, Darrell T. & Marie Joseph Dubois. 1969. *Nengone Dictionary. Part I: Nengone-English* (Pacific Linguistics Series C – Books. n° 9). Canberra: The Australian National University.

Tuldava, Juhan. 1994. *Estonian Textbook. Grammar, Exercises, Conversation* (Indiana University Uralic and Altaic Series 159). Bloomington (Ind.): Indiana University, Research Institute for Inner Asian Studies.

Ultan, Russell. 1978. The nature of future tenses. In Joseph H. Greenberg, Charles Ferguson & Edith Moravcsik (eds.), *Universals of Human Language. Vol. 3: Word Structure*, 83–123. Stanford: Stanford University Press.

van der Auwera, Johan, Andreas Ammann & Saskia Kindt. 2005. Modal polyfunctionality and Standard Average European. In Alex Klinge & Henrik Høeg Müller (eds.), *Modality. Studies in Form and Function*, 247–268. London: Equinox.

van der Auwera, Johan & Vladimir A. Plungian. 1998. Modality's semantic map. *Linguistic Typology* 2: 79–124.

Verspoor, Marjolijn, René Dirven & Günter Radden. 2004. Putting concepts together: syntax. In René Dirven & Marjolijn Verspoor (eds.), *Cognitive Exploration of Language and Linguistics*, 2nd rev. edn. (Cognitive Linguistics in Practice 1), 75–100. Amsterdam & Philadelphia: John Benjamins.

Wade, Terence. 2011. *A Comprehensive Russian Grammar* (Blackwell Reference Grammars). Oxford: Wiley-Blackwell.

Wade, Terence & Nijole White. 2004. *Using Russian Synonyms*. Cambridge: Cambridge University Press.

Wälchli, Bernhard. 2001. A typology of displacement (with special reference to Latvian). *Sprachtypologie und Universalienforschung* 54 (3): 298–323.

Wälchli, Bernhard & Michael Cysouw. 2012. Lexical typology through similarity semantics: toward a semantic map of motion verbs. *Linguistics* 50 (3): 671–710.

Wilkins, David P. & Deborah Hill. 1995. When "go" means "come": questioning the basicness of basic motion verbs. *Cognitive Linguistics* 6 (2–3): 209–259.

Dictionaries and corpora

COCA: The Corpus of Contemporary American English.
    http://corpus.byu.edu/coca/ (accessed 30 September 2013)
GG-B: Gearrfhoclóir Gaeilge-Béarla (Short Irish-English Dictionary).
    Dublin: Government Publications, 1981.
ORD: Oxford Russian Dictionary.
    http://www.oxfordlanguagedictionaries.com (accessed 30 September 2013)
RNC: Russian National Corpus.
    http://ruscorpora.ru/en/index.html (accessed 30 September 2013)

Caterina Mauri and Andrea Sansò

Go and *come* as sources of directive constructions[1]

1 Introduction:
motion deixis and directive speech acts

Being crucial to the management of interpersonal relationships, directive speech acts (orders, suggestions, exhortations) are very frequent in everyday conversation. Directive forms (imperatives, hortatives, jussives, etc.)[2] are often among the simplest verbal forms of a language, and this is especially true in the case of 2nd person (singular) directives, which in most languages correspond to the verbal root (or to a minimally marked form of the verb). Frequency and simplicity are among the reasons why such forms are particularly subject to processes of diachronic renewal. Moreover, ordinary requirements of politeness usually make the use of flat imperatives inappropriate in normal conversation and speakers are therefore prone to find indirect means to reach their illocutionary goals: highly frequent indirect speech acts may become conventionalized and thus become systematically associated with a directive illocutionary force.

The patterns by which various morphosyntactic strategies are exploited to convey orders are known from a considerable amount of mostly language-specific pragmatic analyses (see, for instance, the survey in Aikhenvald 2010:

---

1 This paper is the result of joint work by the two authors. However, for academic purposes, Caterina Mauri is responsible for Sections 2 and 4 and Andrea Sansò is responsible for Sections 1 and 3. We wish to thank two anonymous referees for their insightful comments on a previous draft of the article. The usual disclaimers apply.

2 The term "imperative" is normally reserved for directive forms in which the intended performer of the action is the addressee (*go!*), whereas the labels "hortative" and "jussive" are generally used in grammars to indicate 1st person plural directives (*let's go!*), and 3rd person directives (*let him/her/them go!*) respectively. This terminological variety reflects the fact that forms encoding directive speech acts addressed to different performers are seldom formally homogeneous within a given language. In this paper, however, we will adopt the label *directive(s)* to refer to the set of forms that encode positive directive situations in a language (i.e. to the exclusion of so-called prohibitives), because there are both cases in which a given directive strategy extends non-randomly from one person to another (see, for instance, Mauri & Sansò 2011: 3504, 3506, and *passim*), and languages in which a formally homogeneous directive paradigm for all the persons exists (van der Auwera et al., 2003: 50). These facts are suggestive of the existence of a semantic/conceptual core common to all directive situations, independently of the performer, which might be concealed by the plethora of terms used to refer to forms encoding them.

346–350). In Mauri and Sansò (2011) we have presented a detailed account of the recurrent processes leading to the emergence and conventionalization of directive strategies based on a large language sample and on the available cross-linguistic evidence. These processes include:

(i) the *cooptation* of strategies originally attested in indirect speech acts through conventionalization of pragmatic implicatures; the source strategies in these cases are primarily devoted to the expression of futurity/imminence (e.g. future constructions), or to the expression of the speaker's wish (e.g. optative constructions);

(ii) cases of *insubordination*, i.e. processes in which syntactically embedded directives (e.g. complement clauses after manipulative or desiderative predicates) become syntactically independent directive clauses; and

(iii) cases of *grammaticalization*, i.e. processes in which various source constructions involving a limited number of lexical sources develop directive functions. The source constructions share a twofold internal structure consisting of two events (preliminary action and ordered event), and the directive form referring to the preliminary action grammaticalizes into a general directive marker.

Along with permissive verbs (*let/allow*) and verbs of saying (*tell*), directive forms of deictic motion verbs are by and large one of the most frequent lexical sources in the processes of grammaticalization of directives (Mauri and Sansò 2011: 3496–3502) alluded to in (iii). As will be discussed below, this fact may be either interpreted as a piece of evidence in favour of the versatility of these two verbs, which are involved as lexical sources in plenty of grammaticalization processes, or may be suggestive of a closer connection between deictic motion and directive speech acts.

The literature on directive speech acts has not failed to acknowledge that motion deixis is relevant for this type of speech acts. It is well-known, for instance, that in many languages there are directional affixes denoting, among other meanings, motion away from or towards the speaker that are incompatible with forms other than directives (Aikhenvald 2010: 136–138; cf. (1)), and that it is cross-linguistically very frequent to find suppletive directive forms for the two verbs 'go' and 'come' (Veselinova 2007: 139; Aikhenvald 2010: 33–37; cf. (2)–(3)):

(1) Tariana (Arawak)

a. *pi-ñha-si*
2SG-eat-PROXIMAL.IMP
'Eat here!'
(Aikhenvald 2010: 136)

b. *pi-ñha-kada*
2SG-eat-DISTAL.IMP
'Eat over there!'
(Aikhenvald 2010: 136)

(2)   Modern Greek (Indo-European, Hellenic)

      'come'

erx-ese	come-PRS.IND.2SG
erx-ete	come- PRS.IND.2PL
ela	come:IMP.2SG
ela-te	come:IMP-IMP.2PL

      (Veselinova 2007: 137)

(3)   Yucatec (Mayan)

    a. root *b'in* 'go' → imperative   *xen* 'go!'

                              hortative   *ko'ox* 'let's go (you and I)';

                                                    ko'on-e'ex 'let's go (you all and I)'

                                                       (Hofling and Ojeda 1994: 279)

    b. root *tal* 'come' → imperative   *ko'oten* 'come!'

                                                        (Hofling and Ojeda 1994: 284)

Suppletive directives for verbs of motion outnumber suppletive directives for other verbs, representing 70% of suppletive imperatives across languages (Veselinova 2006: 139). As suppletive (and, more generally, irregular) forms tend to correlate with high frequency of occurrence, this fact may be suggestive of a great frequency of orders involving motion away from or towards the speaker in everyday conversation, or, at least, of their *saliency* as directive speech acts.[3]

    In grammaticalization studies too, the existence of pathways of change in which deictic motion verbs are involved as lexical sources of directive forms is widely recognized. Heine and Kuteva (2002), for instance, acknowledge the existence of two paths of semantic change that lead to the development of what they call 'hortative' strategies. In both paths a deictic motion verb is involved as the

---

3 Note, however, that the frequency of suppletive imperatives of 'go' and 'come' may have more complex motivations than the frequency of the corresponding speech acts or their saliency in conversation. Veselinova (2006: 141–146) correctly observes that suppletive imperatives of motion verbs can be the result of the inclusion of exhortative particles (often of unclear origin) into a verbal paradigm: in these cases, it is the ellipsis of the morphological imperative that leads to the reinterpretation of the former particle as an imperative form, and to its integration into the paradigm. Suppletive imperatives may also arise in situations of intense discourse contact ("from a language with greater prestige and whose speakers have more power to the speakers who have less", Veselinova 2006: 147): cf. Bulgarian *ela*, come.IMP.2SG, from Greek *ela*. Still, it is a fact that only with motion verbs (and with the verb 'look') such phenomena (borrowing, integration of particles into the paradigm) are robustly attested, so that in the end these suppletive imperatives can be considered as "lexical expressions for a category that is *highly relevant* to the sense of verbs which express motion, and are obviously *very often used* in the imperative" (Veselinova 2006: 146, [our emphasis]).

lexical source of the construction: *come > hortative* (Heine & Kuteva 2002: 69) and *go > hortative* (Heine and Kuteva 2002: 159). According to Aikhenvald (2010: 346–351), deictic motion verbs have the potential for developing into imperative markers by virtue of their "purposeful overtones" (Aikhenvald 2010: 349), and because "semantics of motion is intrinsically linked to a change of state or creating a new situation" (Aikhenvald 2010: 349). Neither Heine and Kuteva nor Aikhenvald, however, seem to draw any distinction between (i) the development of 'go'/'come' into general directive markers and (ii) the more widespread pattern by which imperatives of motion verbs develop into expressive/emphatic markers with an exhortative meaning (see also Bravo, this volume). The latter path leads to non-obligatory encouragement, exhortative or emphatic devices acting at the discourse level (e.g. as discourse markers) and frequently (but not exclusively) occurring in directive contexts. The former instead is a *bona fide* instance of a grammaticalization process ending up in a new grammatical strategy (e.g. a bound imperative morpheme, a new imperative construction, etc.). Consider the example from Baure in (4): the free particle *pa* (< 'go'), directly preceding the verb, has an emphatic function and can be used to reinforce either an assertion (the two clauses in (4a) are both answers to a question such as "Who will eat it?") or a command (as in (4b)). However, it cannot be argued that *pa* has grammaticalized into a general directive marker, rather its function is similar to that of English *come on* or German *komm* (see exx. (5) and (6)).

(4)   Baure (Arawak)

   a. *pa nti' nikier! pa nti'-niš!*
      pa   nti' nik=ro   / pa   nti'=niš
      EMPH 1SG 1SG.eat=3SG.M   EMPH 1SG=EXCLAM
      'I will eat it!' 'Well, I will!'   (Danielsen 2007: 292)

   b. *to pa pihirikašan nan siy-ye*
      to   pa   pi=hirik-a-ša-no   nan siy-ye
      ART EMPH 2SG=sit-LK-IRR-IMP here chair-LOC
      'Go, sit here on the chair!'   (Danielsen 2007: 292)

(5   German

   a. *Komm, denk darüber nach!*   b. *Komm, geh jetzt!*
      come   think about:it after   come   go   now
      'Come on, think about it!'   'Come on, go now!'

(6)   English

   Come on, finish your essay!

In Mauri & Sansò (2011: 3496–3497), we have argued that the motivation behind these grammaticalization processes cannot simply boil down to the fact that 'go' and 'come', which are said to imply telicity and change of state, have a high potential for grammaticalization as directive markers: such an explanation is simplistic and does not account for a number of facts. For instance, as will become clear in the following discussion, 'go' verbs grammaticalize into directive markers for 2nd person performers and, to a lesser extent, for 1st person plural performers, whereas 'come' verbs develop into directive markers for 1st person plural performers exclusively, i.e. there are some performers that seem to act as bridgeheads for these grammaticalization paths. How can this be explained by simply taking into account the change-of-state semantics of the two verbs?

The aim of this paper is to answer this question by addressing the complex net of factors at play in the development of directive values out of deictic motion verbs. To do this, we will first discuss data from a number of unrelated languages showing how motion verbs may acquire a general (non-motion) directive function, and secondly we will complete the picture by comparing these paths with other diachronic scenarios involving motion verbs as sources of grammatical meanings.

The paper is based on a convenience sample of 200 languages, chosen with a view to maximizing genealogical diversity but with little or no statistical concerns, as we have decided to focus on grammars of languages for which enough data on imperatives and related constructions were available, and we have included grammars of closely related languages whenever it appeared useful to compare diachronic developments in such languages. Directive strategies based on motion verbs are attested in 20 languages of the sample (10%) and are more or less evenly distributed between 'go' and 'come' verbs. We generally followed our primary sources in the evaluation of a given directive form as historically derived from (or synchronically related to) a certain motion construction (mainly cases in which there is a marker which is synchronically polysemous or there is sufficient resemblance between the source construction and the target construction). This allows us to take the source–target relationship for granted. When the grammar is not explicit or simply by-passes the question of the possible lexical origins of a directive marker, insights into the possible diachronic source of a given marker could come from reconstructions within a given language family or from cross-linguistic comparison.

This paper is organized as follows: in Section 2 we examine the grammaticalization paths in which there is a source construction involving some form of 'go' verbs. These paths are compared with other grammaticalization paths involving 'go' as a source meaning. In Section 3 we discuss the grammaticalization of 'come' as a directive marker: it turns out that this verb (or, more precisely, complex constructions formed with a directive form of this verb) gives rise to directive constructions addressed to 1st person plural performers. Some conclusions about these processes are presented in Section 4, where we also try to answer some more general questions concerning the role of the deictic motion semantics of 'go' and 'come' verbs in their reinterpretation as directive markers.

2 "Go" > directive

2.1 Go > itive directive

In some languages, the verb meaning 'go' may give rise to *specialized itive directive markers*, thus maintaining its source motion value. For instance, in Jingulu it is possible to encode directive speech acts addressed to 2nd persons by means of a construction in which the imperative of motion /-yirri/ (lit. 'go.IMP') is suffixed to the verb stem, resulting in directives that involve motion away from the site of commanding ('go and do X!').

(7)　Jingulu (Australian, West Barkly)

　　ngunu　buba　miji-yirri
　　DEM(N)　fire　get-go.IMP
　　'Go get some firewood!'　　　　　　　　　　　　　(Pensalfini 2003: 230–231)

A similar situation is attested in Sipakapense Maya and in Toqabaqita. In Sipakapense Maya there is a special deictic imperative formed by means of the prefix j-, related to the irregular imperative of the verb 'go' (*jat*). This special imperative is possible with all persons:

(8)　Sipakapense Maya (Mayan)

　　a.　*jo', ji'cha'n k'chi' ruk' Liy tla'.*
　　　　jo',　　　j+iY+cha'+n　　　　　　　k'a+chi'　r+uk'　　Liy tla'
　　　　go:1PL.IMP MOT.IMP+3.ABS+talk+AAP then+well 3SG-with Liy over.there
　　　　'Let's go, let's go talk with Liy over there, then'　(Barrett 1999: 89–90)

　　b.　*jilq'o'!*
　　　　j+∅+i+loq'+V'
　　　　MOT.IMP+3SG.ABS+2.ERG+buy+MOD
　　　　'Go buy it!'　　　　　　　　　　　　　　　　　　　(Barrett 1999: 89–90)

In Toqabaqita, the verb *lae* 'go' combines with other verbs to form itive directives for 2nd person and 1st person plural performers:

(9) Toqabaqita (Austronesian, Eastern Malayo-Polynesian, Oceanic)

a. *lae moro   fanga naqa*
    go 2DU.NFUT eat   PFV
    'Go eat now (you two)!'   (Lichtenberk 2008: 857)

b. *lae kulu   qili nguda*
    go PL.INCL.NFUT dig crab
    'Let's go digging for crabs!'   (Lichtenberk 2008: 857)

2.2 Go > simple (non-motion) directive

In a number of languages, 'go' develops into a directive marker *tout court*, without any reference to motion. In Tetun, *bá* 'go' is used after other verbs in commands or invitations for the addressee to do something without the speaker, even in those contexts in which no motion is implied, as in (10):

(10) Tetun (Austronesian, Central Malayo-Polynesian)

imi hán bá
2PL eat go
'You (plural) eat up!'   (Williams-van Klinken *et al.* 2002: 68)

In Vietnamese the motion verb *đi* 'go, go ahead' combines with other verbs (including *đi* itself) to form a directive construction in which the motion component is not necessarily there:

(11) Vietnamese (Austro-Asiatic, Mon-Khmer, Viet-Nuong)

a. *mẹ   đi ngủ đi, khuya rồi!*
    mother go sleep IMP late   PFV
    'Go to bed, mother, it is late'   (Nguyễn 1997: 242)

b. *ăn đi, ăn cho hết   bát canh, con ạ!*
    eat IMP eat for exhaust bowl soup child IMP
    'Eat, sonny, eat the whole bowl of soup'
                                                    (Bystrov & Stankevič 2001: 465–466)

A similar construction is also attested in Cambodian (Spatar 1997), another Mon-Khmer language, where the verb 'go' is the plausible source of a general (non-itive) imperative marker. In Cambodian, orders addressed to 2nd persons may be realized either by means of the bare verb form (identical to the indicative) or by means of the verb form accompanied by dedicated imperative markers (preposed or postposed, Spatar 1997: 119–121). One of these postposed imperative markers, *daw*, is a homonym of the motion verb 'go'. Although no clear diachronic arguments are provided, Spatar (1997: 122) suggests that the directive verb form *daw* 'go!' (exemplified in (12a), followed by the imperative marker *cuh*) and the directive marker *daw* (exemplified in (12b), where the motion component is absent) may be etymologically related. Diachronic evidence from other genetically close languages (e.g. Vietnamese above) makes Spatar's hypothesis highly plausible.

(12) Cambodian (Austro-Asiatic, Mon-Khmer, Khmer)

    a. *daw phsaːr jaːmuay pangsriː aeng cuh*
       go   market with   sister   you   IMP
       'Go to the market with your sister.'   (Spatar 1997: 120)

    b. *an suːm aːn pantic -pːanheiy aːn daw*
       I   beg read a little okay   read IMP
       'May I read? Okay, read!'   (Spatar 1997: 121)

Directive forms of 'go' may develop into non-motion directive markers also with *1ˢᵗ person plural performers*. In Yucatec there is a rather complex system for 1st person plural directives, involving two suppletive directive forms of 'go' for 1st person plural (*ko'ox* 'let's go [you.and.I]' and *ko'on-e'ex* 'let's go [you.all.and.I]'). In directive situations addressed to the speaker + the addressee, the two suppletive forms are followed by a subordinate clause introduced by the subordinator *j*, forming a general (non-deictic) directive strategy (see (13a,b)). When the verb in the subordinate clause is transitive, as in (13c,d), the picture is slightly more complicated, because two constructions may be used which differ in patient marking suffixes. When the subordinate verb is marked by *-ik* (as in (13c)), the construction only encodes the directive situation, without any reference to motion. On the other hand, when the subordinate patient marker *-e* occurs (as in (13d)), the dislocative semantics is retained and the construction encodes a directive situation in which the realization of the desired SoA requires motion away from the place where the order is uttered.

(13)   Yucatec (Hofling & Ojeda 1994: 284, 285)

a. *ko'ox j*	*k'ay (túun)*	b. *ko'one'ex j*	*k'ay!*
HORT SUBORD	sing then	HORT SUBORD	sing
'Let's sing (then)'		'Let's all sing'	

c. *ko'ox j*	*il-ik!*	d. *ko'ox j*	*il-e!*
HORT SUBORD	see-PPM	HORT SUBORD	see-SPM
'Let's see (about) it!'		'Let's go see it!'	

The cross-linguistic data discussed in Sections 2.1 and 2.2 provide evidence for a number of paths involving 'go' as a source of directive markers:

(14)   a.   GO$_{[DIRECTIVE.2PERSON]}$ DO X > 2ND PERSON <u>DEICTIC</u> DIRECTIVE   [e.g. Jingulu]

b.   GO$_{[DIRECTIVE.2PERSON]}$ DO X > <u>DEICTIC</u> DIRECTIVE FOR ALL PERSONS
                                                         [e.g. Sipakapense Maya]

c.   GO$_{[DIRECTIVE.2PERSON]}$ DO X > 2ND PERSON <u>NON-DEICTIC</u> DIRECTIVE
                                         [e.g. Tetun, Vietnamese, Cambodian]

d.   GO$_{[DIRECTIVE.1ST.PLURAL]}$ (AND/IN ORDER TO) DO X
      > 1ST PERSON PLURAL <u>DEICTIC</u> DIRECTIVE   [e.g. Yucatec]

e.   GO$_{[DIRECTIVE.1ST.PLURAL]}$ (AND/IN ORDER TO) DO X
      > 1ST PERSON PLURAL <u>NON-DEICTIC</u> DIRECTIVE   [e.g. Yucatec]

In our sample there is no clear evidence to establish whether at least some of the paths in (14) can be conflated together. For instance, it is not clear whether the use of 'go' as an itive directive marker can be considered as an obligatory preliminary stage for the use of 'go' as a general, non-deictic directive marker: if this was the case, (14a) and (14c) could be thought of as two subsequent stages along the same path. Similarly, it is not clear whether the development of a deictic imperative out of a form originally meaning 'go' necessarily starts from 2nd person directives, and then extends to other performers: in this case, (14b) would represent the second step of the path in (14a).

A number of further questions arise as to the nature and motivations of the development of 'go' into a directive marker. Firstly, it is debatable whether the grammaticalization of 'go' into a directive marker is an independent one or it is connected to the well-known pattern by which 'go' grammaticalizes into an aspectual prospective marker. A connection between the two paths has been explicitly postulated by Craig (1991) in Rama, where the verb 'go' is said to be involved in a case of "polygrammaticalization", i.e. as a set of grammaticalization chains originating from the same particular lexical morpheme. The morpheme in question is *ba(ng)*, a suppletive form of the verb *taak* 'go' (which nowadays only survives in the 1st + 2nd person directive form *bang* 'let's go'). *Bang* undergoes grammaticalization as a prospective marker and as a marker of 1st person plural directives in which the meaning of motion is still retrievable, as in (15b).

(15) Rama (Chibchan)

    a. *tiiskama ni-tanang-bang*
       baby   I-look_at-ASP
       'I'm going to look at the baby'   (Craig 1991: 457)

    b. *mwaing yairi s-tuk-bang*
       we   soup   1PL-drink-IMP
       'Let's (go) drink our soup!'   (Craig 1991: 485)

According to Craig, although various analyses of the relative timing of the two grammaticalization paths are possible, the two paths are interconnected, and the fact that the motion meaning is still preserved in 1st person plural directives formed with *-bang* suggests that "the use of *bang* in first person imperative ... is the closest link between the free lexical motion verb *bang* and a bound aspect/mood marker *-bang*" (Craig 1991: 485). In the languages of our sample in which a 'go' > directive path is attested, however, there are no cases in which the same verb is also the source of prospective and future markers. Therefore, the existence of a path "'go' > directive" in a language does not entail the existence of a path "'go' > future/prospective" in the same language, and the two paths are only very loosely related. Whether this is due to the inherent goal-orientation of verbs meaning 'go', i.e. to the fact that such verbs, representing the most basic encoding of the cognitive schema SOURCE-PATH-GOAL happen to be good candidates for grammaticalization in functional domains (such as futurity and commands) in which the achievement of a goal is a salient component, as Kuteva (2001: 22) observes for the grammaticalization path "'go' > future", cannot be established without considering any single grammaticalization process in its own respect.

    It is also tempting to think of the grammaticalization paths involving 'go' as a source as cases of serial verb constructions (henceforth SVCs), i.e. as sequences of verbs "which act together as a single predicate, without any overt marker of coordination, subordination, or syntactic dependency of any other sort" (Aikhenvald 2006: 1), especially given the fact that some of the languages discussed in this section (e.g. Vietnamese, Tetun) have SVCs. Directional motion

verbs are frequently involved in SVCs, and these constructions may grammaticalize into aspectual constructions: in other words, it cannot be excluded that
the SVC verb + 'go' grammaticalizes first into an aspectual construction with a
prospective/future meaning (much in the same way as "be going to" grammaticalizes into a future/prospective marker in English), and then, due to its inherent
future-projection, the construction is used to encode directive situations.

An analysis of the patterns exemplified in this section as resulting from the
grammaticalization of SVCs into aspectual constructions, however, is problematic. Take, for instance, Tetun. The motion verb *bá* in Tetun forms SVCs in which
it follows other motion verbs indicating direction, as in (16a). Moreover, *bá* par-
ticipates in another type of SVC, exemplified in (16b); in this type of construction
it precedes another verb forming with it a non-contiguous structure, as demonstrated by the fact that postverbal adverbs can be optionally placed after either
the first or the second verb:

(16)   Tetun

    a. *nia   sae   fali   bá*
       3SG ascend again go
       'He went up again.'   (Hajek 2006: 243)

    b. *sira [bá (fali) hariis] (fali) iha   tasi*
       3PL go again bathe   again LOC sea
       'They went to swim in the sea again.'   (Hajek 2006: 243)

The directive construction with *bá* differs from both these types of SVCs: on the
one hand, *bá* appears after the other verb, as in (16a) and unlike (16b), but unlike
the serial verb construction in (16a) directive *bá* combines with all verbs and is
not limited to motion verbs; on the other hand, adverbs in the directive construction (such as, e.g., *lai* 'first', and *dei* 'only') appear after *bá* (Lumien van Klinken
1999: 244), thus showing that this verb forms a tighter syntactic unit with the
other verb than it does in SVCs such as those exemplified in (16b).

To sum up, there are no reasons to think of the grammaticalization path
"'go > directive" as being necessarily related to other grammaticalization paths
involving 'go' as source meaning. A tentative explanation of the process(es) of
grammaticalization described in this section should instead consider a simple
fact: in directive speech acts the addressee often needs to move away from the
place where the speaker utters his/her order as a preliminary action necessary to
bring about the desired SoA. In most cases, the directive strategies employed by
the speaker leave this need for dislocation unexpressed and implicit: when it is
explicit, however, i.e. when a sequence of two verbs is used (*go and do x/go do x*),

the verb expressing dislocation can be easily reinterpreted as a general directive marker. In other words, the frequency with which in directive situations the realization of the order implies a dislocation of the performer may be speculatively considered as a prerequisite for the construction [*go* do X] to be processed as a single unit and, subsequently, for the verb meaning 'go' to be reanalyzed as having a general (i.e. non-dislocative) directive function.

This conclusion is corroborated by the existence of similar processes of weakening of motion verbs. In English there is a construction (called the *go get* construction or the "double verb construction") which encodes a single event made up of a main predicate with associated motion ('go' and the main verb in this construction behave syntactically as a single unit, see Nicolle 2007: 54–58):

(17) English

   a. *We go watch a match every week.*
   b. *Did she go buy apples?*

It has been convincingly shown that this construction has its most likely source in imperatives (Nicolle 2007: 54), and has then extended to declarative clauses. Nicolle (2007) explains the kind of semantic development of *go get* constructions as involving "a subjectified construal of both the action of moving and the other event [in which] the perspective of the conceptualizer becomes incorporated into the description of the event described by the main verb, whilst less prominence is given to the act of physical movement" (Nicolle 2007: 58, adapted). In other words, it is the salience of the deictic dimension in directive situations that is responsible for the reinterpretation of a motion verb in a chain of verbs as marking the point of view of the speaker rather than motion proper. 'Go eat' (and its counterpart 'come eat') no longer expresses motion + another action, but simply the fact that the eating must be done somewhere else (or where the speaker is situated in the case of 'come eat'): the "function of the deictic movement verb has changed whilst its semantic content remains unchanged" (Nicolle 2007: 58). If the analysis of *go get* as deriving from "go and get" through conjunction elision is correct (but see the discussion in Nicolle 2007), the semantic change is accompanied by a structural change resulting in a tighter construction. A similar weakening of the motion component can be hypothesized for 'go' verbs that undergo grammaticalization as directive markers: by using 'go' + another verb in a command the speaker not only orders a motion action to the performer, but also casts her-/himself as the deictic centre of the order. In the course of time, the motion component may become secondary and the simple deictic anchoring connected to the verb 'go' may become central, giving rise to dislocative directives such as those exemplified by Sipakapense Maya (*do x somewhere else*). In their turn, dislocative directives can loose their deictic meaning and be reanalyzed as plain directives. Overtones of anger and disapproval, correlated with the 'subjective' construal of distance between the speaker and the addressee, may also arise at this stage and take over the original motion meaning. Although there is no conclusive evidence that this process has taken place in the cases discussed in this section, the process of weakening of meaning involved in this process is the same as in other grammaticalization paths involving 'go' as a source, and could tentatively be assumed to characterize the grammaticalization path 'go' > directive as well.

3 "Come" > directive

The 2nd person directive form of a verb meaning 'come' (strictly intended as 'motion towards the speaker') develops into a marker of directive situations with 1st person plural performers in which no motion towards the speaker is implied. The source constructions in this path are a family of complex constructions in which the addressee is invited to move towards the speaker, in order to undertake the desired action together with her/him ('come [and] (we will) do X', 'come in order to do X', 'come do X', etc.).

Let us consider Tetun again: besides the grammaticalization of *bá* as a directive marker for 2nd persons (example (10) in the preceding section), in this language there is also a directive strategy addressed to the speaker + the addressee that derives from the grammaticalization of the 2nd person directive form of 'come', *mai* (18a-b). The situation in (18a), in which *mai* is followed by the verb *bá* used in its lexical value of 'go', virtually implies a displacement by the addressee, i.e. this sentence can be used if the addressee is asked to join the speaker in performing the desired action, consisting in a displacement away from the speaker's place together with her/him (although this is not a necessary implication). In (18b), instead, the situation does not presuppose any motion towards the speaker, and *mai* is simply employed as a general directive marker for 1st person plural performers.

(18)   Tetun (Austronesian, Central Malayo-Polynesian)

    a. *ema   tene   ita   r-ak   "mai ita   bá nebá"*
       person invite 1PL.INCL 3PL-say come 1PL.INCL go there
       'People invite us saying "Let's go over there."' (motion implied)
                                         (Lumien van Klinken 1999: 208)

b. *mai   ita   hamulak*
   come 1PL.INCL pray
   'Let's pray.' (no motion implied)   (Lumien van Klinken 1999: 208)

Such complex constructions are still transparent in some cases, as in (19) and (20). In Leti, directives addressed to 1st person plural performers consist of two clauses conjoined by *=po* 'and then', the first of which shows the directive form of the verb 'come' inflected for person (2nd singular or plural), while the second one has a verb inflected for 1st person plural inclusive. In fast speech, the verb 'come' may occur uninflected, that is, without 2nd person singular or plural agreement markers.

(19)   Leti (Austronesian, Central Malayo-Polynesian)
      mmüapo tamtïètano
      mu-ma=po   ta-mtïètna=o
      2SG-come=then   1PL.INCL-sit=IND
      'Let's sit down.'   (van Engelenhoven and Williams-van Klinken 2005: 753)

In Ewe, the imperative of the verb 'come' is followed by an optional linker and by a verb inflected for 1st person plural imperative or subjunctive. This biclausal structure still expresses a complex situation made up of two distinct events. Yet, this structure is systematically used to encode orders to 1st + 2nd person performers.

(20)   Ewe (Niger-Congo, Kwa)

      vǎ/mi-vá   *(né)   mí-ḍu/mí-a-ḍu-i*   *nú*
      come.IMP.2SG/2PL-come   LK   1PL-eat/1PL-SBJV-eat-3SG   thing
      'Let's eat something/Come, let's eat!'[4]
                         (Ameka 2008: 155; see also Agbodjo and Litvinov 2001: 395)

---

4 Ewe SVCs with *va* followed by another verb may "either express concrete motion or the fact that something eventually happened" (Essegbey 2004: 474), as in the following example:

(i) *Kofi va   kpɔnɔvi-a*
    K.   come see sibling-def
    'Kofi came and saw his sibling/Kofi eventually saw his sibling.'

Although Ameka (2008: 156) does not attach any significance to the lack of the overt linker in structures such as (20), it must be remarked that the structure without the linker cannot be equated with a SVC, since in this case the second verb in the chain would remain uninflected. Therefore, it must be excluded that *va* has an aspectual meaning also when used in combination with other verbs in 1st + 2nd person directives.

In some languages, the construction derived from the 2nd person imperative of 'come' may co-exist with another strategy, and in such cases it is frequently typical of colloquial speech. A case in point is Modern Hebrew. In Modern Hebrew the future is normally used to convey orders to 1st person plural performers (21a). In the colloquial language, the future can be used in combination with the imperative form of the verb *ba'* 'come' (21b,c). This form can distinguish number and gender in the singular (*bo'* 'come:IMP.2SG.M'; *bo'i* 'come:IMP.2SG.F'; *bo'u* 'come:IMP.PL'), the choice depending on the number/gender of the addressee as in the following examples:

(21)   Modern Hebrew (Afro-Asiatic, Semitic)

a. *"n-ikanes   po"   ...ve-'arba't-am   nixns-u   le-mis'ad-a*
   FUT.1PL-enter here ...and-four-they enter-PST.3PL DIR-restaurant-F
   '"Let's drop in here" ... and the four of them entered the restaurant'
   (future verb form)   (Glinert 1989: 123; see also Malygina 2001: 271)

b. *bo'   n-ešev   ba-mxonit, xom gehinom baxuc*
   come:IMP.2SG.M FUT.1PL-sit in-car   hot hell   outside
   'Let's sit in the car, it's hot like hell in the street'
   (Glinert 1989: 123; see also Malygina 2001: 271)

c. *'im ken, bo'   n-itxalef   ba-tafkid-im*
   if   yes come:IMP.2SG.M FUT.1PL-exchange INSTR-role-PL.M
   'If so, let's swap our roles'
   (Glinert 1989: 123; see also Malygina 2001: 271)

The various manifestations of the grammaticalization path 'come' > directive all involve *a biclausal construction grammaticalizing into a monoclausal construction*: in all these processes, the verb originally meaning 'come' is reanalyzed as a marker of 1st + 2nd person directive, so that it is the whole configuration 'come + 1st person plural verb' that eventually conveys the directive meaning.

(22)   COME$_{[DIRECTIVE.2PERSON]}$ (AND/IN ORDER TO) DO$_{(1PL)}$ X

> 1ST + 2ND PERSON DIRECTIVE

The path schematized in (22) is fostered by the fact that situations in which the addressee is invited to join the speaker (i.e. to move towards her/him) in order to bring about the desired SoA together and orders addressed to the speaker + the addressee are functionally similar. Both situations indeed entail that the speaker and the addressee join one another before undertaking the requested action together. Such functional similarity motivates the processing of [*come* do$_{[1PL]}$ X] as a single unit, thus preparing the ground for the reanalysis of the verb meaning 'come' as a 1st person plural directive marker. As in the case of 'go' described above, the motion component becomes secondary in this grammaticalization path, and phenomena of loss of categorial status of the imperative of 'come' (e.g. loss of inflection, as in Leti fast speech) may accompany its reinterpretation as a directive marker.

The structure "come$_{IMP}$ + 1st person plural verb" is attested as a non-conventionalized way to convey orders to 1st person plural performers also in conversational data from some European languages. In spoken English, for instance, 1st person plural directives with *let's* are sometimes reinforced by the imperative of 'come', as in (23), whereas in some vernacular varieties of English (e.g. in Jamaican English) "come + 1st person plural indicative" is used as a strategy to convey orders to the speaker + the addressee (exx. (24)–(25)):

(23) *I'm naturally Scottish so that's erm **Come let's** hear your Scottish accent. No Why not? Hannah does that a lot, right, she goes to America and she comes back with an American accent, she goes to Scotland, she comes back with a Scottish accent* (British National Corpus; Chris, student, 15 years old, North-west Midlands)

(24) *If skin is to cut with lash, then **come we lash** the skin till water come down and wet the land* (lyrics from a sacrifice chant of Pocomania rituals, St. Thomas, Jamaica; http://www.fromjamaica.com/planet/blog/post/4949/)

(25) ***Come we go** down a Unity* (lyrics from a folk song; Cassidy 2007: 144)

Similarly, in colloquial French, the sequence *viens + on va faire x* ("come$_{IMP.2SG}$ + we are going to do x") is used as an expressive command strategy for 1st person plural performers, not necessarily in contexts in which the addressee is requested to move to the speaker's site:

(26) *"Ohlala, un tremblement de terre !!", "**Viens on va mettre à jour** notre statut sur Facebook !!"* (title of a Facebook fan page)
'Huh, an earthquake! Let's update our Facebook status!'

(27) *C'est facile à faire pour elle. Elle est l'adulte, elle a un grand pouvoir. Elle va créer des activités communes où elle va demander à l'enfant de participer innocemment : « **viens on va faire** des confitures ensemble », « **viens on va faire** la cuisine ensemble », « **viens on va faire** de la couture ensemble », « **viens on va faire** le ménage ensemble ».* (http://le-zinc-du-matin.over-blog.com/article-petite-fable-educative-45683810.html)

'It's easy for her to do it. She's the adult, she's got a special power. She's going to plan some common activities and she's going to innocently ask the baby to take part in them: "let's make some preserves together!", "let's cook together!", "let's sew together!", "let's do the housework together!"'

4 Conclusions

Data discussed in Sections 2 and 3 show that the development of directive strategies from 'come' and 'go' verbs is plausibly triggered by specific, recurrent conditions of directive speech acts, closely connected to the appeal conveyed to the hearer and to the identity of the performer. We are however left with a more general question: to what extent are the diachronic paths described determined and/or constrained by the original meaning of 'come' or 'go'? Can we account for the various developments by reference to their persistent original lexical semantics?

In the paths analyzed in this paper, 'come' and 'go' become the source of directives by virtue of the frequent connection between directive situations and some motion requested to the performer, thus suggesting that it is the 'displacement' component of these verbs that is crucially associated with directives. The logic underlying such recurrent association can be described as follows. In every directive situation, the speaker conveys an *appeal* to the addressee(s) to help make the desired SoA true and *expects* the desired SoA to be brought about right away. The source constructions discussed here contain themselves an *appeal to the addressee* to do something in order for the desired SoA to be brought about. The appeal refers to a preparatory condition (in the sense of Searle 1969: Ch. 3) through which the addressee favours the realization of the order, namely a *displacement*: 'go in order to realize the order', 'come in order to realize the order'. Motion occurs very frequently as a preliminary action in directive situations, and this is probably the motivation underlying the reanalysis of 'come' and 'go' as general directive markers.

The original lexical semantics of 'go' and 'come' is still observable in the first stage of their grammaticalization path, when the complex constructions [COME and/in order to DO X] and [GO (and/in order to) DO X] are systematically employed to convey ventive and itive/dislocative directive situations. Yet, their original lexical semantics is completely lost once they grammaticalize into general (non-motion) directive markers, nor is the directive function itself inherently connected to some notion of motion.

A provisional answer to the question of whether the various developments can be explained by reference to the persistent original lexical semantics of 'come' and 'go' could therefore be negative. The paths described are not *per se* determined by the original meaning of 'go' and 'come', but these verbs rather enter the process of grammaticalization because they imply some displacement, and displacement is *frequently necessary* in directive situations in order to realize the order. Clearly, the inherent semantics of the verbs makes their occurrence in directive situations frequent, but it is such *frequent co-occurrence* that triggers their reanalysis as directive markers.

However, the picture gets more complex if we consider whether and how the semantics of 'come' and 'go' may *constrain* the paths described. As widely argued throughout the paper, there appear to be a clear specialization of 'come' verbs for directives addressed to 1st person plural performers, and 'go' verbs for directives addressed to 2nd person performers and 1st person plural performers. In other words, the two lexical sources are not simply reanalyzed as directive markers *tout court*, but are reanalyzed as directive markers mostly when the performer coincides with one (or both) *speech act participant(s)*, and they do not extend to orders addressed to 3rd parties. This restriction is not attested in other paths from other lexical verbs, such as for instance *let* and other causative/ manipulative stems, which may evolve into directive markers available for all persons (Mauri & Sansò 2011: 3502ff; see also Mauri & Sansò 2012).

Given the fact that such restriction appears to be characteristic of directives derived from 'come' and 'go', it might be connected to the lexical semantics of the verbs, especially to their deictic component. Such a component only makes sense to performers who share the communicative situation with the speaker, since 3rd parties might already be distant from the place where the directive speech act is uttered and could therefore not be able to identify the deictic origo. Crucially, the fact that addressees must have direct access to the spatial deictic information of the speech act, at least in the source construction, could also constrain the successive diachronic developments of 'come' and 'go' as general directive markers, restricting the use of motion and non-motion directive markers derived from 'go' and 'come' to directive situations addressed to speech act participants, i.e. 1st and 2nd persons.

Therefore, we may provide a second, more complex answer to the question of whether the various developments can be explained by reference to the persistent original lexical semantics of 'come' and 'go', following our twofold analysis. First, a distinction has to be made between (i) the explanation of why 'come' and 'go' verbs are recurrent diachronic sources for directives and (ii) the explanation of why directives derived from 'come' and 'go' are restricted to orders addressed to speech act participants. Once such a distinction is made, we argue that the answer is negative in one case but positive in the other. In particular, the reason why 'come' and 'go' may be reanalyzed into directives is *not* connected to their lexical semantics, but rather to their frequent occurrence in directive situations. However, their original deictic semantics plausibly *plays a role* in constraining the *possible extensions* of their reanalysis, restricting the use of directives derived from 'come' and 'go' to orders addressed to speech act participants.

Abbreviations

AAP	absolutive antipassive
ASP	aspectual marker
EMPH	emphatic
EXCLAM	exclamative
HORT	hortative
INSTR	instrumental
LK	linker
MOD	modal suffix
MOT	motion
NFUT	non-future
PPM	proximal patient marker
PFV	perfective
SPM	subordinate patient marker
SUBORD	subordinator

References

Agbodjo, Kofi H. & Viktor P. Litvinov. 2001. Imperative sentences in Ewe. In Viktor S. Xrakovskij (ed.), *Typology of imperative constructions*, 390–403. Munich: Lincom Europa.

Aikhenvald, Alexandra Y. 2006. Serial verb constructions in typological perspective. In Alexandra Y. Aikhenvald & Robert M. W. Dixon (eds.), *Serial Verb Constructions. A Cross-linguistic Typology*, 1–68. Oxford: Oxford University Press

Aikhenvald, Alexandra Y. 2010. *Imperatives and commands*. Oxford: Oxford University Press.

Ameka, Felix K. 2008. Aspect and modality in Ewe: A survey. In Felix K. Ameka & Mary E. Kropp Dakubu (eds.), *Aspect and modality in Kwa languages*, 135–194. Amsterdam: John Benjamins.

Barrett, Edward R. 1999. *A grammar of Sipakapense Maya*. Austin: University of Texas at Austin dissertation.

Bystrov Igor S. & Nonna V. Stankevič. 2001. Imperative in Vietnamese. In Viktor S. Xrakovskij (ed.), *Typology of imperative constructions*, 461–474. Munich: Lincom Europa.

Cassidy, Frederic G. 2007. *Jamaica Talk. Three hundred years of the English language in Jamaica*. Kingston: University of West Indies Press.

Craig, Colette G. 1991. Ways to go in Rama: a case study in polygrammaticalization. In Elizabeth C. Traugott, & Bernd Heine (eds.), *Approaches to Grammaticalization*, 455–492. Amsterdam: John Benjamins.

Danielsen, Swintha. 2007. *Baure. An Arawak language of Bolivia*. Leiden: CNWS Publications.

Essegbey, James, 2004. Auxiliaries in serializing languages: on COME and GO verbs in Sranan and Ewe. *Lingua* 114: 473–494.

Glinert, Lewis. 1989. *The grammar of Modern Hebrew*. Cambridge: Cambridge University Press.

Hajek, John. 2006. Serial verbs in Tetun Dili. In Alexandra Y. Aikhenvald & Robert M. W. Dixon (eds.), *Serial Verb Constructions. A Cross-linguistic Typology*, 239–253. Oxford: Oxford University Press.

Heine, Bernd & Tania Kuteva. 2002. *World Lexicon of Grammaticalization*. Cambridge: Cambridge University Press.

Hofling, Charles A. & Fernando L. Ojeda. 1994. Yucatec Maya imperatives and other manipulative language. *International Journal of American Linguistics*. 60 (3): 272–294.

Kuteva, Tania. 2001. *Auxiliation: An enquiry into the nature of grammaticalization*. Oxford: Oxford University Press.

Lichtenberk, Frantisek. 2008. *A grammar of Toqabaqita*. Berlin & New York: Mouton de Gruyter.

Lumien van Klinken, Catherine. 1999. *A grammar of the Fehan dialect of Tetun*. Canberra: Pacific Linguistics.

Malygina, Ljudmila V. 2001. Imperative sentences in Modern Hebrew. In Viktor S. Xrakovskij (ed.), *Typology of imperative constructions*, 268–299. Munich: Lincom Europa.

Mauri, Caterina & Andrea Sansò. 2011. How directive constructions emerge: Grammaticalization, constructionalization, cooptation. *Journal of Pragmatics* 43: 3489–3521.

Mauri, Caterina, & Andrea Sansò. 2012. The reality status of directives and its coding across languages. *Language Sciences* 34: 147–170.

Nguyễn, Đinh-Hoà. 1997. *Vietnamese*. Amsterdam: John Benjamins.

Nicolle, Steve, 2007. The grammaticalization of tense markers: A pragmatic reanalysis. *Cahiers Chronos* 17: 47–65.

Pensalfini, Rob. 2003. *A grammar of Jingulu, An Aboriginal language of the Northern Territory*, Canberra: Pacific Linguistics.

Searle, John R., 1969. *Speech Acts: An Essay in the Philosophy of Language*. Cambridge University Press, Cambridge.

Spatar, Natalja M. 1997. Imperative constructions in Cambodian. *Mon-Khmer Studies* 27: 119–127.

van der Auwera, Johan, Nina Dobrushina & Valentin Goussev. 2003. A semantic map for Imperative-Hortatives. In Dominique Willelms, Bart Defrancq, Timothy Colleman & Dirk Noel (eds.), *Contrastive Analysis in Language. Identifying Linguistic Units of Comparison*, 44–68. Palgrave, New York.

van Engelenhoven, Aone & Catherine Williams-van Klinken. 2005. Tetun and Leti. In Alexander Adelaar & Nikolaus P. Himmelmann (eds.), *The Austronesian Languages of Asia and Madagascar*, 735–768. London: Routledge.

Veselinova, Ljuba N. 2006. *Suppletion in verb paradigms. Bits and pieces of a puzzle*. Amsterdam: John Benjamins.

Williams-van Klinken Catherine, John Hajek & Rachel Nordlinger. 2002. *Tetun Dili. A grammar of an East Timorese language*. Canberra: Pacific Linguistics.

Discourse functions

Ana Bravo
The Spanish auxiliary *ir* 'to go': from resultative motion verb to focus marker[1]

1 Spanish standard constructions with the auxiliary verb *ir* 'to go' + infinitive and standard grammaticalization paths

Spanish presents two clearly different constructions with the auxiliary verb *ir* 'to go' plus an infinitive.[2] In one of them *ir* expresses either prospective aspect or future tense – depending on the author – in the same way that its English and its French counterparts do, as is shown in (1):[3]

(1)　a.　*{Va / Iba} a llover.*
　　　b.　*It {is / was} going to rain.*
　　　c.　*Il {va / allait} pleuvoir.*

The second construction, recognized as productive and different from the prospective periphrasis only in a few works (Gómez Torrego (1999), Fernández de Castro (1999) and RAE-ASALE (2009)), is exemplified in (2):

(2)　*La　pelota　rebotó　　　　　　　y　fue　　　　　　　a　dar*
　　　The　ball　　bounce.3SG.PAST.PFV　and　go.3SG.PAST.PFV　to　hit.INF
　　　contra　la　ventana.
　　　against　the　window[4]
　　　'The ball bounced and it ended up hitting the window.'
　　　'The ball bounced and it happened to hit the window.'

1 I am very grateful to Paloma Andrés, Ignacio Bosque, Brenda Laca, Elena de Miguel and Manel Pérez-Saldanya for their valuable comments and discussion on the topic, as well as for their help in collecting the examples. I am also deeply in debt to two anonymous reviewers as well as to the editors of this volume, and, in particular to Jenneke van der Wal, whose pertinent remarks have substantially improved the shortcomings of the first version of this paper. All errors are mine only.
2 The term *construction* is used just as a descriptive label equivalent to 'syntactic string'.
3 Some recent works on contemporary Spanish *ir a* + infinitive are Laca (2005), Camus (2006), Bravo (2008) and RAE-ASALE (2009: 2154–2160), to cite just a few. Diachronic issues are specially addressed in Aaron (2006), Mellis (2005, 2006) and Pérez-Saldanya (2008).
4 I am assuming that *to* is the allative preposition correspondent to the Spanish directional preposition *a*, and not part of the infinitive. Although nothing important hinges on the

In this case, the construction with *ir* is aspectually perfective. In addition, it is said to typically highlight the situation referred to with the infinitive by presenting it as the last one in a sequence of previous eventualities (here the bouncing of the ball). For this reason it is considered to be a synonym to *acabar* 'to end' + gerund, Eng. *end (up)* + *-ing*, that is, a sort of a discourse marker along the proposal of Dietrich (1973) for Sp. *acabar* + gerund, and not a perfective marker, so (2) is equivalent to (3):

(3) *La pelota rebotó y acabó dando contra la ventana.*
     'The ball bounced and it ended up hitting the window.'

In Section 3.1 I will depart from this analysis and I will defend that *ir* in (2) is a resultative semi lexical verb (IR$_{res}$).

Apart from the prospective and the resultative constructions in (1) and (2), the Spanish auxiliary *ir* 'to go' may function as a focus marker in a construction that has passed almost unnoticed as such until now.[5] An example is given in (4), where the brackets and the subscript *f* indicate a focused constituent:

(4) *Fue   a llover   [el   día de mi boda]$_f$*
     go.AUX.3SG.PAST.PFV to rain.INF the day of my wedding
     'Of all the days of the year, it had to rain my wedding day.'

For the construction with the form *ir* 'to go' + *y* 'and' + a tensed verb, as in *Juan va y se cae* 'John goes and falls', Arnaiz and Camacho (1999) have argued that the auxiliary *ir* functions as a topic auxiliary; however, if there is a topic, a focus is also to be expected, so a relationship may be asserted to exist between the auxiliary verb in (4) and this topic auxiliary.[6] Nevertheless, the study of both the grammatical properties of this construction and the possible connections among resultative, sequential and focus markers lays outside of the scope of the present investigation.

---

decision, nevertheless it has not necessarily to be like that, as Eckardt (2006: 115, 119 fn.15) has pointed out (also Roberts and Roussou (2003: 103–110)).

5 In Mexico, Central America and most parts of the Caribe the focus auxiliary is *venir* 'to come' (RAE-ASALE 2009: § 28.8j):

(i) *El   carro se   nos   vino   a romper   [en el   peor momento]$_f$.*
     The car SE.REFL we.DAT come.3SG.PAST.PFV to break.INF in the worst moment
     'The car had to get broken in the worst moment'

6 The *ir* in this construction can be considered as an instance of the grammaticalization path that turn 'go' verbs into sequential markers or markers of textual connectivity (see Bybee, Perkins and Pagliuca (1994: 59), Heine and Kuteva (2002: 156–157) and Bourdin (2008)).

The aim of this paper is twofold. First, it attempts to describe the focus construction (IR_{focus}) in (4) as both semantically and syntactically independent from the resultative construction in (2) in synchronic terms. If I am right, then Spanish *ir* offers additional support for recent studies showing that 'go' verbs can also grammaticalize into focus markers (Devos and van der Wal (2010) for the Bantu language Shangaci, and Carlson – in this volume – for Supyire).

Secondly, it aims at describing the possible grammaticalization trend followed by the focus construction. As will be shown, the focus construction (IR_{focus}) develops out of the resultative one (IR_{res}).[7] Specifically, the process will be analyzed as an instance of a semantic change that – following Eckardt (2006)– takes place under syntactic reanalysis. It will, in addition, turn out from my research that, although some semantic features of the lexical motion verb *ir* (IR_{lex}) form the basis for the development of IR_{res}, these are absent in IR_{focus}, a proposal that challenges the semantic retention hypothesis (Bybee, Perkins and Plagiuca 1994), if it is correct. The consequences that follow for a theory of grammaticalization will be examined along with the conclusions in the last part of this contribution.

This chapter is organized as follows. In Section 2 I present the basic postulates on grammaticalization that I assume; in Section 3 the syntactic and semantic properties of the two constructions will be given; Section 4 is devoted to explaining how the focus construction develops out of the resultative construction. In Section 5 I present a summary with the major findings.

2 Some assumptions about grammaticalization

There are by now some widely accepted hypotheses concerning the phenomenon of grammaticalization and, for this reason, in this paper I will assume them without further discussion.[8] Hence, I stick here to the very general definition of grammaticalization as a linguistic mechanism by virtue of which some lin-

---

7 It should be noted that, as far as I know, we still don't know the diachrony of the resultative construction, maybe because it has not been yet recognized as such. Pérez-Saldanya (2003: 78, fn.10 and p.c.) maintains that the resultative construction and the purposive (perfective in his analysis) construction are independent one of the other. The description in Section 3.1 supports this hypothesis. See specially Section 3.1.5.

8 This does not amount to saying that there is no discussion at all, but it is not the purpose of this paper to go over the different problems that the notion of grammaticalization raises. Some of them are critically reviewed in Haspelmath (1999), Campbell (2001), Heine (2001) and Eckardt (2006: 47–51), among many other references.

guistic element develops into something more grammatical.[9] In the following, I will concentrate on the properties of what Eckardt (2006) calls "semantic change under reanalysis", which is the sort of language change that is operating in the phenomenon under study (as opposed to analogy or borrowing) and I will rely mainly on Harris and Campbell (1995) and Eckardt (2006).[10]

3.1 Reanalysis: definitions and implications

There is no unique definition of reanalysis (see Traugott and Trousdale (2010: 33) for a brief overview). Langacker's characterization is one of the most cited: a "change in the structure of an expression or class of expressions that does not involve any immediate or intrinsic modification of its surface manifestation" (Langacker 1977: 58). Eng. *be going to*, and equally Sp. *ir a* + infinitive, offers a very well known example of reanalysis, that is, of a reorganization of the underlying structure that leaves the surface structure unaffected – (5) is from Hopper and Traugott (2003: 2–3) and (6) has been adapted from Pérez-Saldanya and Hualde (2003):

(5) a. [*I am going* [*to marry John*]].
     b. [*I am going to*] *marry John*]].

(6) a. [$_{Sentence1}$ *Yo$_i$ voy a* [$_{Sentence2}$ *Ø$_i$ casarme con Juan*]]]. (=5a)
     b. [$_{Sentence1}$*Yo$_i$* [$_{Aspectual Phrase}$ *voy a* [*yo$_i$ casarme con Juan*]]]. (=5b)

In formal approaches to language, and to language change, reanalysis affects constituency ("rebracketing"), hierarchical structure, category labels and grammatical structure, including selectional and combinatorial properties (Harris and Campbell (1995: 62–65), Eckardt (2006: ch. 1 and 2), see also Roberts and Roussou (2003: Introduction)).

Reanalysis, consequently, produces a second analysis that continues alongside the former structure (Harris and Campbell 1995: 72). In fact, as Fischer (2007: 145) observes, strictly speaking, reanalysis may not exist. That is, a speaker who

---

9 A detailed overview of the evolution of the theory can be found in Hopper and Traugott (2003: ch. 2). A summary of the definitions is given in Campbell and Janda (2001).
10 The way reanalysis and grammaticalization are related to each other has been extensively discussed in the relevant literature. See, among many others, Haspelmath (1998), Campbell (2001), Roberts and Roussou (2003: 1–2), Eckardt (2006: 22, 27), de Smet (2009) and Traugott and Trousdale (2010: 33–35), and references therein.

innovates does not substitute structure represented in (5a) and (6a) above for those represented in (5b) and (6b), abandoning as a consequence the structures in (a). Instead, reanalysis brings about a new construction type (also Harris and Campbell 1995: 70–71). Eckardt (2006: ch. 1 and 2), on her part, emphasizes the fact that "meaning change under reanalysis can lead to denotations that had no previous conceptual status and only become a desirable denotatum in the course of the reanalysis in question" (Eckardt 2006: 45–46). In this contribution I will defend that this is the case for the change $IR_{res} > IR_{focus}$.

The existence of multiple analyses of a sentence structure has other practical as well as theoretical consequences, such as the need for specifying whether the relation between the old item and the new one (*be going to* in (5) and *ir a* in (6)) is one of homonymy, polysemy or both – if the whole process of grammaticalization is considered. Following Traugott and Trousdale (2010: 32), and Fischer (2007: 145), I accept as correct the hypothesis that both items – in this case IR_{res} and IR_{focus} – are related by homonymy (see also Hopper and Traugott 2003: 77–78).

Eckardt (2006) adopts a compositional semantic approach in order to make the change under study as explicit as possible. She assumes that speakers are "*somehow* able to make the required semantic shifts" (Eckardt 2006: 3; emphasis in the original). More specifically, Eckardt argues – and this is her theory's main point – that if a combination of words is given a new structure, as soon as it receives a new meaning, a semantic equation is created that the speaker must resolve much in the same way as he resolves a mathematical equation like $5 + 3 + x = 12$: "The (understood) meaning of the overall sentence and the meanings of the stable parts will determine the 'missing bit', i.e. the hypothetical new meaning x for the item-under-change. Speakers can bridge the gap between sentence and word" (Eckardt 2006: 13). Roberts and Roussou (2003: 15) seem to share the same hypothesis when making reference to a 'substring of the input text'. I agree that such a degree of specificity in the description is necessary and hence, it will also be the approach adopted here.

Another hypothesis that Eckardt puts forward is that these supposed new meanings are not at all provisional, vague or subject to further adjustments. On the contrary, "speakers use the newly emerged words, constructions or phrases with great confidence and conciseness. Grammaticalization [...] and other instances of reanalysis generally do not evoke a feeling of uneasiness in those who use the new item" (Eckardt 2006: 13). In other words, right from the initial stages of change the grammatical content of the new item is fully specified in the speaker's lexicon.

Two consequences follow from the theory just sketched: one theoretical, and one empirical. Theoretically, change can only be discrete, and hence, abrupt

(Eckardt 2006: 55, 236, 239–242). As this is still an unsettled question, I am just going to adopt it as a consequence of working within a formal framework, but for a recent overview, see Traugott and Trousdale (2010). Empirically, in semantic change under reanalysis there are a pre-stage, the morphosyntactic and semantic situation before the change, and a post-stage, the morphosyntactic and semantic situation after the change, and both are equally specific and concise in meaning and they need to be described as such. In the change under examination, IR_{res} is the pre-stage and IR_{focus} is the post-stage. Section 3 below is devoted to make the grammatical content of these two stages as explicit as possible.

In the next section I discuss the issue of what triggers the grammaticalization process, an equally debated question.

2.2 Why? Reanalysis as grammaticalization of inferences

There are different accounts that try to explain what triggers reanalysis. In Eckardt (2006), taking as the departing point Traugott and Dasher's Generalized Invited Inferences theory (Traugott and Dasher 2001), it is argued that meaning change under reanalysis is driven by pragmatic inferencing and subsequent conventionalization. This pragmatically inferred new proposition must be supported both by the context and by the syntactic and semantic structure of the construction under change. That is, reanalysis begins when the speaker adopts "a tentative new semantic and syntactic analysis for some given sentence", a new semantic analysis that must be "pragmatically salient" (Eckardt 2006: 234). The schema in (7) shows that pragmatic inferencing functions as a bridge between the pre-stage and the post-stage (Eckardt 2006: 239):

(7) Step 1: non ambiguous PRE-STAGE[11]
    Be going to: meaning 'motion'. Lexical verb.

    Step 2: ambiguous PRE-STAGE
    Pragmatic inferencing + onset context + syntactic reanalysis.

    Step 3: POST-STAGE
    Be going to post-stage: Target meaning: 'imminence'.
    Target category: auxiliary verb.

According to Eckardt (2006: 9–11, 34–46), hence, the following scenario is necessary in order for a syntactic reanalysis with a concomitant semantic change to

---

11 For a detailed analysis, see Eckardt (2006: ch. 6).

happen —see also Section 4. Firstly, there must be some communicative situations where the word under change is used. Secondly, the entire sentence containing the old word must give rise to pragmatically driven inferences. These pragmatically driven inferences convey information beyond the literal meaning expressed by the sentence. Up to this point, the hearer has access to two messages: the literal message and a side message. In the last step, the hearer, under certain circumstances, would feel "invited [...] to adopt a new lexical entry to her mental lexicon" (Eckardt 2006: 9). With such an operation, the surface form of the word under change is paired with the new syntactic and semantic information. Crucially, the hearer will make this move "even though she initially understood the sentence on the basis of the old lexical entry for the item. Otherwise she would not have understood anything" (Eckardt 2006: 9).

Given that not every situation of pragmatic inferencing is also a situation that triggers reanalysis it becomes evident that there must be something else in addition to these pragmatic invited inferences. Eckardt (2006) argues that this extra requisite is what she calls "the onset context of reanalysis" (Eckardt 2006: 10, 42, 50–54): this is the "context of use that offered the right kind of structural and semantic ambiguity plus instigation factors", that is, factors dependent on specific utterances of the old construction such that they invite the hearer to change her lexicon.[12] Finally, it is accepted that reducing processing efforts must somehow play an important role in reanalysis (Kuteva 2001: 179; Eckardt 2006: 244–247).

3 The resultative construction and the focus construction: semantic and syntactic properties

Recall that one of Eckardt's strongest theses is that meaning change under reanalysis proceeds in two discrete stages (a pre-stage and a post-stage), plus a trigger, and that the speaker possesses specific lexical information about the semantic and syntactic nature both of the old word and the new word (see Section 2.1 above). The description of the syntax and the semantics of IR_{res} and IR_{focus} will show that, in effect, they must be kept apart.

---

12 On the differences between Eckardt's onset context and Heine's (2002) "bridging context" see Eckardt (2006: 51–53).

3.1 The resultative construction

3.1.1 Introduction

In this section I present the syntactic and semantic properties of IR$_{res}$. I particularly concentrate on those properties relevant for the topic under discussion. I contend that IR$_{res}$ is a semi lexical motion verb with its own argument structure and different from IR$_{lex}$: IR$_{res}$ forms a complex predicate with its complement (a Goal Chain) and is not agentive. In the last part of this section I very briefly address the problem of the relationship between IR$_{lex}$ and IR$_{res}$. My analysis is that they are independent one of the other both in synchronic and diachronic terms.

3.1.2 Some data and one hypothesis

Example (2) is repeated below as (8):

(8)   *La   pelota rebotó   y   fue   a dar*
       The ball   bounce.3SG.PAST.PFV and go.3SG.PAST.PFV to hit.INF
      contra la ventana.
      against the window
      'The ball bounced and it ended up hitting the window.'
      'The ball bounced and it happened to hit the window.'

Examples in (9) are taken from different sources and different stages and varieties of Spanish:

(9)   a. *Mas el Rey le dio al cavallo en el rostro con la espada tal golpe, que la no pudo sacar, y el cavallo enarmonóse y **fue caer** sobre el cavallero.*
        (Garci Rodríguez de Montalvo, *Amadís de Gaula*, libros I y II, end of 13th century, CORDE)
        'But the King gave the horse such a strike with his sword that he was not able to take it out, so the horse reared up and ended up falling over the knight.'[13]

    b. *Los peñascos rodaban precipicio abajo, hasta saltar en el vacío e **ir a chocar** en la pared del otro cerro.*
       'Stones rolled down the precipice, fell into the space and ended up hitting the wall on the other hill.'

---

13 Translations are approximate.

c. *En lo más vivo de su soliloquio, vaciló y **fue a chocar** contra la puerta.*
(B. Pérez Galdós, *Miau*, 1888, CORDE)
'In the middle of his soliloquy, he happened to totter and as a result he crashed against the door.'

d. *Los muebles [...], llevados por el viento, **habían ido a caer** en pleno campo.* (A. Carpentier, *El Siglo de las luces*, 1962, via Google, 14.04.2012)
'All the furniture [...], taken away by the wind, had gone and fallen right in the countryside.'

e. *Pasó el proyectil zumbando sobre nuestras cabezas y **fue a estallar** a escasos metros del casco de la nave.* (Eduardo Mendoza, *El último trayecto de Horacio*, 21st century, via Google, 03.04.2012)
'The projectile whizzed over our heads and it ended up exploding close to our boat.'

As becomes clear in the correspondent translations, it seems that *ir* is a (semi-) lexical verb expressing motion (see (9d)) and introducing a result (see (9c)). To that effect, compare the sentences in (9) with the sentences in (10):

(10)   a. *Ejemplos hay de guerreros insignes que **han ido a ocupar** lugar preferente en el Cielo, sólo por una buena batallita ganada contra herejes.*
(B. Pérez Galdós, *El equipaje del rey José*, 1875, via Google 14/04/12)
'There are examples of notable warriors who have ended up occupying a preferential place in the sky thanks only to one battle won against the heretics.'

b. *[El] ardor revolucionario que **fue a encender**, lejos de sus lares, el ánimo excelso de...* (L. Villanueva, *Vida del valiente ciudadano General Ezequiel Zamora*, 1898, via Google, 12/04/12)
'The revolutionary fervour that happened to light, far away from their houses, the sublime courage of...'

Apparently in all of the examples in (9), but not in those of (10), there is a path traversed by the subject. In fact, for the resultative construction I propose the analysis in (11):

(11) The resultative construction

1. It consists of two subevents: a process, introduced by IR$_{res}$, and a resultant state, selected by IR$_{res}$ as an inherently directed motion goal verb.

    a. The process will be interpreted as a subevent of motion if a locative preposition is selected by the infinitive verb (as in (12a)).

    b. Otherwise it will be interpreted as the process preceding a subsequent event (as in (12b)).

2. Any property of this construction can be explained in terms of the syntax and the semantics of IR$_{res}$.[14]

Syntactically (elaborating on Ramchand 2008: ch. 5):

(12) a. *La pelota fue a dar contra la ventana.* (=8)

$[_{VPProcess}$ Fue$_j$ $[_{ResultativeP}$ a$_j$ $[_{VP}$ la pelota $[v°_j$ dar $[_{ResultativePP}$ contra$_j$ [DP la ventana]]]]]].

b. *El ardor fue a encender el ánimo.* (=10b)

$[_{VPProcess}$ Fue$_j$ $[_{ResultativeP}$ a$_j$ $[_{VP}$ el ardor $[v°_j$ encender [DP el ánimo]]]]]].

I take as a point of departure the following assumptions regarding the semantics of inherently directed motion verbs in general, and of *ir* 'to go' in particular.

(13a) is the conceptual structure (Jackendoff 1990) for the motion verb *ir* 'to go' as in *Juan fue a la biblioteca* 'John went to library'. (13b) could be the conceptual structure of *ir* 'to go' when it selects for an infinitive as in *Juan fue a comprar pan* 'John went to buy bread':

(13) a. $[_{Event}$ IR$[_{-Here}]$ $([_{Object}$ X], $[_{Path}$ A (Ø [Place])])].

    b. $[_{Event}$ IR $([_{Object}$ X], [Event])].[15]

---

14 An anonymous reviewer correctly points out to me that the role the perfective aspect plays in the meaning of IR$_{res}$ cannot be obviated. The same reviewer observes that closely related to this point is the fact that the temporal relation between the two subevents is one of quasi-simultaneity, something I would take as evidence in favour of analyzing IR$_{res}$ as a semi lexical verb. Unfortunately, I will not be able to deal with any of these issues here. A detailed discussion can be found in Melis (2005, 2006).

15 It is not that obvious that the preposition *a* 'to' in Spanish introduces a Path in *Juan fue a comprar.* In French, as well as in Medieval Spanish, there is no preposition at all. Regarding Eng. *to*, recall what was said in note 3. If a conceptual structure such a (13a) is assumed for this construction, with Place being substituted by Event, sentences as **Juan fue hacia comprar* lit. *John went towards to shop* could be expected to be possible along with *Juan fue hacia Madrid*

In accordance with the lexical semantics of *ir*, the situation described by the infinitive denotes the goal of the path. In effect, inherently directed motion verbs are said to lexically incorporate the goal. In addition, as is well known (Talmy 2000, 2: 49–53, Demonte 2011 and references cited therein)), Sp. *ir* merges the Motion and the Path components. More specifically, it has lexically incorporated a resultative path, which explains that, in the absence of an explicit PP (as in *Juan fue* lit. 'John went'), the only possible interpretation is one in which the PP denotes a specific goal introduced by the directional preposition *a*. Hence *Juan fue* must be interpreted as *Juan fue a* x 'John went to x' where the x denotes a specific place.[16] The preposition *a* 'to' denotes the goal of a Path and selects, in its turn, a resultative preposition, which in Spanish is realized as Ø (see Jackendoff 1990, Zwarts 2010 to cite just a few). The main difference between (13a) and (13b) is, hence, that as long as the second conceptual constituent in (13b) does not denote a Path, but an Event, it cannot denote a location either. If its meaning is not locative, it cannot, in consequence, be understood that the Theme ends up in this location. In short, to the extent that the second argument of *ir* 'to go' in (13b) is not a location the resultative meaning is absent from (13b):

(14)

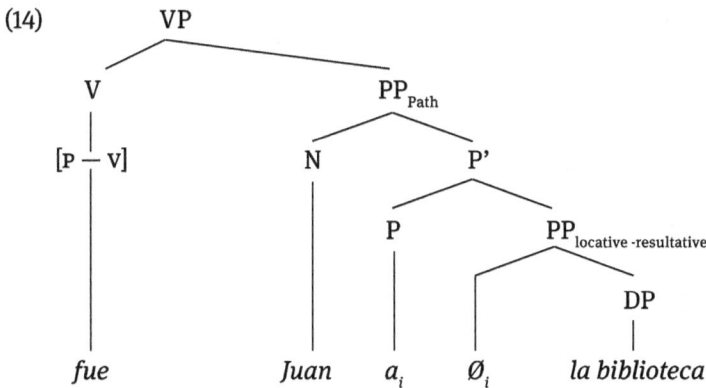

Going back to IR$_{res}$, I argue that in spite of its surface similarity with the construction in which *ir* takes an infinitive, it shares more properties with *ir* as a lexical motion verb with the conceptual structure of (13a). This is, in effect, the way the contrast in (15) must be interpreted:

---

lit. *John went towards Madrid*. But this is not the case. My hypothesis is, hence, that they are two different objects (see Bravo 2008: ch. 7 for further argumentation). The current analysis defends, instead, a metaphorical reinterpretation of the denotation of the infinitive as a Place (or a Goal) – see Olbertz (1998: 233–234) Melis (2005, 2006), Pérez Saldanya (2008).

16 Arguments in favour of the directionality of Spanish *a* 'to/at' are examined in Torrego (2002) and Demonte (2011), among others; see also Zubizarreta and Oh (2007: 152).

(15) a. *Juan fue a comprar pan, pero finalmente no lo compró.*
       'John went to buy bread, but he finally didn't buy it.'

      b. *Juan fue a París * pero no llegó a París.*
       'John went to Paris but he did not arrive to Paris.'

      c. *Juan dio tres vueltas y fue a chocar contra la puerta, *pero no chocó.*
       'John spun three times before going and hitting the door, but he didn't
       hit it.'

It is (15a) which is deviant with respect to the lexical verb with a spatial PP in
(15b). IR_{res}, on its part, aligns with the inherently directed motion verb *ir* of (13a).
From (15c) it can be concluded that the construction denotes a telic event (more
or less complex, as it will be explained) and that it implies the attainment of the
goal.

3.1.3 The subevent of motion

There exist at least three potential counterarguments for the hypothesis
advanced in (11). I will first present them and I will show that they allow for an
explanation that is compatible with the hypothesis that IR_{res} denotes a subevent
of motion.

In the first place, the infinitival complement cannot be substituted by
adónde 'where':

(16) *¿Adónde fueron los muebles?# A caer en medio del campo.* (=(9d))
       'Where did all the furniture go? To fall right in the middle of the country-
       side.'

However, this is as expected if IR_{res} selects for a resultant state (see (12)) and not
for an argument denoting a Path, as lexical *ir* does (see (13a)).[17]

Secondly, if there were a subevent of going, it should be visible for different
grammatical processes, a prediction that is not born out. For example, the two
events cannot be expressed independently by two clauses, as the ungrammaticality of (17) shows:

---

17 In any case, in as much as there is a lot of variability in the possibilities these test of sub-
stitutions offer, they are not very useful. Thus the it-clefted version of *¿Adónde fue? A comprar*
'Where did he go? To buy' is much worse: ??/* *A comprar es adonde fue* 'It is to buy where he
went'.

(17)   *El chocó contra la puerta a consecuencia de un evento de ir.*
        'He ran into the door as a consequence of an event of going.'

English causative resultatives and other resultatives, on the contrary, not being lexically determined, allow for such a paraphrase (see Levin and Rappaport (1995: 58), among many others):

(18)   a. *John hammered the metal flat.*
            'John hammered the metal and this caused it to become flat.'

        b. *John danced out of the room.*
            'John went out of the room by dancing.'

However, as Levin and Rappaport (1995: 58) recall, a paraphrase with the two events is never available when the resultant state is lexically implied by the semantics of the predicate. That is, *John went to Paris* cannot be paraphrased as 'The event of John's going caused John to be in Paris'. Thus, the restriction in (17) is not particular of IR$_{res}$. Furthermore, if it is a restriction that follows from the semantics of *ir*, this would suggest that IR$_{res}$ shares with the motion verb *ir* this particular feature of its semantics, namely, it would also have lexically incorporated a resultative path.

   Thirdly, adjuncts modifying this subevent of going should be accepted, but they are not:

(19)   a. *Juan fue a comprar el pan {en autobús / andando / a paso rápido}*
            'John went to buy the bread by bus', 'John ran to buy the bread',
            'John walked quickly to buy the bread.'

        b. *La pelota fue dando botes a dar contra la ventana.* (see (8))
            'The ball bounced to hit the window.'

        c. *Las piedras fueron rodando a caer por el precipicio.* (see (9b))
            'The stones rolled to fall over the precipice.'

The impossibility of combining with manner adjuncts that modify the subevent of going is only partially true, as the examples in (20) show:

(20)   a. *Las piedras fueron, rodando, a chocar contra la pared.*
            'The stones went and hit against the wall by rolling.'

        b. *La pelota, dando botes, fue a dar contra la ventana.*
            'The ball went and hit against the window by bouncing.'

In (20) the adjunct modifies the whole VP (the VP Process in (12)), and not only the motion verb, and the sentence is well formed. Thus, the question now is what makes (20) grammatical. The answer is the moving subevent introduced by resultative *ir*. Hence, it is not that there is not a moving subevent, but that *ir* introduces a defective motion verb (V1), and not a complete VP, into which the lexical verb (V2) and the preposition incorporate to form a goal resultative (directional or not) chain. This chain is very similar to the Tense-Chain of Guéron and Hoekstra (1988), as the syntactic structure in (12) shows.[18] The situation denoted by V2 and its complements is interpreted in terms of describing the endpoint of the previous process of displacement. The inherently directed resultative prepositional phrase licenses the selectional restrictions of IR_{res} via syntactic incorporation of V2 into V1.

In effect, another argument in favour of analyzing *ir* as a resultative motion verb in (12) is the fact that the number of verbs that enter in this combination is very reduced as well as the prepositional phrases they accept as complements: *chocar contra* ('to crash against, hit against)'), *{dar / clavarse} {contra ~ en}* ('to {hit ~ stick} {against ~ on}), *{salir / entrar} por* ('to go {in ~ out} through'), *{caer / aterrizar} {contra ~ en ~ sobre ~ dentro}* ('to fall / to land' {against ~ into ~ inside }'). Crucially, the prepositions the infinitive combines with are all prepositions that denote either a Path and a Location or just a Location. Gawron (1986), in fact, proposes that it is the preposition itself that introduces the element of motion, as in *John breaks the vase against the floor* (with motion of the object), vs. *John breaks the vase* (without motion).[19] Hence, both V2 and the preposition contribute the resultative locative meaning required by IR_{res} compositionally in the syntax. As expected, if neither V2 nor the preposition conveys this meaning, the process denoted by IR_{res} will be just interpreted as a previous subevent.

Finally, prepositions such as *de* 'from' or *hacia* 'towards' are rejected either on semantic grounds (the Source meaning of *de* being incompatible with the directed motion content of *ir*) or due to aspectual reasons in the case of *hacia*, a non delimited preposition.

One more property may be associated with the existence of a subevent of going: the absence of agentivity. This is the topic of the next section.

---

18 See Cardinaletti and Giusti (2001) for other examples of semi-lexical motion verbs.
19 See also Zwarts (2000). For Jackendoff (1990: 53) selectional restrictions are already in the semantics of the predicate.

3.1.4 Semantic unaccusativity and the lack of agentivity

In the construction with IR$_{res}$ the subject cannot be the initiator or the controller – whether internal or external (see Levin and Rappaport Hovav (1995: 91)– of the displacement, that is, it is not a semantic agent, contrary to what happens with lexical *ir*:

(21)   a. *Juan fue a Madrid para visitar a sus padres.*
          'John went to Madrid in order to visit his parents.'

       b. #*Juan tropezó y fue a caer en un charco para divertir a sus amigos.*
          'John stumbled and he decided to fall into the puddle in order to amuse his friends.'

If the subject is able to decide the goal of the displacement, as in (21), only the meaning correspondent to *ir* as a lexical motion verb remains available. Similarly, depending on whether the subject in (22) can control the goal of the trajectory, the sentence will be interpreted as referring to a motion event, as in (22a), or to the resultant state, as in (22b):

(22)   *Juan fue a encender los ánimos revolucionarios.*

       a. 'John went somewhere in order to light the revolutionary spirit'
       b. 'It happened that John in the end lit the revolutionary spirit'

Obviously, if the subject is [-animate], the resultative interpretation is the preferred, if not the only possibility:

(23)   *La noticia fue a encender los ánimos revolucionarios.*
       'The news had as a consequence that it lit the revolutionary spirit'

This lack of agentivity correlates, crucially, with the semantic unaccusativity of motion verbs (Levin and Rappaport Hovav 1995: 162–165). In fact, the hypothesis that I want to defend here is that the absence of agentivity is a consequence of IR$_{res}$ being a motion verb. This is to be expected if IR$_{res}$ is syntactically defective and does not project a complete vP (see (12)). Above IR$_{res}$ we would hence not find any projection hosting the instigator feature (an Initiator Phrase in terms of Ramchand 2008). There seems to be a strong correlation between being a semantically unaccusative motion verb and introducing a process that in turn selects a result.

    To sum up, IR$_{res}$ presents the following properties. The verbal phrase it heads describes a complex event consisting of a subevent of going and a subevent that denotes the end point of this displacement through the preposition selected by V2. As an inherently directed motion verb IR_{res} is semantically unaccusative. The motion denoted is not internally caused nor controlled. The endpoint is attained (see (15c)). As long as there is a subject that moves along a path, the subject measures out the event, what allows to interpret the subevent as a process.

3.1.5 Where does IR_{res} come from?

Although it is not very frequent, 'go' verbs can grammaticalize into perfective, completive, anterior or past markers in general (Bybee, Perkins and Pagliuca 1994: ch. 3); when this is the case, it seems that they do so as emphatic particles or, at least, they can convey an expressive meaning (Ebert 1987). Likewise, IR_{res} might well have developed out of IR_{lex}. However, there exist two arguments, one empirical and one theoretical, against this analysis. I very briefly present the two of them below.

i)   Inherently directed motion verbs, as *ir*, in spite of the fact of being unaccusative, can be used agentively (see, among others, Jackendoff (1990) and Levin and Rappaport (1995: 162–163)), which amounts to defending that somewhere in the derivation there is a projection hosting this feature. The path $IR_{lex} > IR_{res}$ implies the suppression of this extra projection. Nevertheless, from a theoretical point of view, this step seems to be unmotivated and rather "expensive": it dispenses with an extra feature that it is not in the lexical semantics of the verb, but which is added to. To undo something done before might be thought of as a forward-backward movement, and hence, as expensive. The question is whether *ir*, at least in Spanish, has been in any stage of the language an unaccusative verb with no agentive properties on the part of the subject.

ii) Historically, both IR_{res} and IR_{lex} are available from the very beginning. See also the discussion in Section 5.1

My claim, hence, is that IR_{res} develops as an independent semi lexical verb different from IR_{lex}.

3.2 The focus construction

The focus construction with *ir* was illustrated in (4) above, repeated here as (24), and further examples below, see especially (32):

(24) *Fue*   *a llover*   [*el   día de mi   boda*]$_f$.
      go.AUX.3SG.PAST.PFV to rain.INF the day of my wedding
      'Of all the days of the year, it had to rain on my wedding day.'

My claim is that *ir* in (24) functions as a scalar focus marker. As such it is specified with the features [+focal], [+scalarity] in the lexicon. In syntax it will head its own functional projection. My analysis relies on the fact that IR$_{focus}$ shares with other focus markers, such as *only, even...*, at least the following relevant properties, which I number from 1 to 5.[20]

1) Its semantic effect is contributing a set of alternative propositions of the same type of the ordinary proposition (Rooth 1994: 276; König 1991: 32). It also presupposes the corresponding sentence without *ir* and is distinct from it. Finally, as other focus particles (*only, even*), IR$_{focus}$ requires a focus constituent in its environment to associate with; otherwise, the sentence is ungrammatical.

2) It shares also with other focus particles the feature of being scalar: it induces an ordering ranking into the set of alternative propositions (Hoeksema and Zwarts 1991; König 1991: 37–42).

3) The propositions in the set of alternative propositions are ordered in such a way that IR$_{focus}$ locates the referent of the focalized constituent in the lower point of the scale. That is, the value of the focus signaled by IR$_{focus}$ ranks low in the scale. It is what König (1991: 43–46) describes as the 'evaluative component' of focus particles.

4) The set of alternative propositions is contextually given (König 1991: 35–37).

5) The abstract focus feature *f* is expressed by an appropriate prosodic pattern, (Erteschik-Shir 1997: 2, 124; Zubizarreta 1998: 17, 88; among many others). In Spanish, the prosodic prominence corresponds to the rightmost constituent (Zubizarreta 1998: 20–22, 75–77).

These five properties allow us to correctly explain the meaning of IR$_{focus}$ in (24).

---

20 I cannot go into the relation between IR$_{focus}$ and the auxiliary verb *tener que* 'to have to', which is the expression that appears in the English glosses. It could be argued that there must also be a modal component of strong deontic necessity. As Brenda Laca (p.c.) points out to me, the situation referred to is described as being the result of the interaction of two contradictory forces or, more exactly, two forces acting in opposite directions (just the opposite of causal chains, see Copley and Harley 2011). One of these forces is bouletic, belongs to the speaker and is always the less strong. This would account for the evaluative (negative) meaning. In any case, an account for the quantificational force (i.e the focus component) of the construction is needed.

Considering property (1), IR_{focus} has the general function of evoking (salient) alternatives. In the example under consideration, the constituent in focus is *el día de mi boda* 'my wedding day' and the alternatives obtain through substitution of this expression by other expressions of the same logical type: *(en) el día de mi cumpleaños* 'on my birthday', *el jueves* 'on Thursday', *en mayo* 'on May'. In fact, the expression that better translates IR_{focus} into English is precisely *of all*, which explicitly introduces this quantificational meaning.

IR_{focus} also asserts the correspondent proposition without the focus particle: *El día de mi boda llovió* 'On my wedding day it rained'. It also seems that it IR_{focus} could belong to the group of the restrictive focus particles since it might imply that none of the alternatives other than the asserted satisfies the open proposition, although this does not seem completely right. In effect, the proposition *Fue a llover el día de mi boda* does not seem to entail that there are no other days in the relevant period of time in which it rained. In any case, it is obvious that the proposition with IR_{focus} is informatively more relevant than the one without it.

With respect to the need to have an associate, this requirement explains the ungrammaticality of the sentence in (25):

(25) **El día de mi boda*   *fue*   *a llover.*
      the day of my wedding go.AUX.3SG.PAST.PFV to rain.INF

This fact is surprising considering that Spanish is often considered a language with flexible word order. As expected, in the absence of *ir* both orders are possible:

(26) a. *Llovió*   *el día de mi boda.*
       rain.3SG.PAST.PFV the day of my wedding
       'It rained on my wedding day.'

    b. *El día de mi boda*   *llovió.*
       the day of my wedding rain.3SG.PAST.PFV
       'It rained on my wedding day.'

If *ir* in (24) is a focus marker, it requires a constituent on focus to associate with. Assuming that the VP is a not suitable candidate,[21] the ungrammaticality of the sentence receives a straightforward explanation. I will go over the restriction on what can be on focus below (see example (31)).

---

21 I cannot offer an explanation for this restriction. In any case, caribean SER_{focus} 'to be' is subject to the same constraint. See Camacho (2006).

Properties (2) to (4) have to do with the set of alternatives. First of all, the alternatives are ordered along a scale of opportunity, convenience or appropriateness. Secondly, the focused constituent ranks always low in the scale, hence it is interpreted to be the value the least appropriate to fill the open place in the proposition ('It rained on x'). That is, any other value on the scale (my birthday day, my neighbor's wedding day, the day I graduated...), would have been a preferable candidate for the variable, which explains the fact that the focused valued is the more disliked. As a consequence, the sentence might also be interpreted as expressing surprise.

Actually, if the value of the focused constituent ranks low in the scale, it would be expected that any other element with the opposite meaning, that is, a focus maker ranking high, such as *incluso* 'even', would be incompatible with IR_{focus}.[22] Example (27) shows that this is indeed the case:

(27) **El año pasado fue   a llover*
      the year past   go.AUX.3SG.PAST.PFV to rain.INF
      incluso [el día de mi boda]ᵣ
      even   the day of my wedding

This valorative meaning may also be explicit:

(28) *Fue a aparecer **en el peor momento**.* (NGLE: § 28.8j)
      'Of all of the moments of the day, s/he had to appear at the worst moment'

Finally, the set of alternatives is contextually given, that is, the alternatives are normally restricted to the universe of discourse. In effect, the possible alternatives that constitute the domain of quantification obviously are not all the days in the history of the Earth, but only those relevant for the speakers (the speaker's whole life, the current year or any other period of time in which the day the speaker got married is included...). This context-dependency is made explicit in the examples in (29):

(29) a. *Después de varios meses sin llover, fue a llover [el día de mi boda]ᵣ*
         'It had been months since it didn't rain and it had to rain on my wedding day.'

      b. *Entre todos los días del año, fue a llover [el día de mi boda]ᵣ*
         'Of all the days of the year, it had to rain on my wedding day.'

---

22 I owe the argument to Jenneke van der Wal.

To sum up, the meaning of IR_{focus} can be as defined in (30):

(30) IR_{focus} combines with a sentence S containing a constituent in focus.

$[[IR_{focus}\ S]]^\circ$
asserts $[[S]]^\circ$

presupposes:

(i) No p in $[[S]]^f$ holds true
(ii) All p in $[[S]]^f$ are more desiderable, less striking, than $[[S]]^\circ$

Regarding the syntax of the focus marker, I have already shown that the VP alone cannot function as the associate (see example (25) above)). This restriction, that must be interpreted as a restriction on what can be taken as the assertion, affects IR_{focus} and, apparently, other particularizers with a similar meaning: *precisamente* 'precisely', *justo* 'not any other but; of all *x*':

(31) **El   día   de   mi   boda   precisamente   llovió.*
      my   day   of   my   wedding   precisely   rain.3SG.PAST.PFV

Crucially, if this is the case, the restriction is semantic in nature and hence it has nothing to do with the meaning of *ir* as an inherently directed motion verb.

Any other syntactic constituent, either in the VP or adjoined to it, can be the associate. In the examples below the focus constituent is the subject (32a), the internal argument (32b), a selected PP (32c), a temporal adjunct (32d) and a locative adjunct (32e):

(32) a. *Fue a romper el coche [Juan]$_f$.*
          'Of all the people I know, it is John who had to break my car.'

      b. *En medio de tan brillante juventud, ha ido a elegir [un hidalguillo gallego]$_f$.*
          (J. de Espronceda, *Amor venga sus agravios*, via Google 14/04/2012)
          'Out of all those brilliant youths, she has had to choose a nobody.'

      c. *Sintió vergüenza de haberle ido a acusar [de un asesinato que...]$_f$.*
          (A. Trapiello, *Los amigos del crimen perfecto*, 2003, via Google 14/04/12)
          'He was ashamed because, of all of the crimes he could blame him for, he had accused him precisely of a crime that...'

      d. *¡Qué bestia y qué bruto era! Ir a espantar la caza [en el preciso instante en que...]$_f$.* (B. Lillo, *Sub Sole*, 1907, via Google 12/04/2012)
          'What an ignoramus and a brute! He had to chase away the hunt precisely when...'

e. *Juan fue a comprar el pan [en el supermercado]*,.
   'Of all the places where J. could have bought the bread, he had to buy it
   at the supermarket.'

Taking into consideration a restriction similar to the one shown in (25), Camacho (2006) has argued for an analysis of a verbal focus marker as heading its own projection (an inflectional phrase) adjoined to the verbal phrase and where both the focus marker and the associate are generated. However, as long as IR$_{focus}$ carries the temporal and aspectual information of the sentence, it must check these features along the derivation and, hence, an adjoined XP may not be the correct place for it to be generated. Furthermore, no other auxiliary verb including epistemic modal verbs, may occur above IR$_{focus}$ modal verbs, as is well known, are said to end up in a very high position in the left periphery. Finally, it is incompatible with both sentential negation and constituent negation, all of which indicates that at least at LF it must occupy the head of a Focus projection high in the left periphery and check its focus feature in a specifier-head relation with an operator, but I leave this question open:

(33) a. **Debió   de ir   a llover   [el día de mi boda]*,. Ep*/De*
         must.3SG.PAST.PFV of go.INF to rain.INF the day of my wedding

   b. **No fue   a llover   el día de mi boda.*
      NEG go.AUX.3SG.PAST.PFV to rain.INF the day of my wedding

As I will show in the next section, not only the semantics but also distributional data as in (33) help to support the hypothesis that IR$_{res}$ and IR$_{focus}$ must be kept apart. This proposal is discussed in the next section.

3.3 The resultative construction versus the focus construction

Apart from their semantics, there are other differences that separate the two constructions, of which I will discuss only one. The resultative construction but not the focus construction (see (33) above) may be in the complement of an epistemic modal —deontic modals being excluded for semantic reasons:

(34) *La pelota debió de ir a chocar contra la ventana (porque el cristal está roto).*
     'The ball must have ended up hitting the wall (because the glass is broken).'

Syntactically, this property clearly indicates that IR_{res} is located below IP both in overt syntax and in covert syntax, an analysis that the possibility of being negated confirms:

(35)　*Los informes indican que el avión no fue a caer al precipicio, por lo que su búsqueda continúa.*
　　　'The reports indicate that the airplane did not fall into the precipice, which explains the fact that they are still looking for it'.

To sum up, IR_{res} and IR_{focus} each head their own projection. IR_{res} heads a lexical projection just below the functional area of the sentence and forms a chain in syntax with the heads of both the infinitive and the (locative or goal oriented) preposition. IR_{focus} heads a focus projection high in the sentence.

4 From being resultative goal oriented to being a focus marker

The distance between the two constructions, both in semantic and in syntactic terms (see Section 3), seems too strong to claim that IR_{focus} has developed out of IR_{res}. However, this is the hypothesis that I will defend here, that the path followed by IR_{focus} is as stated in (36):

(36)　resultative goal oriented verb > focus marker

With respect to the diachrony of the process, the first examples I have found correspond, as expected, to ambiguous examples and are from the 16th century; in the 17th they are still ambiguous; from the 18th century I have not been able to find any example, but examples from the very beginning of the 19th century show that the new construction is already incorporated in the grammar of the speakers. Examples in (37) below illustrate both ends of the process:

(37)　a.　*¡Miren dónde fue a dar con su belleza / [...], / sino en todo un capón [...]!*
　　　　　　　　　　　　　　　　　　(F. de Quevedo, 1597–1645, CORDE)
　　　　　'Look where all her beauty has ended, in an extremely ugly man.'

　　　b.　*En medio de tan brillante juventud, ha ido a elegir [un hidalguillo gallego]$_f$.*
　　　　　(J. de Espronceda, *Amor venga sus agravios*, 1838, via Google 14/04/2012)
　　　　　'Out of all those brilliant youths, she has had to choose a nobody.'

4.1 The pre-stage

I have argued (see Section 3.1) that the resultative goal-oriented motion is an independent development of the verb *ir* with the conceptual structure in (13a) (*Juan va al mercado* 'John goes to the market, John is going to the market'). The purposive construction (*Juan va a comprar el periódico* 'John goes to buy the newspaper, John is going to buy the newspaper'), on the other hand, has the conceptual structure in (13b). The possibility for the internal argument to act as the controller of the situation is a property characteristic only of the latter. That is, only purposive *ir* is agentive.

Another consequence that follows from this situation is that only with IR_{res} is the achievement of the goal asserted in the same way as it is in *Juan fue a Madrid* 'John went to Madrid' and does not have to be inferred (see the discussion about example (15)).[23] The examples in (38) show this different behaviour:

(38)   a.   Purposive *IR*

Fue ferir *a un cavallero* [...]***, pero no le empesció.***
(Anonymus, *El libro del caballero Cifar*, 1300–1305, 11v)[24]
'He tried (went) to wound a knight, but he didn't succeed.'

b.   Resultative IR

*Mas el Rey le dio al cavallo en el rostro con la espada tal golpe, que la no pudo sacar, y el cavallo enarmonóse y **fue caer** sobre el cavallero.*
(Garci Rodríguez de Montalvo, *Amadís de Gaula*, libros I y II, end of 13th century, CORDE)
'But the King gave the horse such a strike with his sword that he was not able to take it out, so the horse reared up and ended up falling over the knight.'

So, the motion verb in (38b) functions as a semantic unaccusative motion verb that selects for a directional or locative PP. And this is the only possible interpretation of *fue caer* in (39b). The first ambiguous example is the one in (37a) and comes from the 17th century. The properties of the onset context will be reviewed in the next section.

---

23 This pragmatic inference, on the contrary, is on the basis of the development of the perfective meaning of *anar* 'to go' in Catalan and, as such, can be cancelled (see Pérez Saldanya and Hualde 2003 and Pérez-Saldanya 2008: 166–167).
24 Example number (11b) in Pérez-Saldanya (2008).

4.2 The onset context: triggering the inference

4.2.1 Contexts with inherently negative meaning

The main difference between the example in (38b) and the one in (37a), repeated here as (39), is that the former does not allow for the interpretation 'Of all of the places to fall onto, he had to fall precisely onto the knight'. Only (39) permits the interpretation of a contrast with an alternative situation. To the extent that in both sentences *ir* denotes a subevent of motion that selects for a goal, it is IR_{res}. In addition to this, (39) admits the interpretation in which the situation of the woman getting married to an extremely ugly man is negatively evaluated by the speaker. More precisely, the poet is not only informing us about a situation that has taken place, as in (38b); he is also presupposing that there must have been other possible situations that could have also been able to qualify as possible results and as such they would have been all preferable to the one that finally turned out to take place. So we are allowed to infer that there had to be other candidates and that any of them would have been more convenient, considering the extraordinary beauty of the woman referred to.

(39) *¡Miren dónde **fue a dar** con su belleza / [...], / sino en todo un **capón** [...]!*
                                                                (1st half of 17th century)
    'Look where all her beauty has ended, in an extremely ugly man.'

The first conclusion, then, is that inferences are triggered in the presence of words with an inherently negative meaning, such as the despective word *capón* 'ugly man' in (39). However, word order – as a reflex of another phenomenon related to information structure and type of the sentence– is also crucial in triggering inferences.

4.2.2 Other triggers: absence of explicit locative or directional prepositions and word order

In the two examples below an explicit directional or locative preposition is lacking:

(40) a. *Puso Dios un cuchillo de fuego a la puerta del paraíso terre-
        nal porque nadie **osase ir a comer** del árbol de la vida.*
        (Fray A. de Guevara, *Epístolas familiares*, 1521–1543, CORDE)
        'God left a knife of fire at the Paradise in Earth in order to avoid that
        anyone would dare to go (there) and eat from the tree of life.'

b. *¿Qué es esto que llego a oír? Mucho **le ha ido a decir** en ganarme por la mano.* (F. de Rojas Zorrilla, *La traición busca el castigo*, 17th century, 1st half, via Google, 16/04/12).
'What am I hearing? He has gone and told him many things in order to win me.'

In both examples in (40) *ir* can be interpreted with the purposive meaning of (38a). In addition, the inference that eating from the tree of life is the last place from which one should eat is also available for (40a). In that case the ambiguity follows from the absence of an explicit locative preposition that would, otherwise, have forced the interpretation of *ir* as in (38a), that is, as a motion verb. But the ambiguity in (40a) arises also from the presence of elements in the context that support the inference that the situation is negatively evaluated by the speaker, namely, the preventive expression *(no) osar* 'not dare to do something'.[25] In spite of the concurrence of these two elements, the purposive interpretation is still the preferred one, due to the presence of a locative preposition in the previous sentence. It is also the less expensive one in terms of context.

For (40b), however, I propose that the situation is a bit different. On the one hand, from the context it can be deduced that the speaker is upset. Hence, it is possible to assert that the evaluative content – that someone has told more things than he was either allowed or expected to– is an inference and that *ir* is still functioning as a motion verb. Nevertheless, the word order of the sentence, with the direct object *mucho* 'many things, things in a big quantity' in a position identified as a focus position also plays a crucial role. In effect, in terms of the model of change proposed by Eckardt (2006), it could well be the case that this is the sort of context in which the interpretation of the new unit in terms of the semantic and syntactic properties of the old unit, that is, as a motion verb, is more costly. In another words, the speaker – or the hearer, if we are to follow Kuteva (2004: ch. 6)[26] – must have already assigned to *ir* the grammar of a focus marker and concomitantly to that syntactic change, there has been a semantic change. Unless the context clearly forces the interpretation in which there is displacement of the subject along a path, the possibility that the syntactic change has already taken place cannot be disregarded. Note that this is precisely the

---

25 Preventive statemens in contemporary Spanish are in fact expressed by *ir + infinitive* in the negative: *no vayas a* 'don't go and'.
26 Kuteva (2001: ch. 6) argues that some onset contexts are of the kind that the hearer reorganizes the old construction in order to solve a mismatch between the speaker's communicative intentions – not explicitly stated – and her own inferences.

main difference between (39) and (40b). Example (41), from the last part of the 17th century, offers good evidence that this must be the case:

(41) *¿Dónde vas, o con qué intento / al campo del enemigo / **te has ido a meter**?*
       (A. Moreto y Cabaña, *El licenciado vidriera*, 1676, via Google, 16/04/12)
       'Where are you going, or in order to do what, have you entered the enemy's field?' / 'Where are you going, or in order to do what, have you precisely gone into the enemy's field?'

Although *ir* in this sentence might refer to a motion event, the fact is that the word order of the sentence – and probably also the perfect tense –, with the goal occupying the focus position, overrides any interpretation in which *ir* does not function as a focus marker. Compare to that effect sentence (41) with sentence in (42), in which the locative PP is not focalized and *ir* describes a motion event:

(42) *¿Con qué intento **te has ido a meter** al campo del enemigo?*
       'You went into the enemy's field, what for?'

To sum up, even if it could be the case that *ir* is already functioning as a focus marker by the end of the 17th century, on the basis of the examples on hand it can only be concluded that it was an interpretation available in the presence of the appropriate triggers. This situation will have entirely changed by the beginning of the 19th century.

4.3 The post-stage

The examples below – chronologically ordered – show that IR_{focus} is already a new unit in the grammar. On the one hand, the scalar presupposition contributed in the precedent centuries either by emphatic focusing or negative words is now expressed by *ir* alone. No specifically favouring context is needed. On the other hand, IR_{focus} combines with predicates such as *quedar mal* 'to look like a fool' that are rejected by motion verb *ir* (43a). Finally, there appear modifiers as *justamente, precisamente* 'precisely' (see (43a) and (43b)) that reinforce the scalarity of IR_{focus} (see also example (28) above):

(43) a. ***Me fue a hacer** quedar mal, **justamente** cuando estaba yo queriendo quedar bien con su prima.* (J. J. Fernández de Lizardi, *El Periquillo Sarniento*, 1816, via Google, 16/04/2012)
            'He made me to look like a fool precisely when I was trying to make a very good impresion on his cousin.'

b. [*El crítico*] **fue a alabar precisamente** *como la mejor pieza...*
(J. E. Hartzenbusch, *Ensayos poéticos y artículos en prosa, literarios y de costumbres*, 1843, via Google, 14/04/12)
'Among all his writings, the critic praised as the best composition precisely the one that...'

c. *¡Oh! amor, dónde te* **has ido a anidar...**
(E. Cambaceres, *Música sentimental*, 1884, via Google, 16/04/2012)
'Oh love! Among all the hearts in the world, you have nested in the least expected one'

5 Some possible consequences concerning the grammaticalization process

In this paper I have examined two different constructions with the verb *ir* + infinitive in Spanish. I have shown that *ir* as a resultative verb introduces a process (consisting in a displacement of the subject or not) and selects for a goal situation that qualifies as a result. Secondly, in order to obtain this interpretation, the subject cannot be interpreted as an agent (intentional or not). This requirement follows from the unaccusativity of *ir*. Regarding *ir* as a focus marker, it is an independent construction: syntactically, IR_{focus} occupies a position in the left periphery of the sentence and heads a focus projection at least at logical form. It develops out of the resultative construction no earlier than at the 18th century in contexts characterized for having either a constituent already in focus or some negative words that allow for the relevant pragmatic inference. The pragmatic inference triggers syntactic reanalysis of IR_{res} as IR_{focus} in order for the sentence to make sense, and, concomitantly to it, the semantic change.

There are some consequences – of which here I am offering just a very short overview – that follow from the present study if it is on the right track. First of all, it seems evident that there is little of the semantics of *ir* as an inherently directed motion verb, as defined in (13a), in the semantics of *ir* as a focus marker, as defined in (30). The meaning of *ir* as a focus marker is a new concept that, as Eckardt (2006: 46) puts it, only becomes a desirable denotatum "in the course of the reanalysis in question". That is, the feature of scalarity among different alternatives can only be explained by taking into consideration the grammaticalization process, and not the meaning of motion *ir* independent of context. To put it in other words, from the point of view of the theory assumed here, there is nothing in the meaning of *ir* that, in isolation, helps to understand its grammar as a focus marker. The fact that in some varieties of American Spanish *venir* 'to come' is used instead of *ir* 'to go' (see above note 5) would support this conclusion, although a deep investigation about the origins of this construction is needed before arriving to any definite conclusion.

However, when it comes to the hypothesis of the semantic retention in Bybee, Perkins and Pagliuca (1994), the conclusion can be quite the opposite. In effect, the equations "inherently directed motion = selecting for a focus" and "goal (or end point) = focus constituent" seem to be easy to reach. But if this is right, it is also right that it is only by using a metaphor – which not everybody has to share, by the way – that we can explain the equation. Thus, the metaphoric reasoning could be something like focus constituents are the equivalent in the discourse to the privileged points in the space selected by the lexical verb IR. However, the assumptions we need to make are a lot and do not allow to reach any interesting generalization.

It could be argued that formal versions of the semantic retention hypothesis, as in von Fintel (1995), Guéron (2000), Roberts and Roussou (2003) to cite just a few examples, may be more illuminating. In fact, this theory allows us to explain the properties of some aspectual periphrases in a rather straightforward way. For example, in those cases where the aspectual feature of atelicity or durativity remains as a feature (see for example Squartini (1998) and RAE-ASALE (2009)). The problem with $IR_{lex} > IR_{focus}$ is that it is not that evident which is the feature that is kept, and how we explain the movement from one notional area (location, telicity, perfectivity) to another (the left periphery), apart from the widely accepted fact that grammaticalization goes from the more concrete to the more abstract. However, as long as in Caribean Spanish the focus auxiliary is *venir* 'come' (see fn. 5) and this difference has no consequences for the meaning of the construction, we might conclude that telicity is the relevant feature. In effect, what the two verbs share is not obviously their deictic orientation, which is exactly the opposite for each of them, but their *aktionsart*, since in the absence of any other specification, both *ir* and *venir* are inherently telic (see the discussion for *ir* in Section 3.1).

The question may also be asked in a different way: do we expect discourse markers – so to speak – grammaticalized from non telic 'go' verbs? For instance, accordingly to Carlson (this volume), Supyire's 'go' grammaticalizes into a "speech act intensifier" through an intermediate step as a degree intensifier. For Carlson, the relevant lexical feature in allative *sa* 'go' is that of "distance from the speaker" and, at the same time, the existence of an end point. In addition, the intensifier *sa* develops out of the perfective form. If this is the case, then we can expect a correlation between telicity or boundedness and developing into a discourse marker. In spite of this, Carlson's contribution also confirms that only in the course of the process of grammaticalization may the new meaning be expected to arise, and this new meaning cannot be explained only taking into consideration the semantics of the lexical verb.

To sum up, I consider that, in this particular grammaticalization process the semantic retention hypothesis might not be very helpful in the task of understanding why 'go' ends up being a focus marker, which does not amount to denying its validity in general. If a process of grammaticalization is considered as a *continuum*, the semantic retention hypothesis helps in understanding what happens from one step to the other. However, it might not render the same results if there are many steps in between what we consider are both ends.

In addition to this, the precedent assertions have to be combined with what is already known about the different lexicalization patterns of a motion event. The question, thus, is if we may expect different results depending on these different lexicalization parameters or not. Let me illustrate this very briefly with a minimal example. Both Spanish and French are *Verb-framed* languages (Talmy 2000, 2: ch. 3), that is, they merge the Motion and the Path components in the main verb (see Section 3.2); English, on the contrary, is a *Satellite-framed* language. Both French and Spanish have developed the IR_{res} construction and the IR_{focus} construction, but English has not. One possible interpretation it that there is no reason at all and that the process is rather arbitrary. Another one, highly speculative, is that the different lexicalization patterns these languages show do in fact play a role and allow us to explain the reason why a construction is present in one language but not in other. In our case, having the Path incorporated into *ir, venir* or *aller* would be on the basis of IR_{res} (see Section 3.2.). English, in turn, being a satellite-framed language would not be able to develop a unit similar in grammar and semantics to IR_{res}. However, this is an extremely speculative hypothesis which calls for a wider cross linguistic research.

In any case, the link between the two categories (goal and focus) is always established *a posteriori*.

On the other hand, the results of the research do confirm that change occurs in one discrete step, from being a goal oriented resultative to being a focus marker, and that from the very beginning of the change the new meaning is not at all vague, or provisional and subject to a further adjustaments. In effect from the very first examples (see Section 4.3), the grammatical properties of IR_{focus} have remained the same.

Finally, as long as pragmatic inferencing is crucial in this sort of change (see Section 4.2), I concur with Eckardt (2006: 247), who argues that language change driven by pragmatic inference is "typically an adult process", as children are lacking both the world knowledge and the pragmatic skills necessary to accomplish such a process.

Sources

CORDE (= Real Academia Española: Corpus diacrónico del español).
http://www.rae.es (accessed 12 April 2012)
CREA (= Real Academia Española: Corpus de referencia del español actual).
http://www.rae.es (accessed 12 April 2012)

References

Aaron, Jessica E. 2006. *Variation and change in Spanish future temporal Expression*. New Mexico: University of New Mexico Ph.D. dissertation.
Bourdin, Philippe. 2008. On the grammaticalization of 'come' and 'go' into markers of textual connectivity. In María José López-Couso & Elena Seoane (eds.), *Rethinking Grammaticalization. New perspectives* (Typological Studies in Language 76), 37–59. Amsterdam & Philadelphia: John Benjamins.
Bybee, Joan L., Revere D. Perkins & William Pagliuca. 1994. *The Evolution of Grammar: Tense, Aspect and Modality in the Languages of the World*. Chicago: University of Chicago Press.
Camacho, José. 2006. In *situ* focus in Caribbean Spanish: Towards a unified account of focus. In Nuria Sagarra & Almeida Jacqueline Toribio (eds.), *Selected Proceedings of the 9th Hispanic Linguistics Symposium*, 13–23. Somerville, MA: Cascadilla Proceedings Project.
Camacho, Jose & Alfredo *Arnaiz*. 1999. A *topic auxiliary* in Spanish. In Javier Gutiérrez-Rexach & Fernando Martínez-Gil (eds.), *Advances in Hispanic Linguistics. Papers from the 2nd Hispanic Linguistics Symposium,* 317–331. Boston: Cascadilla Press.
Campbell, Lyle. 2001. What's wrong with grammaticalization? *Language Sciences* 23 (2–3): 113–162.
Campbell, Lyle & Richard D. Janda. 2001. Introduction: conceptions of grammaticalization and their problems. *Language Sciences* 23 (2–3): 93–112.
Camus Bergareche, Bruno. 2006. «*Ir a* + infinitivo». In Luis García Fernández (ed.), *Diccionario de perífrasis verbales*. Madrid: Gredos.
Cardinaletti, Anna & Giuliana Giusti. 2001. "Semi-lexical" motion verbs in Romance and Germanic. In Norbert Corver & Henk C. van Riemsdijk (eds.), *Semi-Lexical Categories: The Function of Content Words and the Content of Function Words* (Studies in Generative Grammar 59), 371–414. Berlin & New York: Mouton de Gruyter.
Copley, Bridget & Heidi Harley. 2011. Force dynamics for event semantics: Reifying causation in event structure. Ms., CNRS/Paris 8 and Department of Linguistics, University of Arizona. Available at http://semanticsarchive.net/Archive/jkwNGM5N/CopleyHarley2011.pdf.
De Smet, Hendrik. 2009. Analysing reanalysis. *Lingua* 119: 1728–1755.
Demonte, Violeta. 2011. Los eventos de movimiento en español: construcción léxico-sintáctica y microparámetros preposicionales. In Juan Cuartero Otal, Luis García Fernández & Carsten Sinner (eds.), *Estudios sobre perífrasis y aspecto*, 16–42. Munich: Peniope.
Devos, Maud & Jenneke van der Wal. 2010. 'Go' on a rare grammaticalisation path to focus. *Linguistics in the Netherlands* 27: 45–58.
Dietrich, Wolfang. 1973. *Das periphrastische Verbalaspekt in den romanischen Sprachen*. Tübingen: Max Niemeyer. Spanish version: *El aspecto verbal perifrástico en las lenguas románicas*. Madrid: Gredos, 1975.
Ebert, Karen. 1987. Discourse function of motion verbs in Chadic. *Afrikanistische Arbeitspapiere* 10: 53–72.

Eckardt, Regine. 2006. *Meaning Change in Grammaticalization: An Inquiry into Semantic Reanalysis*. Oxford: Oxford University Press.

Erteschik-Shir, Nomi. 1997. *The Dynamics of Focus Structure* (Cambridge Studies in Linguistics 84). Cambridge: Cambridge University Press.

Fernández de Castro, Félix. 1999. *Las perífrasis verbales en el español actual*. Madrid: Gredos.

Fischer, Olga. 2007. *Morphosyntactic Change: Functional and Formal Perspectives* (Oxford Surveys in Syntax and Morphology 2). Oxford: Oxford University Press.

Gawron, Jean Mark. 1986. Situations and prepositions. *Linguistics and Philosophy* 9: 427–476.

Guéron, Jacqueline. 2000. From need to necessity: A syntactic path to modality. *Belgian Journal of Linguistics* 13: 63–87.

Guéron, Jacqueline & Teun Hoekstra. 1988. T-Chains and the Constituent Structure of Auxiliaries. In Anna Cardinaletti, Giuliana Giusti & Guglielmo Cinque (eds.), *Constituent structure. Papers from the 1987 Glow conference*, 35–100. Dordrecht: Foris.

Gómez Torrego, Leonardo. 1999. Los verbos auxiliares. Las perífrasis verbales de infinitivo. In Ignacio Bosque & Violeta Demonte (eds.), *Gramática descriptiva de la lengua española* (Colección Nebrija y Bello), 3323–3389. Madrid: Espasa.

Harris, Alice C. & Lyle Campbell. 1995. *Historical Syntax in Cross-Linguistic Perspective* (Cambridge Studies in Linguistics 74). New York: Cambridge University Press.

Haspelmath, Martin 1998. Does grammaticalization need reanalysis? *Studies in Language* 22 (2): 49–85.

Haspelmath, Martin. 1999. Why is grammaticalization irreversible? *Linguistics* 37 (6): 1043–1068.

Havu, Jukka. 1997. *La constitución temporal del sintagma verbal en el español moderno*. Helsinki: Academia Scientiarum Fennica.

Heine, Bernd. 2001. On the role of context in grammaticalization. In Ilse Wischer & Gabriele Diewald (eds.), *New Reflections on Grammaticalization: An Inquiry into Semantic Reanalysis* (Typological studies in language 49), 83–102. Amsterdam & Philadelphia: John Benjamins.

Heine, Bernd. 2003. On degrammaticalization. In Barry J. Blake & Kate Burridge (eds.), *Historical Linguistics 2001: Selected Papers from the 15th International Conference on Historical Linguistics* (Current Issues in Linguistic Theory 237), 163–180. Amsterdam & Philadelphia: John Benjamins.

Heine, Bernd & Tania Kuteva. 2002. *World Lexicon of Grammaticalization*. Cambridge: Cambridge University Press.

Hoeksema, Jack & Frans Zwarts. 1991. Some remarks on focus adverbs. *Journal of Semantics* 8: 51–70.

Hopper, Paul & Traugott, Elisabeth C. 2003. *Grammaticalization* (Cambridge Textbooks in Linguistics). Cambridge: Cambridge University Press.

Jackendoff, Ray. 1990. *Semantic Structures*. Cambridge, MA: The MIT Press.

König, Ekkehard. 1991. *The Meaning of Focus Particles. A Comparative Perspective*. (Theoretical Linguistics.) London: Routledge.

Kuteva, Tania. 2004. *Auxiliation: An Enquiry into the Nature of Grammaticalization*. Oxford: Oxford University Press.

Laca, Brenda. 2005. Périphrases aspectuelles et temps grammatical dans les langues romanes. In Hava Bat-Zeev Schyldkrot & Nicole Le Querler (eds.), *Les périphrases verbales* (Linguisticae investigationes. Supplementa 25), 47–66. Amsterdam: John Benjamins.

Langacker, Ronald W. 1977. Syntactic reanalysis. In Charles Li (ed.), *Mechanisms of Syntactic Change*, 57–139. Austin: University of Texas Press.

Levin, Beth & Malka Rappaport Hovav. 1995. *Unaccusativity. At the Syntax-Semantics Lexical Interface*. Cambridge, MA: The MIT Press.

Melis, Chantal. 2005. El aspecto y la gramaticalización del nexo *a* en la construcción VMVT + infinitivo. In Margaret Lubbers Quesada & Ricardo Maldonado (eds.), *Dimensiones del aspecto en español*, 55–97. México: Universidad Nacional Autónoma de México / Universidad Autónoma de Querétaro.

Melis, Chantal. 2006. Verbos de movimiento. La formación de los futuros perifrásticos. In Concepción Company Company (ed.), *Sintaxis histórica del español. Primera parte: La frase verbal*, 873–968. México: Fondo de Cultura Económica/Universidad Nacional Autónoma de México.

Olbertz, Hella. 1998. *Verbal periphrasis in a functional grammar of Spanish* (Functional grammar series 22). Berlin & New York: Mouton de Gruyter.

Pérez-Saldanya, Manuel. 2003. La gramaticalización del verbo *ir* en construcciones narrativas del español. *Medievalia* 35: 62–89.

Pérez-Saldanya, Manuel. 2008. Entre *ir* y *venir*: del léxico a la gramática. In Concepción Company Company & José G. Moreno de Alba (coords.), *Actas del VII Congreso Internacional de Historia de la Lengua Española*, vol. 1, 159–184. Madrid: Arco Libros.

Pérez- Saldanya, Manuel & José I. Hualde. 2003. On the origin and evolution of the Catalan periphrastic preterit. In Claus D. Pusch (ed.), *Verbalperiphrasen in den (ibero) romanischen Sprachen*, 46–70. Hamburg: Buske.

RAE-ASALE (= Real Academia Española / Asociación de Academias de la Lengua Española). 2009. *Nueva gramática de la lengua española*. Madrid: Espasa.

Ramchand, Gilian. 2008. *Verb Meaning and the Lexicon: A First-Phase Syntax*. (Cambridge Studies in Linguistics 116). Cambridge: Cambridge University Press.

Roberts, Ian & Anna Roussou. 2003. *Syntactic Change: A Minimalist Approach to Grammaticalization* (Cambridge Studies in Linguistics 110). Cambridge: Cambridge University Press.

Rooth, Mats. 1994. Focus. In Shalom Lappin (ed.), *The Handbook of Contemporary Semantic Theory* (Blackwell Handbook in Linguistics), 271–297. Oxford: Blackwell.

Talmy, Leonard. 2000. *Toward a Cognitive Semantics*. Cambridge, MA: The MIT Press.

Torrego, Esther. 2002. *Aspect in the prepositional system of Romance*. In Teresa Satterfield, Christina Tortora & Diana Cresti (eds.), Current Issues in Romance Languages. *Selected papers from the 29th Linguistic Symposium on Romance Languages* (Current Issues in Linguistic Theory 220), 337–357. Amsterdam: John Benjamins.

Traugott, Elizabeth C. & Richard B. Dasher. 2001. *Regularity in Semantic Change* (Cambridge Studies in Linguistics 96). Cambridge: Cambridge University Press.

Traugott, Elizabeth C. & Graeme Trousdale. 2010. Gradience, gradualness and grammaticalization: How do they intersect? In Elizabeth C. Traugott & Graeme Trousdale (eds.), *Gradience, gradualness and grammaticalization* (Typological Studies in Language 90), 19–44. Amsterdam: John Benjamins.

Von Fintel, Kai. 1995. The formal semantics of grammaticalization. In Jill N. Beckman (ed.), *Proceedings of the 25th Meeting of the North East Linguistics Association* (NELS 25), vol. 2, 175–190. Amherst, MA: Graduate Student Linguistics Association.

Zubizarreta, María Luisa. 1998. *Prosody, Focus, and Word Order*. Cambridge, MA: The MIT Press.

Zubizarreta, María Luisa & Eun Oh. 2007. *On the Syntactic Composition of Manner and Motion*. Cambridge, MA: The MIT Press.

Zwarts, Joost. 2000. External arguments. In Peter Coopmans, Martin Everaert & Jane Grimshaw (eds.), *Lexical Specification and Insertion* (Current Issues in Linguistic Theory 197), 429–457. Amsterdam & Philadelphia: John Benjamins.

Zwarts, Joost. 2010. A hierarchy of locations: evidence from the encoding of direction in adpositions and cases. *Linguistics* 48 (5): 983–1009.

Kelsey Daniels
On the grammaticalization of *venga* 'come' as a discourse marker in Peninsular Spanish

1 Introduction

In contemporary Peninsular Spanish, *venga* (from the motion verb *venir* 'come') is frequently heard in interpersonal discourse having little to do with motion toward the deictic center. In fact, Cestero Mancera and Moreno Fernández (2008: 76), summarizing the work of several other scholars (e.g. Herrero 2002; Martín Zorraquino and Portolés Lázaro 1999; Santos Río 2003; Calsamiglia and Tusón 1999; and Cestero Mancera 2005), list at least seven discourse uses of *venga* in Peninsular Spanish, such as: acceptance, acceptance with reservation, rejection, pleas, encouragement, instruction, and interactional expressions such as leave-taking and turn-taking.

While many scholars have analyzed the synchronic state of *venga* as a discourse marker, few have analyzed its diachronic development. Blas Arroyo (1998) created a personal corpus of spoken instances of *venga* and discussed its common discursive uses at the time, noting briefly the origin of *venga* from an imperative construction and the impact of its conative semantics (i.e. desiderative meaning) on its development. Additionally, Company Company (2004) surveyed the grammaticalization of seventeen Spanish verbs (including *venir* 'come') in their various roles as discourse markers. However, when examining the specific changes which led to the discourse usage of the verbs in her study, she focused specifically on *anda* 'walk' and *sepa* 'know'.

The historical development of discourse particles more generally has been the subject of much research since Schiffrin (1987) first brought the topic to the center of linguistic inquiry (cf. Brinton 2001 for an overview). Since that time, studies such as Traugott (1995) have sought to identify the grammaticalization pathways which have led to the development of some textual discourse markers in English. Additionally, Brinton's (1996) volume analyzed the development of both textual and interpersonal discourse markers in the history of English.

However, to my knowledge, there has been no in-depth historical analysis of the grammaticalization (or pragmaticalization)[1] of *venga* as an interpersonal discourse marker in Peninsular Spanish. Thus, the aim of this paper is two-fold:

---

1 I use the term "grammaticalization" in this paper to refer to the wider process of grammatical change which encompasses the development of pragmatic material (cf. Diewald 2011, Traugott 2007).

a) to examine the origin of the use of the Spanish ventive, *venga* 'come', as an interpersonal discourse marker and b) to discuss the mechanisms of semantic change in the diachronic development of *venga*.

Using data gathered from three Spanish corpora, the Corpus del Español (CDE), the Corpus Diacrónico del Español (CORDE), and the Corpus de Referencia del Español Actual (CREA), I analyze the grammaticalization of *venga* into a discourse marker. I propose two diachronic paths which explain the present-day use of *venga*: (1) optative[2]>indirect request>acceptance of an offer>discourse marker of agreement>discourse marker of conversation closing, and (2) imperative>hortative[3]>discourse marker of disagreement.

While I recognize the influence of persistence of the original lexical semantics in shaping certain aspects of the development of *venga* into a discourse marker, I argue that other mechanisms of change, specifically (inter)subjectification, the conventionalization of conversational implicatures (Traugott 1989; Traugott and Dasher 2002), and metaphorical extension are the primary participants in the grammaticalization processes[4] observed here.

I conclude the paper by surveying similar discursive uses of 'come' in other languages to suggest that the pathways proposed here could be more universal.

The structure of this paper is as follows: Section 2 contains information about the data collection and methodology, Section 3 discusses the diachronic development of the Spanish optative form of *venga* as a discourse marker, Section 4 examines the development of the imperative form of *venga (ya)* as a separate discourse marker, Section 5 summarizes the historical development and discusses the extent to which the original lexical semantics and other mechanisms of semantic change influence this diachronic path, Section 6 offers a brief survey of similar uses of 'come' in other languages, and Section 7 provides some concluding remarks.

---

2 From the Latin tradition, the optative and the imperative are considered to be two uses (or meanings) of the subjunctive (van der Auwera and Shalley 2004: 87–88). Thus, verbs marked for the optative or the imperative appear to be identical morphologically. However, for the purpose of this paper, I have chosen to use the terms outside of their traditional senses in order to distinguish between the two historical sources of *venga* as a discourse marker. In this paper, I use the term "optative" to refer to main clause uses of the subjunctive in the third person. I use the term "imperative" to refer to main clause uses of the subjunctive in the second person.
3 The term "hortative" in its present usage does not refer to the first person, plural imperative. Rather, it is used (similar to Heine and Kuteva 2002: 69–70) to refer to a solidarity marker used in conjunction with canonical (second person) imperatives (cf. 'imperative marker' in Aikhenvald 2010: 346–347).
4 I use the term "process" here in the sense it is commonly used in a grammaticalization framework, that is, to refer to diachronically adjacent steps in some overall change (see e.g. Smith 2011: 277–278).

2 Data collection and methodology

The data were gathered using three Spanish corpora: the Corpus del Español which contains data from the 1200s – 1900s (CDE), the Corpus Diacrónico del Español (CORDE) which contains data from 1491 – 1974, and the Corpus de Referencia del Español Actual (CREA) which contains data from 1974 – 2004.

In both the CDE and the CREA, dates for the oral data are not available. Because of this fact and because of the fact that mixing oral and written genres in a diachronic analysis would likely skew the timeline, I have chosen to look primarily at narrative texts[5] as well as a few theatrical texts. As is well known, the tension between written and spoken data is a serious problem of historical linguistic inquiry. I believe that my focus on written genres for this study allows me not only to establish a finer temporal trajectory for the changes I am studying, but also to extrapolate my findings to other languages. The fact that some of my data include theater texts also suggests that the data, though written, are not completely incompatible with the spoken language of the time.

Given that the use of *venga* as a discourse marker is specific to Peninsular Spanish (see Company Company 2004: 45), only data from Spain were analyzed. Because the CDE does not allow searches for written data to be sorted by country, the primary diachronic corpus used for historic data was the CORDE. Historical texts dated prior to 1492 in the CDE were occasionally used. We can be certain that these texts exemplify Peninsular Spanish (as opposed to Latin American varieties) given that they were created before Spanish influence in Latin America.

3 From optative to discourse marker of conversation closing

The first cline that I propose for the development of *venga* into a discourse marker is that of optative>indirect request>acceptance of an offer>discourse marker of agreement>discourse marker of conversation closing. There appear to be three points on the cline which are all considered structural optatives: optative, indirect request, and acceptance of an offer. There are two points on the cline that fall under the category of discourse marker: the discourse marker of agreement and the discourse marker of conversation closing.

---

5 In certain contexts in which the dates were not necessary for the diachronic analysis, I have made reference to the oral data as a means of fleshing out my analysis.

3.1 Optative

According to the corpus data, in the thirteenth century *venga* was used both in imperatives and optatives. The examples in (1)–(3) illustrate early uses of the optative.

(1)   *Et   venga   el   santo amor de=l   mundo que es bueno...*
      and come:3SG.OPT the holy love of=the world that is good
      'And may the holy love of the world that is good come...'

(CDE: 13th Century)

(2)   *Diziendo venga   pues ya   la   muerte quando querra.*
      say:PROG come:3SG.OPT then now the death   when   want:3SG.FUT
      'Saying may death come then whenever it may.'   (CDE: 14th Century)

(3)   *Vengan   labradores   y   traigan   mucho hierro...*
      come:3PL.OPT farmworkers and bring:3PL.OPT much   iron
      'May farmworkers come and bring lots of iron...'   (CDE: 1564)

Notice at this point that *venir* agrees in number with its subject. Also, it seems that the subject of the clause could frequently be abstract nouns such as *love* or *death*, as in (1) and (2).

3.2 Indirect requests

By the middle of the eighteenth century, *venga* acquired a pragmatically peculiar usage. In this period, the optative was used to make an indirect request that the addressee bring a specified object to the speaker. Examples of the use of *venga* to make requests are found in (4)–(7).

(4)   *"Venga,   por Dios, ese papel"* ... *Tomó=le,*
      come:3SG.OPT by God   that paper   take:3SG.PRET=it
      leyó=le,   releyó=le...
      read:3SG.PRET=it read:3SG.PRET=it
      '"May that paper come, by God"...He took it, read it, and reread it...'

(CORDE: 1758)

(5) ¡Fuera   los higos secos! Y   luego venga   café...
     out.with the figs   dried   and then   come:3SG.OPT coffee
     'Out with the dried figs! And then may coffee come (bring coffee)...'
                                                        (CORDE: 1850)

(6) "Venga,   venga   la   carta," dijo
     come:3SG.OPT come:3SG.OPT the letter   say.3SG.PRET
     Torquemada inquieto y   ansioso.
     Torquemada   restless and anxious
     "'Come, may the letter come (bring the letter)," said Torquemada restless
     and anxious.'   (CORDE: 1894)

(7) A: *Para que veas   que te= quiero,   te=   voy*
         for   that see:2SG.SBJV that you= love:1SG.PRS you= go:1SG.PRS
         a dar una prueba de mi cariño.
         to give a   proof   of my affection
         'So that you see that I love you, I am going to give you a proof of my
         affection.'

     B: *Venga   la   prueba.*
         come:3SG.OPT the proof
         'May the proof come.'   (CORDE: 1929)

It seems that in making indirect requests, syntactically, the optative still agrees
with a third person subject (which is the item that the speaker wishes to come
towards him or her). Semantically, *venga* retains the majority of the original
meaning of the verb in that it is used to request physical movement of the theme[6]
(i.e. the desired item) through space toward the goal (i.e. the speaker). However,
the command is pragmatically used to make an indirect request to the addressee
that he or she bring the object to the speaker.

3.3 Acceptance of an offer

By the middle of the nineteenth century, *venga* was used to accept an offer, as
shown in (8)–(9). Though it appears that *venga* simply expresses acceptance, at
this point in the diachronic development, the construction was an optative with
an elided grammatical subject, as the example in (10) illustrates.

---

6 I use theme here to refer to the semantic role assigned to persons or items which change
locations.

(8)   A: *Paquita,   querrás   un pollito,   ¿no es verdad?*
            Paquita   want:2SG.FUT   a   chicken:little   NEG is right
            'Paquita, you will want a little chicken, isn't that right?

      B: *¡Venga!*
            come:3SG.OPT
            'May it come!'   (CORDE: 1842–1851)

(9)   A: *¿Quieres   llevár=te=la?*
            want:2SG.PRS   take:INF=you=it
            'Do you want to take it (the chicken)?'

      B: *¿Cómo no? Venga.*
            how   NEG come:3SG.OPT
            'Why not? May it come.'   (CORDE: 1897)

(10)   A: *Eso   me= recuerda,   Víctor, la   leyenda de=l*
            that me= remind:3SG.PRS Victor   the   legend   of=the
            fogueteiro que tengo   oída   en Portugal.
            Fogueteiro that have:1SG.PRS heard in Portugal
            'That reminds me, Victor, of the legend of the fogueteiro that I have
            heard in Portugal.'

      B: *Venga.*
            come:3SG.OPT
            'May it come.'

      A: [Speaker A goes on for three sentences without telling the legend]

      B: *Pero venga la   leyenda.*
            but come:3SG.OPT the   legend
            'But may the legend come.'   (CORDE: 1914)

In example (10), the first response of Speaker B appears to use *venga* in a manner that is simply an acceptance of Speaker A's statement. However, the second response of Speaker B confirms that *venga* has not yet been reanalyzed. Rather, Speaker B's second utterance suggests that he had simply elided the subject of the optative. The use of *venga* to accept an offer is present in the corpus through the 1960s as shown in (11).

(11)   A: *¿Quieres   café?*
            want:2SG.PRS coffee
            'Do you want coffee?'

B: *Venga.*
come:3SG.OPT
'May it come.' (CORDE: 1962)

3.4 Discourse marker of agreement

In the late 1980s and early 1990s, *venga* began to be used as a discourse marker which expressed acceptance of an addressee's proposal as shown in examples (12)–(16). In this stage, *venga* was not used as an optative, expressing a wish that the theme move toward the goal (i.e. the speaker). Rather, it was used to accept the addressee's command or suggestion.

(12) A: *Pues compra=me   un perrito...*
      well buy:2SG.IMP=me a   dog:little
      'Well then buy me a little dog.'

   B: *Venga,   te=   compro   el   perrito...*
      come.DM you= buy:1SG.PRS the dog:little
      'Okay, I will buy you a dog.' (CREA: 1989)

(13) A: *¿Nos= vamos   a comer   juntas?   Te=   invito.*
      REFL= go:1PL.PRS to eat:INF together you= invite:1SG.PRS
      'Are we going to go eat together? I'll pay for you.'

   B: *Venga.   Pero a   escote.*
      come.DM but   by neck
      'Okay. But we'll each pay our own.' (CREA: 1990)

(14) A: *Tendrías   que pagar=me...*
      have:2SG.COND to   pay:INF=me
      'You would have to pay me.'

   B: *Venga,   te=   pago, ¿cuánto quieres?*
      come.DM you= pay how.much want:2SG.PRS
      'Fine, I'll pay you, how much do you want? (CREA: 1992)

Example (15) illustrates that *venga* has lost its paradigmatic autonomy (Lehmann 1995) given that it does not agree with the second person plural informal pronoun. Finally, example (16) illustrates that as a discourse marker, *venga* can occur in both the left-detached and right-detached positions. Blas Arroyo (1998) notes that the use of *venga* in the right-detached position as in (16) also marks turn-taking between interlocutors.

(15) A: *¿Queréis   que nos   acerquemos?*
       want:2PL.PRS that REFL come.closer:1PL.SBJV
       'Do you all want us to move closer?'

    B: *Venga,   sí.*
      come.DM yes
      'Okay, yeah.'   (CREA: 2001)

(16) *Bueno, esperamos   a=l   día veintinueve, venga.*
    good   wait:1PL.PRS to=the day twenty.nine come.DM
    'Okay, we will wait until the twenty ninth, alright.'   (CDE: 20th century)

3.5 Discourse marker of conversation closing

The discourse use of *venga* in conversation closing seems to have arisen from its use to mark acceptance; however, more corpus data are needed to confirm this diachronic development. Given that the corpora only contain data through 2004, much of the recent development of *venga* as a discourse marker awaits further study. However, given the current data set, I posit that *venga* first signaled agreement between the interlocutors and subsequently came to signal that the conversation could be concluded because both interlocutors were in agreement as shown in example (17).

(17) A: *Oye, si vas   a Penyeta, a ver si me= miras   eso.*
       INT if go:2SG.PRS to Penyeta to see if me= look:2SG.PRS that
       'Hey, if you go to Penyeta, let's see if you can show me that.'

    B: *Sí, no te=   preocupes.   La semana*
      Yes NEG you= worry:2SG.IFL.PROH the week
      que viene   iré   y   te= lo= miraré.
      that come:3SG.PRS go:1SG.FUT and you=it=look:1SG.FUT
      'Yeah, don't worry. This coming week, I'll go and I'll show it to you.'

    A: *Venga.*
      come.DM
      'Okay.'

B: *Bueno, hasta luego.*
   DM   until then
   'Alright, see you later.'

A: *Hasta luego.*
   until then
   'See ya.'   (Blas Arroyo 1998, spoken data)

In this conversation, Speaker A requests that Speaker B do something for her. Speaker B assures her that he will do it and Speaker A responds with *venga*. Blas Arroyo (1998) states that this use of *venga* is an empty phrase which functions as an offer to close the conversation. However, it seems rather that Speaker A uses *venga* to signal her acceptance of Speaker B's promise to accommodate her request. Subsequently, once both are in agreement (which is signaled by *venga*), they close the conversation. Thus, in example (17), *venga* functions both to express agreement and to signal a close of the conversation.

While Blas Arroyo's (1998) comment on constructions like (16) and his examples from spoken data like (17) illustrate that the use of venga in turn-taking and conversation closing were well-attested in the spoken language by 1998, the first written examples of venga used to signal conversation closing are found in the corpus in 2001 as shown in (18) (which represents half of a telephone conversation).

(18)   A: *¿Sí?... Bien... Aquí, muy a gusto...   Muy acogedor...*
        yes   well   here very to pleasure very cozy
        No, todavía no he   firmado... ¡Pues cuando
        no still   no 1SG.AUX sign:PERF well   when
        me= llamen!   Sí, sopa... con jamoncito... Venga,
        me= call:3PL.SBJV yes soup with ham:little   come.DM
        adiós y   no me= llames   más aquí...
        bye   and NEG me= call:2SG.PROH more here
        'Hello?... Good... Here, very pleased... Very cozy... No, I still haven't signed... Well, whenever they call me! Yes, soup with a little ham... Okay, bye and don't call me here again.'   (CREA: 2001)

Notice that *venga* is not used as a replacement for other conversation closing expressions such as *adiós* 'goodbye' or *hasta luego* 'see you later'. Instead, it occurs just prior to those conversation closing expressions as an initial signal of the close of the conversation. This use of *venga* before conversation closing expressions in interpersonal discourse is frequently heard in spoken Peninsular Spanish today.

4 From imperative to discourse marker of disagreement

The second cline that I propose for the diachronic development of *venga* as a discourse marker is imperative>hortative>discourse marker of disagreement. Within the hortative stage, hortative markers appear on both imperatives and prohibitives. Furthermore, in this cline, the discourse marker signals disagreement with a proposal or stance of the addressee.

4.1 Imperative

The corpus data for the imperative construction illustrate that prior to the nineteenth century, *venga* was used as a canonical imperative (i.e. second person) commanding movement toward a specified goal. However, at this point, the goal was not necessarily toward the speaker as shown in (19).[7]

(19) *Venga*   *a la   cárcel.*
      come:2SG.FRL.IMP to the jail
      'Come to jail.'   (CORDE: 1609)

The example in (19) illustrates that *venga* is used to command physical movement through space toward the specified goal *la cárcel* 'the jail'. However, it is not clear whether or not the speaker is in the same location as the goal.

4.2 Hortative

The second point on the grammaticalization cline is the hortative. At this point, *venga* marks imperatives which are instructions to the addressee, requests that the addressee fulfill the speaker's desire, or reassurance that the addressee can do the task in question. It is important to note that in the hortative stage, the use of *venga* is not reactive. The speaker simply uses it to exhort the addressee to comply with his desires without taking into account the desires of the addressee.

---

7 Lewandowski (2007) notes that the *Diccionario de Autoridades* of the Real Academia Española (1739) states that *venir* 'come' communicated the same motion toward a goal as *llegar* 'arrive'. It was not until the 19th century that Spanish literary historian Juan Antonio Pellicer discovered that *venir* 'come' carried deictic meaning (Pellicer 1800, quoted in Lewandowski 2007).

With respect to the development of the imperative to the hortative, it seems that the hortative arose in the mid-nineteenth and early twentieth centuries out of contexts in which two commands were present: first, that the addressee should physically move toward the speaker, and second, that the addressee should carry out a subsequent task. In other words, sources of the hortative use appear to be directives such as *venga* (*y*) + IMPERATIVE 'come (and) do X' as shown in (20)–(22).

(20) el Boyero le= decía; venga, hijo,
the Boyero him= say.3SG.IMPF come:2SG.FRL.IMP son,
tome *una lección, y* *cargaban* *juntos.*
take:2SG.FRL.IMP a lesson and load:3PL.IMPF together
'Boyero told him, "Come, son, learn a lesson" and they loaded together.'
(CDE: 1850)

(21) *¡Venga* *aquí, Ferragut...* *Venga* *y* *no*
come:2SG.FRL.IMP here Ferragut come:2SG.FRL.IMP and NEG
sea *niño!*
be:2SG.FRL.PROH child
'Come here, Ferragut...Come on and don't be a baby!' (CORDE: 1918)

(22) *¡Venga* *y* *asóme=se* *a la cocina*
come.2SG.FRL.IMP and lean.in:2SG.FRL.IMP=REFL to the kitchen
y *mire* *las alacenas...*
and look: 2SG.FRL.IMP the cupboards
'Come and lean into the kitchen and look at the cupboards...' (CORDE: 1921)

In this early usage, *venga* still agrees morphologically with the subsequent command, i.e., both imperatives (or the imperative and the prohibitive) are marked for second singular formal. Thus, it may still be syntactically considered an imperative.

As the examples in (23)–(27) show, in the hortative stage, *venga* is syntactically independent (i.e. occurs in the left-detached position offset by a pause) and no longer agrees with the subject of the subsequent imperative (i.e. *venga* is marked for second singular formal, whereas the other imperatives are marked for second singular informal). Further, (23) illustrates that *venga* no longer communicates physical movement toward the speaker. If this were the case, the speaker in (23) would be commanding the addressee to move both toward and away from him. Although the left-detached position is the most common location for the hortative, *venga* can also be found in the right-detached position as in (26). Example (27) illustrates that *venga* can mark both canonical imperatives and non-canonical imperatives.

(23)   *Pero venga,   muéve   =te*
       But come.HORT move:2SG.IFL.IMP =REFL
       'But, come on, move!'   (CORDE: 1958)

(24)   *Venga,   venga,   pon   =me el   café*
       come.HORT come.HORT put:2SG.IFL.IMP =me the coffee
       y   calla.
       and be.quiet:2SG.IFL.IMP
       'Come on, put (bring) me a coffee and be quiet.'   (CORDE: 1968)

(25)   *Venga,   piensa.*
       come.HORT think:2SG.IFL.IMP
       'Come on, think.'   (CDE: 20th Century)

(26)   *Venga,   cuénta=nos=lo,   venga.*
       come.HORT tell:2SG.IFL.IMP=us=it come.HORT
       'Come on, tell us (it), come on.'   (CDE: 20th Century)

(27)   *Pues venga,   vámo=nos   ya.*
       well come.HORT go:1PL.IMP=REFL now
       'Well come on, let's go already.'   (CORDE: 1956)

Two particular uses of *venga* from the mid-twentieth century should be mentioned here. Both instances include the optional intensifier *ya* 'now'. First, *venga (ya)* was frequently used to encourage the addressee to hurry along whatever activity he or she was completing or to hurry along to the next activity, as in (28). And second, *venga (ya)* was often used in prohibitive hortative constructions as in (29).

(28)   *Algunos viajeros empezaban   a estar impacientes.*
       some   travelers begin:3PL.IMPF to be   impatient
       "Venga   ya, hombre, ¿nos vamos   o no?"
       come.HORT now man   REFL go:1PL.PRS or NEG
       'Some travelers began to get impatient. "Come on, man. Are we going or
       not?"   (CORDE: 1958)

(29)   *Venga   ya, no digas   tonterías.*
       come.HORT now NEG say:2SG.IFL.PROH foolish.things
       'Come now, don't say foolish things.'   (CORDE: 1962)

Notice in (29) that the use of *venga* prior to a prohibitive, while still encouraging the addressee to comply with the desires of the speaker, expresses disagreement between the interlocutors. The speaker does not approve of the actions of the addressee and thus commands him to stop. This use of *venga* to express disagreement is crucial to the diachronic development of the discourse marker of disagreement.

4.3 Discourse marker of disagreement

The third and final point on the cline is that of discourse marker of disagreement. According to the corpus data, it seems that this discourse marker arose in the mid to late twentieth century. While the hortative was used to encourage the addressee to comply with the desires of the speaker, the discourse marker of disagreement is used as a reactive expression which conveys disagreement with the stance or proposal of the addressee as in (30).

(30) A: *tengo que salir   ahora con mi coche a ese lío.*
          have to   go:INF now   with my car   to that mess
          'I have to go out now with my car to that mess.'

      B: *Venga,   hombre, yo me= quedo   aquí.*
          come.DM man   I REFL= stay:1SG.PRES here
          'No way, man, I'm staying here.'   (CDE: 20th Century)

Although this does not have to be the case, the emphatic particle *ya* frequently occurs after *venga* when it expresses disagreement as in (31)–(33). For this reason, it seems that the discourse marker of disagreement actually arose out of the prohibitive use of *venga*.

(31) *¿Después de todo no   piensas   pagar   el*
        after   of all NEG think:2SG.PRS pay.for:INF the
        servicio? ¡Venga   ya!
        service   come.DM now
        'After all that you don't think to pay for the service? Come on!' (CREA: 1988)

(32) *¿Es que creéis   que me= chupo   el dedo?*
        is.it that believe:2PL.PRS that REFL= suck:1SG.PRS the thumb
        ¡Venga   ya...!
        come.DM now
        'Is it that you all think that I'm stupid? Come on!'   (CREA: 1989)

Table 1. Summary of diachronic changes from optative to discourse marker of acceptance

Optative	Indirect Request (1758)	Acceptance of an offer (~1842)	Discourse marker of agreement (1989)	Discourse marker of conversation closing (2001)
Syntactic – Dependent – Takes a third person subject (frequently an abstract noun)	**Syntactic** – Dependent – Takes a third person subject (usually a physical object)	**Syntactic** – Dependent – Takes a third person subject (the offered item) – Subject is often elided	**Syntactic** – Independent – Offset by pause indicated by a comma – Takes no subject – Loss of paradigmatic autonomy	**Syntactic** – Independent – Offset by pause indicated by a comma – Takes no subject – Loss of paradigmatic autonomy
Semantic – Physical or metaphorical movement toward a goal – Theme: the grammatical subject	**Semantic** – Physical movement through space toward a goal (i.e. the speaker) – Theme: the desired object	**Semantic** – Physical movement toward speaker – Theme: the previously offered item (e.g. coffee)	**Semantic** – Empty – No movement toward the speaker encoded – No theme	**Semantic** – Empty – No movement toward the speaker encoded – No theme
Pragmatic – Expresses a wish or a desire of the speaker	**Pragmatic** – Makes an indirect request	**Pragmatic** – Accepts the addressee's offer (i.e. it is a reactive expression) – Subjectified form of optative	**Pragmatic** – Agrees to the addressee's request or command – Intersubjectified form of acceptance	**Pragmatic** – Marks agreement between interlocutors and the closure of a conversation – Intersubjectified form of acceptance

(33) *¿Te=   piensas   que yo me=   voy   a   creer*
      REFL= think:2SG.PRS that I   REFL= go:1SG.PRS to believe:INF
      que tú   has   dejado   a   Pablo? Venga   ya,   Lulú!
      that you 2SG.AUX leave:PERF DAT Pablo come.DM now Lulu
      'Do you think I'm going to believe that you left Pablo? Come on, Lulú!'

(CREA: 1989)

5 Mechanisms of semantic change in the development of the discourse marker

The purpose of this section is to summarize the diachronic changes of *venga* in both clines and to discuss various semantic analyses which can account for this development of the discourse marker.

5.1 Summary of development from optative to discourse marker of acceptance and conversation closing

Before discussing the influence of the original semantics on the development of *venga* as a discourse marker, I want to summarize the diachronic changes discussed in Section 3. Table 1 summarizes the various stages in the development of *venga* from optative to discourse marker. Within each category, the syntactic, semantic, and pragmatic statuses of *venga* are shown. The date of the first appearance of each use in the corpus is shown below the heading.

5.2 Discussion of mechanisms of semantic change

Between each point on the grammaticalization cline, there appear to have been various mechanisms of semantic change at work. Each stage of the grammaticalization cline is discussed below. Each section contains a syntactic, semantic, and pragmatic summary according to the information in Table 1 followed by a discussion of the semantic changes which occurred at that point.

5.2.1 From optative to indirect request

In the optative form, *venga* was syntactically dependent as a constituent of the verb phrase. It was marked for third person agreement with the subject of the clause. Semantically, the optative expressed physical or metaphorical movement of a desired entity toward a goal. Pragmatically, the optative expressed a wish or desire of the speaker.

Around the mid-eighteenth century, persistence of the original lexical semantics of the construction and pragmatic inference intertwined to create an indirect request. With regard to the original lexical semantics, in both the optative and the indirect request constructions, there was an expression of a desire that something or someone move toward the speaker. However, in the indirect request construction, the speaker invited the addressee to pragmatically infer that he was a making a request that the addressee bring the desired item, as in (34).

(34) *¡Fuera   los   higos secos!   Y   luego venga   café...*
      out.with the   figs   dried   and then   come:3SG.OPT coffee
      'Out with the dried figs! And then may coffee come (bring coffee)...'
                                                                    (CORDE: 1850)

Conventionalized conversational implicatures or invited pragmatic inferences are one of the main mechanisms of semantic change and the rise of subjectification (Traugott 1989; Traugott and Dasher 2002). Beginning at this point in the development of *venga*, the process of subjectification can be seen. According to Traugott (2010: 35), subjectification is the process by which "meanings are recruited by the speaker to encode and regulate attitudes and beliefs". Thus, in the case of *venga*, subjectification is the process by which the original lexical semantics of *venga* are replaced by elements of meaning which express the speaker's desires. This process is evidenced by the fact that the speaker extends the use of *venga* to express that he wants the addressee to bring him the theme. To summarize, before the mid-eighteenth century there was a persistence of the original lexical semantics of *venga* along with an invited pragmatic inference which expressed the speaker's desire that the addressee bring a desired item (subjectification).

5.2.2 From indirect request to acceptance of an offer

In indirect requests, *venga* was syntactically identical to the optative. However, its subject was often a physical object rather than an abstract noun or person. Semantically, it expressed a desire for physical movement of an object toward the speaker; however, pragmatically, it was used to make an indirect request that the interlocutor bring the desired object to the speaker.

Around the mid-nineteenth century, there was an expansion in the pragmatic environments in which the construction occurred. At this point, the original lexical semantics of *venga* still remained. In other words, the speaker still expressed a desire for something to move towards him or her. Thus, there were no semantic changes from the previous point on the cline. The only difference between the two constructions was that *venga* became used reactively to respond to an offer rather than simply to make a request as in (35).

(35) A: *Eso me= recuerda,   Víctor, la   leyenda   de=l*
       that me= remind:3SG.PRS Victor the legend   of=the
       fogueteiro que tengo   oída   en Portugal.
       Fogueteiro that have:1SG.PRS heard in Portugal
       'That reminds me, Victor, of the legend of the fogueteiro that I have heard in Portugal.'

     B: *Venga.*
       come:3SG.OPT
       'May it come.'

     A: [Speaker A goes on for three sentences without telling the legend]

     B: *Pero venga   la   leyenda.*
       but come:3SG.OPT the legend
       'But may the legend come.'   (CORDE: 1914)

Thus, though there were no semantic changes during this period, the pragmatic environments of the construction expanded.

5.2.3 From acceptance of an offer to discourse marker of agreement

At the acceptance of an offer stage of the cline, *venga* still behaved syntactically like an optative. However, the subject of the clause with *venga* was often elided as in (35). Semantically, it encoded physical movement through space toward the goal (i.e. the speaker) by the theme that had been offered in the previous utterance. Pragmatically, *venga* was used to accept an offer of another interlocutor.

Around the late twentieth century, a loss of the original semantics of *venga* occurred as well as an addition of a conventionalized conversational implicature by the process of intersubjectification. More specifically, with the usage of *venga* to accept an offer, the implicature of the speaker to the addressee was 'Yes, I want X' as in (36).

(36) A: *¿Quieres   café?*
      want:2SG.PRS coffee
      'Do you want coffee?'

    B: *Venga.*
      come:3SG.OPT
      'May it come.'   (CORDE: 1962)

As a result of this process of intersubjectification, the construction acquired the semantic content of agreement. As mentioned above, in accepting an offer the subject of the *venga* clause was frequently elided. Therefore, *venga* itself carried the implicature of agreement as in (37). Once it acquired this semantic content, *venga* lost its original lexical semantics of movement toward the speaker.

(37) A: *Pues compra=me   un perrito...*
      well buy:2SG.IMP=me a   dog:little
      'Well then buy me a little dog.'

    B: *Venga,   te= compro   el   perrito...*
      come.DM you= buy:1SG.PRS the dog:little
      'Okay, I will buy you a dog.'   (CREA: 1989)

Traugott (2010: 35) defines intersubjectification as the process by which the subjectified meanings "may be recruited to encode meanings centered on the addressee." Although Traugott (2010) considers intersubjectified forms mainly to be those that express the speaker's awareness of the 'face' or 'self-image' of the addressee, I consider the intersubjectified form of *venga* to be one which expresses the desires of the speaker in relation to the desires of the addressee. Thus, in (37), *venga* is used to comply with the desires or commands of the addressee; whereas previously, *venga* was used only to encode the beliefs or desires of the speaker. Thus, to summarize, at this stage in its development, *venga* became used to express agreement to a request or a command of the addressee by the process of intersubjectification, and it lost much of its original semantic content.

5.2.4 From discourse marker of agreement to discourse marker of conversation closing

As a discourse marker of agreement, *venga* was syntactically independent. It predominantly occurred in the left-detached position offset by a pause.[8] As an independent particle, it did not take a subject and it lacked agreement marking with other constituents in the clause. Semantically, it was empty, encoding no physical or metaphorical movement of the addressee or another object toward the speaker. Pragmatically, *venga* functioned to signal an agreement by the speaker to carry out the desires of the addressee. The use of *venga* as a discourse marker seems to be an intersubjectified form of the acceptance construction.

Around the late twentieth and early twenty-first centuries, the discourse marker of conversation closing arose out of the discourse marker of agreement. As a discourse marker of conversation closing, *venga* was nearly identical syntactically and semantically to the discourse marker of agreement, but it had acquired the pragmatic function of closing a conversation or signaling turn-taking (especially when used in the right-detached position). In many cases, *venga* still expressed agreement with the interlocutor; however, as a result of its frequent collocation in speech with conversation closings, *venga* had come to signal that both interlocutors were in agreement about the subject under discussion and that the conversation could be terminated.

5.3 Summary of development from imperative to discourse marker of disagreement

Again, before discussing the influence of the original semantics of *venga* on its diachronic development, I first offer a chart in Table 2 which summarizes the historical changes of the construction. Each stage (i.e. imperative, hortative, and discourse marker) contains information about the syntactic, semantic, and pragmatic statuses of the construction. The date of the first appearance of each use in the corpus is shown below the heading.

---

8 Smith (2012) suggests that the tendency for developing pragmatic markers to appear in detached positions is due to the effects of Bybee's (1985) Relevance Principle. While the Relevance Principle predicts that verbal morphology affecting the stem most often will appear closer to that stem, its effect on pragmatic markers is that it motivates them to appear in clause-adjacent positions since their function is, in some sense, to "inflect" the entire utterance (see also Traugott 2001). Thus, the appearance of *venga* in detached positions is further evidence of its pragmaticalization.

Table 2. Summary of diachronic changes from imperative to discourse marker of disagreement

Imperative	Hortative (1958)	Discourse marker of disagreement (1988)
Syntactic – Dependent – Takes a second person subject	***Syntactic*** – Independent – Loss of morphological agreement, takes no subject – Often in left-detached position – Typically followed by an imperative – Similar to double imperatives, simply juxtaposed	***Syntactic*** – Independent – Often in left-detached position – Takes no subject
Semantic – Physical movement through space toward the speaker – Theme: the addressee	***Semantic*** – Metaphorical movement toward desires of the speaker – Theme: addressee's epistemological stance	***Semantic*** – Possible metaphorical movement toward desires of the speaker or possibly semantically empty – Possible theme: addressee's epistemological stance
Pragmatic – Make commands	***Pragmatic*** – Non-reactive – Speaker requests alignment of the addressee's desires – Mitigates a subsequent command – Subjectified form of imperative	***Pragmatic*** – Reactive – Expresses disagreement with the addressee's epistemological stance – Intersubjectified form of hortative

5.4 Discussion of the original lexical semantics and other mechanisms of semantic change

Like the last cline, between each point of the grammaticalization, there appear to have been various mechanisms of semantic change at work. Again, each stage of the grammaticalization cline is discussed below, and each section contains a syntactic, semantic, and pragmatic summary according to the information in Table 2, followed by a discussion of the semantic changes which occurred at that point.

5.4.1 From imperative to hortative

In the imperative stage, *venga* took a subject. Semantically, it expressed physical movement through space toward a goal. Pragmatically, it was used to make commands on the addressee.

As mentioned in Section 4.2, the hortative seems to have originated around the mid-nineteenth century from directive clauses which contained multiple commands as shown in (38).

(38) *el   Boyero le=   decía;   venga,   hijo,*
      the Boyero him= say.3SG.IMPF come:2SG.FRL.IMP son,
      tome   una lección, y   cargaban   juntos.
      take:2SG.FRL.IMP a   lesson and load:3PL.IMPF together
      'Boyero told him, 'Come, son, learn a lesson' and they loaded together.'
                                                   (CDE: 1850)

In these cases, the addressee was first commanded to move physically closer to the speaker and then commanded to complete another action. However, in situations in which physical movement was not necessary, *venga* was reanalyzed as emphatically marking the following imperative.

This innovation and reanalysis can be attributed to two semantic changes that took place during this period: metaphorical extension and conventionalization of conversational implicatures by the process of subjectification. First, the original lexical semantics of *venga*, which communicated physical movement through space toward the speaker, were metaphorically extended to communicate movement of the addressee's epistemological stance toward the epistemological stance of the speaker. Second, two implicatures of the imperative were conventionalized in speech by the process of subjectification. The implicatures of the imperative were that: (1) The speaker wanted the addressee to do X, and (2) the speaker believed the addressee had the ability to do X. That is, the original semantics of *venga* indicating physical movement toward the speaker became bleached in favor of the implicatures of the imperative (i.e. 'I want you to do X' or 'You have the ability to do X'). These implicatures were retained (as part of the process of subjectification) in the hortative use of *venga* in which the speaker encouraged the addressee that he wanted her to complete the task, as in (39).

(39)   *Pero venga,   muéve   =te*
         but   come.HORT   move.2SG.IFL.IMP =REFL
         'But, come on, move!'   (CORDE: 1958)

It is important to note that since all imperatives carry these two implicatures, any imperative can be recruited for this hortative usage. It is perhaps then frequency of use or the fact that "[semantic] motion is intrinsically tied to a change of state or creating a new situation" or that "motion conspires with instigation" (Aikhenvald 2010: 349) which can account for the fact that motion verbs are often selected for this usage. Or, as Mauri and Sansó (this volume) discuss, it is perhaps the fact that displacement is frequently a necessary preliminary action in directive situations that contributes to the usage of motion verbs in these contexts.

5.4.2 From hortative to discourse marker of disagreement

In the hortative stage, *venga* was syntactically independent, lacking morphological agreement and taking no subject. It often occurred in the left-detached position before another imperative. Semantically, it expressed the speaker's desire for the metaphorical movement of the addressee toward his or her epistemological stance. Thus, the theme of the command was the epistemological stance of the addressee. It was a subjectified form of the imperative, whereby the speaker encoded his own attitudes and beliefs and regulated those of the addressee. Pragmatically, it was non-reactive—that is, it was not offered in response to an opinion of the addressee. Furthermore, pragmatically, the speaker requested alignment of the addressee's desires with his own, and he mitigated his subsequent command.

     A natural extension of the hortative use of *venga* was the prohibitive use as shown in (40). Both the prohibitive and the hortative exhort the addressee to comply with desires of the speaker by following the subsequent command.

(40)   *Venga   ya,   no   digas   tonterías.*
         come.HORT now NEG say:2SG.IFL.PROH foolish.things
         'Come now, don't say foolish things.'   (CORDE: 1962)

The discourse marker of disagreement arose in the late twentieth century, from the prohibitive use of *venga*. This reanalysis can be attributed to metaphorical (or metonymic)[9] extension of conventionalized conversational implicatures. First, the prohibitive use of *venga* carried at least two implicatures: (1) The speaker did not want the addressee to do X, and/or (2) the speaker wanted the addressee to stop doing X, and/or (3) the speaker did not agree with what the addressee was doing. This third implicature was carried over to the discourse marker of disagreement by way of metaphorical extension. Thus, the speaker used *venga (ya)* to express disagreement with the thoughts of the addressee rather than the actions of the addressee, as in (41). With this metaphorical extension from action to thought complete, *venga (ya)* gained greater syntactic freedom and was used in syntactic environments separate from imperatives and prohibitives, as in (41).

(41) ¿*Después de todo no piensas   pagar   el*
      after   of all NEG expect:2SG.PRS pay.for:INF the
      servicio? ¡Venga   ya!
      service   come.DM now
      'After all that you don't expect to pay for the service? Come on!'

      (CREA: 1988)

The process of intersubjectification can be seen in the fact that this construction was the first point on this cline in which *venga* was used as a reactive expression to the thoughts or beliefs of the addressee; previously, *venga* was used only to express the desires of the speaker. Thus, the intersubjectified form of *venga* to express disagreement did not have to regulate the beliefs or attitudes of the addressee but rather it could simply express the beliefs or attitudes of the speaker with respect to the beliefs or attitudes of the addressee. It is noted in Table 2 that the discourse marker of disagreement expressed either a desire for metaphorical movement toward the speaker's epistemological stance or was empty. This is due to the fact that occasionally when the speaker used *venga* as a discourse marker of disagreement, he intended to convince his addressee to change her position; however, in other instances, the speaker's intent was merely to express disagreement without necessarily changing the opinion of the addressee.

---

9 Goossens (1995: 176), in keeping with standard definitions, distinguishes metonymy from metaphor in that metaphor links two different domains (i.e. the physical world vs. the thought world); but, metonymy links items within a single domain (i.e. PERSON: physical body vs. epistemological stance). For this purpose of this paper, I have considered the distinction between the physical and epistemological as being in separate domains. Thus, I have chosen to call it metaphorical extension.

In summary, metaphorical extension and conventionalized conversational implicatures brought about by the process of intersubjectification interacted to form the discourse marker of disagreement.

6 Similar discursive uses of 'come' in other languages

In an effort to examine the possible cross-linguistic universality of the proposed clines and mechanisms of semantic change, I present here data from other languages which use 'come' in interactional and discursive functions similar to *venga*.

As in the early stages of the first grammaticalization cline of *venga* from optative to discourse marker of acceptance, Tok Pisin uses 'come' to make indirect requests as shown in (42). The example in (43) seems to suggest that this construction has begun to grammaticalize into a marker of acceptance as well.

(42) *Saksak i-kam.*
 sago   PRED-come
 'May sago come (Give me sago).'
                    (Tok Pisin, Don Daniels 2012, personal communication)

(43) A: *Bai   yu   kaikai saksak?*
      would you eat   sago
      'Would you like to eat sago?'

   B: *Kam.*
      come
      'Come (yes).'   (Tok Pisin, Don Daniels 2012, personal communication)

Furthermore, like the final stages of the first cline proposed in this paper, Flemish uses 'come' (along with the French borrowing *allé* 'go') to express acceptance with reservation toward requests, as in (44) and (45). The parentheses indicate that *kom* can optionally be used in discourse in those positions. Notice that in (45) *kom* can be used in either the left-detached or right-detached positions, which is evidence for its pragmaticalized status. The fact that both 'come' and 'go' are used in the same utterance as discourse markers of acceptance also supports the claim that it is the conventionalization of conversational implicatures of the construction rather than simply the lexical semantics of the verb which influences the grammaticalization pathway to discourse marker.

(44) *Allé (kom), 't is goe. Ik zal het dan wel doen.*
go come it is okay I FUT it then PRT do
'Well, ok fine, I'll do it then.'

          (Flemish, Aelbrecht 2011, personal communication)

(45) *Allé (kom), ik zal u helpen, (kom).*
go come I FUT you help come
'Alright, I'll help you.' (Flemish, Aelbrecht 2011, personal communication)

Looking now at the second cline from imperative to discourse marker of disagreement, the use of 'come' as a hortative in languages other than Spanish has long been attested. With the hortative, 'come' is used to mitigate a subsequent imperative, encourage the addressee of his or her abilities, or comply with the speaker's desires as shown in examples (46)–(49):

(46) *Come on. Let's think.*   (COCA: 2011)

(47) *dɔ̀ gɔ!*
come go
'(Come on), go!'   (Baka, Heine and Kuteva 2002: 70)

(48) *Komm, denk darüber nach!*
come think about:it after
'Come on, think about it!'   (German, Heine and Kuteva 2002: 69)

(49) *Komm, geh jetzt*
come go now
'Come on, go now!'   (German, Heine and Kuteva 2002: 70)

Finally, English and Flemish use 'come' in reactive ways in discourse to express disagreement with the epistemological stance of the addressee as in (50)–(52). Although (50) is structurally used with a prohibitive similar to the hortative construction, semantically and pragmatically it expresses disagreement with the beliefs of the addressee. Thus, like Spanish, the prohibitive construction seems to be a possible source for the discourse marker of disagreement.

(50) *Kom, jong, nie onozel doen.*
come INT NEG silly do
'Come on, don't be silly.'

          (Flemish, Aelbrecht 2011, personal communication)

(51) *'I don't want anyone to lose their job, whether they're a federal employee or not,' Boehner said. 'But come on, we're broke.'* (COCA: 2011)

(52) A: *I mean, people will just be trampling the box office to get in.* (sarcastically)
B: *You know how they get.*
A: *Oh, come on, Hoda.* (COCA: 2011)

While these examples suggest a cross-linguistic tendency to use 'come' as a discourse marker, they also suggest a strong need for more discourse data for lesser-studied languages of the world. These interactional and discourse usages are often not cited in reference grammars; however, they are essential to our understanding of grammaticalization, pragmaticalization, and language change more broadly. Thus, my hope is that this paper will serve as an impetus for further research into interpersonal discourse in the world's lesser-studied languages.

7 Conclusion

In this paper, I have argued for two grammaticalization clines involving Peninsular Spanish *venga* 'come': (1) optative > indirect request > acceptance of an offer > discourse marker of agreement > discourse marker of conversation closing, and (2) imperative > hortative > discourse marker of disagreement. These pathways are summarized in the timeline in Figure 1.

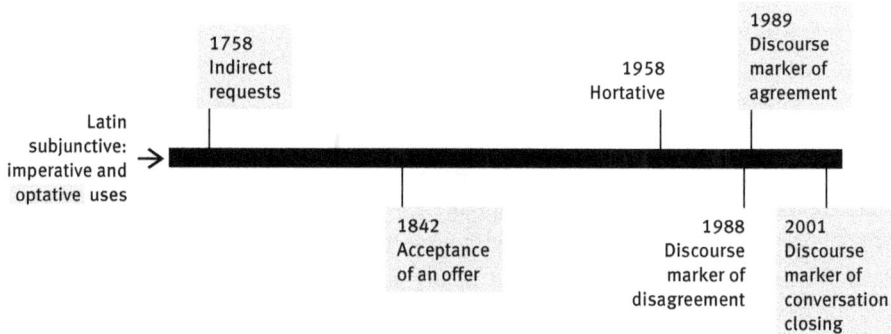

Figure 1. Timeline of diachronic changes of *venga*

Furthermore, I have argued that metaphorical extension and the conventionalization of conversational implicatures brought about by the processes of subjectification and intersubjectification were the mechanisms of semantic change at work in the diachronic development of *venga* as a discourse marker. Finally, I have illustrated similar uses of 'come' in a number of other languages to illustrate the possible cross-linguistic universality of these diachronic pathways.

Beyond establishing the diachronic development of *venga* as a discourse marker, a number of questions for further study remain. Specifically, more research is needed to determine the difference between the use of *venga* in the left and right peripheries and the effect of the peripheries on the development of *venga* as a discourse marker (e.g. Traugott 2012). Furthermore, the historical interaction between both grammaticalization clines warrants further investigation beyond the scope of this paper.

Acknowledgments

I would like to thank Don Daniels, Robert McLaughlin, Benjamin Schmeiser, and two anonymous reviewers for their helpful comments on previous drafts of this paper. I would also like to thank the audience members of my presentations at the Graduate Institute of Applied Linguistics Academic Forum and the 44th Annual Meeting of the Societas Linguistica Europaea for their many profitable suggestions. I am also grateful to Juan Navarro Martinez for his assistance with the Spanish translations in this paper. Finally, I owe special gratitude to K. Aaron Smith for his guidance and support throughout the research and writing process and for his many revisions on previous drafts of this paper. All remaining errors or inaccuracies are my own.

Abbreviations

COND	conditional
DM	discourse marker
FRL	formal
HORT	hortative
IFL	informal
IMP	imperative
INT	interjection
OPT	optative
PRED	predicate marker
PRET	preterite
PROH	prohibitive
PRT	particle
SBJV	subjunctive

Sources

Davies, Mark. 2002. Corpus del Español: 100 million words, 1200s–1900s.
    http://www.corpusdelespanol.org/x.asp.
Davies, Mark. 2008. The Corpus of Contemporary American English (COCA): 385 million
    words, 1990–present. http://www.americancorpus.org.
REAL ACADEMIA ESPAÑOLA: Banco de datos (CORDE) [en línea]. *Corpus diacrónico del
    español.* http://www.rae.es (accessed July 2011)
REAL ACADEMIA ESPAÑOLA: Banco de datos (CREA) [en línea]. *Corpus de referencia del
    español actual.* http://www.rae.es (accessed July 2011)

References

Aikhenvald, Alexandra Y. 2010. *Imperatives and Commands.* Oxford: Oxford University Press.
Blas Arroyo, José Luis. 1998. A case of pragmatic variation: On the increase in meaning of a
    discourse marker in contemporary Spanish. Structural and sociolinguistic aspects.
    Analecta Malacitana 21(2): 543–571.
Brinton, Laurel J. (ed.). 1996. *Pragmatic Markers in English: Grammaticalization and dis-
    course functions.* Berlin & New York: Mouton de Gruyter.
Brinton, Laurel J. 2001. Historical discourse analysis. In Deborah Schiffrin, Deborah Tannen, &
    Heidi Hamilton (eds.), *Handbook of Discourse Analysis*, 138–160. Malden, MA: Blackwell.
Bybee, Joan L. 1985. *Morphology: A study of the relations between meaning and form.*
    Amsterdam: John Benjamins.
Calsamiglia, Helena & Amparo Tusón. 1999. *Las Cosas del Decir: Manual del análisis del
    discurso.* Barcelona: Ariel.
Cestero Mancera, Ana María. 2005. *Conversación y Enseñanza de Lengua Extranjeras.*
    Madrid: Arco/Libros.
Cestero Mancera, Ana María & Francisco Moreno Fernández. 2008. Usos y funciones de vale
    y ¡venga! en el habla de Madrid. *Boletín de Lingüística* 20(29), 65–84. Caracas: Universi-
    dad Central de Venezuela.
Company Company, Concepción. 2004. Gramaticalización o desgramaticalización? Reanáli-
    sis y subjetivización como marcadores discursivos en la historia de Español. *Revista de
    Filología Española* 84: 29–66.
Diewald, Gabriele. 2011. Pragmaticalization (defined) as grammaticalization of discourse
    functions. *Linguistics* 49(2). 365–390.
Goosens, Louis. 1995. From three respectable horses' mouths: Metonymy and conventional-
    ization in a diachronically differentiated data base. In Louis Goussens, Paul Pauwels,
    Brygida Rudzka-Ostyn, Anne-Marie Simon-Vandenbergen & Johan Vanparys (eds.), *By
    Word of Mouth: Metaphor, Metonymy and Linguistic Action in Cognitive Perspective*,
    175–204. Philadelphia: John Benjamins.
Heine, Bernd & Tania Kuteva. 2002. *World Lexicon of Grammaticalization.* New York: Cambridge
    University Press.
Herrero, Gemma. 2002. Aspectos sintácticos del lenguaje juvenil. In Félis Rodríguez (ed.), *El
    Lenguaje de los Jóvenes*, 67–96. Barcelona: Ariel.
Lehmann, Christian. 1995. *Thoughts on Grammaticalization.* Munich: LINCOM Europa.

Lewandowski, Wojciech. 2007. Toward a comparative analysis of coming and going verbs in Spanish, German, and Polish. Barcelona: Universitat Autònoma de Barcelona Master's thesis.

Pellicer, Juan Antonio. 1800. *Vida de Miguel de Cervantes Saavedra*. Madrid: D. Gabriel de Sancha.

Pinkster, Harm. 1988. *Lateinische Syntax und Semantik*. Tübingen: Francke.

Real Academia Española. 1979. *Diccionario de Autoridades* (1726–1739). Madrid: Gredos.

Santos Río. 2003. *Diccionario de Partículas*. Salamanca: Luso Española de Ediciones.

Schiffrin, Deborah. 1987. *Discourse Markers*. Cambridge: Cambridge University Press.

Smith, K. Aaron. 2011. Grammaticalization. *Language and Linguistics Compass* 5/6: 367–380.

Smith, K. Aaron. 2012. New perspectives, theories and methods: Frequency and language change. In Alexander Bergs & Laurel J. Brinton, English Historical Linguistics (HSK 34.2), Volume II, 1531–1545. Berlin & Boston: de Gruyter.

Traugott, Elizabeth Closs. 1989. On the rise of epistemic meanings in English: An example of subjectification in semantic change. *Language* 65: 31–55.

Traugott, Elizabeth Closs. 1995. The role of the development of discourse markers in a theory of grammaticalization. Paper presented at International Conference on Historical Linguistics XII, Manchester.

Traugott, Elizabeth Closs. 2001. Legit counter examples to unidirectionality. Paper presented at Freiburg University, October 17th 2001.

Traugott, Elizabeth Closs. 2007. Discussion article: Discourse markers, modal particles, and contrastive analysis, synchronic and diachronic. *Catalan Journal of Linguistics* 6: 139–157.

Traugott, Elizabeth Closs. 2010. (Inter)subjectivity and (inter)subjectification: A reassessment. In: Hubert Cuyckens, Kristin Davidse & Lieven Vandelanotte (eds.), *Subjectification, Intersubjectification and Grammaticalization*, 29–74. Berlin & Boston: Mouton de Gruyter.

Traugott, Elizabeth Closs. 2012. Intersubjectification and Clause Periphery. In Lieselotte Brems, Lobke Ghesquière, & Freek van de Velde (eds.), *Intersections of Intersubjectivity* (special issue of *English Text Construction* 5:1), 7–28.

Traugott, Elizabeth Closs & Richard B. Dasher. 2002. *Regularity in Semantic Change*. New York: Cambridge University Press.

van der Auwera, Johan & Ewa Schalley. 2004. From optative and subjunctive to irrealis. In Frank Brisard, Michael Meeuwis & Bart Vandenabeele (eds.), *Seduction, Community, Speech: A Festschrift for Herman Parret*, 87–96. Amsterdam: John Benjamins.

Zorraquino Martín, María Antonia & José Portolés Lázaro. 1999. Los marcadores del discurso. In Ignacio Bosque & Violeta Demonte (eds.), *Gramática Descriptiva de la Lengua Española*, Vol. 3. 4051–4213. Madrid: Espasa Calpe para la Real Academia Española.

Robert Carlson

The grammaticalization of 'go' as an intensifier in Supyire

1 Introduction

Like other northern and central Senufo languages, Supyire[1] has two verbs roughly meaning 'go'. The great majority of verbs in these languages have two forms: a base form and a derived form used with imperfective aspect. The two 'go' verbs in Supyire are *kare* (impfv. *kɛ́ɛ́gɛ́*) and *shyɛ*,[2] (impfv. *sí ~ se*). In current Supyire, the two verbs are very similar in meaning, and they are interchangeable in a wide variety of constructions. There is some comparative evidence, however, that they were semantically different at a previous stage of the language. In his lexical list of Minyanka, the Senufo language spoken to the north of Supyire, Cauvin (1980) translates the Minyanka cognate *karì* as *'partir'* and *šɛ* as *'aller'*. Similarly, in his dictionary of Cebaara, the Senufo language spoken to the south of Supyire, Mills (2003) glosses *kåari* as *'aller, s'en aller, partir'*, while *sɛ́ɛ* is glossed *'visiter, aller à, aller dans, se rendre à'*. It is thus likely that at an earlier stage, Supyire *kare* meant 'go (away from here)' or 'leave (the deictic center)', while *shyɛ* meant 'go to (a locative goal)'. In current Supyire, both *kare* and *shyɛ* can occur with (examples 1 and 2) and without (examples 3 and 4) a mentioned locative goal. Without a specified locative goal, *kare* is sometimes best translated as "leave" (example 5).[3]

(1) *Mìi à   moblíge ywɔ nahá Fáágá   ná mà kàrè Sukwol' e.*
     I   PRF bus   take here Farakala at and go Sikasso to
     'I took a bus here in Farakala and went to Sikasso.'

---

1 Supyire is a northern Senufo language spoken by about 500,000 people in southeastern Mali. The place of Senufo languages within Niger-Congo is disputed. Although they were formerly classified in the Gur family (cf. for example Naden (1989), following Bendor-Samuel (1971)), current thinking is inclined to consider the Senufo group as coordinate with Gur and Adamawa and possibly Kru, both falling under a West Volta-Congo grouping (cf. the classification proposed by Segerer (n.d.)). I have no relevant data on 'go' verbs for southern Senufo languages. The variety of Supyire described in this chapter is that spoken in the Kampwo region, to the west of the city of Sikasso.
2 [ɛ] does not contrast with [a] after a palatalized consonant (though it does elsewhere). Thus *shyɛ* is variously pronounced [ʃʲɛ] or [ʃʲa] or anywhere in between.
3 *Kare* (N=1195) is roughly twice as frequent in the text database (see below) as *shyɛ* (N=680).

(2) *Kà pi í shyɛ́ kacèège e mà sàa ŋwɔ̀hɔ̀nì.*
and they NARR go meadow to and AND.IMPFV hide.IMPFV
'Then they went to the meadow and began to play hide and seek.'

(3) *Kà Cin sí ŋ́káré, maá ḿpá ná cèmpèèyi shùùnnì í.*
and Leopard NARR go and.NARR come with bushbuck two with
'The Leopard went and came back with two bushbuck.' [speaking of going hunting]

(4) *Ku canŋa nùmpanŋa na, kà pi í shyá, pi ɲɛ à yafyîn*
that day tomorrow at and they NARR go they NEG PRF thing
ta mɛ́.
get NEG
'The next day, they went, but didn't get anything.' [speaking of going fishing]

(5) *Kà pi í ú shyɛ́ɛ́ré sèl' è, kà u ú ŋ́káré.*
and they NARR him thank truth in and he NARR go
'They thanked him very much, and then he left.'

In addition to these two lexical verbs, Supyire also has an auxiliary-like andative *sá* and a highly grammaticalized serial verb *sa*, both of which are etymologically related to *shyɛ*.[4] The andative *sá*, which can usually be translated as 'go VERB', is an example of grammaticalization very much "on the beaten path". The same cannot be said for the serial verb *sa*, which is the subject of this paper. The central claim put forward here is that *sa* has developed a cluster of semantic and pragmatic functions which can loosely be described as "intensifying".

The etymological connection between *sá*, *sa*, and *shyɛ* is not obvious at first sight, and must therefore be justified. This forms the topic of Section 1.1. The auxiliary *sá* and the serial verb *sa* occur in similar but slightly different syntactic contexts. The constructions in which they appear are briefly described in Sections 1.2 and 1.3.

Section 2 describes the various functions that "intensifier" *sa* has in current Supyire. These can be summarized as follows: (i) A content-oriented or semantic function of intensifying some gradable concept which occurs in the same sentence. This function is described in Section 2.1. (ii) A pair of speech-act or prag-

---

4 Supyire has two phonetically identical but behaviorally different mid tones, labeled "strong" and "weak" in Carlson (1994). The weak mids undergo many more tone rules than the strong ones. *Shyɛ* and *sa* are both weak mids. The rules affecting both weak mids and high tones have the effect that in many contexts *sa* and *sá* actually have the same tone (either low or high).

matic functions: (a) an epistemic function of strengthening an assertion in the face of the addressee's skepticism ("believe me"); this is described in 2.2.1; (b) a deontic function of strengthening a directive or an interrogative ("do what I want" and "answer me") in the face of the addressee's reluctance to comply; this is described in Sections 2.2.2 and 2.2.3.

A tentative story of the development of this cluster of meanings is given in Section 3. An account is offered there of how "go to" might have developed into "more than usual", and how that in turn might have developed into "speech act intensifier". It must be admitted at the outset that there are no historical documents available which could give direct evidence of the order of appearance of the various functions of *sa*. The account given in Section 3 must therefore be taken as only one possibility, although I think that it is a plausible one.

The data in this chapter come from two sources. One is a text database containing texts recorded and transcribed over the last 30 years in the Kampwo region. This database currently has slightly over 50,000 clauses. Around 2% of clauses contain either an andative *sá* or an intensifying *sa*.[5] There are around 980 examples of andative *sá* and 140 of intensifying *sa* in the database.[6] The other source of both data and insights is my colleague Ali Sanogo, with whom I am preparing a bilingual dictionary of Supyire. Every aspect of the analysis has been discussed with Mr. Sanogo, as will be evident in the following pages.

1.1 The etymological source of *sa*

Both of the verbs *kare* and *shyɛ* can be reconstructed at least for proto-North/Central Senufo, and probably for proto-Senufo as well. Cognates of *shyɛ* in other Senufo languages are: *séɛ* (Cebaara, Central Senufo), *síɛ 'procéder'* (Nyarafolo, Southern Senufo), *sye* [ʃe] 'go' (Pilara, Southern Senufo), and *šɛ* [ʃɛ] (Minyanka, Northern Senufo). In Supyire, a regular sound change which diphthongized long stressed vowels has led to cognate sets such as the following:

(6) Cebaara   *káa*   'mâcher'
     Nyarafolo   *káa*   'manger'
     Pilara   *ká*   'eat (meat)'
     Jimini   *ká*   'chew'

---

5 Some of these are phonetically *rá* since unstressed auxiliaries beginning in [s] are frequently rhotacized.

6 The exact number of each is not possible to ascertain due to possible transcription errors, especially in texts transcribed decades ago, and very occasional ambiguities.

Karaboro	*kaa*	'manger de la viande'
Supyire	*kya*	'eat (meat)' [kxa]
Minyanka	*xa*	'manger (viande)'

(7) | Cebaara | *lɛɛ* | 'être vieux; mûrir' |
Nyarafolo	*liɛ*	'vieillir; mûrir'
Pilara	*lɛ̂*	'ripe; old'
Jimini	*lɛ̂*	'be old'
Karaboro	*lɛ̂ɛ̂*	'être vieux'
Supyire	*lyɛ*	'be old; age'
Minyanka	*lɛ*	'être vieux'

Thus it is likely that the ancestor of Supyire *shyɛ* was close to Cebaara *sɛ́ɛ*.[7] Andative *sá* is almost certainly a reduced, unstressed descendant of this lexical verb.[8] It is a very old grammaticalization which can be reconstructed for proto-Senufo since it occurs in southern languages (Jimini *sa*[9] ; Nyarafolo *sá* [10]), central (Cebaara *sá* (Mills 2003, *ad loc.*)) as well as the northern language Supyire. In contrast, the grammaticalization of intensifying *sa* must be comparatively recent, since, to the best of my knowledge, it occurs only in Supyire. There is no trace of it in the best documented languages, Minyanka and Cebaara, which are also among the most closely related to Supyire. It is much more likely that it is a new development in Supyire rather than that it is an older grammaticalization dating back to, say, proto-northern Senufo or proto-Senufo which has subsequently disappeared elsewhere except in Supyire. However, when more data from southern Senufo languages is available, this hypothesis may have to be revised.

As noted above, andative *sá* is auxiliary-like. What this means syntactically will be explained in the next section. In contrast, intensifying *sa* is a defective verb: it occurs only as the first verb in a serial verb construction (see Section 1.3 below). It is therefore significant that it has the same tone (weak mid) as *shyɛ*. If Supyire weak mid tone results from a split of an original high tone into a high tone and a weak mid tone, as suggested by Garber (1987), then it is likely that

---

7 Supyire "weak" mid tone (the tone of *shyɛ*) regularly corresponds with Cebaara high tone. Alveolar consonants cannot occur with palatalization or labialization in Supyire. The shift from [s] to [ʃ] is thus regular.
8 The difference in tone between the auxiliary *sá* and the lexical verb (with (weak) mid tone) is paralleled by a similar difference between the venitive auxiliary *pá* and the lexical verb *pa* 'come' (the latter having (strong) mid tone), which are obviously also etymologically related.
9 Matthieu Ouattara, personal communication.
10 Linnea Boese, personal communication.

intensifying *sa* did not develop from the andative *sá*, but rather stems directly from the lexical verb **sɛ́ɛ* after the tonal split which left the latter with a weak mid tone. From a semantic point of view, therefore, the intensifying function most likely developed from the lexical meaning 'go to (a locative goal)'. Admittedly, this scenario is speculative and open to revision if other comparative evidence comes to light.

One final detail should be noted. Both andative *sá* and intensifying *sa* must have developed from the perfective form of the source verb, plausibly reconstructed as **sɛ́ɛ*, rather than from the imperfective form, which must be reconstructed as **sée* or **síi* (cf. Cebaara *sée*, Nyarafolo *síi*, Supyire *sí*). This is likely for phonological reasons ([a] < [ɛ] is more plausible than [a] < [e] or [i]) and from the fact that neither can follow an imperfective auxiliary (both can only occur in clauses with perfective aspect).[11] Andative *sá* itself has an imperfective form *sáa* (or *sàa*, see example 2) which must be followed by an imperfective verb (see next section). Intensifying *sa* has no imperfective form.

1.2 Andative *sá* (the "beaten path")

The older andative *sá* is distinguished not only tonally but also by construction from intensifying *sa*. Andative *sá* behaves like an auxiliary in that it requires a nasal prefix on an immediately following verb (i.e. unseparated from the auxiliary by a direct object[12]) which begins with a voiceless stop (p, t, c, or k). This prefix has no tone of its own, instead taking the tone of whatever precedes it. This prefix appears in intransitive clauses and in clauses where the direct object has been fronted for focus. Examples (8) through (13) show this prefix on the verb *kare* 'go' (imperfective *kéégé*) following a variety of auxiliaries. Example (14) shows that this prefix also follows andative *sá*.

(8)　　*U*　　　*màha*[13]　*ŋ-kare.*　　　　　　　　　　　　　　HABITUAL
　　　　he/she　HAB　　IP-go
　　　　'He/She (habitually) goes.'

---

11 The imperfective of *shyɛ* has been grammaticalized in Supyire with other functions, notably as a future auxiliary *sí*, a subjunctive auxiliary *sí*, and the narrative auxiliary *sí*. Both of the latter have undergone considerable phonological erosion, so in the examples presented in this chapter they do not often appear in their original *sí* form.

12 Basic clausal constituent order in all Senufo languages is fairly rigid: S Aux (O) V X. Only the direct object precedes the verb, and nothing else can come between the auxiliary and the verb. Most languages have at least one mood in which there is no auxiliary.

13 Orthographic *h* between two vowels represents a glottal stop [ʔ].

(9) *U   na   ŋ-kéégé.*   PROGRESSIVE
he/she PROG IP-go.IMPFV
'He/She is going/leaving.'

(10) *U   ná   ŋ́-káré.*   PAST
he/she PAST IP-go
'He/She went/left.'

(11) *U   ahá   ŋ́-káré ...*   CONDITIONAL
he/she COND IP-go ...
'If/She he/she goes/leaves ...'

(12) *Kà   u   ú   ŋ́-káré.*   NARRATIVE
and he/she NARR IP-go
'Then he went/left.'

(13) *Mu   à   yaa   mu   ú   ŋ́-káré.*   SUBJUNCTIVE
you PRF should you SBJV IP-go
'You should go/leave.'

(14) *U   a   sà   ŋ̀-kàrè.*[14]   ANDATIVE
he/she PRF AND IP-go
'He went.'

No lexical verb can be followed by the intransitive prefix in this way. In requiring the intransitive prefix, andative *sá* thus patterns like an auxiliary.

Another respect in which andative *sá* is like an auxiliary is that it has an imperfective form *sáa* (or *sàa* in some tonal contexts; see (2) above for an example). The imperfective suffix *-a* which derives this form may also be added to the conditional auxiliary *ká ~ ahá* to create an imperfective form *káa ~ aháa*, and to the habitual auxiliary *màha*, to create an imperfective form *màhaa*.

Andative *sá* is unlike regular auxiliaries in that it is itself normally preceded by an auxiliary, as for example in (14), where it is preceded by the perfect auxiliary. The position immediately following an auxiliary may only be occupied by an intransitive verb or by a direct object. In this respect *sá* is more verb-like

---

14 Andative *sá* has low tone in this example because the low tone of the preceding perfect auxiliary *à* has spread onto it (while the mid tone of the pronoun subject has spread onto the perfect auxiliary).

than ordinary auxiliaries. Examples (15–17) illustrate andative *sá* following auxiliaries:

(15) *Wùu màha sá   ɲáára caangé e.*   following HABITUAL[15]
    we   HAB   AND walk   market in
    'We go walk around in the market.'

(16) *Mu ahá   sá   yí jwú wà   à ...*   following CONDITIONAL
    you COND AND it say INDEF to
    'If you go tell anyone ...'

(17) *kà   u   ú   sá   ɲ̀-cwó nɔ̀ɲi yàsìnìɲké na.* following NARRATIVE
    and she NARR AND IP-fall man bed   on
    'she went and fell onto the man's bed.'

Furthermore, andative *sá* is found in some positions where auxiliaries do not occur, but where a verb is expected. In (18) it follows the same subject connective *mà* which signals both continuity of subject and tense, aspect, and modality from the preceding clause. Aside from andative *sá* and venitive *pá*, this connective can only be followed by a direct object or a verb. Example (19) illustrates a frequent construction in which this type of *mà* clause follows the conjunction *fó* 'until' when the following clause has the same subject as the main clause. Example (20) shows another frequent construction in which andative *sá* follows the connective in the middle of a serial verb construction, a position where auxiliaries may not occur.[16]

(18) *Kà u ú   fé   à   kàrè mà   sà   nɔ̀   tábacíge na ...*
    and he NARR run SCN go and.ss AND arrive doka.tree at
    'then he went running and came to the doka tree ...'

(19) *Kà pi í   lí dírí fó mà   sà   cānŋke kwɔ̀.*
    and they NARR it pull till and.ss AND day   finish
    'They pulled it till the day ended.'

---

15 Note that habitual cannot be analyzed as a species of imperfective aspect in Supyire. It can cooccur with both perfective aspect, as in this example, and with imperfective aspect (in which case the auxiliary is *màhaa*, with an imperfective suffix). Andative *sá* and intensifying *sa* may only occur with the perfective form of the habitual. For a discussion of the category habitual cross-cutting the aspectual distinction perfective/imperfective, see Dahl (1985).
16 Examples (19) and (20) illustrate a temporal (hence metaphorical) use of the andative.

(20) *Kà pi sanmpíí sì m̀-pà̠ a sà̠ ŋ̀-kwɔ̀ wuru ŋgé cógóŋi na.*
and they rest   NARR IP-come SCN AND IP-finish that that[17] manner on
'The rest of them all came in the same way.'

These data show that andative *sá* is like an auxiliary in some respects and like a verb in others. In contrast, intensifying *sa*, to which we now turn, is more consistently verb-like.

1.3 Intensifying *sa* ("off the beaten path")

Intensifying *sa* occurs in only one syntactic position: it is always the first verb in a serial verb construction.[18] It is like andative *sá* in that it normally requires a preceding tense, aspect, or mood auxiliary. It is unlike *sá* in that it must be followed by a serial verb connective,[19] and cannot be followed directly by a verb (with or without the intransitive prefix). The construction in which it occurs thus has the following form: S AUX *sa* SCN (O) VERB X.

There are two serial verb connectives: *à* and *a*.[20] The first occurs in clauses with perfect, habitual, conditional, narrative, or past auxiliaries. The second occurs in imperative and subjunctive clauses.[21] Examples of serial constructions

---

17 Supyire has two series of demonstratives: (i) a series of "discourse" or "endophoric" demonstratives, pointing to a referent mentioned or evoked in the preceding discourse (*wuru* in this example); (ii) a series of "exophoric" demonstratives, normally pointing to a referent in the speech situation. The two not infrequently occur together, as here, with a kind of emphatic endophoric meaning, viz. "that very ..." or "that same ..."

18 The serial construction of which it is a constituent may itself be embedded as the second constituent of another serial construction. However, *sa* cannot occur as the final verb of a serial construction.

19 Supyire serial verb constructions in most tense-aspect-moods require a connective (historically probably derived from a VP conjunction), which typically cliticizes onto the first verb.

20 The second of these is the subjunctive serial connective, which has no tone of its own. It always takes the final tone of the preceding word.

21 In future, potential, and prohibitive clauses there is no serial connective. Instead, each verb in the construction takes the future intransitive prefix if it is not preceded by a direct object. This prefix differs from the non-future intransitive prefix in that it is prefixed to all verbs no matter what their initial consonant, whereas the non-future intransitive prefix occurs only on verbs beginning with a voiceless stop. In these future-oriented clauses the syntactic difference between andative *sá* and intensifying *sa* is neutralized. Following a future auxiliary, both *sá* and *sa* become *zà* (from *m̀-sá* and *m̀-sa*, the future low-tone nasal prefix voicing the initial fricative and bequeathing its tone and then disappearing). Since the following verb invariably takes the future intransitive prefix, instead of the voiceless-stop-only intransitive prefix (expected after *sá*) or a serial connective (expected after *sa*), there is no formal way to tell the difference between the two. Because of this formal ambiguity, the analysis presented in this chapter does not use any clauses with future or potential tense or prohibitive mood.

with *à* are given in (21) and (22), and with *a* in (23) and (24). In (22) and (24), the first verb of the serial construction is the intensifier *sa*.

(21) *Pi   pun' á   kàr' à   mu yaha númê.*[22]
      they all PRF go SCN you leave now
      'They have all gone away and left you now.'

(22) *K' a   sà   a   pèè.*[23]
      it PRF INT SCN be.big
      'It is really big.'

(23) *Ku nèèn' à   wíí.*[24]
      it taste SCN look
      'Taste it and see.'

(24) *Bàbá, mu ú   sá   á   wíí.*[25]
      Papa, you SBJV INT SCN look
      'Papa, you really should look.'

2 Types of intensification with *sa*

There are two main functions of intensifying *sa*. One can be characterized as more semantic or content-oriented,[26] with a meaning translatable as 'very' or 'really'. This requires some gradable quality or action within the sentence, which is asserted to be "more than usual". Ali Sanogo labels this the *sa fànhàlewu* 'strenghening *sa*', literally, 'the force-putting *sa*', from *fànhà* 'power, force' + *le*

---

22 The Supyire orthography writes final unstressed vowel assimilation as if it were elision. In this example, *kare* acquires a low tone from the preceding perfect auxiliary, which itself takes a high tone from the preceding word *puní*. The final vowel of *kare* assimilates to the serial connective in vowel quality, but not in tone, and the final vowel of *puní* similarly assimilates in quality to the perfect auxiliary. Thus the sequence *puní + à + kare + à + mu* ... is phonetically [punáákàraàmu ...].
23 In this example, the low tone perfect auxiliary has given its tone to the following *sa*, and itself takes the mid tone of the preceding pronoun. The mid tone of the *sa* is in turn realized on the following serial connective *à*, whose low tone is realized on the following verb *péè*.
24 In this example, the high tone verb *nééné* 'taste' becomes low because the preceding direct object pronoun ends in a floating low tone. The low tone spreads onto the subjunctive serial connective *a*.
25 In this example, the high tone of the subjunctive auxiliary spreads onto the following *sa* and continues onto the following connective *a*.
26 Compare agent-oriented modality in Bybee et al.'s classification (1994).

'put in' + *wu* 'adjectivizing suffix'. The idea is that the speaker is strengthening some part of the utterance.

The other function can be characterized as more pragmatic or interlocutor-oriented.[27] In this function, the speaker strengthens the speech act which the utterance is intended to accomplish. There are in fact two subfunctions here which depend on the speech act intended by the speaker. In declaratives and polar questions, the function of the *sa* can be characterized as epistemic. In statements the speaker strengthens an assertion in the face of a perceived inclination on the part of the addressee to disbelieve the assertion. Sanogo calls this type the *sa dádáwú* 'sa for believing', from reduplicated *dá* 'believe' + *wu* 'adjectivizing suffix'. Especially strong examples he calls *kakyanhaladádáwú* 'sa for believing something astonishing', from *kakyanhala* 'astonishing situation or event'.

In polar questions, it is the speaker rather than the addressee who exhibits incredulity. *Sa* polar questions are uttered in contexts where the addressee has made an assertion which the speaker/questioner finds difficult to believe. The question is thus posed with some urgency: do you really *mean* that? Sanogo calls this type *sa jwumɔ fànhə̀nyahawu* 'sa which increases the force of the speech'. *Jwumɔ* is a nominalization of the verb *jwo* 'speak, say'. *Fànhə̀nyahawu* is composed of *fànhà* 'force, power' + *nyaha* 'be much, cause to be much' + *wu* 'adjectivizing suffix'. This label does not allude to the fact that the object of the query is actually the truth of an assertion made previously by the addressee.

In imperatives, hortatives, and other directives the speaker also strengthens the manipulative speech act. This type of function can be broadly characterized as deontic: the speaker urges the addressee to do what the speaker wants. Sanogo calls this type the *sa fànhàcyáncyánwú* 'force-imposing *sa*', from *cyán* 'cause to fall', used in the expression *fànhà cyàn wà nà,* 'force someone (to do something)', literally 'cause force to fall on someone'.

Examples of *sa* in these functions are given in the following two sections. It is worth pointing out that the distinction between semantic and pragmatic in the above characterizations is not categorical, which is why I have used the expressions "more semantic" and "more pragmatic".[28] In the so-called semantic case the assertion of a more than usual degree crucially depends on the speaker's assessment of what the addressee regards as "usual". Of course conventionality enters into this assessment, but cannot account by itself for the subtle use of 'strenthening *sa*' in actual discourses.

---

27 Compare speaker-oriented modality in Bybee et al. (1994). In the present case, the function is intersubjective in the sense that the speaker is assessing the beliefs or willingness of the addressee, and shaping the utterance accordingly.

28 On the non-categorical boundary between semantics and pragmatics, see Givón (2001), Langacker (2008).

2.1 *Sa fànhàlewu*: "strengthening *sa*"

As noted above, the *sa fànhàlewu* requires the presence of something gradable which can be strengthened. The simplest cases are those in which the verb which follows *sa* is stative and denotes some gradable quality. Compare the following examples, (25) and (27) with an unmodified stative verb, with (26) and (28) with the addition of *sa:*

(25) *K'à   tɔɔn.*
     it PRF be.long
     'It is long / tall.'

(26) *K'a   sà   à   tɔɔn.*
     it PRF INT SCN be.long
     'It is very long / tall.'

(27) *Mu   a   pèè.*
     you PRF be.big
     'You are fat.'

(28) *Mu   a   sà   a   pèè.*
     you PRF INT SCN be.big
     'You are very fat.'

Both of these verbs evoke extension in space. The gradable quality may also be non-spatial, as shown in the following examples:

(29) *K'a   sà   a   ɲàànà   ɲáíɲáí.*[29]
     it PRF INT SCN be.red.hot very.red.hot
     'It is extremely hot.'

(30) *Mu   pyig'   á   sà   a   kyàn!*
     your child PRF INT SCN be.rebellious
     'Your child is very rebellious.'

(31) *Wùù pi   à   pyi li   baríni   i   ké, wùu a   sà   a   cwɔ̀nrɔ̀.*
     we they PRF be that house.DIM in REL we PRF INT SCN be.squeezed
     'We who were in that tiny house were very squeezed.'

---

29 *Ɲáíɲáí* is an intensifying ideophone which is specific to the verb *ɲááɲá* 'be or become red hot'.

(32) *Mu jwúmpe kà   sá à   ɲyaha,*
    your speech COND INT SCN be.much
    sùpyíibíí sàhà   màha mpáa ntɔre mu   wúmpe e mɛ́.
    people   no.longer HAB VEN count your POSS in NEG
    'If you talk too much (lit. If your speech is very much), people will eventu-
    ally no longer pay attention to what you say.'

Any action which can be performed with more or less force can be intensified
with *sa*. Compare examples (33) and (35) without *sa* with (34) and (36) with *sa*.

(33) *U a   bààrà.*
    he PRF work
    'He worked.'

(34) *U a   sà a   bààrà.*
    he PRF INT SCN work
    'He worked very hard.' or 'He worked a lot.'

(35) *Wùu à   ɲaara.*
    we PRF walk
    'We walked.'

(36) *Wùu a   sà ā   ɲaara.*
    we PERF INT SCN walk
    'We really walked.' (=We walked a long way.)

Sa may also be used to indicate that a patient is more affected by the action
denoted by the verb:

(37) *L' a   mìì fyá.*
    it PRF me frighten
    'It scared me.'

(38) *`Ndémù l' a   sà a   mìì fyá   ke dɛ́,   supyibōni.*
    what   it PRF INT SCN me frighten REL EXCLAM people.killing
    'What really scared me was the killing.'

A patient may be more affected by the application of more force:

(39) *Pi a   ù   bwɔn.*
    they PRF him hit
    'They beat him.'

(40) *Pi   a   sà   a   ù   bwɔ̀n.*
they PRF INT SCN him hit
'They really beat him.'

The gradable element which attracts the intensification of *sa* may be something other than the main verb. Adverbial serial verbs, for example, can be intensified with *sa*. Compare the following pair of examples:

(41) *U   a   sòl'   ã̀   kàrè.*
he PRF do.early SCN go
'He left early (in the morning).'

(42) *U   a   sà   a   sòl'   ã̀   kàrè.*
he PRF INT SCN do.early SCN go
'He left really early.'

The gradable element may be a quantifier in the subject:

(43) *Pi   niɲyahara   a   tɛ̀ɛ̀n.*
they many   PRF sit
'Many of them have sat down.'

(44) *Pi   niɲyahara   a   sà   a   tɛ̀ɛ̀n.*
they many   PRF INT SCN sit
'Most of them have sat down.'[30]

It can be the direct object. Compare the following examples:

(45) *Pi   a   pèènte le   mìì ì.*
they PRF honor put me in
'They honored me.' Lit. 'They put honor in me.'

(46) *Pi   a   sà   a   pèènte le   mìì ì.*
they PRF INT SCN honor put me in
'They honored me very much.'

---

30 *Niɲyahara* is morphologically an adjective derived from the verb *ɲyaha* 'be much/many'. It is not quite the equivalent of "many" in example (43) in that in Supyire it denotes a quantity greater that 50%. Ali Sanogo gave hypothetical proportions for these examples: 40 out of 50 for (43) and 45 out of 50 for (44). In view of these proportions, perhaps a better English translation for (38) would be 'Most of them have sat down', and for (44) 'Almost all of them have sat down.'

(47) *U   à   kacɛnnɛ   pyi mìi á.*
      he PRF good.deed do me to
      'He did a good thing for me.'

(48) *`Ndé kacènni   u   a   sà   ā   pyi mìi á ke,*
      that good.deed he PRF INT SCN do me to REL
      Kile ù   lì fwòòní tò   ù   á   kacènnè.
      God   he its debt   cover him to good.deed
      'May God repay him with good for the very good thing he did for me.'

Degree intensifiers like English *very* are sometimes said to indicate a degree higher than the norm – an instance of the "up is more" metaphor, sometimes illustrated with a diagram like the following in the Cognitive Grammar tradition:

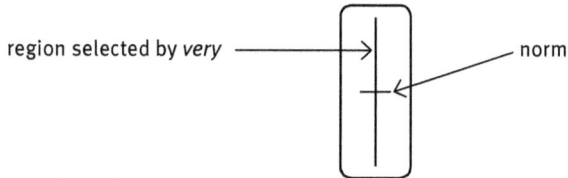

Figure 1. Degree above the norm

Degree intensifying expressions in Supyire in contrast evoke a horizontal rather than a vertical conceptual space. In this conceptualization, a greater degree is viewed as farther from the speaker. Note the following paraphrases of (22) (repeated here as (49)), supplied by Ali Sanogo:

(49) *K' a   sà   a   pèè.*
      it PRF INT SCN be.big
      'It is really big.'

(50) *K' a   pèl'³¹ a   tòrò.*
      it PRF be.big SCN pass
      'It is very big.'

(51) *K' a   pèl'   ā   nɔ   tɛgèni na.*
      if PRF be.big SCN arrive limit   at
      'It is very big.'

---

31 The verb *péè* 'be big' is underlyingly *péle*. The medial [l] regulary elides except when a clitic with an unstressed initial vowel follows, as here.

All three expressions illustrated in (49) through (51) evoke the gradable concept *péè* 'be big' as a space that recedes from the conceptualizer. In this conceptual space, the greater the distance from the conceptualizer the greater the degree of intensity. All three expressions also evoke fictive[32] motion. The conceptualizer sequentially scans[33] the conceptual space, starting from the nearest part of the conceptual space (corresponding to a lesser degree), and going further away towards the far boundary of the space which corresponds to a high degree of intensity. This basic scenario is evoked in slightly different ways in each case. In example (50) the verb *toro* 'pass' evokes a "norm" in the middle of the conceptual space.[34] The instance in question is beyond this norm. The conceptualizer scans the conceptual space until the mid-point norm is passed:

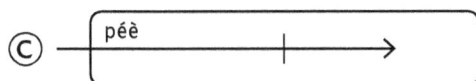

Figure 2. *toro* 'passing beyond the norm'

In example (51) the postpositial phrase *tɛgɛ̀ni na* 'at the limit/boundary' evokes the far boundary of the gradable category, where the maximal degree is to be found. The fictive motion reaches or arrives at this maximal region. Here the gradable quality or action in question must be thought of in relation to a specific type of entity or situation, in which there is actually a farthest limit either possible or desirable for the category. Although in the abstract some concepts like "be long" and "be big" do not have an inherent farthest limit, for a specific category of things, such as human beings, "be tall" and "be big/fat" are limited: in experience people just do not exceed a certain height or size. Other concepts like "be white" or "be short" do have an inherent limit, and these concepts may have been the ones with which the expression "arrive at the limit" in the sense of intensification may have arisen.

In contrast to example (50), *sa* in (49) does not directly evoke a norm, nor does it directly refer to a farther boundary of the gradable concept, as does (51). However, *sa* retains the goal-orientedness of the orginal *shyɛ* 'go to', and it thus evokes fictive motion that is directed away from the conceptualizer towards some goal. It prompts scanning that reaches the region of the gradable concept that is

---

32 See Talmy (2000) for the concept of fictive motion. Cf. also Matlock (2004).
33 See Langacker (2005, 2008) for the concept of scanning.
34 Compare the development of French *très* 'very' from Latin *trans* 'across, on the other side', similarly evoking a passing beyond an implicit norm.

farthest from the conceptualizer. Thus all three degree expressions "carry" the conceptualizer into the same region of the conceptual space.

Related to the conceptualization of greater degree as farther distance is the conceptualization of *comparison* as "passing". Consider the following example:

(52)   *Yịncwōŋi, lir' ā yịncwōŋi ŋgé ta ú à pa ké,*
     cowife   this PRF cowife that find she.COMP PRF come TIME
     'The cowife, meanwhile her cowife had come,

     ur' a sà a pyàŋi cù fó mà tòrò u wùubíí na.
     she PRF INT SCN child hold up.to and.ss pass her POSS at
     she took care of the child much more than she took care of her own children.'

The activity of holding a child, meaning in this context caring for the child, is gradable: it can be done to different degrees. In this example, extracted from a folktale, the mother of the child has died, and the mother's cowife takes better care of the orphaned child than she does of her own children. The comparison is expressed with the preposition/conjunction *fó* 'as far as (a location); until (a point in time)' introducing a clause with the verb *toro* 'pass'. This evokes a conceptualization in which the fictive motion continues into an area of the conceptual space which is beyond the degree of the standard of comparison (the degree to which the cowife cares for her own children). The *sa* may be understood as indicating that the fictive motion (that is, the scanning through the conceptual space to reach the intended degree) goes a long way past the standard of comparison.[35]

Comparison of degree is not necessarily cued with the verb *toro* 'pass'. In the following example, *laaga* 'distance' and *tɔɔn* 'be long' are used to evoke the same type of comparative scanning:

(53)   *Waga a sà ā yaa mà laaga tɔɔn Bàmàkwo na.*
     Ouaga PRF INT SCN be.made and.ss distance be.long Bamako at
     'Ouagadougou is much more developed than Bamako.' Literally: 'Ouagadougou has been very constructed and made the distance far from Bamako.'

---

35 The fact that the cowife takes care for the orphaned child more than she takes care of her own children is very unexpected in the context of Supyire folktales, where the evil cowife plays a role similar to the evil stepmother in European folktales. This unexpectedness is also potentially indicated by *sa*, a function discussed in Section 2.2.1. This example is in fact a bridging example, in which both the degree enhancement ("take very good care of") and the speech act enhancement ("you may find this astonishing, but it is in fact true") functions are available. This type of bridging example is discussed in Section 3.

Comparison can be indicated by the addition of a *na*-marked postpositional phrase by itself, as shown by the following examples:

(54) *Waga   à   yaa.*
      Ouaga   PRF   be.made
      'Ouagadougou is developed.'

(55) *Waga   à   yaa   Bàmàkwo na.*
      Ouaga   PRF   be.made   Bamako   at
      'Ouagadougou is more developed than Bamako.'

The addition of *sa* in (53) indicates a greater degree ("very developed"), and the addition of *mà laaga tɔɔn* 'and make the distance long' indicates that the degree predicated of the theme in is far beyond that of the standard of comparison. The fictive motion scanning to reach the degree being asserted thus moves through the conceptual space, passes the standard of comparison, and continues for a long distance.[36]

To recapitulate, it seems that development of *sa* 'go to' into a degree intensifier is based on the same basic metaphor of a horizontal conceptual space receding from the conceptualizer as the expressions using *toro* 'pass' and *nɔ tɛgèni na* 'arrive at the limit' and *laaga tɔɔn* '(go) a long way'. In all of these expressions, the farther away from the conceptualizer that the motion is scanned, the greater the degree of the gradable concept. As argued above, the ways in which these various expressions of degree use this basic metaphor differ slightly from each other. The fictive motion evoked by *sa* traverses the conceptual space away from the conceptualizer towards the far boundary of the gradable concept in question. *Sa* by itself does not seem to evoke a norm somewhere in the middle of this conceptual space, the way *toro* 'pass' does. In the sense that it implies motion towards some location, it resembles *nɔ tɛgèni na* 'arrive at the limit', though unlike that expression it does not evoke arrival at the destination, but only motion towards it.

---

36 This example, which is extracted from a conversation, was preceded by a statement to the effect that Malians in general believe that Mali is more developed than Burkina Faso. The news that the capital of Burkina Faso is in fact more developed from an infrastructure point of view than the capital of Mali is thus quite unexpected. The speaker had recently visited Ouagadougou for the first time, and was speaking to an addressee who had never been there. (53) can thus be interpreted as another bridging example, since it potentially has both the degree enhancing interpretation ("very much more developed") and the speech act enhancing interpretation ("you may not believe this, but I tell you it's true").

2.2 Speech act intensifying *sa*

In addition to indicating a greater degree of some gradable concept in the clause, *sa* may also be used to increase the force of the speech act of the utterance in which it is inserted. This is a move in the direction of intersubjectification, in the sense that the speaker assesses that the added force is necessary to overcome some resistance or reluctance on the part of the addressee. This type of development has been repeatedly noted in grammaticalization.[37] As noted above, the effect of the modification cued by *sa* depends on the speech act involved. The three main speech acts of statement, question, and command will be dealt with in the following sections. There is undoubtedly more to be discovered on the interaction of *sa* with speech acts other than these three basic ones, but these will have to await further investigation.

2.2.1 *Sa dádáwú* 'believe me'

In indicative sentences, *sa* may function to reinforce the force of the assertion. This is typically in the face of reluctance (either real or anticipated) on the part of the hearer to believe the assertion. Consider the following extract from a conversation. Person A is recounting a bus trip that he had taken in Ivory Coast, from Bouaké to Abidjan, where the conversation took place. In the interest of saving space, I have given A's first contribution only in English.

(56) A: It was we five people who were in the bus. The driver, his assistant, a
          friend of theirs, and we two: me and a girl.

   B: *Hán!*
       What!

   A: *Wùù kɔ́nní p'   a   sà   a*
       we   TOP   they PRF INT SCN
       'It was in fact only we who

---

37 I use the term intersubjectification in the sense of Traugott and Dasher (2002) and Traugott (2010). In the latter work Traugott presents evidence that intersubjective polysemy (where a linguistic form signals that the speaker is taking into account the beliefs or self-image of the addressee) historically arises after subjective meaning (where the speaker expresses her/his own evaluation). If this hypothesis is generalizable, then it supports the proposal advanced here that the degree-enhancing function of *sa,* which is more subjective in Traugott's terms, arose historically before the speech-act enhancing function, where the *sa* comes to be used to counter a belief or attitude of the addressee.

B: [*'Ooyì!*

A: [<u>*pyi*</u> *Abijàn   shyèebíí.*
  be Abidjan goers.the
  were going to Abidjan.

  Nótɛ,   mɔbílíge numpuŋk' á <u>*sà   a   yìr'*</u> *àní   Bwɔke e*
  anyway bus   empty   PRF INT SCN leave there Bouaké in
  In any case, the bus actually left Bouaké empty

B: *na   ma.*
  PROG come.IMPFV
  'coming.'

A: *na   ma   àmɛ̃, fó   nahá, Abijàn   ì.*
  PROG come.IMPFV thus till here Abidjan in
  coming like that, all the way here to Abidjan.'

B: *`Ɔɔɔ́n!*
  Wow!

B's initial exclamation shows that he was astonished by what A had just said. To underline the assertion he had just made, A uses *sa* in his next contribution, in response to B's incredulity. B interrupts A's turn with another exclamation, and A continues with another assertion underlined with *sa*. B continues to be surprised through the end of the extract given here. It is this type of *sa* which Ali Sanogo calls *kakyanhaladádáwú*, '*sa* for believing something astonishing'.

Note that at the time of A's first use of *sa*, all the propositional information in the *sa* clause is already known to B. Similarly, in the second *sa* clause, the propositional information is simply an obvious inference from information already asserted previously. This is typical of epistemic *sa* clauses: their function is not to impart some new information, but to insist on the truth of the assertion.

This interaction with already-known information makes the function of *sa* in negative clauses much more likely to be epistemic rather than degree intensifying. The speech act of "negative assertion"[38] normally takes place against the background of the hearer's presumed or likely belief in the positive counterpart of the negative clause. This means that the speaker assumes that the hearer knows or can easily infer the propositional content. In this discourse environment, *sa* most naturally takes on the function of underlining the negative

---

38 For an insightful treatment of negatives from a discourse-pragmatic point of view, see Givón (2001).

assertion. Consider the following extract from the same conversation that (56) was taken from. In this example, A tells of another trip from the Mali border to Bouaké, in the center of the Ivory Coast.

(57) A: *Mìi a   jyè   lire ǹdé   mobílǐni i   mà pa   Bwɔke e ké,*
     I   PRF enter that that[39] car   in and come Bouaké in TIME
    wà   ɲyɛ a   mìi yígé mɛ,
    someone NEG PRF me ask NEG
    'From the time I entered that car till I arrived in Bouaké, no one asked me for money.'[40]

    B: *Hán!*
     'What!'

    A: *Mìi ɲyɛ a   yìgè mɛ. Mìi à   pa   nɔ   Bwɔke e.*
     I   NEG PRF ask NEG I   PRF VEN arrive Bouaké in
     'I was not asked for any money. I eventually arrived at Bouaké.'

    B: *`Ŋkàà k' à   pyi nùntàngà.*
     but   it PRF be luck
     'That was lucky!'

    A: *Mìi ɲyɛ a   <u>sà   a   yìgè</u> mɛ, áli   daashí[41] wúyó ná mɛ.*
     I   NEG PRF INT SCN ask NEG even 5.francs POSS at NEG
     'I was not asked for money at all, not even for five francs.'

It is clear that by the time A utters the clause with *sa* (the last clause in the extract), the hearer has heard all of the propositional information already. The *sa* simply reinforces the negative assertion. I have tried to indicate this reinforcement with *at all* in the free translation.

Negative assertion renders very unlikely the interpretation of *sa* in a degree enhancing way, even when there is a gradable element in the clause. Compare the corresponding negatives of examples (41) and (42) above:

(58) *U ɲyɛ a   sòl'   a   kàrè mɛ.*
    he NEG PRF do.early SCN go   NEG
    'He didn't leave early.'

---

39 See note 17 above.

40 The verb *yígé* 'ask' is used here to refer to police 'asking' for (i.e. extorting) money at road blocks.

41 In Supyire, as in most surrounding languages, the smallest unit of money is the five franc piece.

(59) *U ɲyɛ a sà a sòl' ǎ kàrè mɛ.*
    he NEG PRF INT SCN do.early SCN go NEG
    'He did *not* leave early.'

Although in (42) the first interpretation that comes to mind is that the gradable element 'early' is intensified ('very early'), in (59) this interpretation ('not *very* early, only a little early') is all but unavailable. Instead, the hearer is entitled to infer that 'he' not only did not leave early, but in fact 'he' left late (that is, later than expected, or later than had been arranged). This inference is stronger in (59) than in (58), where the hearer is only entitled to infer that 'he' did not leave early (i.e. 'he' probably left at the expected time).

Although in an example like (59) the negation all but eliminates the degree enhancing interpretation of *sa*, the corresponding positive in (42) does not preclude an assertion enhancing interpretation. Even though the degree enhancing interpretation is the most likely, and the first one that comes to mind when the sentence is encountered in isolation, with enough context any such sentence can be understood with an epistemic "believe me" sense. Thus (42) could be interpreted as 'He really left early,' as well as 'He left really early.' Similarly, (26) could be 'It really *is* long (believe me)!' as well as 'It is very/really long,' and (28) could be 'You really *are* fat (although you don't think so)!' as well as 'You are really fat.'

2.2.2 *Sa jwumɔ fanhaɲyahawú* 'answer me now'

The most common function of polar questions is to query the truth value of the corresponding indicative. In this environment, *sa* has a function similar to that of the *sa dádáwú* 'believe me *sa*' in indicatives. However, whereas in statements the incredulity, real or potential, is on the part of the addressee, in questions it is rather on the part of the speaker. The speaker is thus querying the truth of an assertion or an assumption that has arisen in the preceding discourse, because the speaker finds the information astonishing or otherwise difficult to believe. Consider the following examples:

(60) *Cyi à byanhara cyiyè nà.*
    they PRF be.close themselves at
    'They are similar[42] to each other.'

---

42 This is an instance of a "similar is close in space" metaphor. The example originally came from a discussion about the differences between the past and the present. The "they" thus refers to "times" or "epochs".

(61) *Cyi à   byanhara cyiyè   nà la?*
they PRF be.close themselves at QUES
'Are they similar to each other?'

(62) *Cyi a sà à   byanhara cyiyè   nà la?*
they PRF INT SCN be.close themselves at QUES
'Are they actually similar to each other? (I can hardly believe it.)'

Ali Sanogo makes the following comment on the use of *sa* in (62):

(63) *Jwufoòŋi na   sɔ̀nŋì   na cyi ɲɛ à   byanhara*
speaker PROG think.IMPFV that they NEG PRF be.close
cyiyè   nà mɛ,
themselves at NEG
'The speaker thinks that they are not similar to each other,

lire e u   à   yibigé fànhe ɲyaha   ɲwɔshwɔɔré dì
this in he/she PRF question force increase answer   SBJV
ŋ̀kàn fwɔ́fwɔ́.
give quickly
therefore he/she has increased the force of the question so that the answer
will be given quickly.'

This shows that the incredulity of the speaker/questioner also lends some urgency
to the question speech act, similar to the urgency noted below for imperatives.

Note that the verb *byanhara* in examples (60–62) is a gradable stative verb.
Thus (62) could be intrepreted as 'Are they very similar?' as well as 'Are they
actually similar?' Although this kind of ambiguity is frequently resolved in the
contexts of actual discourses, bridging examples do exist in natural discourse.[43]
These are discussed in Section 3. The first *sa* clause in the following extract from
a conversation (the same one from which (56) and (57) were extracted) clearly
shows that the intention of the speaker is to enhance the speech act rather than
the degree of the gradable verb. In this extract, person A is recounting a bus trip
he took from Sikasso, in Mali, to Abidjan, in the Ivory Coast. At a police check
point in the Ivory Coast, the driver of the bus refused to pay a bribe in order to
pass.

---

43 The degree-intensifying interpretation of *sa* appears to be more available in polar questions than it is in negative statements, though this is an issue that needs further investigation.
It may be that the degree to which the corresponding declarative is implied is less strong in
polar questions than in negative statements.

(64) A: *Pi   à   shofɛríɲi bwɔn waní.*
     they PRF driver.the hit   there
     'They beat the driver there.'

    B: *Mà <u>sà   a   ù</u>   bwɔ́n yábàlè?*
     and INT SCN him hit   FOC
     'They actually *beat* him?'

    A: *Mà <u>sà   ā̀   u</u>   bwɔn*
     and INT SCN him hit
     'They actually beat him'

    B: *hm̄*
     huh!?

    A: *mìì ɲyíí ... Mu ɲyíí ɲyɛ mìì nà,*
     my eye   your eye be   me   on
     [false start] 'As surely as you see me here

     mìì i   yi   yu   àmɛ̄,
     I.SUB PROG them say.IMPFV thus
     talking to you,'

    B: *Mm̀.*
     Unhun.

    A: *pi   à   shofɛríɲi bwɔn ...*
     they PRF driver.the hit
     'they beat the driver.'

In this exchange it is clear that B finds A's initial assertion astonishing, and indicates this not only with intonation, but also with focus on the verb (indicated by the focus adverb *yábàlè*) and by using *sa*. Although the verb refers to an activity which can be carried out with varying degrees of intensity (cf. example (40), with the same verb), the degree enhancing interpretation is virtually ruled out. Note that speaker A in his reply uses *sa* to reinforce his original assertion, in the face of the incredulity of speaker B. Moreover, he goes on to insist that, astonishing as the assertion is, he really does stand by it: "As surely as you see me here talking to you ..."

Although Ali Sanogo is quite happy to produce intensifying *sa* in content questions, the only naturally occurring example in the text database is the following:

(65) *Ntɛɛncwɔ́, jò   u   a   sà   à   mu jyiile yɛ?*
     N   who he/she PRF INT SCN you cross QUES
     'Nteencwo, who *really* took you across?'

This example comes from a folktale in which a woman (Nteencwo) has managed to reach her village from the other side of a swollen river, and she is asked by a series of people (her father, her mother, her brother) who it was who had helped her to cross the river. In each case she replies, "No one. God helped me cross." At last her lover asks her the same question, to which she gives the same reply. He then asks (65). Clearly he does not believe her previous assertion.[44] The *sa* signals both his incredulity and urgency in asking.

2.2.3 *Sa fànhàcyáncyánwú* 'do what I want'

In commands, where the speaker is attempting to get the hearer to do something, the *sa* has the function that Ali Sanogo calls *fànhàcyáncyánwú* 'force-imposing'. With both imperatives and hortative subjunctives, *sa* increases the *fànhà* 'force' of the manipulative act. Consider the following pair of imperatives:

(66) *Tɛɛn!*
     sit
     'Sit down!'

(67) *Sa   a   tɛɛn!*
     INT SCN sit
     '*Do* sit down!' or 'Sit down!!!'

The addition of *sa* in (67), according to Ali Sanogo, "causes more force to fall" on the addressee. An imperative with *sa* would normally be used in a context where the addressee has exhibited some reluctance to comply. For example, a child may have been requested to sit still and failed to do so, and an adult may utter (67) with some impatience. The use of *sa* does not necessarily imply irritation on the part of the speaker, however. (67) could also be uttered to a visitor who has been invited to sit down but declined. The speaker may urge the addressee to sit down and stay for a while.

Subjunctives with a second person subject may be used in Supyire for polite requests. An example is (24), repeated here as (68) for convenience:

---

44 He is right to doubt her first answer, since in fact she was taken across the river by a crocodile, which enjoined her to tell no one.

(68) *Bàbá, mu ú sá á wíí.*
      Papa, you SBJV INT SCN look
      'Papa, you really should look.'

This example comes from a narrative in which, prior to (68), a child has repeatedly come and requested her father to go look at something, but the father, who
was engaged in conversation with his friends, has failed to comply. Finally the
child introduces urgency into her request with the addition of *sa*. The use of
bàbá, a term of affection and respect, shows that the child is not being disre-
spectful in making the urgent request.

The use of *sa* normally implies that the speaker wishes the addressee to comply
quickly. Frequently there is the added implication that the addressee ought to have
acted sooner (at least in the opinion of the speaker). Note the added context in the
following examples, which would typically be uttered by an adult to a child:

(69) *Sa a fùkínàɲi mìnì, numpilàge na wwuu.*
      INT SCN lamp light night PROG get.dark.IMPFV
      'Light the lamp! It's getting dark.'

(70) *Kàlagé tèèbwɔɔnní na ntuuli, sa a ku bwɔn.*
      sorghum time.hit PROG pass.IMPFV INT SCN it hit
      'The time to pound[45] the sorghum is passing, so pound it!'

So far all the examples given have had second person subjects. *Sa* may also be
used to reinforce the directive speech act with first and third person subjects. In
the following hortative example taken from an interview concerning education,
the hortative speech act is marked by the use of the non-declarative form[46] of first
person plural subject and the absence of any auxiliary (as in the imperative):

(71) *Wuu sa a li yaha kàlìŋ' á pèè, ŋkàà ɲjyìɲi*
      we.NDEC INT SCN it believe education PRF be.big but food
      u a sìì yyahayyèrèɲí na.
      it PRF be front at
      'We really ought to consider that although education is important, food is
      the most important thing of all.'

---

45 This is to remove the grains from the ears. This must be done early enough in the day to
allow time for the grains to be pounded (*sú*) into flour which then needs to be cooked for the
evening meal.
46 First and second person pronouns have special non-declarative forms which may be used
(but are not required) in questions and directives. In the plural, these pronouns are distinguished from ordinary pronouns only by tone. Thus the ordinary forms of the 1st and 2nd
plural pronouns are *wùu* and *yìi*, and the non-declarative forms are *wuu* and *yii*.

In the preceding context the speaker has been defending his decision not to put all his children in school, arguing that he needs some of his children to help him farm so that the whole family will have food. He obviously thinks that his interlocutor, the interviewer, disapproves of his not having put all his children in school, and here urges him to admit that food is a more fundamental need than education.

The "force-imposing" *sa* may also occur with third-person subjects in indirect speech, where they correspond to second person imperatives or subjunctives in direct speech. The following example is taken from a folktale. The speaker, Hyena, is urging the other animals to let him eat Hare.

(72)   Kà   Zàntùŋɔ̀ dì   jwò, ɔnhɔ, pi sa a   u   kan uru sí
       then Hyena NARR   say no   they INT SCN him give he FUT
       ǹtíì   ù   numpurùŋi kùn.
       straightaway him raw   munch
       'Then Hyena said, no, they [the assembly of wild animals] really should give him [Hare] to him to eat raw right on the spot.'

In the preceding context, the wild animals had captured Hare and were debating what to do with him. Most were leaning towards throwing him into the dew-covered grass (because Hare had been begging them not to, claiming that dew was harmful to him), whereas Hyena had been urging them to hand Hare over to him to eat then and there (reported by the narrator in direct speech: "No! Give him to me to eat raw!"). The other animals were disinclined to accept Hyena's proposal (and in fact they end up throwing Hare into grass), so Hyena reinforces his directive with a *sa,* reported by the narrator as indirect speech.

The context of a manipulative speech act does not totally exclude the possibility of a degree enhancing interpretation of *sa* if there is a gradable element in the clause. For example, in an utterance such as (73), supporting context is required to decide on the correct interpretation:

(73)   Sa a   lyí!
       INT SCN eat
       'Eat!'

Sa in this utterance may have a speech act enhancing interpretation, for example 'Eat (even though you don't want to)!' or 'Eat (now/quickly, don't delay any further—we need to go)!' But equally it may have a degree enhancing interpretation, for example 'Eat away/up! (There is plenty.) / You are very welcome to eat your fill. / You need to eat more food now to keep up your strength. / etc.).' Bridging examples of this sort are discussed in the next section.

3 Motivating the change

By way of conclusion, we return now to the question raised in Section 1, namely what plausible story can be told of how *sa* might have developed from "go to (a destination)" to "a greater degree" and "believe me (although you find it difficult)", "do you really mean what you say (it seems incredible)?", and "do this (even though you don't want to)"? The first step of the development was suggested in Section 2.1, where it was claimed that intensifying *sa* should be seen as evoking the metaphorical conceptualization of the gradable quality, event, or situation as a space that recedes from the conceptualizer and is traversed in a fictive motion such that the farther from the conceptualizer the greater the degree. The 'go to' evokes a trajectory away from the conceptualizer towards an unspecified goal which carries the fictive motion towards the far boundary of the conceptual space. This much of the story seems straightforward, though in the current state of Supyire, due to phonological changes, *sa* 'intensifier' and *shyɛ* 'go' are now formally different. Historical documents are not available which might show bridging examples that could be construed both as actual motion and degree-enhancing.

Once degree of intensity was conceptualized as the traversing of a metaphorical space, the stage was set for the transfer from a "content-based" usage to a "speech-act" based usage. The conceptual space receding from the conceptualizer is now the degree of force employed in the speech act, whether enhanced assertion in the face of the addressee's inclination not to believe, enhanced interrogation in the face of a difficult-to-believe assertion, or enhanced manipulation in the face of the addressee's disinclination to act.

Several cases of potential ambiguity have been noted above, where a single form could have either a degree enhancing interpretation or a speech act enhancing interpretation. It was pointed out, for example, that (26) could be interpreted as either 'It is really/very long,' or 'It really is long.' These observations have been based on judgments by Ali Sanogo and others. It remains to be shown that bridging examples—in which either interpretation is possible—actually occur in natural discourse. Consider the following, from an interview of a well-known singer. The interviewer's question is given in English translation to save space:

(74) A: Grandmother, have you ever come across a song that wasn't good, but you fixed it till you made it good, so that people liked it? Did you ever fix one like that?

     B: *Mìi màha li yaa. Mìi màha sá á lìrè yàa.*
         I   HAB it fix I   HAB INT SCN that fix
         (i) 'I fix it. I fix it very well.'
         (ii) 'I fix it. I *do* fix it.'

In view of the preceding question, interpretation (ii) is probably more available. However, the degree enhancing interpretation (i) is certainly possible, and in fact, both interpretations can be available together (i.e. something like 'I *do* fix it very well.') A similar example is the following. The preceding speaker has just said "and then someone comes along and ruins everything".

(75) *Sèèŋí na y' ā   waha.   Y' a   sà   à   waha.*
      truth on it PRF be.hard   it PRF INT SCN be.hard
      (i) 'Really, it's hard. It's really hard.'
      (ii) 'Really, it's hard. It really is hard.'

Here the adverbial postpositional phrase *sèèŋí na*, roughly equivalent to 'truly', 'really' in English or '*vraiment*' in French, is a paraphrase of the speech act enhancing *sa*. If the *sa* in this example is of the speech act variety, the second sentence is roughly the equivalent of the first, and so (ii) is definitely one possible interpretation. It cannot be totally ruled out, however, that the speaker intended the *sa* as a *fànhàlewu*, since *waha* 'be hard, be difficult' is eminently gradable, so (i) is also a possibility. As with the preceding example, both interpretations may be present ('It really is very hard.')

As a final instance of this type of bridging example, consider the following extract from a conversation:

(76) A: *Na wà mù à   pyi Bàan   kúŋɔ́ ná ò,*
        that one also PRF be Gana.PL bank at INTER
        'They say there is also someone in Gana country,[47]

      ceèŋi wà u   a   sà   à   lyɛ   mà   lyɛ   mà   lyɛ.
      woman one she PRF INT SCN be.old and.ss be.old and.ss be.old
      a certain woman who is very, very old.[48]

      Numpécíny' a   sà   ǹtɔɔn.
      toenails   PRF AND IP.be.long
      Her toenails have become[49] long.

---

47 Lit. 'at the bank/shore of the Gana people'. Gana is the dialect of Bambara spoken immediately to the west of Kampwo Supyire. The largest river in the area, the Bagoé, traverses Gana country, hence the reference to the "bank (of the river)".
48 Repetition of the VP (here literally 'she is very old and old and old') may indicate a greater degree. The co-occurrence with *sa* makes this an exaggerating predication.
49 Andative *sá* (here low tone because it follows the perfect auxiliary) here indicates entry into a state.

Pi màhaa u yìgè na sùnnì.
they HAB.IMPFV her take.out.IMPFV PROG make.offerings.to.IMPFV
They take her out and offer sacrifices to her.'

B: *Màha u yig' à sun wá?*
HAB her take.out SCN make.offerings.to QUES
'Take her out and offer sacrifices to her?'

A: *Numpécyínyi y' a <u>sà à tɔnn'</u> à pyi kacyiin fíígé.*
toenails they PRF INT SCN be.long SCN be fetish like
(i) 'Her toenails are very long, so they are like a fetish.[50]'
(ii) 'Her toenails really are so long they are like a fetish.'

B: *Na Bàan kúŋɔ́ ná wa?*
that Gana.PL bank at QUES
'In Gana country?'

In this exchange, B clearly finds A's story astonishing. The first *sa* that A uses is clearly a degree enhancing *sa*. The second one could have either a degree enhancing function (i) or a speech act enhancing function (ii). Given B's astonishment, perhaps (ii) is favored, yet once again (i) cannot be ruled out, and in fact the two interpretations may coexist.

As further bridging examples, recall the comparatives in (52) and (53). In both cases these examples could be construed as indicating both greater degree of a gradable element (taking care of a child in (52) and being developed in (53)) and as indicating greater force in making an unexpected assertion.

All these bridging examples point to a connection between the semantic and pragmatic functions. A degree much greater (or "farther", to keep the Supyire metaphor) than the norm is in itself unusual and therefore more noteworthy. From the point of view of the addressee, insofar as it is unexpected, it is newsworthy. The farther through the category that the fictive motion is scanned, the more newsworthy the instance. It seems that in such discourse-pragmatic contexts *sa* developed the function of marking an assertion of remarkable degree, and from there was generalized to marking a remarkable assertion in which no semantic degree was involved.

The same kind of bridging examples as noted above with indicatives are also possible with imperatives and hortatives. The following example, taken from a conversation, was addressed to Ali Sanogo by an old man:

---

50 A *kacyiin*, here translated 'fetish', is a human-made 'power object' to which offerings—typically blood sacrifices—are made. A *kacyiin* is normally kept hidden away, often in a special house, and is only brought out in the open when sacrifices are to be offered to it.

(77) *Ma   sa   a   tíí   lè!*
  you.NONDECL INT SCN be.straight FOC
  (i) 'You should be very honest!'
  (ii) 'You really must be honest!'

The context does not allow a clear decision as to the intentions of the speaker—either of these interpretations is possible, and Ali himself is not sure which is the right one. From a practical point of view, the advice given is not very different in the two interpretations. In the same way that has occurred in declaratives, through bridging usages like this, *sa* has taken on the function of enhancing the manipulative speech act.

It is significant that Ali Sanogo uses the concept of *fànhà* 'force' in speaking of both types of enhancement. For the degree enhancing *sa*, his label (*fànhàlewu*) indicates that *fànhà* is being 'put' (*le*) into the utterance—specifically into the part of the utterance that cues a gradable concept. In explanation of the assertion enhancing *sa*, Sanogo offers the following:

(78) *Jwofoòŋi màha fànhà le jwumpé e, lógófóóŋi dì   dá   pú ná.*
  speaker HAB force put speech in hearer   SBJV believe it at
  'The speaker puts force into the speech so that the hearer will believe it.'

Here the addressee's reluctance to believe is conceptualized as an obstacle that must be overcome through the application of more force. It is not clear how this metaphorical "force dynamic" conceptualization[51] relates to "fictive motion" conceptualization of *sa*. Perhaps the connection is that going farther takes more energy. In any case, Ali Sanogo's analysis draws a clear connection between the two functions.

---

51 For "force dynamics" in conceptualization, see Talmy (2000).

Abbreviations

AND	andative
COMP	complementizer (high tone on subject pronoun)
COND	conditional mood auxiliary
DIM	diminutivizing suffix
FOC	focus particle
HAB	habitual tense auxiliary
IMPFV	imperfective verb form or verb suffix
INT	intensifying *sa*
INTER	turn taking interjection
IP	intransitive prefix
NARR	narrative tense auxiliary
NDEC	non-declarative form of a pronoun (used in questions and hortatives)
NEG	negative marker (either negative auxiliary or negative clause final marker)
PRF	perfect tense-aspect auxiliary
PL	plural
POSS	possessum pronoun
PROG	progressive aspect auxiliary
QUES	clause final interrogative particle
REL	relative clause marker
SBJV	subjunctive mood auxiliary
SCN	serial verb connective
SS	same subject
TIME	time clause marker
TOP	topic marker
VEN	venitive auxiliary

References

Bendor-Samuel, John. 1971. Niger-Congo, Gur. *Current Trends in Linguistics* 7: 141–178.

Bybee, Joan, Revere Perkins & William Pagliuca. 1994. *The evolution of grammar: tense, aspect, and modality in the languages of the world.* Chicago: Chicago University Press.

Carlson, Robert. 1994. *A grammar of Supyire.* Berlin & New York: Mouton de Gruyter.

Cauvin, Jean. 1980. *L'image, la langue et la pensée. Vol. 2: Recueil de proverbes de Karangasso.* St. Augustin: Anthropos-Institut.

Dahl, Osten. 1985. *Tense and aspect systems.* New York: Blackwell.

Garber, Anne. 1987. A Tonal Analysis of Senufo: Sucite dialect (Gur; Burkina Faso). Urbana: University of Illinois dissertation.

Givón, Talmy. 2001. *Syntax: an introduction.* Amsterdam: Benjamins.

Langacker, Ronald. 2005. Dynamicity, fictivity, and scanning: the imaginitive basis of logic and linguistic meaning. In Diane Pecher & Rolf A. Zwaan (eds.), *Grounding cognition: the role of perception and action in memory, language, and thinking*, 164–197. Cambridge: Cambridge University Press.

Langacker, Ronald. 2008. *Cognitive grammar: a basic introduction.* Oxford: Oxford University Press.

Matlock, Teenie. 2004. The conceptual motivation of fictive motion. In Günter Radden & Klaus-Uwe Panther (eds.), *Studies in linguistic motivation (Cognitive Linguistics Research 28)*. Berlin & New York: Mouton de Gruyter.

Mills, Richard. 2003. *Dictionnaire sénoufo-français: sénanri—parler tyébara (Côte d'Ivoire): avec un index français-tyébara.* Cologne: Rüdiger Köppe.

Naden, Tony. 1989. Gur. In John Bendor-Samuel (ed.), *The Niger-Congo languages*, 140–168. Lanham: University Press of America.

Segerer, Guillaume. n.d. Les langues Niger-Congo. http://www.nigercongo.com/nc_classific.pdf (accessed 7 August 2012)

Talmy, Leonard. 2000. *Toward a cognitive semantics. Volume I: Concept structuring systems.* Cambridge, MA: MIT Press.

Traugott, Elizabeth. 2010. (Inter)subjectivity and (inter)subjectification: a reassessment. In Kristin Davidse, Lieven Vandelanotte & Hubert Cuyckens (eds.), *Subjectification, inter-subjectification and grammaticalization*, 29–74. Berlin & New York: Mouton de Gruyter.

Traugott, Elizabeth & Richard Dasher. 2002. *Regularity in semantic change.* Cambridge: Cambridge University Press.

Maud Devos
Motion verbs in Shangaci: lexical semantics and discourse functions

1 Introduction

Bantu languages use different means to structure discourse. To begin with, it is a well-known fact that verbal inflection in Bantu can express more than TAM categories alone. Schadeberg (2003: 151) mentions a range of other functions, one of which is embedding in the discourse. Next, a number of recent articles make clear that demonstratives are an important text structuring device in Bantu languages (Levinsohn 2010: 148–149, Meeuwis and Stroeken 2012, Nicolle 2007, 2012, Van der Wal 2010, 2013). Although Shangaci, the Eastern Bantu language studied in this paper, has tenses which carry the storyline and others which describe backgrounded events as well as demonstratives with non-situational uses (Meeuwis and Stroeken 2012: 148), it has an even more important means of structuring the discourse: the motion verb.

In Shangaci, motion verbs expressing 'go', 'come' and 'enter' are particularly frequent in narrative discourse. Section 3 of this paper discusses textual and interpersonal uses of these verbs in narratives and more spontaneous discourse types. In order not to fall into the trap of misconceiving the grammaticalization paths followed by motion verbs because of a misunderstanding of their lexical semantics (Wilkins and Hill 1995), the paper starts with a description of the lexical uses of Shangaci basic motion verbs (cf. Section 2).

2 Lexical-semantics of motion verbs in Shangaci

In Shangaci the motion verbs *entta* 'go to', *lawa* 'leave (for)', *ta* 'come' and *ingela* 'enter' developed grammatical uses. Contrary to expectation these uses do not pertain to TAM but rather to discourse. This section takes a closer look at the lexical-semantics of these motion verbs. As is made particularly clear by Wilkins and Hill (1995: 215), the semantics of a single motion verb cannot be understood without taking into account the larger system of basic motion verbs. Section 2.1 therefore considers a set of 9 motion verbs in Shangaci and discusses the way their uses relate to each other. It is a well-known fact that lexical items may continue to exist and undergo changes after they have developed grammatical uses (cf. 'divergence' (Hopper 1991: 22)). The synchronic meanings of *entta* 'go to', *lawa* 'leave (for)', *ta* 'come' and *ingela* 'enter' may thus not be identical to the ones that instigated the grammaticalization processes. I therefore do not restrict myself to a synchronic analysis of the selected basic motion verbs but add, when possible, insights from a historical / comparative point of view. A summary of the lexical-semantic findings is given in Section 2.2. Section 2.3 indicates which of these verbs enter into processes of grammaticalization leading to TAM or other uses and what the selection of these particular verbs tells us about source items in general.

2.1 Basic motion verbs in Shangaci

Following Talmy (1985: 60–61) a basic motion event refers to an object moving along a path with respect to another object and it is analyzed as having four components: 'Figure' (i.e. the moving object), 'Path' (the trajectory followed), 'Motion' (including manner of motion) and 'Ground' (i.e. the reference object, typically Source or Goal). In this paper 'basic motion verbs' denote a motion event in which none of the four components is very specific. Verbs like *thira* 'run' or *tuthunya* 'limp', which include manner of Motion, are therefore excluded. Likewise verbs which specify the Path taken, as in *zungulela* 'walk around something' or *lookha* 'cross', are not considered. Also not included are verbs like *phattuwa* 'come out (moon)', which refer to the movement of a specific Figure. Finally, if the verb refers to motion with respect to a specific Ground, it is not taken into account. Such is the case for *vuuwa* 'come out of water', for which the Source can only be water. Eventually this leaves us with a subset of 9 motion verbs. Table 1 lists the verbs in question together with their approximate meanings and the number of times they appear in my database.[1]

---

1 The study of motion verbs in Shangaci is based on their occurrences in a database containing more or less 8,000 fully glossed sentences consisting of 30,400 running words. Of those 8,000 sentences 3,000 are isolated elicited sentences serving mainly as illustrative sentences for Shangaci verbs. The remaining 5,000 sentences are part of nineteen folk tales, twelve recipes, eighteen accounts of various activities and three short dialogues, all of which were collected during two fieldwork trips by the author, one in 2004 and the other in 2007. Note that the numbers in the third column concern only independent lexical uses not grammaticalized ones.

Table 1. Shangaci basic motion verbs

entta	go to	282
lawa	leave (for)	344
enttetta	move	54
enttettattetta	walk, walk around	7
vira	pass	94
inkela	enter	6
ta	come	326
fiya	arrive	250
lamuwa	leave	141

2.1.1 Two GO verbs: *entta* & *lawa*

The basic motion verbs *entta* and *lawa* display a similar syntactic distribution: they can both be followed by a locative argument or a subordinate clause (each typically referring to the goal of the motion) and they can both be used on their own. Below we try to find out what motivates the choice between *entta* and *lawa* in these three structures in order to understand the semantic relation between the two 'go' verbs.

As can be seen in (1) and (2) both *entta* and *lawa* can be used on their own (i.e. without a locative argument or a subordinate clause following them).

(1) *ki-tt-eéntt-él-a   w-on-a   mí-rákho z-áangu*
  SBJ_{1SG}-PRS-go-APPL-FV NP_{15}-see-FV NP_4-trap PP_4-POSS.$_{1SG}$
  'I am going to look at my traps'

  eentt-aá-ni, n-lunyaánka
  go-IMP-PLA NP_1-husband.mine
  'Go, my husband!'

(2) *mií-fwa   za   táána   y-aa-ri   púré-wó   aá-tthu*
  NP_4-death PP_4.of yesterday PP_2-PST-be many-LOC$_{17}$ NP_2-people
  Yesterday, at the mourning place, there were a lot of people.

  weéyo w-oó-láaw-a   ãã   k-oó-láaw-a
  you SBJ_{2SG}-PST-go-PFV yes SBJ_{1SG}-PST-go-PFV
  'Did you go? Yes, I went.'

Whereas the use of *lawa* is very common in this environment, the use of *entta* is more restricted. In fact, *entta* is only regularly used on its own in the imperatival mood (cf. (1)). Other instances of *entta* without a following locative complement or subordinate clause have an idiomatic reading. (3), in which *entta* is used to express 'cut' is a case in point.

(3)   *afatáári o-kí-tíis-el-e*   *ií-su*   *yá*   *w-eéntt-a*
      better   SBJ$_{2SG}$-OBJ$_{1SG}$-bring-APPL-SBJV NP$_7$-knife PP$_7$.of NP$_{15}$-go-FV
      'You'd better bring me a knife that cuts.'

The verb *entta* is more typically used with a locative argument referring to the goal of the motion, as illustrated in (4). As can be seen in (5), *lawa* can occur in the same structure.

(4)   *o-tt-étt'*   *ó-n-liímpu*
      SBJ$_{2SG}$-PRS-go-FV NP$_{17}$-NP$_3$-well
      Are you going to the well?

(5)   *o-ttí-láw'*   *ó-n-liímpu*
      SBJ$_{2SG}$-PRS-go-FV NP$_{17}$-NP$_3$-well
      'Are you going to the well?'

A closer examination shows that locative arguments of *entta* and *lawa* are different syntactically, pragmatically and semantically. On a syntactic level, locative arguments of *entta* can be considered core arguments, whereas locative arguments of *lawa* are peripheral.[2] As was said above the use of *entta* without a locative argument (or subordinate clause) following it is very restricted. Moreover, when *entta* is used on its own the locative goal is understood from the context. In (1), it is clear that the husband is urged not simply to go away but to go to his traps. In (2), where *lawa* is used on its own, the locative goal can also be understood from the context. However, this is not always the case, as (6) shows. A host, who sees his guest standing up, asks whether he is going (i.e. leaving). No locative goal is stated in the context.

(6)   *o-ttí-laáw-a?*   *w-éntt-á*   *vaaí?*
      SBJ$_{2SG}$-PRS-go-FV   NP$_{15}$-go-FV   where
      'Are you going?'   'Going where?'

Interestingly, when the guest answers by saying 'going where?', he uses the verb *entta*. This brings us to the pragmatic difference between the locative arguments of *entta* and *lawa*. A locative goal following the verb *lawa* cannot be focused.

---

2 Dixon's terminology (2010: 122–128) is adopted here.

The inherently focused question word *vai* 'where?' can only be used with *entta*, not with *lawa*. The possible answers to the questions in (4) and (5), given respectively in (7) and (8) also show that a locative argument is new information only when following *entta*.

(7)   *waalá ki-tt-éntt'*   *ó-muúti*
      not   SBJ$_{1SG}$-PRS-go-FV NP$_{17}$-NP$_3$-town
      'No, I am going **home**.'

(8)   *khancúuwi*   *nkhámá ki-ttí-laáw-a*
      I.do.not.know if   SBJ$_{1SG}$-PRS-go-FV
      'I do not know whether I am going.'

Finally, there is also a semantic difference between the locative arguments of *lawa* and *entta*. Locative arguments of *entta* always refer to the Goal of the motion. With *lawa* this is typically but not always the case. When *lawa* is used in the imperative mood, the locative argument (implied or stated) always refers to the Source of the motion, as shown in (9).

(9)   *va-ncé*   *v-aángu'*   *pha*   *law-a-nií-vo*
      NP$_{16}$-home PP$_{16}$-POSS$_{1SG}$ PP$_{16}$.DEM$_i$ go-IMP-PLA-LOC$_{16}$
      'Go away from my home!'

Similarly, *lawa* can be used to refer to things coming out of the body. This is shown in (10), where the locative argument is a core argument and refers to the person who is bleeding.[3] (11) illustrates the use of the lexicalized causative *laza*. It expresses 'remove from, cause to come out of' and not 'make go to'.

(10)   *zi-ṅ-láw-a*   *taámu*
      SBJ$_{10}$-OBJ$_1$-go-PF NP$_{10}$.blood
      'Blood comes out of him.'

(11)   *w-á-láz-e-mu*   *maá-ti*   *va-nkááma*
      SBJ$_{2SG}$-DIST-remove-SBJV-LOC$_{18}$ NP$_6$-water NP$_{16}$-bilge
      'Go scoop the water from the bilge.'

---

3 When *entta* is used with a locative core argument referring to the human body, it refers to motion inside and not out of the body, e.g. *taámu khinímwééntta mwásá wá wúma mitíínga* 'his blood does not circulate well because of dry veins'.

Possibly, this variation in the semantics of the locative arguments used with *lawa* is indicative of a change in the argument structure of the verb. Whereas *lawa* used to take locative arguments referring to the Source of the motion, it is now more typically used with locative arguments referring to the Goal of the motion and reference to the Source of the motion (outside of imperative constructions and idiomatic expressions where the source is the human body) is only possible with applicative derivation, as in (11).[4]

(12)　*mbuúkhu a-law-eel-e*　　*va-ń-ttúpha va-áwe*
　　　NP$_{1a}$.rat　SBJ$_1$-go-APPL-PFV　NP$_{17}$-NP$_3$-hole　PP$_{16}$-POSS$_1$
　　　'The rat has come out of his hole.'

Comparative evidence can help to substantiate this claim. Cognates of *lawa* (i.e. reflexes of common Bantu **dàg* (Bastin et al. 2003, Guthrie 1970: 132) in Bantu languages most frequently express 'bid farewell, take leave', as illustrated for the Tanzanian Bantu language Nyakyusa in (13).

(13)　Nyakyusa (Niger-Congo, Bantu, M31)

　　　nu-n-dag-íle　　　　　　　*pa　Ipinda*
　　　SBJ$_{1SG}$-OBJ$_1$-say.goodbye-PST　NP$_{16}$ Ipinda
　　　'I bade him farewell in Ipinda.'　　　　　　(Felberg 1996: 66, gloss added)

However, in some other East African languages a metonymical shift appears to have occurred and the verb refers to the consequence of taking leave, i.e. the actual leaving (cf. Mwini *lawa* 'go / come out', move from', Ngazidja *lawa* 'leave, come from', Kagulu *lawa* 'leave' (Petzell 2008: 216) and Shambala *awa* 'set out, come from' (Besha 1993: 81)). As can be seen in (14) and (15) from Mwini and Ngazidja, respectively, the locative argument refers to the Source of the motion.

(14)　Mwini (Niger-Congo, Bantu, G403)

　　　ka　apo　　wa-chi-law-a　　　waa-nthu　wa-wili
　　　from　PP$_{16}$.DEM$_{ii}$　SBJ$_2$-PST-come.from-FV　NP$_2$.person　NP$_2$.two
　　　'From there, two people came out.'
　　　　　　　　　　(Kisseberth and Abasheikh 2004: 243, gloss added)

---

4 This change in the argument structure of *lawa* could be a consequence of the so-called 'goal-bias' in the encoding of motion events. As shown by i.a. Stefanowitch and Rohde (2004) and Lakusta and Landau (2011) languages typically display an asymmetry between Source and Goal Paths as people tend to include Goal paths but omit Source paths when describing motion events.

(15)   Ngazidja (Niger-Congo, Bantu, G44)

tsi-law-a   *Ungudya*
SBJ$_{1SG}$-come.from-PRS Unguja
'I come from Unguja.'   (Chamanga and Gueunier 1979: 166, gloss added)

In Shangaci a further change has occurred, with the locative argument now referring to the Goal, except for some idiomatic cases in which it (still) refers to the Source.

I now turn to the third context in which both *entta* and *lawa* can be used, i.e. with a subordinate clause referring to the goal of the motion. This type of construction is most frequently found when *entta* or *lawa* are in a directive mood (i.e. go and/to do X!). Interestingly, *entta* and *lawa* display a complementary distribution in this context: *entta* can only be used with second person directives in the imperative mood whereas *lawa* is restricted to first person plural directives in the subjunctive mood (i.e. co-hortatives), as seen in (16) and (17), respectively.[5]

(16)   *entt-á   w-á-xúm-e   pheéra*
go-IMP SBJ$_{2SG}$-DIST-pick-SBJV NP$_{10}$-guave
'Go pick guaves.'

(17)   *n-law-éé-ni   n-á-xúm-e   mi-xúumo*
SBJ$_{1PL}$-go-SBJV-PLA SBJ$_{1PL}$-DIST-pick-SBJV NP$_4$-fruit
'Let's go pick fruit.'[6]

I can think of several reasons for this complementary distribution. A first one lies in the persistent semantic difference between the locative arguments of *entta* and *lawa*. As mentioned before, *lawa*, when used in the imperative mood, expresses 'go away, leave' without an implied locative Goal (cf. (9)). This does not combine well with a subordinate clause specifying the goal of the motion. Next, as will be discussed below, *lawa* occurs very often in serial verb constructions.

---

5 The same complementary distribution is found in Makonde with the verb *uka* 'leave (for)' and the verb *wena* (a cognate of Shangaci *entta*) 'go (to)' being used in co-hortatives and (second person) imperatives, respectively (Guerreiro 1963: 36, 37).
6 The first person plural subjunctive form of *lawa* shows signs of grammaticalizing into a co-hortative marker in Shangaci. In (17) the subjunctive following it includes a distal marker, which indicates that the joint action takes place at a distance from the deictic centre. However, the distal marker can be omitted, in which case the motion element is demoted and the primary emphasis is on the mutual encouragement (i.e. 'let's'). This becomes particularly clear when *lawa* combines with another motion verb, for which see (53).

In such constructions the subject as well as the TAM specifications of the verbs typically stay the same. This could explain the non-occurrence of *lawa* in utterances like the one in (16) where a subjectless imperative combines with a second person singular subjunctive. Finally, there could be a pragmatic motivation as well. In (16) the the picking of the guaves constitutes the most important information, whereas in (17) the focus is more evenly distributed between the 'going together'-part and the 'in order to do what'-part. *lawa* thus not only shows a dispreference to combine with a focused locative argument (6)) but also with a focused subordinate clause.

Non-directive forms of *entta* and *lawa* can also be followed by a subordinate (infinitival) clause referring to the goal of the motion, as seen in (18) and (19), respectively. However, the applicative of *entta* (i.e. *enttela*) is more regularly used in this context, for which see (20).

(18) *ki-tt-étt-á*   *w-iipheéy-a*
      SBJ$_{1SG}$-PRS-go-FV NP$_{15}$-cook-FV
      'I am going to cook.'

(19) *si-ń-láw'*   *o-swaáli*
      NEG.SBJ$_{1SG}$-PRS-go-FV NP$_{15}$-pray
      'I am not going to pray.'

(20) *a-lamuw-u*   *ttáapha*   *eentt-el-e*   *w-iipheéy-a*
      SBJ$_1$-leave-PFV PP$_{16}$.DEM$_{ie}$ SBJ$_1$.go-APPL-PFV NP$_{15}$-cook-FV
      'He left right here and went to cook.'

To sum up, although *entta* and *lawa* are used in similar contexts they are semantically different. *entta* expresses movement towards a goal which typically represents new information and can be focused. *lawa* typically refers to movement away from the deictic centre and while a goal can be expressed it cannot be focused.[7]

---

[7] As was pointed out to me by Philippe Bourdin, one should be careful when glossing a motion verb as 'go away from the deictic centre'. Often, verbs that receive this gloss are not deictic at all (see also Botne's (2005) analysis of Chindali verbs of motion referred to in the Introduction of the present volume) or can more appropriately be defined as expressing movement towards a place different from the deictic centre. In Shangaci, however, the meaning of *lawa* is well-rendered by 'movement away from the deictic centre'. This is confirmed by the fact that when *lawa* combines with a locative Source, the latter has to coincide with the deictic centre (either the place where the speaker is and where he wants the addressee to leave from (9) or the human body (10)).

2.1.2 To MOVE (around): *enttetta* & *enttettattetta*

The verbs *enttetta* and *enttettattetta* are lexicalized reduplicatives of *entta* and *enttetta*, respectively. Where *entta* expresses going towards a goal, its lexicalized reduplicated form *enttetta* is a more general motion verb, essentially expressing 'to move'. In (21) for example, a negative form of *enttetta* is used to express that one stayed in the same spot and did not move around.

(21) *ya súbúúhu s-eenttett-ééni*   *k-oo-kheréngúl-a z-ombo z-áangu*
     since morning NEG.SBJ$_{1SG}$-move-PFV SBJ$_{1SG}$-PST-brim-FV NP$_{10}$-pot PP$_{10}$-POSS$_{1SG}$
     'Since the morning, I have not moved. I have been making the brims of my pots.'

When *enttetta* is used, the emphasis is not on the source or the goal of the motion but rather on the movement itself and the way it takes place. Hence, it can be used to express motions like 'to walk', 'to swim', 'to spread (of fire)' and 'to run (of machines)'. An example of the latter meaning is given in (22).

(22) *roróójw' eti*   *e-s-eentteett-e*
     NP$_9$.watch PP$_9$.DEM$_i$ SBJ$_9$-NEG-move-SBJV
     'May this watch stop running.'

In some cases the motion component is absent altogether and the verb refers to a way of being or to how something happened, as illustrated in (23) and (24), respectively. The latter use typically occurs at the end of a story as a kind of a closing sentence ('that is how it went').

(23) *ontúúle a-tt-eénttétt-a*   *teitééi n' ontúúle*
     PP$_1$.DEM$_{iii}$ SBJ$_1$-PRS-move-FV how   with PP$_1$.DEM$_{iii}$
     'How is that one related to that one?'

(24) *tí z-éenttett-ee-zo*   *n-fálúume na n-lweéle*
     COP SBJ$_{10}$-move-PFV-REL$_{10}$ NP$_1$-king   and NP$_1$-sick
     'That is how things went between the king and the sick person.'

The verb *enttettattetta* is a lexicalized reduplicate form of the verb *enttetta*. It has a more specific meaning than *enttetta* as it always refers to walking or walking around (visiting people).

(25) *si-na   y   óo-rampalaál-a*
NEG_{1SG}-have PP₉.CONN NP₁₅-lie.down-INF
'I cannot lie down

waalá si-na   yá   w-éenttettáttéett-a
nor   NEG_{1SG}-have PP₉.CONN NP₁₅-walk-INF
nor can I walk (around).'

In sum, the verb *enttetta*, a lexicalized reduplicated form of *entta* 'go to', is used as a generic motion verb (i.e. 'move'). The verb *enttetta* itself also has a lexicalized reduplicated form *enttettattetta*, which means 'walk (around)'.

2.1.3 To ENTER or to PASS: *ingela* & *vira*

Non-grammaticalized uses of *ingela* occur very sparingly in my database. They always refer to motion into something, as illustrated in (26). The notion of entering is more frequently expressed by *entta* 'go to' or *vira* followed by a locative argument referring to a place inside, as seen in (27) and (28) respectively.

(26) *o-si-íngéel-e   o-káatth' ukhuúno k-aa   wáazu*
SBJ_{2SG}-NEG-enter-SBJV NP₁₇-room here   SBJ_{1SG}-be open
'Do not enter this room, I am naked!'

(27) *z-aw-éntt-á   m-mú-rúupa z-oónxi*
SBJ₈-PST-go-FV NP₁₈-NP₃-bag NP₈-all
'They (fish) were all going into the bag.'

(28) *ki-viír-e   n-nyúumpa   ttúumpho*
SBJ_{1SG}-pass-SBJV NP₁₈-NP₉.house PP₁₈.DEM_{iie}
'May I enter the house?'

The verb *vira* more typically expresses 'pass'. Its locative argument (explicit or implicit) refers either to the location that is passed by (cf. Ground) or to the Path taken, as seen respectively in (29) and (30).

(29) *a-vir-i   muú-tthú' pha?*
SBJ₁-pass-PFV NP₁-person PP₁₆.DEM_i
'Has a person passed here?'

(30) *a-vir-i   siímba   n-táriíkhi*
SBJ₁-pass-PFV NP_{1a}.lion NP₁₈-NP₉.road
'A lion passed along the road.'

When the locative argument refers to the Path, it takes a class 18 locative nominal prefix, which in Shangaci (and in Bantu languages more generally, cf. Meeussen 1967: 103–104) refers to a location inside. This suggests immersion in the pathway, which might not be very obvious in example (30) where a road is followed but it becomes clearer in (31), where a person passes through the wood.

(31) ki-<u>vir</u>-i   n-tthunttu   ńtthúunttu mpákhá magáariípi
     SBJ$_{1SG}$-pass-PFV NP$_{18}$-NP$_9$.wood RED   until   afternoon
     'I passed through the woods until late afternoon.'

It is probably this idea of being immersed in the Path that made it possible for *vira* to express 'enter'. Note that in the closely related language Koti, *ingela* is not (or is no longer) used and *vira* is polysemous between 'pass' and 'enter' (Schadeberg and Mucanheia 2000: 229).

Just like *enttetta* 'move', *vira* can be used to refer to the way things go. The locative argument, *nhali* in (32) is used as a metaphor for the course of events.

(32) ti   mw-ényé   a   mií-nko   n-hál'   a-ń-vír-aá-mo
     COP NP$_1$-owner PP$_1$.O NP$_4$-greed NP$_{18}$-place SBJ$_1$-PRS-pass-FV-REL$_{18}$
     'That is how it goes with a greedy person.'

To conclude, the verb *vira* expresses passing by a Ground or along a Path. Although *ingela* specifically expresses 'enter', the latter notion is more regularly expressed by *vira* and to a lesser extent also by *entta* 'go to'.

2.1.4 To COME: *ta*

The verb *ta* is typically used to refer to motion towards the deictic centre (mostly the speaker), as seen in (33).

(33) w-ii-ń-síngán-á   ń-yó   w-áangu   aá-<u>t</u>-e
     SBJ$_{2SG}$-COND-OBJ$_1$-meet-FV NP$_1$-wife PP$_1$-POSS$_{1SG}$ SBJ$_1$-come-SBJV
     'If you meet my wife, she should come.'

When the Goal of the motion is the deictic centre, it can be left unexpressed as in (33). The singular imperative of *ta*, however, always includes the Goal of the motion. As can be seen in (34) the imperative is a fused form consisting of the verb *ta* and the demonstrative *okhuno* expressing 'here'.

(34) *ṭukhún'*   *ókírúule*
come.here.IMP SBJ$_{2SG}$-OBJ$_{1SG}$-take.from.head-SBJV
'Come here to take the load from my head!'

Explicit reference to the speaker requires applicative derivation, as in (35).

(35) *nyoókha*   *y-aa-nttó-kí-ṭ-eél-a*
NP$_9$.snake SBJ$_9$-PST-FOC-OBJ$_{1SG}$-come-APPL-FV
'A snake was coming towards me.'

When the Goal of the motion is left unexpressed, *ta* can take other locative arguments referring to the Path or to the Source of the motion, as seen in (36) and (37), respectively.

(36) *muú-tthú*   *a-ń-ṭ-aá*   *o-táriíkh'*   *ukhu*
NP$_1$-person SBJ$_1$-PRS-come-FV.REL NP$_{17}$-NP$_9$.road PP$_{17}$.DEM$_i$
'A person that comes along this road ...'

(37) *w-á-thímb-e*   *n-líimpu aápho*   *a-ń-t-á-vo*
SBJ$_{2SG}$-DIST-dig-SBJV NP$_3$-well PP$_{16}$.DEM$_{ii}$ SBJ$_1$-PRS-come-FV-REL$_{16}$
naáttyuúttyu
NP$_{1a}$.fountain
'Go dig a well where water is coming out!'

The verb *ta* can also combine with a subordinate clause referring to the goal or the reason for the coming. This is illustrated in (38). However, there is a preference to use the applicative of *ta* in this type of structure. (39) is a case in point.

(38) *ílá yoówó khúlá siikhu*   *a-núu-ta*   *o-kí-tháramuúl-a*
but they each NP$_9$.day SBJ$_2$-PRS-come-FV NP$_{15}$-OBJ$_{1SG}$-bother-FV
'But they, each day, they come to bother me.'

(39) *k-oó-ṭ-él-e*   *uu-cheliís-a*
SBJ$_{1SG}$-PST-come-APPL-PFV NP$_{15}$.OBJ$_{2SG}$-greet-FV
'I came to greet you.'

To conclude, *ta* most typically expresses motion towards the deictic centre.

2.1.5 Beginning and endpoint of a motion: *lamuwa* & *fiya*

The verbs *lamuwa* and *fiya* refer to motion in situ and do not involve movement along a Path. They are included in the list because they are very often used in combination with basic motion verbs and, at least *lamuwa*, could even come to include a Path.

Cognates of the verb *lamuwa* in closely related languages refer to 'wake (intransitive), rise, get up' (cf. Swahili *amka* 'wake, get up' (Johnson 1951: 13) and Koti *lankha* 'rise, get up' (Schadeberg and Mucanheia 2000: 224). In present day Shangaci this is (still) one of the meanings of *lamuwa* but not the most frequent one. Examples are given in (40) and (41), in which *lamuwa* refers to 'wake up' and 'get up', respectively.

(40) namárókolo a-*lamuuw*-u   n'   óo-suthuúw-a
     NP₁ₐ.hare   SBJ₁-leave-PFV with NP₁₅-jump-FV
     'The hare woke up with a jump.'

(41) oo-lál-á   naá   eex-i   weéyo o-*lamuuw*-u
     SBJ₁-OBJ₂SG-sleep-PFV with.you SBJ₁.end-PFV you   SBJ₂SG-leave-PFV
     'He sleeps with you, finishes and then you get up.'

The fact that the lexicalized causative form *lamusa* means 'wake (transitive)' or 'lift' points towards 'wake (intransitive), get up' as the original meaning of *lamuwa*. More evidence for 'wake, rise' being the original meaning of *lamuwa* is found in its frequent use before reported discourse constructions. This is probably due to the fact that people, especially in formal settings, stand up before speaking. In (42) the hare gets up before addressing the crowd. In other examples the combination of *lamuwa* and reported discourse is a metaphor like 'taking the floor' and does not necessarily involve any actual movement on behalf of the speaker.

(42) a-lamuuw-u   namárókolo er-i: aph'   aátthu ...
     SBJ₁-leave- PFV NP₁ₐ.hare   SBJ₁.QV-PFV: PP₁₆.DEMᵢ NP₂-person ...
     'The hare got up and said: "The people here ...".'

The more frequently attested meaning 'leave' is probably a metonymical extension from 'get up' as 'getting up' is often associated with 'leaving'. If a locative argument is expressed, it always refers to the place someone or something leaves from as is the case in (43).

(43)   *ki-<u>lámúw</u>-ee-vo*   *Parápaátho aa-ri*   *a-si-ná-jíibu*
     SBJ$_{1SG}$-leave-PFV-REL$_{16}$ P.   SBJ$_1$.PST-be SBJ$_1$-NEG-UPFV-answer
     'When I left Parapatho [Angoche], he had not yet answered.'

When used to express 'leave', *lamuwa* is very often followed by a motion verb, typically a 'go' verb or *ta* 'come' as seen in (44) and (45), respectively.

(44)   *meéxó*   *n-ttóo-<u>lamuúw</u>-a*   *nii-láw-á*   *sáfári*   *y-éetthu*
     tomorrow SBJ$_{1PL}$-FOC-leave- FV SBJ$_{1PL}$.SUB-go-FV NP$_9$.journey PP$_9$-POSS$_{1PL}$
     'Tomorrow we will leave and go on our journey.'

(45)   *taán'*   *etíile*   *ki-<u>lámúw</u>-ee-vo*   *ki-t-aánk-a ...*
     yesterday PP$_9$.DEM$_{iii}$ SBJ$_{1SG}$-leave-PFV-REL$_{16}$ SBJ$_{1SG}$-come-DUR-FV
     'Yesterday when leaving and coming ...'

The composite meaning 'leave and come' can also be expressed by *lamuwa* alone. In (46), for example, *lamuwa* not only refers to the event of leaving Nacala but also to the journey home. It can thus incorporate a Pathway which is typically directed towards the deictic centre. As such, *lamuwa* can be used to express where someone or something came from, as (47) illustrates.

(46)   *ki-<u>lámúw</u>-áank-a* *Nakhaála k-oó-sámbal-iiw-a*   *m-pháári*
     SBJ$_{1SG}$-leave-DUR-FV N.   SBJ$_{1SG}$-PST-make.drunk-PASS-PFV NP$_{18}$-NP$_9$.ocean
     'When coming from Nacala, I got seasick.'

(47)   *moór'*   *opúule*   *o-<u>lámúw</u>-u*   *váaí*
     NP$_3$.fire PP$_3$.DEM$_{iii}$ SBJ$_3$-leave-PFV where
     'Where has this fire come from?'

Interestingly, when an applicative extension is added to *lamuwa*, a human argument is added referring to the Goal rather than to the Source, as seen in (48). In fact, the meaning of *lamuwela* is very similar to the meaning of *entta*.

(48)   *ki-tti-ń-lámuw-el-a*   *á-kí-liv-e*   *n-zúrúkhu w-áangu*
     SBJ$_{1SG}$-PRS-leave-APPL-FV SBJ$_1$-SUBS-pay-SBJV NP$_3$-money PP$_3$-POSS.$_{1SG}$
     'I am going to him so that he gives me my money.'

Contrary to *lamuwa*, which typically refers to the beginning of a motion, *fiya* describes its endpoint. As can be seen in (49), *fiya* expresses 'arrive' and the locative argument, if present, always refers to the place one arrives at.

(49) *n-oówéleel-e*   *mpákhá* *o-fíy-á*   *va-lí-vúula*
    SBJ$_{1PL}$-swam-PFV until   NP$_{15}$-arrive-FV NP$_{16}$-NP$_5$-island
    'We swam until we arrived at an island.'

The verb *fiya* often follows a 'go' verb or *ta* 'come', to indicate the actual arrival at the Goal. This is illustrated in (50) and (51) which express 'go and arrive' and 'come and arrive', respectively.

(50) *a-laáw-é*   *n'*   *oo-fiíy-á* ...
    SBJ$_1$-go-SBJV and   NP$_{15}$-arrive-FV
    'He should go and upon arriving ...'

(51) *n'*   *oo-t-á*   *n'*   *oo-fiíy-á*   *a-ń-síngan-a*
    and NP$_{15}$-come-FV and NP$_{15}$-arrive-FV SBJ$_1$-OBJ$_1$-meet-PFV
    'Upon coming and arriving, he met him.'

To express arrival at a human Goal an applicative extension is added to *fiya* as seen in (52). The applicative verb is sometimes used with a more idiomatic meaning of 'being enough', illustrated in (53).

(52) *násaámbi* *o-ní-kí-fiy-eél-a*   *miíyo* *u-cá*   *w-aángu*
    now   SBJ$_3$-PRS-OBJ$_{1SG}$-arrive-APPL-FV I   NP$_{11}$-rice PP$_{11}$-POSS$_{1SG}$
    'Now, I will receive my rice.' (litt. 'now my rice will arrive on me')

(53) *siíma*   *e-ńttó-ni-fiy-eél-a*
    NP$_9$.porridge SBJ$_9$-FOC.PRS-OBJ$_{1PL}$-arrive-APPL-FV
    'The porridge will be enough for us.'

To conclude, *lamuwa* and *fiya* typically refer to the beginning and the end of a motion. They often combine with basic motion verbs and *lamuwa* can even come to include a reference to a Path.

2.2 Summary

The preceding sections have shown that basic motion verbs in Shangaci form a complex network of closely related meanings which are best defined in relation to one another, with *entta* and *lawa* being an exemplary case.

    Another, less anticipated finding, is the instability of the lexical semantics of motion verbs, and more specifically their Ground component, i.e. the orientation of the motion. This becomes especially clear when looking at the motion verbs from a comparative angle. The Shangaci verb *entta* is strongly oriented towards a Goal but probably once had a more generic meaning, i.e. 'walk, travel' (Guthrie 1970: 214), which in present day Shangaci is expressed by the reduplicated form *-enttetta*. *lawa*, on the other hand, derives from a verb oriented towards the Source (cf. Section 2.1.1) but can be used in Shangaci with a locative Goal, with the meaning 'come from, leave from' being rendered by *lamuwa* (cf. Section 2.1.5). A similar shift is attested in other Eastern Bantu languages. In Nyakyusa, for example, the verb *buuka* related to Proto-Bantu *bʊ́ʊ́k* 'rise up' (Guthrie 1970: 64) is used to express 'go (to)' (Mwangoka Ngapona and Voorhoeve n.d.: 32).

The verb *vira* 'pass' appears to be taking over the meaning of *ingela* 'enter', thus adopting a locative Goal. This expansion has been accomplished in Koti where *vira* means 'pass' as well as 'enter' (Schadeberg and Mucanheia 2002: 229). In other Eastern Bantu languages different shifts occur with the cognates of Shangaci *vira* and *ingela* expressing 'go (to)' (cf. Chewa *pita* 'go (to)' (Paas 2004: 378) and Makhuwa *kela* 'go' (Katupha 1983: 139)). In sum, Shangaci motion verbs form an unstable network of related meanings. The instability appears to be driven by a reorientation or a stronger orientation towards a locative Goal.

2.3 Which Shangaci motion verbs take part in grammaticalization processes?

Of the 9 basic motion verbs listed in table 1, 4 take part in grammaticalization processes, i.e. *entta* 'go to', *lawa* 'leave (for)', *ta* 'come' and *ingela* 'enter'. The present result of the ongoing grammaticalization is a complex two-verb predicate. The motion verbs function as syntactic main verbs or auxiliaries and are followed by a content verb which occurs in its infinitival form or has the same subject and TAM-specifications as the auxiliary motion verb. Table 2 lists all six constructions and gives an indication of their grammatical meaning. Note that *entta* and *ta* each occur twice, once with an applicative extension and once without.

The first two constructions as well as the second use of the last construction express TAM-meanings and will not be further discussed in this paper. An example of each is given below. In Section 2.1 it was said that *enttela* often takes an infinitival complement referring to the goal of the motion. In (54) the combination is grammaticalized, it does not express actual motion but refers to an imminent future.

(54) *í*   *panelá*   *y-aángu*   *e-n-éenttel'*   *o-ttokoótth-a*
      EX NP$_9$-pot PP$_9$-POSS$_{1SG}$ SBJ$_9$-PRS-be.about.to-FV NP$_{15}$-boil.over-FV
      'Oh oh, my pot is about to boil over!'

Table 2. Grammaticalized constructions involving motion verbs

construction	grammatical meaning
-enttela + infinitive	imminent future
-tela + infinitive	certain future
-entta + infinitive	verb focus
-ingela + infinitive	pragmatic marker
-ta$_i$ + inflected verb$_i$	pragmatic marker
-lawa$_i$ + inflected verb$_i$	pragmatic marker
	co-hortative marker

Similarly, an infinitive introduced by *tela* often refers to the goal of the coming (cf. (39)). In (55) *tela* followed by an infinitive expresses a certain future rather than an actual motion.

(55)   *ki-tti-tél-á   w-aariíti*
       SBJ$_{1SG}$-PRS-will-FV NP$_{15}$-know.by.heart
       'I will learn it by heart'

When a first person plural subjunctive of *lawa* is followed by a another first person plural subjunctive (without distal marking cf. (17)), *lawa* has a cohortative meaning: it urges the speaker as well as the addressee(s) to perform the action expressed by the main verb.

(56)   *oóntu   a-laaw-a   n-law-é-ní   ni-ruúti*
       PP$_1$.DEM$_i$ SBJ$_i$-go-PFV SBJ$_{1PL}$-go-SBJV-PLA SBJ$_{1PL}$-return.SBJV
       'She has gone. Let's go back!'

The question I want to address in this section is whether there is something in the lexical semantics of the four motion verbs in Table 2 which makes them more prone to grammaticalization than the other basic motion verbs. In studies on grammaticalization, source concepts are often described as general and/or basic (cf. Heine, Claudi and Hünnemeyer 1991: 32–36, Bybee, Perkins, and Pagliuca 1994: 9–12, Hopper and Traugott 1993: 154–155).

If we assume frequency to be a good criterion for the generalness of a verb, then grammaticalizing motion verbs indeed appear to be more general in Shangaci than non-grammaticalizing ones (cf. Table 1), *ingela* 'enter' being the only exception. It was shown that *vira* 'pass' and *entta* 'go to' are taking over the lexical meaning of *ingela* which could have caused a drop in frequency.

The fact that I describe all 9 motion verbs as basic appears to be in line with the assumed basicness of source items. However, motion verbs in Shangaci (and other Bantu languages) do not constitute prototypical basic vocabulary as their meanings are unstable and one motion verb can adopt the meaning of another one. Next, the derived verbs *tela* and *enttela*, describing 'motion in order to', can hardly be described as 'irreducible notions' (Bybee, Perkins, and Pagliuca 1994: 10). Also, the most basic motion verb -*enttetta* 'move' does not grammaticalize and *ingela* 'enter', which does take part in grammaticalization, describes a rather specific motion.

In more specific studies dealing with the grammaticalization of 'come' and 'go', the deictic nature of the latter is often seen as a crucial factor in their grammaticalization, especially into markers of tense and aspect (i.a. Emanatian 1992: 22). Although I do think that deixis plays a role, it does not appear to play a crucial role in the grammaticalization of future markers in Shangaci, as both 'go to' and 'come' are source items for future grams (cf. (54) and (55), respectively).[8] Also, of the two 'go' verbs, *lawa* is the most deictic one as it typically expresses motion away from the deictic centre. However, *entta* rather than *lawa* grammaticalizes as a future marker.

What appears to be more important than deixis, basicness, and maybe also generalness, at least for the first four constructions in Table 2, is whether the motion verb can take a core argument referring to a (locative or non-locative) Goal. The first four verbs in Table 2 are all syntactically appropriate in this sense. As for the two remaining verbs, they do not take a core argument and hence cannot combine with an infinitive. As will be shown below, deixis features more prominently in their grammaticalization (into pragmatic markers).

3 Non-TAM functions of Shangaci motion verbs

Motion verbs and especially verbs glossed as 'come' and 'go' are known to develop into grammatical markers of tense and aspect (cf. Bybee and Dahl 1989, Bybee, Perkins, and Pagliuca 1994, Heine and Kuteva 2002). Grammatical targets different from tense and aspect have not gone unnoticed (cf. Devos and Van der Wal 2010, Ebert 1987, 2003, Bourdin 2008, Nicolle 2002, 2007 to cite some studies pertaining to African languages) but they figure much less

---

8 See Heine et al. (1991: 38) for a similar case in the Ugandan language Kuliak.

prominently in the grammaticalization literature. This section aims to contribute to the knowledge of these lesser known grammaticalization paths by looking at the last three grammatical constructions in Table 2. For a discussion of the use of *entta* as a verb focus marker the reader is referred to Devos and Van der Wal (2010). The verbs *lawa* 'leave (for)', *ta* 'come' and *ingela* 'enter' take part in grammaticalization processes leading to 'pragmatic markers' which serve to structure the discourse and / or express the attitudes of the speaker. Following Brinton (1996: 30–40) I use the term pragmatic marker to refer to elements with textual and / or interpersonal functions.[9] One typical feature of pragmatic markers is their optionality (Brinton 1996: 44). Because of this and because of their pragmatic function, they are often not considered a genuine part of a language's grammar. As a consequence, diachronic processes leading to pragmatic markers are sometimes referred to as pragmaticalization rather than grammaticalization (cf. Diewald 2011: 373–377 for an overview). However (and in line with i.a. Degand and Simon-Vandenbergen 2011, Diewald 2011, Traugott 1997 [1995], Traugott 2007), I adhere to a broader conception of grammatical material which includes, as formulated by Traugott (2007: 151) 'material that signals the speakers' perspective on the relationship [...] of utterances to each other and to the beliefs of speakers and hearers'. As such, pragmatic markers do fulfill grammatical functions and may also be the result of grammaticalization processes.

Section 3.1 discusses formal characteristics of grammaticalized constructions serving as pragmatic markers in Shangaci. Section 3.2 describes the uses of these grammaticalized constructions in different discourse types (ranging from narrative to more spontaneous discourse). Section 3.3 is a summary and discussion.

3.1 Formal characteristics

As mentioned in Section 2.2, grammaticalized constructions involving motion verbs are of two syntactic types according to the form of the second verb.[10] The auxiliaries *lawa* and *ta* are followed by a content verb with identical subject

---

9 Elements fulfilling these functions are also referred to as 'discourse markers'. Fraser (1996: 186) considers discourse markers to be a special type of pragmatic marker signaling the relationship of the basic message to the foregoing discourse. However, more recent studies usually do not make a significant distinction between discourse markers and pragmatic markers (i.a. Degand and Simon-Vandenbergen 2011: 288).

10 This is in line with Bourdin's crosslinguistic observation that auxiliation (i.e., auxiliary + non-finite verb) and serialization are especially favored structures in the grammaticalization of 'come' and 'go' verbs to textual connectives (Bourdin 2008: 42).

and TAM-specifications. Formal particularities of this type of construction are discussed in Section 3.1.1. Section 3.1.2 looks at *ingela* which combines with an infinitive.

3.1.1 Serial verb constructions

When *lawa* or *ta* is used as a pragmatic marker, it is followed by a verb with the same subject and TAM-specifications. Most typically both verbs are in the Perfective.[11] An important use of the Perfective in Shangaci (and other Bantu languages cf. Crane 2012) is to carry the storyline. Successive Perfectives with the same subject specifications are thus plentiful in Shangaci. An example is given in (57). The crossing of the river and the coming home are subsequent events in the story.

(57) *a-lookhw'*   *aa-t-i*
      SBJ$_1$-cross-PFV SBJ$_1$-come-PFV
      'He crosses the river and comes.'

When the verbs *lawa* or *ta* are used as auxiliaries, morphosyntactic changes take place which are typical for grammaticalization processes. (58) also involves successive Perfectives. However, the tonal pattern is crucially different from the one in (57). The second verb in (58) has a high tone assigned to its first mora, which doubles onto the second mora. In Shangaci nominal arguments of Perfectives (and some other verb forms) can be focused by replacing their lexical high tone(s) (cf.(59a)) by a word-initial high tone (cf. (59b)). The resultant tonal pattern is remarkably similar to the one in (58). In a way, the second verb is 'decategorialized' (Hopper and Traugott 1993: 103–113) in (58). It is no longer an independent verb form but rather a kind of argument of the motion verb. There is also a clear loss in autonomy as nothing can come in between the two verbs in (58), in the same way as nothing can come in between a verb and its focused argument. Moreover, (58) also displays phonological erosion as the auxiliary *lawa* is shortened and both verbs occur in a single phonological phrase (marked by lengthening of the penultimate mora) rather than in two distinct phonological phrases as is typical for Perfectives referring to subsequent events (cf. (57)).

(58) *a-la'*   *á-zúnguluus-u*
      SBJ$_1$-go-PFV SBJ$_1$-turn.around-PFV
      'He turns it around there' / 'And then he turns it around.'

---

11 Other tenses are also possible as seen in (71) and (77) where both verbs occur in the Subjunctive and in (73) where the Durative Situative is used.

(59) a. *ki-rafuun-u*   *li-khólóoma*
    SBJ₁sg-chew-PFV NP₅-young.coconut
    'I have eaten a young coconut (amongst other things)'

    b. *ki-rafun-u*   *lí-khólooma*
    SBJ₁sg-chew-PFV NP₅-young.coconut
    'I have eaten nothing but a young coconut'

3.1.2 Infinitival complement

When *ingela* is used as an auxiliary and takes an infinitival complement rather than a locative argument, it can only occur in the Perfective thus showing clear loss of paradigmatic variability (Lehmann 2005). As an autonomous lexical item, *ingela* is not restricted TAM-wise. Another sign of its (ongoing) grammaticalization is the lack of vowel lengthening following the merger of the subject marker and the verb stem (cf. initial *e* instead of *ee* in (60). In Shangaci vowel merger is normally accompanied by compensatory lengthening, as seen in (61).

(60) *e̱ngel'*   *otthiíra*
    a-ingel-e   *o-tthir-a*
    SBJ₁-begin-PFV NP₁₅-run-FV
    'He started running.'

(61) *mwaána*   *e̱emeele*
    mu-ana *a-emel-e*
    NP₁-child SBJ₁-stand-PFV
    'The child is standing.'

3.2 Functions of *lawa*, *ta* and *ingela* in different discourse types

The auxiliaries *lawa*, *ta* and *ingela* are especially frequent in narrative discourse. Narrative discourse subsumes folktales but also expository discourse (i.e. recipes and descriptions of various activities) (Longacre 1990: 2). The same constructions are also found in more spontaneous discourse types, i.e. short dialogues and isolated utterances.[12] Section 3.2.1 and 3.2.2 look respectively at the functions of *lawa* and *ta* in these different discourse types and Section 3.2.2 does the same for *ingela*.

---

12 My main consultant Jorge Nlapa was very skilled in making spontaneous sounding utterances.

3.2.1. *lawa* 'leave (for)'

As an auxiliary, *lawa* is unevenly distributed throughout my database with a clear preference for narrative discourse. In narratives it can have different functions. First, it can be used as a 'deictic explicator' (Ebert 2003: 112), indicating that an action takes place away from the deictic centre. The most striking use of *lawa* as a deictic explicator occurs when the auxiliary combines with a passive verb. In (62) and (63) the subject of *lawa* undergoes an action and does not itself move (at least not willingly). *lawa* merely serves to indicate that the action takes place 'over there' (and in the same way *ta* indicates that the action takes place 'here', cf. (63) and Section 3.2.2).

(62) *eentt-el-iw-a*   *mbuúzi*
      SBJ$_1$.go-APPL-PASS-PFV NP$_{1a}$-goat
      'A goat is chased,

      a-la   *á-khól-iiw-a*   *a-t'*   *á-xínj-iiw-a*
      SBJ$_1$-go.PFV SBJ$_1$-take-PASS-PFV SBJ$_1$-come.PFV SBJ$_1$-cut-PASS-PFV
      it is caught there and slaughtered here.'

(63) *n-láa*   *li-thímb-íiw-a*   *li-phoóntto* *zí-t-í*   *zi-thúul-iw-a*
      SBJ$_5$-go.PFV SBJ$_5$-dig-PASS-PFV   NP$_5$-pit   SBJ$_8$-come-PFV SBJ$_8$-take-PASS-PFV
      'A pit is dug over there, the things are fetched here

      vií-tthu *zi-láa*   *zi-tthây-íw-a*   *va-li-phóntt' opháale*
      NP$_8$-thing SBJ$_8$-go.PFV SBJ$_8$-put-PASS-PFV NP$_{16}$-NP$_5$-pit PP$_{16}$.DEM$_{iii}$
      and put in the pit over there.'

As a deictic explicator *lawa* can also follow an undirected motion verb, like *lamuwa* 'leave', to indicate that the subsequent action takes place away from the deictic centre. An example is given in (64).

(64) *a-lamuuw-u* *a-law'*   *á-khóz-o*   *m-aáti*
      SBJ$_1$-leave-PFV SBJ$_1$-go.PFV SBJ$_1$-heat-PFV NP$_6$-water
      'He leaves and heats the water over there.'

When *lawa* repeats rather than complements a preceding motion verb, as in (65), it is redundant in that it is no longer crucial for the expression of distance away from the deictic centre.

(65) *a-law'*   *o-sáanko*   <u>*a-law'*</u>   <u>*á-ń-singan-a*</u>   *mw-eénye*
      SBJ$_1$-go.PFV   NP$_{17}$-oracle   SBJ$_1$-go.PFV   SBJ$_1$-OBJ$_1$-meet-PFV   NP$_1$-owner
      'He goes to the oracle and meets the owner.'

Instead, it gains importance as a marker of subsequent actions. In (66a–d) *lawa* functions as a textual connective. Someone sets out on a journey and the repeated occurrences of *lawa* indicate that the subsequent actions take place during the journey.

(66) a) *alawaa*   'She leaves ...'
      b) <u>*alaw'áńsingana*</u> *nuúnú mmóote*   '... and meets a woman ...'
      c) <u>*alaw'ásíngana*</u> *nyaáma yuúlweénye*   '... and meets a big animal ...'
      d) <u>*alaw'áfíiyi*</u>   '... and arrives ...'

In the preceding examples the auxiliary *lawa* can be interpreted as a sequential marker but it is still harmonious with motion away from the deictic centre. Its use in contexts that do not imply motion away from the deictic centre but only distance in time reveal the metaphorical mapping of distance in space on distance in time. (67) is a case in point. The auxiliary *lawa* is used in combination with a verb expressing 'to bring', which implies motion towards the deictic centre, and thus cannot be interpreted as a marker of distance away from the deictic centre. It solely indicates a lapse in time (rendered by 'so' or 'and then' in the English translation).[13]

(67) [Mariamu: "I do not want those ones (=cuttings). Those ones have been planted by you. I want a seed of an orange and a coconut. One of these is what I want to play with against that person." <u>Inhabitant</u>: "That is how you want it?" <u>Mariamu</u>: "Yes."]

      zi-láa   *zi-tíis-iiw-a*
      SBJ$_{10}$-go.PFV   SBJ$_{10}$-bring-PASS-PFV
      'So, they (the seeds) are brought'

---

13 The utterance in (67) follows a discussion between Mariamu, the protagonist of the story, and the inhabitants of the mysterious prosperous place Mikhintani. Mariamu is in Mikhintani to win a contest in order to gain riches and release her brothers. The contest involves the planting of trees by a guest as well as an inhabitant of Mikhintani. The winner is the one whose tree is the first to bear fruit. Usually the guest are given cuttings of a coconut or an orange tree but Mariamu demands to be given seeds instead and after some discussion thus was done, i.e., the seeds are brought.

A similar case is found in (68). Here, *lawa* combines with the verb *ta* 'come' and likewise cannot imply motion away from the deictic centre. It merely expresses distance in time. This reading is confirmed by the preceding adverbial phrase.[14]

(68) [The eagle gives the needle to the chicken. The chicken takes the needle but because his toes are spread he lets go of it. The chicken starts searching the ground but can't find it]

    mpákhá síkhú   *z-iínkeénye* <u>*a-law'*</u>   *áa-t-i*   *xaága*
    until   NP$_{10}$.day NP$_{10}$-many SBJ$_1$-go.PFV SBJ$_1$-come-PFV NP$_{1a}$-eagle
    'Then, after many days, came the eagle.'

On the whole, the use of *lawa* as a sequential marker is quite restricted in my database. Some stories even go without it. This is not unexpected as the Perfective is perfectly capable of marking subsequent events. Episode boundaries, which typically involve a temporal gap, may be marked by *lawa* (as is the case in (67) and (68)) but the use of *lawa* is far from being obligatory in this context. In fact, *ingela* more regularly marks episode boundaries (cf. Section 3.2.3). The use of *lawa* appears to be preferred when the lapse in time coincides with an important turn in the course of events. In (67) *lawa* marks the arrival of the 'winning seeds' which foretell the victory of Mariamu after both her brothers lost the contest and in (68) the coming of the eagle after the chicken has lost the needle starts an eternal quarrel between the two of them. Other examples are given in (68) and (69). In both examples *lawa* introduces a pivotal event in the story. In (69) the loosing of the chain 'unchains' a war and in (68) the coming of the rainy season means the end of the idleness of the cricket and the beginning of a good time for the ant.

(69) [I want to tell the story of Makhoni, Mogincual and Shangaci in a time when people were always having wars. One war occurred because of a woman. She was a white woman who married in Makhoni.]

    <u>*o-láa*</u>   *o-ń-vúluuw-u*   *o-xangá*   *w-áawe*
    SBJ$_{14}$-go.PFV SBJ$_{14}$-OBJ$_1$-fall-PFV NP$_{14}$-bead PP$_{14}$-POSS$_1$
    'And she lost her chain.'

---

14 The utterance in (68) is taken from a story about an eagle and a chicken who used to be friends. One day the chicken borrows the needle of the eagle to mend her wings and fly like the eagle does. She loses the needle and when the eagle finds out about it, an eternal quarrel begins.

(70) [The ant agrees to gather fishbones and put them aside in his house. The cricket, on the other hand, applies himself to singing. Every day he does nothing but singing]

mpákhá	íi	e-láa	e-fíy-í	íi-ta
until	EX	SBJ₇-go.PFV	SBJ₇-arrive-PFV	NP₇-rainy.season

Until, ohoh, the rainy season arrives.

As noted above, *lawa* is rarely used in more spontaneous speech types. However, there are some examples which suggest that *lawa* can acquire overtones of emotional distance and express the disapproval of the speaker. In (71) *lawa* could be interpreted as a deictic explicator. The addressee (=Mariamu) is advised not to accept cuttings 'over there' in Mikhintani. However, I feel that the presence of *lawa* in this context emphasizes that agreeing to accept cuttings would be a very unwise thing to do.

(71) *w-ii-fíy-á*   *Mikhinttáani*
SBJ₂ₛG-CON-arrive-FV Mikhinttani
'When you arrive in Mikhintani,

o-si-law-e   *w-á-khúpaali*   *w-iíkh-íw-a*
SBJ₂ₛG-NEG-go-SBJV SBJ₂ₛG-DIST-agree.SBJV NP₁₅-give-PASS-FV
don't you agree to be given

ví-tthú *z'* *oo-zál-íiw-a*
NP₈-thing PP₈-of NP₁₅-give.birth-PASS-FV
things that have come out already (=cuttings)!'

In (68) *lawa* cannot be interpreted as a deictic explicator as it combines with the verb *ta* 'come'. It could be said to mark a lapse in time and thus function as a sequential marker. However, I again feel that *lawa* has an interpersonal function here: it helps to express the sheer astonishment of the speaker with the described event.

(72) *awú-t-í*   *muú-tthu* *a-k-iíy-éele*
SBJ₁.PST-came-PFV NP₁-person SBJ₁-OBJ₁ₛG-steal-APPL-PFV
'A man came, stole from me

a-law'   *áa-t-i*   *theéna* *thuúnto* *a-k-iíy-éel-e*
SBJ₁-go.PFV SBJ₁-come-PFV again PP₁.DEM_ile SBJ₁-OBJ₁ₛG-steal-APPL-PFV
'and dared to come and steal from me again!'

In (71) and (72) the interpersonal uses of *lawa* are hard to pin down as they occur in environments that are compatible with its other uses as either a deictic explicator (cf. (71)) or a sequential marker (cf. (72)). Example (73) is more revealing in this respect. At first sight, *lawa* could be interpreted as marking distance away from the deictic centre. The Ostrich, who is being addressed by the Hare, got himself trapped 'over there'. However, at this point of the story both the Hare and the Ostrich are standing close to the trap and the Hare wants the Ostrich to show him how exactly he got himself trapped. *lawa* thus does not appear to refer to distance in space. I think it mainly helps to express how stupid the Hare thinks the Ostrich was to get himself trapped that way. In other words, in (73), the interpersonal use of *lawa* prevails.

(73)　*wé　w-oó-réntt-e teéí*
　　　you　SBJ$_{2SG}$-PST-do-PFV how
　　　'You, what did you do

　　　o-law-ángá　　*o-fiy-él-él-anga*　　　　　　*o-séy-iíw-a*
　　　SBJ$_{2SG}$-go-DUR-FV　SBJ$_{2SG}$-arrive-APPL-APPL-DUR-FV　NP$_{15}$-tie-PASS-FV
　　　to end up getting yourself trapped'

3.2.2 *ta* 'come'

Like *lawa*, the auxiliary *ta* is largely restricted to narrative discourse in which it is less differentiated functionally than *lawa*. It is mainly used as a deictic explicator, indicating that an event takes place towards the deictic centre. As could already be seen in (62) and (63), *ta* can, just like *lawa*, be used in combination with a passive verb. In such cases *ta* makes clear that the subject undergoes an action at or nearby the deictic centre and basically expresses 'here'. Next, and again like *lawa*, *ta* can follow a motion verb to indicate that the motion takes place towards the deictic centre. (74) is a case in point.

(74)　*a-zunguluuw-u*　　*a-t'*　　　　*á-cí-réey-e*
　　　SBJ$_1$-turn.around-PFV　SBJ$_1$-come.PFV　SBJ$_1$-REFL-put.on.head-PFV
　　　'He turned around and came with a load on his head.'

Through the use of *ta* we know that the hare turns around to face home (i.e. the deictic centre). Unlike *lawa*, *ta* can be used as a purpose marker. Probably, the origin of the latter function lies in its use after a verb of going; when someone goes and does something in order to come back and perform a related action. Sequences like the one in (75) occur frequently in my database.

(75) *a-laaw'*   *a-thuul-u*   *a-tíis-i*
SBJ$_1$-go.PFV SBJ$_1$-fetch-PFV SBJ$_1$-bring-PFV
'She goes and fetches (the pots), brings them

<u>*á-t-í*</u>   <u>*a-xínj-í*</u> *mi-puttú z-áaya*
SBJ$_1$-come-PFV SBJ$_1$-cut-PFV NP$_4$-base PP$_4$-POSS$_1$
and (comes and) cuts their bases.'

In (76) the subject of *ta* is not the person who fetched the water. Rather, water is brought to her. In this context *ta* is devoid of motion and starts to function as a purpose marker.

(76) *a-láa*   *a-ttékh-íw-a*   *maá-ti*   *a-tíis-iw-a*
SBJ$_6$-go.PFV SBJ$_6$-fetch-PASS-PFV NP$_6$-water SBJ$_6$-bring-PASS-PFV
'Water is fetched there, it is brought

<u>*ki-t-i*</u>   <u>*k-óos-o*</u>   *ma-ziíwa*
SBJ$_{1SG}$-come-PFV SBJ$_{1SG}$-wash-PFV NP$_6$-breast
so I can wash my breasts.'

In spontaneous speech this use of *ta* prevails. Often both verbs are in the subjunctive (cf. (77)), which by itself can express a purposive meaning (for more on the use of the subjunctive in Shangaci, see Devos 2008). The presence of *ta* emphasizes the connection with the previous action.

(77) *k-aw-ééntt-el-e*   *o-ranttey-a fuúmba*
SBJ$_{1SG}$-PST-go-APPL-PFV NP$_{15}$-lay-FV NP$_9$-mat
'I went to lay down a mat

wírá aá-tthu   <u>*á-t-é*</u>   *eekhál-ée-vo*
that NP$_2$-person SBJ$_2$-come-SBJV SBJ$_2$-sit-SBJV-LOC$_{16}$
so the people could sit down'

Finally, *ta* is frequently used after an independent lexical instance of *ta*, as illustrated in (74).

(78) *aa-t-í*   <u>*a-t' á-k-éemel-eel-e*</u>
SBJ$_1$-come-PFV SBJ$_1$-come.PFV SBJ$_1$-OBJ$_{1SG}$-stand-APPL-PFV
'she came, she came and stood before me

a-si-k-áambel-ang-a   *ií-tthu*
SBJ$_1$-NEG-OBJ$_{1SG}$-tell-DUR-FV NP$_7$-thing
without saying anything.'

Unlike *lawa* (cf. (66)), this iterated use of *ta* does not develop into a marker of subsequent actions towards the deictic centre. It mostly takes part in a kind of a ready formula that allows the narrator to gather his thoughts (cf. 'floor holder' in Table 3). The latter use is illustrated in (79). The formula 'X comes, X comes and arrives and upon coming and arriving' occurs recurrently in many stories.

(79) *aa-t-i*   <u>*at'*</u>   <u>*á-fíiy-i*</u>
     SBJ$_1$-come-PFV   SBJ$_1$-come-PFV   SBJ$_1$-arrive-PFV
     'He comes, comes and arrives,

     n'   *oo-t-á*   *n'*   *oo-fíiy-a*
     and   NP$_{15}$-come-FV   and   NP$_{15}$-arrive-FV
     and upon coming and arriving, ...'

3.2.3 *ingela* 'enter'

Prata (1987), who was the first to publish Shangaci data, gives 'begin' as a translation equivalent for *ingela* when used in combination with an Infinitive. My data confirm that *ingela* can serve as an ingressive aspectual marker. Often, *ingela* marks the last in a series of events. Whereas the preceding event(s) is/are regarded as completed, the presence of *ingela* emphasizes the initial phase of the last event and does not imply its completion. (77) and (78) are cases in point.

(80) *a-nttó-xééz-a*   *o-ń-xóm-o*   *mw-iíwa*
     SBJ$_1$-FOC-play-FV   SBJ$_3$-OBJ$_1$-pierce-PFV   NP$_3$-thorn
     She was playing, a thorn pierced her

     <u>*engel'*</u>   *o-láw'*   *o-muú-ti*   *a-lil-áank-a*
     SBJ$_1$.begin.PFV   NP$_{15}$-go-FV   NP$_{17}$-NP$_3$-home   SBJ$_1$-cry-DUR-FV
     and she went home crying.

(81) *aantiikh-i*   *na*   *w-iíx-a*   <u>*engel'*</u>   <u>*o-sáyeél-a*</u>
     SBJ$_5$.write-PFV   and   NP$_{15}$-end-FV   SBJ$_1$.begin.PFV   NP$_{15}$-sweep-FV
     'She wrote and upon finishing, she started sweeping.'

However, in many cases *ingela* cannot be interpreted as an ingressive aspectualizer. In (82), for example, it is used in combination with a punctual event which prevents an ingressive reading. What is more, it is itself followed by a series of events.

(82) *ki-law-a*   *kí-rámbalaal-a*   *thoní thoní thoní*
      SBJ$_{1SG}$-go-PFV SBJ$_{1SG}$-lay.down-PFV IDEO
      '[After having fun] I went to sleep

      k-engel'   *o-síl-á*   *khomaála*
      SBJ$_{1SG}$-begin.PFV   NP$_{15}$-hear-FV hello
      when suddenly I heard: "Hello!"

      ki-sisimuuw-u   *ki-n-síngán-a*   *pep' áali*   *ki-n-táhíri*
      SBJ$_{1SG}$-wake-PFV SBJ$_{1SG}$-OBJ$_{1SG}$-meet-PFV NP$_{1A}$.senior Ali SBJ$_{1SG}$-OBJ$_{1SG}$-ask-PFV
      hábaári
      NP$_{9}$-news
      I woke up, met sir Ali and greeted him.'

The question now is what function *ingela* has when an ingressive interpretation is not possible. A couple of factors indicate that *ingela* primarily serves as a narrative device in Shangaci. First, *ingela* has a skewed distribution with the highest density occurring in narrative discourse. Next, as an auxiliary *ingela* always occurs in the Perfective which in Shangaci mainly functions to move the plot forward. When taking a closer look at *ingela* in narratives, it becomes clear that it occurs mainly at episode boundaries and more specifically sets the scene for a new episode. This can be related to its use as an ingressive marker. In the latter use *ingela* refers to the beginning of a (single) action. In a narrative this action does not stand on its own but sets the scene for a number of related events.

One of the longer narratives in the database illustrates the 'demarcating' (cf. Brinton 1996: 77) use of *ingela* nicely. It tells the story of three siblings, two male twins and a sister. The twins want to go to far away Mikhintani to play a game, earn money and return prosperous. When the brothers fail and get caught in jail, the sister also leaves for Mikhintani and not only wins the game, which women are normally not allowed to play, but also manages to free her brothers and take them back home. The twins, however, leave her behind somewhere in the middle of the ocean. With the help of a turtle she eventually gets home and the twins are cast off. The auxiliary *ingela* is used at every episode boundary. Its first occurrence introduces the journey of the first twin brother (cf. (83a), whereas the second one refers to him being caught in jail. In (83b) *ingela* introduces the journey of the second brother, who again ends up in jail. In (83c) *ingela* sets the scene for the journey of Mariamu, the sister, who does not go straight to Mikhintani but meets an old man, an old woman (cf. (83d)) and a whale (cf.(83e)), receiving good advice from each of them. Before arriving in Mikhintani she dresses up as a boy. This is crucial for her to play the game and is also introduced by *ingela*, as seen in (83f). She then wins the game and rewards are given to her (cf. (83g)). Together with her brothers she sets off for the journey home (cf. (83h)). On the way the sister leaves the ship to go pray on a sandhill (cf. (83i)). It is then that the brothers leave her behind and go home (cf. (83j)). Mariamu is saved by a turtle whose arrival is also introduced by *ingela*, as seen in (83k). Mariamu continues her journey on the back of the turtle (cf. (83l)), who leaves after putting her ashore (cf. (83m)). Mariamu goes home and her twin brothers are cast off (cf. (83n)).

(83)   a.   *engel'olaáwa mikhinttááni*
          'He goes to Mikhinttani.'

       b.   *engel'ottítthíma eenttánká mikhinttááni*
          'He flies off to Mikhinttani.'

       c.   *attitthiimi engel'olaáwa mikhinttani*
          'She flies off to Mikhinttani.'

       d.   *engel'olaáwa nuúnu maríyáámu ... alaw'áńsingana nuúnú mmóóte*
          'Sister Mariamu goes ... and meets a woman.'

       e.   *engel'olaáwa ... alaw'ásíngana nyaáma yuúlweénye*
          'She goes ... and meets a huge animal.'

       f.   *engel'osícúweeya*
          'Now she is unrecognizable.'

       g.   *engel'owiíkhiíwa*
          'She is rewarded.'

       h.   *engel'olaáwa*
          'She leaves.'

       i.   *engel'olaáwa aláw'ásíngána livúula*
          'She goes and finds an island.'

       j.   *éngél'olaáw'omuúti*
          'They go home.'

       k.   *na nkaásá engel'oóta*
          'And then the turtle comes.'

       l.   *engel'olaáwa ttittittittittitti*
          'She goes home fast.'

       m.   *alamuuwu ngaása engel'olaáwa*
          'And so the turtle leaves'

       n.   *ttaáphaalé ambá éngél'olaáwa*
          'And right there the brothers leave.'

The clauses containing *ingela* (83a–n) all introduce pivotal events in the story. In fact, they can serve as a summary of the narrative, which is often mentioned as a defining characteristic of pivotal events (cf. Longacre 1990: 5, Brinton 1996: 45). However, as is typical for pragmatic markers in general and for Shangaci pragmatic markers in particular, the use of *ingela* as an episode boundary marker is not obligatory. A narrator may choose not to mark the beginning of a new episode or to mark it by another pragmatic marker (like *lawa* 'leave for', cf. Section 3.2.1). The extraction of clauses containing *ingela* thus does not always yield a good abstract of the narrative. Moreover, it is sometimes hard to decide between an aspectual and a pragmatic reading. Both uses occur in narratives (cf. divergence) and especially with dynamic events one reading does not exclude the other. The pragmatic reading prevails with more punctual events.

In shorter narratives and more spontaneous speech types the demarcative function of *ingela* often acquires an element of surprise and typically marks an unexpected turn in the course of events. (82) is a case in point. An additional example is given in (84).

(84) *k-oo-réntt-á*　　　*ki-som-aánk-a*
      SBJ$_{1SG}$-PST-do-FV SBJ$_{1SG}$-read-DUR-FV
      'I was reading,

      engel'　　　　*oó-t-a*　　　*n-laámu*　　　*a-k-aáx-íis-i*
      SBJ$_1$.begin.PFV NP$_{15}$-come-FV NP$_1$-brother.in.law SBJ$_1$-OBJ$_{1SG}$-leave-CAUS-PFV
      but then my brother-in-law came and made me stop.'

When the unexpectedness coincides with a negative evaluation of the event, the use of *ingela* comes very close to the interpersonal use of *lawa* described in Section 3.2.1. In (85) and (83) the unexpected event introduced by *ingela* is clearly disapproved of.

(85) *yeéne oó-kí-singan-a*　　　　　*k-eéméel-é*
      he   SBJ$_1$.PST-OBJ$_{1SG}$-meet-APPL-PFV SBJ$_{1SG}$-stand-SIT.PFV
      'He met me while standing

      engel'　　　　*o-kí-fúny-a*　　　*nguúwo*　　*m-ma-pháaja*
      SBJ$_1$.begin.PFV NP$_{15}$-OBJ$_{1SG}$-pull.up-FV NP$_{10}$-clothes NP$_{18}$-NP$_6$-thigh
      and he pulled my clothes up as high as my thighs!'

(86) *ki-ttóow-ir-a*　　　*k-iirán-áang-á*
      SBJ$_{1SG}$-FOC-QV-FV SBJ$_{1SG}$-call-DUR-FV
      'Although I was calling,

      engel'　　　　*o-sí-kí-jiibu*
      SBJ$_1$.begin.PFV NP$_{15}$-NEG-OBJ$_{1SG}$-answer-FV
      she did not respond.' [15]

---

15 The quotative verb *ira* is used as an adverbial clause marker in (86) (Devos and Bostoen 2012).

However, the use of *ingela* as a marker of disapproval is hard to pinpoint as it always coincides with unexpectedness.

3.3 Summary

Table 3 summarizes the grammaticalized uses of *lawa*, *ta* and *ingela* in Shangaci. A distinction is made between propositional, textual and interpersonal functions.

Table 3. Grammaticalized uses of Shangaci motion verbs

auxiliary	propositional	textual	interpersonal
lawa	deictic explicator	text cohesion marker	marker of disapproval
		sequential marker	
		episode boundary marker (pivotal events)	
ta	deictic explicator	purpose marker	–
		floor holder	
ingela	ingressive aspectual marker	scene setter	marker of surprise
		episode boundary marker	

Both Ebert (1987, 2003) and Bourdin (2008) mention textual and interpersonal uses of 'come' and 'go' verbs that are very similar to the ones found for *ta* and *lawa* in Shangaci. Ebert (1987, 2003) describes the use of 'come' and 'go' verbs as deictic explicators in Kera and other Chadic languages. In addition to this, Chadic 'come' and 'go' verbs can be used for the expression of consequence and surprise, respectively. According to Ebert (1987: 69), the anaphoric or iterated use of 'come' and 'go' verbs serves as a linking context between both functions. Bourdin (2008), who looks at textual and related uses of 'come' and 'go' verbs from a cross linguistic perspective, indicates that the 'iteration scenario' could indeed be one of the triggering factors in the grammaticalization of these verbs as markers of textual connectivity. Other possible triggers he mentions are deixis and futurity.

In Shangaci the auxiliaries *lawa* and *ta* are also known to follow independent lexical instances of the same verbs. In the case of *lawa* this repetion can be argued to facilitate the demotion of the motion element and as such can be interpreted as a trigger for the grammaticalization of *lawa* as a sequential marker. However, deixis appears to play a more fundamental role. When *lawa* is used as a deictic explicator the motion element is demoted and emphasis is on the distance in space. The textual and interpersonal uses of *lawa* involve a metaphorical mapping of distance in space on time and emotion, respectively. In the case of *ta* there is no obvious link between its iterated use and its use as a purpose marker. The latter is the result of pragmatic strengthening in scenarios where someone leaves home (or other point of reference), does something to come back home and perform another action. The action performed at home is typically interpreted as a the goal of the previous actions. This idea of finality becomes conventionalized causing *ta* to be used even when no actual motion is involved.

Examples of verbs meaning 'enter' developing pragmatic uses are much harder to find in the grammaticalization literature. However, if one starts from the intermediate stage as an ingressive marker, strikingly similar developments can be found for the ingressive marker *gan* in Middle English (Brinton 1996: 67–83).[16] As indicated by Brinton (1996: 83) *gan* is used textually as a marker of narrative juncture and interpersonally as a marker of internal evaluation.

Table 3 looks like a text book example of the type of unidirectional semantic change associated with grammaticalization (Traugott 1982). However, it should be remembered that all these uses are synchronically attested in Shangaci and thus suggest but do not prove a diachronic development. Moreover, the fact that the interpersonal uses are largely restricted to more spontaneous discourse types suggest the possibility of simultaneous discourse type related developments instead of a single unidirectional development (cf. also Brinton 1996: 277 on the importance of discourse type).

4 Conclusion

This paper describes lexical and grammatical uses of Shangaci motion verbs. It shows that motion verbs in Shangaci form a complex and unstable network of interrelated meanings. The instability mostly involves the type of locative argument a motion verb can (or must) take with apparent preference for including a locative Goal. It is suggested that motion verbs that take a (locative) Goal as a core argument are especially prone to grammaticalization.

The Shangaci motion verbs that develop into pragmatic markers with textual (text coherence, scene setting, episode boundary marking) and interpersonal

---

16 Note that the use of a verb denoting 'movement into' as an ingressive marker is not an uncommon development in African languages (cf. Heine et al. 1993: 271).

(disapproval, surprise) functions are *lawa* 'leave for', *ta* 'come' and *ingela* 'enter'. The pragmatic uses of the latter verb are derived from an intermediate stage as an ingressive marker. However, with *lawa* 'leave for' and *ta* 'come' the discourse uses are directly derived from the motion semantics. Deixis as well as the deictic opposition between the verbs plays a crucial role in their grammaticalization. The paper shows that a good understanding of the contexts in which the lexical items are used is crucial to understand the grammaticalization paths followed by them but the lexical semantics of the source items do not help to delimit possible targets. In Shangaci, for example, both a verb expressing 'enter' and a verb expressing 'leave for' can be used with a disapproving connotation. As if this were not enough, the verb *entta* 'go to', which has grammaticalized as a verb focus marker in Shangaci (Devos and Van der Wal 2010), can also be used disapprovingly, as illustrated in (87).

(87) *miíyó koów-áampel-e*   *o-khuruúpa*
     I   SBJ$_{1SG}$.PST.OBJ$_{2SG}$-tell-PFV NP$_{15}$-plough-FV
     'I told you to pull out the weed

     weéyo *w-entt'*   *o-rézuúla*   *mi-yaní*   *z-áawe*
     you   SBJ$_{2SG}$-FOC-PFV NP$_{15}$-sweep-FV NP$_4$-weed PP$_4$-POSS$_1$
     but you just swept it.'

Finally, the paper indicates that although the different synchronic uses of the Shangaci pragmatic markers appear to suggest a diachronic unidirectional evolution from propositional to textual and interpersonal meanings, there is also the possibility of developments dependent on discourse type.

Abbreviations

EX	exclamation
FV	final vowel
FOC	predicative focus
IDEO	ideophone
NP$_x$	noun prefix of class x
OBJ$_x$	object concord of class x
PP$_x$	pronominal prefix of class x
QV	quotative verb
RED	reduplicated
SIT	situative
SBJ$_x$	subject concord of class x
UPFV	unexpected perfective

References

Bastin, Yvonne, André Coupez, Evariste Mumba & Thilo C. Schadeberg (eds.). 2002. *Bantu lexical reconstructions 3 / Reconstructions lexicales bantoues 3*. Tervuren: Royal Museum for Central Africa, online database: http://linguistics.africamuseum.be/BLR3.html (accessed 30 September 2013).

Besha, Ruth M. 1993. *A classified vocabulary of the Shambala language (with outline grammar)*. Bantu Vocabulary Series 10. Tokyo: ILCAA.

Bourdin, Philippe. 2008. On the grammaticalization of 'come' and 'go' into markers of textual connectivity. In Maria Xosé López-Couso & Elena Seoane (eds.), *Rethinking grammaticalization: new perspectives*, 37–59. Amsterdam: John Benjamins.

Brinton, Laurel J. 1996. *Pragmatic Markers in English. Grammaticalization and Discourse Functions*. Berlin & New York: Mouton de Gruyter.

Bybee, Joan & Östen Dahl. 1989. The creation of tense and aspect systems in the languages of the world. *Studies in Language* 13 (1): 51–103.

Bybee, Joan, Revere Perkins & William Pagliuca. 1994. *The Evolution of Grammar*. Chicago: University of Chicago Press.

Crane, Thera Marie. 2012. *-ile* and the pragmatic pathways of the resultative in Bantu Botatwe. *Africana Linguistica* 18: 41–96.

Degand, Liesbeth & Anne-Marie Simon-vandenbergen. 2011. Introduction: Grammaticalization and (inter)subjectification of discourse markers. *Linguistics* 49 (2): 287–294.

Devos, Maud. 2008. The expression of modality in Shangaci. *Africana Linguistica* 14: 3–35.

Devos, Maud & Koen Bostoen. 2012. Bantu DO/SAY polysemy and the origins of a quotative in Shangaci. *Africana Linguistica* 18: 97–132.

Devos, Maud & Jenneke van der Wal. 2010. 'Go' on a rare grammaticalisation path to focus. *Linguistics in the Netherlands* 27: 45–58. Amsterdam: John Benjamins.

Diewald, Gabriele. 2011. Pragmaticalization (defined) as grammaticalization of discourse functions. *Linguistics* 49 (2): 365–390.

Dixon, R. M. W. 2010. *Basic linguistic theory. Volume 1: Methodology*. Oxford: Oxford University Press.

Ebert, Karen. 1987. Discourse function of motion verbs in Chadic. *Afrikanistische Arbeitspapiere* 10: 53–71.

Ebert, Karen. 2003. 'Come' and 'go' as discourse connectors in Kera and other Chadic languages. In Erin Shay & Uwe Seibert (eds.), *Motion, Direction and Location in Languages: In honor of Zygmunt Frajzyngier*, 111–122. Amsterdam & Philadelphia: John Benjamins.

Emanatian, Michele. 1992. Chagga 'come' and 'go': Metaphor and the development of tense-aspect. *Studies in Language* 16: 1–33.

Felberg, Knut. 1996. *Nyakyusa-English-Swahili and English-Nyakyusa Dictionary*. Dar es Salaam: Mkuki na Nyota Publishers.

Fraser, Bruce. 1996. Pragmatic Markers. *Pragmatics* 6 (2): 167–190.

Guerreiro, M. Viegas. 1963. *Rudimentos de Língua Maconde*. Lourenço Marques.

Guthrie, M. 1970. *Comparative Bantu: an introduction to the comparative linguistics and prehistory of the Bantu Languages, volume 3*. Farnborough: Gregg International Publishers.

Heine, Bernd, Ulrike Claudi & Friederike Hünnemeyer. 1991. *Grammaticalization. A conceptual framework*. Chicago & London: The University of Chicago Press.

Heine, Bernd & Tania Kuteva. 2002. *World Lexicon of Grammaticalization*. Cambridge: Cambridge University Press.

Hopper, Paul. 1991. On some priciples of grammaticalization. In Elizabeth Traugott & Bernd Heine (eds.), *Approaches to grammaticalization*, vol. 1. 17–35. Amsterdam & Philadelphia: John Benjamins.

Hopper, Paul & Elizabeth Closs Traugott. 1993. *Grammaticalization*. Cambridge: Cambridge University Press.

Katupha, José Mateus M. 1983. *A preliminary description of sentence structure in the e-Sáaka dialect of e-Mákhuwa*. London: School of Oriental and African Studies MPhil thesis.

Kisseberth, Charles W. & Mohammad Imam Abasheikh. 2004. *The Chimwiini lexicon exemplified* (Asian and African lexicon 45). Tokyo: ILCAA.

Lakusta, M. Laura & Barbara Landau. 2011. Language and memory for motion events: origins of the asymmetry between source and goal paths. *Cognitive Science* 36 (3): 517–544.

Lehmann, Christian. 2005. Theory and method in grammaticalization. In Gabriele Diewald (ed.), *Grammatikalisierung*. Special issue of *Zeitschrift für Germanistische Linguïstik* 32, 152–187. Berlin & New York: Mouton de Gruyter.

Levinsohn, Stephen H. 2010. Towards a Typology of Story Development Marking. In Karsten Legère and Christina Thornell (eds.), *Bantu Languages*, 143–151. Köln: Rüdiger Köppe.

Longacre, Robert E. 1990. Storyline Concerns and Word Order Typology in East and West Africa. *Studies in African Linguistics*. Supplement 10.

Meeussen, A.E. 1967. Bantu grammatical reconstructions. *Africana Linguistica* 3: 80–122.

Meeuwis, Michael & Koen Stroeken. 2012. Non-situational functions of demonstrative noun phrases in Lingala (Bantu). *Pragmatics* 22 (1): 147–66.

Mwangoka Ngapona & Jan Voorhoeve. n.d. *Cursus Ki-Nyakyusa*. Leiden: Afrika Studie Centrum.

Nicolle, Steve. 2002. The grammaticalisation of movement verbs in Digo and English. *Revue de Sémantique et Pragmatique* 11: 47–67.

Nicolle, Steve. 2007a. The grammaticalization of tense markers: a pragmatic reanalysis. *Cahiers Cronos* 17: 47–65.

Nicolle, Steve. 2007b. Textual functions of Chidigo demonstratives. In Nancy C. Kula & Lutz Marten (eds.), *Bantu in Bloomsburry (*SOAS Working Papers in Linguistics 15*)*, 159–171. http://www.soas.ac.uk/linguistics/research/workingpapers/volume-15/file37806.pdf (accessed 30 September 2013).

Nicolle, Steve. 2012. Semantic-pragmatic change in Bantu -*no* demonstrative forms. *Africana Linguistica* 17: 193–233.

Paas, Steven. 2004. *Chichewa/Chinanja-English dictionnary*. Blantyre: Christian Literature Association in Malawi.

Petzell, Malin. 2008. *The Kagulu language of Tanzania. Grammar, texts and vocabulary*. Köln: Rüdiger Köppe Verlag.

Pires Prata, A. 1987. Análise etno-linguistica do xecado de sangage. *Trabalhos de Arqueologia e Antropologia* 2: 75–96.

Schadeberg, Thilo C. 2003. Historical linguistics. In Derek Nurse & Gérard Philippson (eds.), *The Bantu Languages*, 143–164. New York & London: Routledge.

Schadeberg, Thilo C. & Francisco U. Mucanheia. 2000. *Ekoti: the Maka or Swahili language of Angoche*. Köln: Rüdiger Köppe Verlag.

Stefanowitsch, Anatol & Ada Rohde. 2004. The goal bias in the encoding of motion events. In Gunter Radden & Klaus-Uwe Panther (eds.), *Studies in linguistic motivation*, 249–268. Berlin & New York: Mouton de Gruyter.

Talmy, Leonard. 1985. Lexicalization patterns: semantic structure in lexical forms. In Shopen, Timothy (ed.), *Language Typology and Syntactic Description III: Grammatical categories and the Lexicon*, 57–149. Cambridge: Cambridge University Press.

Traugott, Elizabeth Closs. 1982. From propositional to textual and expressive meanings; Some semantic-pragmatic aspects of grammaticalization. In Winfred P. Lehmann & Yakov Malkiel (eds.) *Perspectives on historical linguistics*, 245–271. Amsterdam & Philadelphia: John Benjamins.

Traugott, Elizabeth Closs. 1997 [1995]. The role of the development of discourse markers in a theory of grammaticalization. Paper presented at ICHL XII, Manchester. http://www.stanford.edu/~traugott/papers/discourse.pdf (accessed 30 September 2013).

Traugott, Elizabeth Closs. 2007. Discussion article: Discourse markers, modal particles, and contrastive analysis, synchronic and diachronic. *Catalan Journal of Linguistics* 6: 139–157.

Van der Wal, Jenneke. 2010. Functions of demonstratives in Makhuwa narratives. *Africana Linguistica* 16: 183–213.

Van der Wal, Jenneke. 2013. (Inter)subjectification and demonstratives as pragmatic particles. *Journal of Historical Pragmatics* 14 (1): 1–44.

Wilkins, David & Deborah Hill. 1995. When "go" means "come": Questioning the basicness of basic motion verbs. *Cognitive Linguistics* 6 (2/3): 209–259.

Conclusion

Maud Devos and Jenneke van der Wal

How far have we come and where do we go from here? Discussion and directions for further research

1 Unusual targets of 'come' and 'go' verbs

The present volume investigated a number of lesser-known grammaticalization paths travelled by 'come' and 'go' in order to reach a better understanding of the nature of these motion verbs and the grammaticalization processes associated with them. Table 1 gives an overview of the unusual targets of 'come' and 'go' discussed in the papers and reflects a first straightforward achievement of the book: it contributes to Heine et al. (1993) and Heine and Kuteva's (2002) lexica of grammaticalization, either by adding targets[1] or by giving typological and/or historical weight to (little) known paths.

Table 1. Unusual targets of 'come' and 'go' discussed in the present volume

Source	Target	Paper
GO	(deontic) passive	Mocciaro
	directive marker (2nd person & 1st person plural)	Mauri & Sansò
	non-epistemic necessive modality	Bourdin
	focus	Bravo
	intensifier	Carlson
	sequential (or episode boundary) marker	Devos
	discourse marker of disapproval	Devos
COME	(modal) passive	Giacalone Ramat & Sansò, Dragomirescu & Nicolae
	copula	Dragomirescu & Nicolae
	directive marker (1st person plural)	Mauri & Sansò
	non-epistemic necessive modality	Bourdin
	purpose	Devos
	discourse marker of acceptance and conversation ending	Daniels
	discourse marker of disagreement	Daniels

---

1 This is especially true for the passive, deontic passive and intensifier uses developing out of source 'go'.

However, as stated in the introduction, our main motivation for bringing together unusual targets of 'come' and 'go' source verbs was not just a typological one. Rather, we hoped that the investigation of lesser-known paths would lead to better insights into certain aspects of grammaticalization. On the one hand, we aimed at questioning the characterization of source items (conveniently referred to as 'come' and 'go' in Table 1): their lexical semantics (basicness, generality & frequency and deixis), persistence effects attributed to them and the role of the morphosyntactic context. On the other hand, we wanted to find out more about the path (i.e. the link between source and target in Table 1): whether it is direct or indirect and what kind of meaning changes it involves. In Sections 2 to 8 we summarize what we believe to be the most important contributions to each of these focal points.

2 Are 'come' and 'go' basic, general and frequent?

In the introduction we mentioned that source items in grammaticalization studies are typically referred to as basic, general and frequent, with frequency often being described as an outcome of generality. What is more, these characteristics are often considered sufficient explanations for the frequent grammaticalization of the source items in question.

For 'come' and 'go' verbs, *basicness*, in the sense of lexical universality, has already been questioned by Wilkins and Hill (1995). Their study makes clear that *come* is not a lexical universal. In the Oceanic language Longgu, for example, 'come' is expressed by *la* 'go, travel' followed by *mai* 'hither', as seen in (1).

(1)   Longgu (Austronesian, Oceanic)

     e   la   mai   Honiara
     3_{SG} go hither Honiara
     'S/He came from Honiara (to here).'   (Wilkins and Hill 1995: 240)

This volume, and especially the papers dealing with lesser-known languages, sheds further doubts on the basicness of 'come' and 'go' verbs. Devos' study considers a group of motion verbs in the Bantu language Shangaci and makes clear that they do not represent prototypical basic vocabulary, as their meanings are unstable and one motion verb can adopt the meaning of another one. This is most clearly reflected in the existence of near-synonymous 'go' verbs. Comparative data show that the 'go' verb *entta* is derived from a generic motion verb meaning 'go, travel, move', whereas the other 'go' verb *lawa* is derived from a verb meaning 'leave from'. In present day Shangaci they can both be used to express 'going to a specified Goal'. A remarkably similar phenomenon is attested in the Senufo language Supyire, which also has two near-synonymous 'go' verbs (Carlson). Again, comparative evidence suggests that the 'go' verb *kare* in an earlier stage meant 'leave', whereas the 'go' verb *shyε* derives from a verb meaning 'go to (a locative goal)'.

In sum, if the basicness of 'come' and 'go' cannot be presupposed, then we agree with Bourdin when he says that, contrary to a widely held assumption, conceptual basicness cannot explain the frequent grammaticalization of 'come' and 'go' verbs.

Generality refers to the supposed abstract nature of the source items and their ability to occur in a wide range of contexts. As indicated in the introduction, frequency could be a good measure of generality. Since most papers concentrate on a specific 'come' or 'go' verb, little attention is paid to relative frequency. However, Dragomirescu and Nicolae explicitly indicate that of the three verbs in Romanian expressing motion towards the deictic centre, *veni* 'come' is the most polysemous one and this fact favored its grammaticalization. Similarly, Devos indicates that the motion verbs that take part in grammaticalization processes in Shangaci are the ones that occur most frequently. Mauri and Sansò also claim that it is the frequent use of 'come' and 'go' in directive situations that cause their grammaticalization as directive markers.

To conclude, generality and, related to it, frequency appear to be more crucial characteristics of 'come' and 'go' source items than basicness. However, the notion of generalization of lexical source items prior to grammaticalization also poses some problems. First, it might be hard to draw the line between generalization as part of lexical meaning change and generalization as part of grammatical meaning change (cf. Section 6). Next, if generalization leads to a fairly abstract source meaning with more concrete realizations in specific contexts, what then can be the role of persistence? We turn to persistence in the following section and to the role of the co-text in Section 5.

3 Persistence effects

Several papers mention persistence of lexical source meanings in the newly developed gram. Persistence effects are most obvious when, as formulated by Hopper (1991: 22), "details of the lexical history [of source items are] reflected in constraints on [their] grammatical distribution". Mauri and Sansò convincingly show that although lexical semantics cannot explain why 'come' and 'go' grammaticalize into directive markers, they do constrain the usage range of the resulting grams. Following Mauri and Sansò's analysis, it is the deictic component which causes 'go' to be preferred for second person imperatives and 'come' for first person plural directive constructions. Mocciaro shows that the restriction of *andare* 'go' passives in Early Italian to events with a negative connotation ultimately goes back to a metaphorical extension of the deictic meaning of *andare* as "movement not towards the speaker's point of view". Another component of the meaning of *andare*, i.e. its source-orientedness (in the sense of Fillmore [1971] 1975), is harmonic with the secondary development into a deontic passive marker. When saying 'the documents should be destroyed' the focus is not on the result of a passive path (cf. 'the documents were destroyed') but on the phase preceding the passive change of state (i.e. the source). Dragomirescu and Nicolae claim that the telicity of Romanian *veni* 'come (i.e. movement towards the deictic centre)' explains why, as a passive marker, it can only combine with telic verbs.

The preceding discussion confirms that 'come' and 'go' source items are not semantically empty and that some components of their lexical meaning, typically deixis, may persist in the derived grams. In the following section we take a closer look at the role of deixis. We have seen that it can be persistent, but can it also explain why 'come' and 'go' verbs grammaticalize (and do so with such "exuberance" (cf. Bourdin))?

4 Deixis

Although most papers do not question the deictic nature of 'come' and 'go' verbs, nor the deictic opposition they are assumed to be in, papers dealing with lesser-known languages confirm Wilkins and Hill's (1995) claim that, if there is a universal deictic opposition between 'come' and 'go' verbs, it is at the level of pragmatic interpretation and not lexical semantics. Devos' paper shows that although the Shangaci verb *ca* 'come' is unambiguously deictic, there are several 'go' verbs which, in appropriate contexts, can be used in opposition to 'come'. The presence of synonymous 'go' verbs in Supyire (Carlson) suggests a similar scenario.

As for the importance of deixis in the grammaticalization paths described, three different positions can be distinguished. First, deixis is thought not to be a triggering factor in the grammaticalization process but may still constrain the usage range of the resulting gram (Giacalone Ramat and Sansò, Dragomirescu and Nicolae, and Mauri and Sansò). Next, deixis is said to play a more or less crucial role in the initial stages of grammaticalization (Mocciaro, Daniels, Bravo, Carlson and Devos) and finally the view that the very frequent grammaticalization of 'come' and 'go' verbs in the languages of the world can only be understood by referring to their deictic nature (Bourdin).

Interestingly, the papers dealing with a passive target exemplify all three positions. First, Giacalone Ramat and Sansò, and Dragomirescu and Nicolae, who discuss the development of passive markers out of 'come' sources, do not consider deixis to be a crucial factor in the grammaticalization process. Rather, metaphorical transfer from 'change of place' to 'change of state' plays a key role in the initial stages of the grammaticalization process. As was discussed in the previous section, Dragomirescu and Nicolae indicate that the deictic nature of the source verbs does restrict the current usage range of the passive markers. Mocciaro also believes that motion not towards the deictic center persists in the passive reading of Italian *andare*-passives. However, contrary to Giacalone Ramat and Sansò, and Dragomirescu and Nicolae, she argues that deixis plays a crucial role in the initial grammaticalization stage as well: the change of state is perceived as a movement from a pre-existing state (=here) towards a new state (non-here). Bourdin, finally, suggests that the cross-linguistic tendency of both 'come' and 'go' verbs to develop into passive markers can be explained by referring to directional deixis. He argues that passive constructions crucially involve a decoupling of Agent and Topic: identification with the Topic, i.e. the endpoint of the "kinesis", results in a ventive construction, whereas identification with the Agent, i.e. the source of the kinesis, results in an itive construction. Although Bourdin's typologically inspired analysis appears to be refuted by two of the three in-depth studies in this volume, further in-depth investigation of passive constructions involving 'come' and 'go' verbs is needed. A phenomenon that could add weight to Bourdin's point of view is the recurrent use of 'come' and 'go'-derived deictic explicators (i.e. expressing 'here' and 'there') in passive(like) constructions, attested in Shangaci (Devos) and in the Chadic language Margi. Compare the Margi example in (2) with the Shangaci example in (3).

(2)   Margi (Afro-Asiatic, Chadic)

    má'yám   à-rá   gù   shír'ù,   kà   mjì   á-sì
    go.PL.IMP CONJ-GO look.for wood   that people PRS-come
    à-ptsà-nyì   *dàrí*
    CONJ-roast-you   with.it
    'Go look for firewood, so that people may [come to] roast you with it (= so you may be roasted with it)'

                                          (Hoffmann 1963: 210–211, cited in Ebert 2003: 118)

(3) Shangaci (Niger-Congo, Bantu)

a-la *á-khól-iiw-a* *a-t'* *á-xínj-iiw-a*
SBJ₁-go.PFV SBJ₁-take-PASS-PFV SBJ₁-come.PFV SBJ₁-cut-PASS-PFV
'[the goat] is caught there and slaughtered here.'

The other papers (dealing with non-passive targets) also exemplify all three positions. Mauri and Sansò, when discussing directive markers developing out of 'come' and 'go' verbs, indicate that rather than deixis more basic motion or change of location triggers the grammaticalization process. They make clear that motion is often a necessary preliminary action to realize an order, which explains the frequent use of 'come' and 'go' in directive situations, which in turn accounts for their reanalysis as directive markers. Bravo's analysis of the grammaticalization of Spanish *ir* 'go' into a focus marker at first sight appears to be very similar to Mocciaro's analysis of the Italian *andare*-passive. Bravo acknowledges an intermediate development to a 'change of state' predicate but at the same time claims that the inherent goal-orientedness of Spanish *ir* is also crucial in the development of the intermediary resultative construction: *ir* selects an infinitive expressing the resultant state due to its inherent goal-orientedness. However, contrary to Mocciaro, Bravo suggests that it is attainment of the Goal or telicity, rather than the position of the Goal with respect to the deictic center that plays a crucial role. She finds proof for this in the fact that Mexican Spanish uses the auxiliary *venir* 'come' (as in (4)) rather than *ir* (as in the Peninsular Spanish example in (5)) to express the same focus meaning. Further research is needed to establish the degree of (semantic and syntactic) equivalence between both constructions.

(4) Mexican Spanish

Fue *a llover [el día de mi boda]ᵣ.*
go.AUX.3SG.PST.PFV to rain.INF the day of my wedding
'Of all the days of the year, it had to rain my wedding day.'

(5) Peninsular Spanish

*El carro se nos **vino** a romper*
The car SE.REFL we.DAT come.3SG.PST.PFV to break.INF
[en el peor momento]ᵣ.
in the worst moment
'The car had to get broken in the worst moment'

The three remaining papers discussing discourse uses of 'come' and 'go' verbs propose that deixis is an important trigger for the grammaticalization process. Daniels suggests that the development of Peninsular Spanish *venga* 'come' into a discourse marker of disagreement initially involves metaphorical movement of the addressee towards the desires of the speaker. For Carlson the development of Supyire 'go' into an intensifier involves metaphorical mapping of 'further away from the speaker' to 'more than usual'. Similarly, Devos claims that the textual and interpersonal uses of Shangaci 'go' involve metaphorical mapping of 'distance in space' to 'distance in time' (sequential marker) and 'distance in emotion' (marker of disapproval), respectively.

Bourdin, from a typological perspective, argues that the cross-linguistically recurrent grammaticalization of 'come' and 'go' verbs is due to their deictic nature and more specifically their goal-orientedness. In his study of necessive markers derived from 'come' and 'go' verbs he argues that all the paths, whether they involve an intermediate stage as a future or a passive marker or not, owe their existence to the goal-orientedness of the source verbs. This leads him to claim that if a non- or weakly deictic verb follows a similar grammaticalization path, as is the case for the Austronesian Dehu verb *tro* 'move' developing into a necessive marker, this can be explained by the 'next best tool principle': faced with the lack of a motion verb denoting directional deixis, Dehu goes for the next best option, which is the generic motion verb *tro*. There could be an alternative way of looking at these facts which is more in line with Wilkins and Hill (1995). Although verbs like Dehu *tro* do not encode directional deixis on a semantic level, they are often used to express movement with respect to the deictic centre and it might well be this frequent deictic connotation which causes them to travel the same paths as 'true deictic verbs'.

5 Co-text

It is well-known that, when considering the input of grammaticalization, it is whole constructions rather than discrete lexical items that should be taken into consideration. In this section we focus on the morphosyntactic co-text of the investigated grammaticalization paths.

As was more or less expected, auxiliation and serialization turn out to be the most common structures (cf. Bourdin 2008, cited in the introduction). However, 'come' and 'go' do not need to enter complex verbal constructions to become grammaticalized. This is shown by the development of a discourse marker of agreement out of a simplex verbal construction consisting of the optative of Spanish 'come' (Daniels).

A next question is whether the morphosyntactic co-text is crucial for the grammaticalization process to come about. When identical constructions involving either 'come' or 'go' verbs evolve into more or less identical targets, it can be assumed that the particular type of co-text in which the verb occurs plays an important role. This is clearly the case when 'come' and 'go' verbs become passive auxiliaries in combination with past participles. Haspelmath's (1990, 1994) claim that it is especially the passive orientation of the past participle that causes a passive reinterpretation is confirmed by all three passive papers. In the same vein, Mauri and Sansò indicate that it is the frequent occurrence of 'come' and 'go' in directive situations that causes them to be reinterpreted as directive markers. Bourdin also indicates that it can hardly be a coincidence that necessive markers developing out of passive constructions involving 'come' and 'go' verbs are all non-perfective and lack an overt Agent phrase.

These examples show that when 'come' and 'go' source items enter complex verbal constructions and subsequently grammaticalize, the grammatical meaning is derived not only from the meaning and morphosyntax of the source item but also from the morphosyntax of the co-text.

6 Direct and indirect paths

The unusual targets of 'come' and 'go' verbs listed in Table 1 are attained directly or indirectly. In the papers collected in this book we have seen examples of 'go' developing directly into a directive (Mauri and Sansò), an intensifier (Carlson) and a sequential marker (Devos). 'Come' can develop straight towards a necessive marker (Bourdin), a directive marker (Mauri & Sansò), a discourse marker of agreement or disagreement (Daniels) and a purpose marker (Devos). Other unusual targets are reached indirectly. As was pointed out in the introduction, indirect paths can be of two types, though the division is not entirely clear-cut.

First, the path can be indirect because of a previous semantic change. This is shown to be the case for the development of a passive auxiliary out of Italian 'come'. Giacalone Ramat and Sansò explicitly argue that Italian *venire* 'come' first develops to a change-of-state verb ('become') and only then continues to develop a passive function.

A second type of indirect path is the result of a start on a more usual grammaticalization path. The development to the less usual target thus involves changes pertaining to the second part of the definition of grammaticalization as formulated by Hopper and Traugott (2003: 231) in which it is said that lexical items, once they have developed a certain grammatical function, can "continue to develop new grammatical functions". In Bourdin's words, the less usual grammaticalization targets "piggyback" on the first (step in the) grammaticalization process. In this way, the typical path 'go' > future can continue to necessity, as shown by Bourdin. This type of indirect path also characterizes Italian *andare* 'go', for which Mocciaro shows that the development to a passive proceeds via a resultative construction of Italian *andare* 'go' + past participle indicating a resultant state. The change to passive hence initiates from the resultative construction, rather than the original motion verb. Interestingly, the grammaticalization of Spanish *ir* 'go' described by Bravo also started out with a change to a resultative meaning, but continued in quite a different way, to become a focus marker. Again, this illustrates an indirect path with an intermediate step: 'go > resultative' followed by 'resultative > focus'.

It should be noted that it is not always straightforward to distinguish between these two types of indirect paths. What determines whether we call 'come' > change-of-state a lexical semantic change and 'go' > resultative a grammatical one? Bravo acknowledges this fuzziness by referring to resultative *ir* in Spanish as a "semi-lexical" verb. Bourdin (inspired by von Fintel 1995) suggests that 'come' and 'go' verbs are latently grammatical or "hybrid" verbs, i.e.; they are lexical in their morphosyntax and grammatical in their semantics.

When working with synchronic data only or with diachronic data covering a limited range of discourse types, it may be difficult to tell direct and indirect paths apart. Devos indicates that although the development of a discourse marker of disagreement out of a sequential marker looks like a typical case of an interpersonal function developing out of a textual function, it might also be the case that there is one function with different interpretations depending on discourse type. Similarly, Carlson argues that the interpretation of the 'go'-derived intensifier in Supyire varies according to the type of speech act it occurs in.

7 Meaning change

Metaphor is often seen as crucial in grammaticalization processes starting out from motion verbs and going towards markers of tense and aspect. An interesting question addressed in this volume is: what is the role of metaphor when less usual targets are considered?

First, all three passive papers make reference to the "change-of-place = change-of-state" metaphor. However, this metaphor does not lead directly to a passive reinterpretation but rather to a change-of-state or resultative intermediate stage. Otherwise, metaphor is said to play a role in only a few paths, which, coincidently or not, all involve developments into discourse markers. Daniels indicates that the development of Spanish *venga* 'come' into a discourse marker of disagreement initially involves the mapping of physical movement of the addressee towards the speaker to movement of the addressee's epistemological stance towards that of the speaker. Carlson claims that Supyire 'go' developed into an intensifier via metaphorical mapping of distance from the speaker on distance from a norm. Similarly, Devos believes that Shangaci 'go' evolves into a sequential marker and a discourse marker of disagreement through metaphorical extension of distance in space to distance in time and emotion, respectively.

Although metaphor does play a role, metonymic processes are considered to be more important in most grammaticalization paths described in this volume. This is visible in the influence of the semantic and pragmatic meaning of the immediate co-text, which is said to be an important trigger for the development of the new grammatical meaning (see also Section 5). Passives derived from a combination of 'come' or 'go' verbs and a past participle owe much of their meaning to the passive orientation of the past participle. Similarly, 'come' and 'go' verbs develop into directive markers because of frequent co-occurrence with directive speech acts (Mauri and Sansò). As mentioned in Section 2, this does not imply that the semantics of 'come' and 'go' are irrelevant for the meaning of the grammatical targets, as they may cause skewed distributional properties of the resulting grams (i.e. persistence effects). Next to the immediate co-text, the use of a source construction in a specific (pragmatic) context is also described as a crucial trigger for meaning change in some of the grammaticalization paths. Bravo, for instance, argues that the use of the resultative construction involving Spanish *ir* 'go' in negatively valued contexts is an important trigger for its (further) grammaticalization into a focus marker. In the same way, Devos argues that the purposive use of Shangaci 'come' derives from a specific context where one goes, does something and comes back (in order) to perform an action. The motion semantics are demoted and the finality is promoted, which leads to a reinterpretation of Shangaci 'come' as a purpose marker.

Another semantic-pragmatic development often associated with grammaticalization is subjectification, and related intersubjectification. These processes refer to the increasing use of a gram to express the speaker's attitudes and beliefs (subjective) or his awareness of the addressee's attitudes and beliefs (intersubjective); see Traugott (2010) and references therein. Although (inter)subjectification was not a major focus of the papers in this volume, those discussing the development of discourse markers do refer to it. Daniels describes the discourse markers of agreement and conversation ending as being intersubjective in meaning. As these discourse markers develop out of an increasingly subjective optative of Spanish 'come', her findings adhere to Traugott's claim that intersubjectification follows subjectification. The same is true for the intersubjective discourse marker of disagreement developing out of a subjectified hortative of Spanish 'come'.

Other intersubjective meanings of discourse markers are attested in Supyire (Carlson) and Shangaci (Devos). The intensifier that developed out of Supyire 'go' has both subjective and intersubjective readings. The subjective intensifier indicates a greater or more than usual degree of some gradable concept within the clause, whereas the more intersubjective one increases the force of the speech act in the face of some reluctance on the part of the addressee. In Shangaci a 'go'-derived discourse marker can be used to mark what the speaker considers to be pivotal events in a narrative, whereas in more spontaneous discourse types it expresses disapproval with the addressee. In Supyire as well as in Shangaci subjective and intersubjective interpretations are often available at the same time. Historical studies like the one by Daniels (and Traugott and others) add weight to Carlson's and Devos' proposal that the intersubjective uses developed out of the subjective ones (although in Shangaci a discourse type-related specialization cannot be excluded).

Bourdin believes that the above processes of metaphor, metonymy and (inter) subjectification cannot explain the development of passive markers out of 'come' and 'go' verbs. Rather than evoking an intermediate change-of-state stage, he argues for an iconic link between deictic motion verbs and passives: the use of 'come' and 'go' verbs "iconically reflects the abstract trajectory resulting from the decoupling of Agent and Topic" (see also Section 4). Bourdin suggests that such an iconic relation is typical of what he refers to as "deep grammaticalization", a process which starts from a latently grammatical source item and leads to a complete break from the referential domain. "Shallow grammaticalization", on the other hand, starts from a lexical source item and results via metaphor, metonymy or (inter)subjectification to a shift from one referential domain to the other.

A last type of meaning change, related to Bourdin's deep grammaticalization, concerns what Haspelmath (2004: 33) refers to as expansion, i.e. the development of new grammatical meanings out of older ones. We have seen a focus marker and a passive marker developing out of an intermediate resultative stage and a future marker that became a necessive one. As indicated by Kranich (2010) these meaning changes have received much less attention in the grammaticalization literature than those pertaining to the early stages of grammaticalization. Kranich (2010), mainly based on the further grammaticalization of perfects, futures and progressives in well-documented languages, proposes that secondary grammaticalization typically involves "objectification" or a loss of subjective meaning. This is not entirely corroborated by the indirect paths presented in this book. Whereas passives can be argued to be more objective than resultatives, this can hardly be said of focus markers.

However, an important problem in this respect is the difficulty of identifying discrete steps on a grammaticalization chain. Is the intermediate resultative construction a fully grammatical one, as argued by Mocciaro for the resultative going towards a passive marker, or is it a hybrid, semi-lexical construction as suggested by Bravo for the resultative leading the way to the focus marker? If we accept Bravo's point of view, then the development of the focus marker in Spanish is not a case of further grammaticalization and subjectification is expected. This still leaves us with necessives developing out of future markers (Bourdin), which appears to be a clear case of ongoing subjectification. If the necessive marker further develops into a run-of-the mill complementizer, as Bourdin shows to be the case for Austronesian Dehu, objectification is still attested but it is arguably hard to predict if and when it will set in. In sum, although we do find evidence for objectification, subjectification may characterize several steps on the grammaticalization chain.

Mocciaro describes another interesting meaning change in the context of expansion, which challenges Hopper and Traugott's (2003: 102) claim that grammatical meaning changes – contrary to lexical ones – do not show narrowing in meaning. She shows that the Early Italian analytic passive with *andare* 'go', although not frequent in use, is not restricted with respect to aspect, the presence or absence of an agent phrase or the lexical semantics of the past participle. In contemporary Italian, however, the construction undergoes semantic specialization: its usage range is retracted rather than expanded (see Haspelmath 2004: 33 on retraction). Present-day Italian pure passives with *andare* 'go' typically combine with past participles expressing a negative value. They cannot take an overt agent and are restricted to perfective aspect, with imperfective aspect triggering a deontic connotation. This clearly is a case of narrowing of meaning in secondary grammaticalization induced by the original lexical semantics of the 'go' verb which metaphorically implies movement not towards the speaker's epistemological stance, and possibly also by competition with the more productive deontic construction and the other Italian analytic passives.

8 Further research

As was stated at the outset of this summarizing chapter, this book investigates a number of lesser-known grammaticalization paths traveled by 'come' and 'go'. We hope that it will lead to more descriptions of related and unrelated unusual grammaticalization processes starting from 'come' and 'go' (or other motion verbs) and also stimulate discussions on the nature of source items and other aspects of grammaticalization (see discussions in the previous sections).

There are four methodological points that emerge from the current volume. First, when studying the grammaticalization of 'come' and 'go', we need "to state, as systematically and precisely as is feasible, what is known about the semantics of any given marker, and in particular about its deictic robustness, when describing the grammaticalization route(s) it has followed" (Bourdin). This needs to be done for each lexical item in each individual language – a point also made by Wilkins and Hill (1995). Second, we need to look at the wider inventory of motion verbs in a language in order to see which part of the semantic space lexical items occupy (Devos). Third, we need to look at grammaticalization in the broader discourse in order to see the less beaten paths to textual markers, information structural markers (topic, focus, contrast) and (intersubjective) pragmatic markers. Finally, we need to be careful to observe all the steps on a grammaticalization path in order to distinguish direct and indirect paths.

A further general question is how supposedly independent grammaticalization paths may influence each other. This applies, for example, to the development of a passive from both 'come' and 'go' as in Italian and to the development of *venga* to two different discourse markers. Should we think of similar and simultaneous developments as different clines, or rather as a complex network of grammaticalization?

More concrete questions of further research that directly concern the paths described in the present volume are the following. Related to the development of passive markers, we may wonder whether constructions involving 'come' or 'go' verbs ever directly develop into passive markers, i.e. without an intermediate stage expressing change of state. Necessive markers, for example, are shown to develop both directly and indirectly (i.e. via a future or passive intermediary stage) out of a 'come' source construction (Bourdin). The existence of such a direct path for passive markers would add weight to Bourdin's idea of an 'iconic' relation (based on goal-orientedness) between verbs of 'coming' and 'going' and passive markers.

Another topic for further research relating to the passive papers but also to the necessive markers discussed in Bourdin concerns the development of modal passives. There appears to be some doubt on how the modal passive relates to the pure passive. Does the former develop out of the latter (as suggested by Bourdin from a typological perspective and by Mocciaro for the Italian go-derived passive) or do they develop separately, and if so does the development occur simultaneously or not? More generally, how does the correlation between motion-derived passives and deontic modality relate to the cross-linguistically attested correlation between passives and potentials (see Shibatani 1985)?

Concerning the paths leading to directive markers (Mauri and Sansò), more in-depth studies could help to establish whether 'go'-derived directive markers necessarily involve an intermediate stage as an itive directive marker. They can also shed more light on whether and how (itive) directive markers extend to other performers.

With respect to grammaticalization in the broader area of discourse, we can ask to what extent these developments are due to their increase in scope and a related independent position in the sentence. Brinton (1996) stresses that pragmatic markers are typically loosely attached to the syntactic structure, e.g. Daniels' *venga*, but Carlson and Devos show that an intensifying function or an indicator of disapproval can also develop when the grammaticalized verb remains at the core of the syntactic structure, functioning as an auxiliary.

Likewise, (inter)subjectivity is said to be related to the left and right periphery of the sentence (Traugott 2012). If information structure is taken as an (inter)subjective concept (cf. van der Wal 2011), what does the functional shift of auxiliary to focus marker (Bravo) tell us about the relation between the formal morphosyntactic developments and (inter)subjectification?

In conclusion, we believe that the less beaten grammaticalization paths can teach us a lot about diachronic developments and their motivations. Some of the less beaten paths appear to be side-tracks of beaten paths (e.g. passive from resultative, or necessive from future), whereas others are genuinely new grammaticalization paths (e.g. to intensifier or focus marker). Some of the developments begin on a known path not only because of the presence of 'come' or 'go', but because of the construction they occur in (e.g. imperative > directive). Some unusual paths were perceived as infrequent, but have been shown to be not that uncommon (e.g. passive > necessive), whereas others still seem to be rare (e.g. discourse-related targets). It is our hope that this picture will become more comprehensive as research continues, the current volume hopefully being one step in that direction.

Abbreviations

CONJ   conjunction

References

Bourdin, Philippe. 2008. On the grammaticalization of 'come' and 'go' into markers of textual connectivity. In Maria Xosé López-Couso & Elena Seoane (eds.), *Rethinking grammaticalization: new perspectives*, 37–59. Amsterdam: John Benjamins.

Brinton, Laurel J. 1996. *Pragmatic Markers in English. Grammaticalization and Discourse Functions*. Berlin & New York: Mouton de Gruyter.

Ebert, Karen. 2003. 'Come' and 'go' as discourse connectors in Kera and other Chadic lan-
guages. In Erin Shay & Uwe Seibert (eds.) *Motion, Direction and Location in Languages:
In honor of Zygmunt Frajzyngier*, 111–122. Amsterdam & Philadelphia: John Benjamins.
Fillmore, Charles J. 1975 [1971]. *Santa Cruz Lectures on Deixis*. Bloomington (Ind.): Indiana
University Linguistics Club.
Haspelmath, Martin. 1990. The grammaticization of passive morphology. *Studies in
Language* 14 (1): 25–71.
Haspelmath, Martin. 1994. Passive participles across languages. In Barbara Fox & Paul J.
Hopper (eds.), *Voice: Form and Function* (Typological Studies in Language 27), 151–177.
Amsterdam: Benjamins.
Haspelmath, Martin. 2004. On directionality in language change with particular reference to
grammaticalization. In: Olga Fischer, Muriel Norde & Harry Perridon (eds.), *Up and down
the cline. The nature of grammaticalization*, 17–44. Amsterdam & Philadelphia: John
Benjamins.
Heine, Bernd & Tania Kuteva. 2002. *World Lexicon of Grammaticalization*. Cambridge: Cam-
bridge University Press.
Hopper, Paul. 1991. On some priciples of grammaticalization. In Elizabeth Closs Traugott &
Bernd Heine (eds.), *Approaches to grammaticalization*, vol. 1, 17–35. Amsterdam: John
Benjamins.
Hopper, Paul & Elizabeth Closs Traugott. 2003. *Grammaticalization*, 2nd edn. Cambridge:
Cambridge University Press.
Kranich, Svenja. 2010. Grammaticalization, subjectification and objectification. In Katerina
Stathi, Elke Gehweiler & Ekkehard König (eds.), *Grammaticalization. Current views and
issues*, 101–122. Amsterdam: John Benjamins.
Shibatani, Masayoshi. 1985. Passives and related constructions: a prototype analysis.
Language 61 (4): 821–848.
Traugott, Elizabeth Closs. 2003. From subjectification to intersubjectification. In Raymond
Hickey (ed.), *Motives for Language Change*, 124–139. Cambridge: Cambridge University
Press.
Traugott, Elizabeth Closs. 2010. (Inter)subjectivity and (Inter)subjectification: A Reassess-
ment. In Kristin Davidse, Lieven Vandelanotte & Hubert Cuyckens (eds.),
Subjectification, Intersubjectification and Grammaticalization, 29–71. Berlin & New York:
Mouton de Gruyter.
Traugott, Elizabeth Closs. 2012. Intersubjectification and Clause Periphery. In Lieselotte
Brems, Lobke Ghesquière & Freek van de Velde (eds.), *Intersections of Intersubjectivity*
(special issue on English Text Construction) 5 (1): 7–28.
Van der Wal, Jenneke. 2011. Information structure, (inter)subjectivity and objectification.
Manuscript.
Wilkins, David & Deborah Hill. 1995. When "go" means "come": Questioning the basicness of
basic motion verbs. *Cognitive Linguistics* 6 (2/3): 209–259.

Subject index

Language index

www.ingramcontent.com/pod-product-compliance
Lightning Source LLC
Chambersburg PA
CBHW070017100426
42740CB00013B/2530